Cistercian Studies Series: Number Sixty-Eight

HEAVEN ON EARTH

CISTERCIAN STUDIES SERIES: NUMBER SIXTY-EIGHT

Heaven On Earth

Studies in Medieval Cistercian History, IX

Edited by E. Rozanne Elder

Cistercian Publications
Kalamazoo, Michigan
1983

+ 1005+

Available in Britain and Europe through

A. R. Mowbray & Co Ltd
St Thomas House   Becket Street
Oxford   OX1 1SJ

These articles were originally presented as papers at the Cistercian Studies Conference held during the Sixteenth International Congress on Medieval Studies, Kalamazoo, Michigan, 7-10 May 1981, and the Seventeenth International Congress on Medieval Studies, Kalamazoo, Michigan, 6-9 May 1982.

Library of Congress Cataloging in Publication Data

Main entry under title:

Heaven on earth.

   (Studies in medieval Cistercian history ; 9)
(Cistercian studies series ; no. 68)
   "Originally presented as papers at the Cistercian Studies Conference held during the Sixteenth International Congress on Medieval Studies, Kalamazoo, Michigan, 7-10 May 1981."
   1. Cistercians--History--Congresses.
I. Elder, E. Rozanne (Ellen Rozanne), 1940-
II. Cistercian Studies Conference (1981 : Kalamazoo, Mich.)   III. Series.   IV. Series: Cistercian studies series ; no. 68.
BX3406.2.H4   271'.12   81-15550
ISBN 0-87907-868-5 (pbk.)   AACR2

Table of Contents

Preface

Heaven on Earth is an apt title, not only for the lead article
here, but for a collection of essays on early cistercian monasticism,
for the founders of the New Monastery left Molesme for the wilderness
precisely in order to create there a lifestyle which would detach
them from the things of this earth and give them a foretaste of
heaven. As the monastery grew to an Order and primitive wooden
dwellings gave way to majestic stone abbeys, this cistercian program of detachment and preparation continued to be articulated by
generations of white monks.

In this volume, the tenth in the Studies in Medieval Cistercian
History subseries, we study aspects of cistercian life and thought
in the 'golden age' of St Bernard and among those who came after
him. We see something not only of the ideals of Cîteaux but some
of its failures. We find Cistercians caught up in the world they
had fled, Cistercians facing the practical realities of making a
living in a not always hospitable environment, Cistercians trying
to share the joys of contemplation and exhorting their brethren to
constancy and simplicity.

These papers were first presented at the 1981 and 1982 Confer-
ences on Cistercian Studies, a part of the annual International
Congress on Medieval Studies at Western Michigan University, Kalamazoo. Cistercian Publications and the Institute of Cistercian
Studies wish to express their appreciation to

--The Medieval Institute of the University and its staff,
--the scholars who present aspects of their research,
--the monks and scholars who chair sessions and keep the
   Conference running smoothly, and
--those who attend sessions and further research by their
   questions and insights.

Over the years the Conference has become something of a family
reunion for North American scholars in cistercian studies, and for
an increasing number of Europeans. Old friends return to share
on-going research, new scholars appear with new interests and enthusiasm. We invite those doing research on topics cistercian to
join us.

E.R.E.

HEAVEN ON EARTH: CELESTIAL AND CENOBITIC UNITY
IN THE THOUGHT OF BALDWIN OF FORD

David N. Bell

ACCORDING TO CHARLES HALLET, Baldwin of Ford's treatise *On the Cenobitic Life*[1] is the most complete study known to him on the theology of communion, community, and the common life. 'It encompasses', he writes, 'not only the different communions which relate to man and the whole history of humanity, but also the communion of the angels and that of the Trinity, the source and origin of all communions.'[2] Yet Hallet makes no attempt to determine Baldwin's sources for this important tractate,[3] nor does he indicate the extent to which Baldwin's ideas can be paralleled in the writings of his contemporaries. One of his studies is concerned with Baldwin's terminology in the *De vita coenobitica*,[4] and the other is little more than a paraphrase of what Baldwin himself has to say.[5] Yet in the view of Amédée Hallier, and others, 'the claim to understand an author's doctrine without having referred to the sources from which he drew it, is a questionable one.'[6] It is like a set of musical variations: unless one is acquainted with the theme, one cannot assess the full originality, or inventiveness of the composer as they are revealed in the elaborations. It seems to me, therefore, that unless we know the sources from which Baldwin derived his ideas and the extent to which his contemporaries were saying the same things, we are in no position to make an estimate of the importance or originality of his thought on the *vita communis*. Paul Diemer speaks of Baldwin as having 'such a profound grasp of the meaning of community life,'[7] and Richard Summers echoes Jean Fourcade in saying of Baldwin's fifteenth tractate that it is a work which, like all his works, deserves to be better known.[8] Robert Thomas speaks of it as a 'chef-d'oeuvre' and says that Baldwin has meditated on the nature of the cenobitic life more than any other Cistercian.[9] This present study proposes to assess the accuracy of these and similar statements.

As we have it now, Baldwin's treatise has certainly undergone editing. In its original form, I feel certain that it comprised three separate sermons, each approximately the same length and each ending with the same pertinent doxology,[10] but by the late twelfth or early thirteenth century,[11] these had been amalgamated to produce what is, on the whole, a consistent treatise with a logical progression of ideas. Its basic structure is threefold, each part corresponding to one stage in the transmission of the common life from the Creator to his creatures. We begin with the common life in the Trinity, move on to the common life of the angels, and conclude with the common life of men upon earth. Among the latter, the most im-

portant were the apostles and the members of the Jerusalem Community:
it is from the apostles themselves, says Baldwin,

> that the common life has received its form and expression,
> its title of honor, the privilege of its high position,
> the testimony of its authority, the protection which de-
> fends it, and the foundation of its hope.[12]

But the apostles received the common life from the angels, and the
angels received it from God, and we may therefore see the common life
as

> a sort of radiance from the eternal light, a sort of emana-
> tion from the eternal life, a sort of effluence from the
> everlasting fountain, from which flow living waters spring-
> ing up into eternal life.[13]

The common life in the Trinity and among the angels is the concern of
the first of Baldwin's three original sermons, and in the second and
third he goes on to discuss the common life among humankind under a
further set of three headings: (1) the common life among all men;
(2) the common life among all christian men; and (3) the common life
among all christian men in religious communities.   All three of these
groups share a common nature *(communio naturae)*, but the last two also share a common grace *(communio gratiae)* and will, in the fulness
of time, share a common glory *(communio gloriae)*.   The source and origin of the common life, therefore, is God himself, 'the perfect model
of any contemplative community.'[14]   It is here that we may begin our
investigation.

'God is life; the holy and indivisible Trinity is one life.   The
Father is not one life, the Son another, and the Holy Spirit a third,
but these three are one life.   Just as they have one common essence
and one common nature, so they have one common life.'[15]   Every other
unity and community is a reflection of this unity and community, and
at the end of all things there will be that one true unity when 'they
shall be one, even as we are one' (John 17:11).   The concept is clearly anticipated in Augustine: we are helped, the bishop says, in understanding how the Father and the Son are two distinct persons yet
one and the same nature by considering the way in which holy men
here on earth are also one and many at the same time:

> For these men were one through their fellowship *(consor-
> tium)* and communion *(communio)* in one and the same nature
> by which all were men.   And if they were sometimes not one
> because of different desires and ideas, or dissimilar opin-
> ions and characters, they will yet be fully and perfectly
> one when they have attained to the goal that God will be
> all in all.[16]

In other words, our *communio naturae* (Augustine's phrase as well as Baldwin's[17]) is not only a reflection of the Trinitarian *communio*, but also a means to its better understanding. Aelred of Rievaulx has a similar idea, but extends it to include not only rational men, but also irrational animals and inanimate objects. All created natures, we are told, have been duly and properly arranged by the Supreme Nature, and his will is that 'peace should encompass all his creatures and society *(societas)* unite them; and thus all creatures would receive from him, who is supremely and purely one, a certain trace *(vestigium)* of that unity.'[18] And once again, just as the unity of the Trinity was the source of all, so the unity of the Trinity is the end of all. Our course in this life is a return to unity, for one thing alone is necessary, 'and this one thing is to be found only in the One, near the One, with the One, in whom there is no change nor shadow of variation.'[19] *Communio naturae*, therefore, anticipates the *communio gloriae* which will be ours at the end of time. It is an eschatological *communio*, and we shall have cause to return to this idea towards the end of our study.

Human unity is therefore a derived unity, a reflected unity, an imitative unity. It flows out, says Baldwin, from the Fount of Life itself.[20] Bernard of Clairvaux puts the matter very clearly:

> Among everything which is rightly spoken of as one, the unity of the Trinity, which is three persons in one substance, holds the highest place. It surpasses the second place in which, conversely, there are three substances in one person in Christ. Furthermore, true and prudent consideration proves that this and whatever else can be spoken of as one is called one not by comparison, but by imitation of that Supreme Unity.[21]

God's unity is the unique unity *(unica unitas[22])*, and as Tarcisius Connor points out, the unity of any community 'reflects in time the life of the Trinity itself.'[23]

From the *unitas* and *communio Trinitatis* the common life is transmitted to the angels, and it follows that

> the common life of the angels is a sort of copy of that common life which is in God, of God, and is God. It is united in perfect peace by the Holy Spirit, who is its love, its bond, and its *communio*.[24]

Among the angels there is true mutual love, and Baldwin echoes Sallust and Aelred in saying that all want the same things and all are averse to the same things.[25]

There is no one here puffed up with pride, no one
consumed with envy, no outbursts of anger, no quar-
rels or discord, no murmurs of impatience, and no
one is defamed by treacherous tongues. Here all is
at peace, all is calm, all is tranquil.[26]

There are common possessions, common benefits, common worship, com-
mon peace, common obedience, common order, and common repose.[27] It
is an ideal community in the true sense of the word, 'and we who are
still upon earth should follow their way of life by [living] the common life after their example.'[28]

The concept of the monastic life as the angelic life is an old
and venerable idea,[29] although it should be clear from what we have
said earlier that far from being restricted to monks, the metaphor
should really apply to the whole of errant humanity. Baldwin's *communio naturae* is true of all men, and we have already seen that Aelred
of Rievaulx thought that God willed for all his creatures *pax, societas,*
and a *vestigium* of his own incomparable unity. The unity of any community, therefore, whether angelic, human, christian, or monastic, is
what it is by imitation of the unity of the Trinity, and the characteristics of the Trinitarian unity are thus the ideal characteristics
of any community. The world, the church, and the cloister are all
reflections one of the other,[30] and if monks should be angels, so too
should we who are not monks, whether we like it or not.[31] John Chrysostom, perhaps more clearly than any other, leaves us in no doubt on
this score.[32]

The apostles were not monks, but the Jerusalem community is the
earthly model for the common life just as the Trinitarian community
is its archetype. The apostles, says Baldwin,

so powerful and so noble, were clothed in virtue from
above, and by the inspiration of the Holy Spirit they
undertook to observe the common life. They confirmed
it by their example, sanctioned it by their conduct,
and handed it down to us so that we might also keep it.[33]

This, too, is a very old tradition,[34] and, as we shall see, the description of the apostolic community in Acts 4:32 has been of fundamental importance in the theology of the *vita communis*. 'You, brothers', says Guerric of Igny, 'who have one heart and one soul just as
you have one house and [a common] property, you, I think, ought especially to glory in [the apostles], for you, like olive branches,
have taken from their root not only the sap of faith, but also a pattern of life and the model (*exemplum*) of your Order.'[35] Baldwin's
doctrine stands precisely in line with this unequivocal statement.

If, for Baldwin and for so many others, the common life is the
angelic life, and the angelic life is the Trinitarian life, it follows

that the force which binds a community together here on earth is
the same force which binds it together in heaven. What is the nature of that force? Baldwin's answer is the straightforward answer of the whole Augustinian tradition: *spiritus sanctus communio
est*.[36] We live in unity of spirit through the one Spirit which
dwells in us.[37] For Augustine, the Holy Spirit is the ineffable
embrace (*complexus*) of Father and Son and their ineffable *communio*.[38]
He is their holiness, goodness, peace, grace, joy, delight, blessedness, and unity.[39] He is whatever is common to both, and is so sub-
stantially.[40] And most importantly, he is also their mutual love,
will, and charity,[41] the charity which is God and is from God and
which, by being poured forth in our hearts, establishes among men on
earth the same unity as may be perceived in the Trinity.

> If, in drawing near to God, many souls are one soul and
> many hearts one heart through charity, what must the
> very fount of charity bring about between the Father and
> the Son? Is there not more reason for the Trinity to be
> one God?... If, then, the charity of God which is poured
> forth in our hearts by the Holy Spirit who is given to
> us (Rm 5:5) makes one soul of many souls and one heart
> of many hearts, how much more are the Father, Son, and
> Holy Spirit one God, one light, one principle?[42]

This Augustinian conception of the Holy Spirit as *communio* and *caritas* lies at the heart of Baldwin's theology of the common life as,
indeed, it lies at the heart of his whole spirituality.[43] God is
charity, and charity is therefore a revelation of God. Any act of
charity is an imitation of God, and to live in charity and unity with
our fellows is to imitate the common life of the Trinity. As Baldwin
says:

> God is charity, and as the apostle says, his charity
> is poured forth in our hearts through the Holy Spirit
> who is given to us. This charity is in us by grace,
> and reveals to us in a certain way the nature of that
> incomprehensible charity which is God himself, whose
> nature is charity or generosity (*benignitas*).[44]

Charity, in short, is the key to community and must stand before all
else. If it does, all else will be properly ordered, for charity
'subjects everything to God in obedience and disposes everything
by its authority.'[45] A community united in charity is like the human body in which each part has its own role, but in which all serve
the common good (Baldwin's analogy reflects both Paul and Augustine[46]);
or otherwise (following Aelred of Rievaulx and a well-established tradition), it is like a harp or zither (*cithara*) in which each string

has its own note, but in which all combine to produce concord and
harmony.[47]
    There is nothing new in this. The concept of love/the Holy
Spirit as the *gluten* or *coagulum* which binds together and unifies
the many to form the one is a commonplace in western spirituality
from the time of Augustine onwards.[48] It is love which forms the
cor unum et anima una of Acts 4:32--a principle and a verse which
lie at the very heart of the religious life.[49] Augustine discusses
it more than fifty times,[50] and, according to William of St Thierry,
it was this verse which animated Bernard in his retreat to Châtillon-
sur-Saône.[51]

> Having just completed his discussion of the *communiones*
> of all mankind and of all Christians, Baldwin continues:
> There is still another form of *communio:* that of those
> who live in a [religious] community. It is said of them:
> 'The multitude of believers had but one heart and one
> soul; no one said that any of the things he possessed
> was his own, but they had everything in common' (Acts
> 4:32). What makes the common life, therefore, is one
> heart, one soul, and having everything in common. Such
> a life is an earthly copy--so far as human weakness
> allows--of the life of the angels.[52]

    This is an important idea and has extremely important consequences,
not least the implication that the coenobitic life is not only useful,
but essential for the formation of the individual and the re-formation
of the image of God. It is through the common life, says Baldwin,
'that those who are set upon earth can begin to be fashioned in the
likeness of the angels of God,'[53] and this world in general and the
cloister in particular can therefore be seen as a true *schola caritatis*
in which we are trained in the practice of patience and charity.[54] Our
fellows are essential to us, and Baldwin explains why:

> Since God has no need of any benefits himself, he has
> put in his place, as it were, our brothers and neigh-
> bors who need these things, so that they might receive
> from us those outstanding benefits which are due to
> him. No one, therefore, should flatter himself that
> he loves God...if he does not love his neighbor...How
> else can he offer benefits to God, except by offer-
> ing them to him in whom God does have a need, who in
> himself needs nothing? It is God who, in his members,
> asks and receives, who is loved or despised. The love
> of our neighbor, therefore, is the tie of love and the
> bond of peace by which we maintain and preserve in our-
> selves the charity of God and unity of spirit.[55]

Again, this is not a new idea. It appears in Augustine,[56] and still more clearly in an important passage in Aelred of Rievaulx. Although God is sufficient to himself in goodness, Aelred says,

> he has extended the abundance of his goodness to his creature, drawing it forth from himself and bestowing its usefulness upon all. But because the rational soul could not bestow anything at all on God, a multitude of creatures were created by him so that in this way a likeness to the divine goodness which is poured out among many might appear in their mutual benefits.[57]

We need out neighbors, therefore, both good and bad: the good may act for us as a stimulus and an example, and the bad, like Christopher Smart's cat, can be 'an instrument for the children to learn benevolence upon.'[58] Furthermore, 'it often happens that when good and wicked are living together communally, the wicked are reformed and the good become better and purer';[59] and even if the wicked remain wicked, they may still be of great benefit to the good.

> In a metalworker's workshop a file is essential. [It is used] to scrape the rust from iron so that it becomes gleaming and polished. The same is true of a wicked man who lives his life as part of a community. Even though he injures himself and seeks to injure others, those he persecutes he also 'files' and purifies.[60]

As Augustine (and others) pointed out, the word *monos* 'one' from which *monachus/monachos*, 'monk', is derived can refer not to the solitariness of a single individual, but to the *una anima* of the coenobitic community.[61] Solitude, said the Cistercians, should not be of the body, but of the mind, and 'we should always flee the society of the wicked with the soul, not always with the body; always by our different way of life, but not always by removing ourselves entirely from their company.'[62] Guerric of Igny is very clear on this point: in the desert of Cîteaux we have the quiet of solitude, yet do not lack the consolation of a pleasing and holy fellowship. Each may sit in solitude and silence, for no one will interrupt him, yet the words of Solomon, 'Woe to him who is alone' (Qo 4:10), cannot be applied to him. We are in a crowd with no turmoil and in a city with no tumult.[63] To live socially, says Bernard, is to learn how to love and to be loved,[64] and Aelred is perhaps still more insistent on this point.[65] As Charles Dumont puts it, 'the monastic community...is to be seen as the milieu, at once necessary and efficacious, for this restoration of the likeness of God which has been lost by the sin of selfishness, egoism, *propria voluntas*, and singularity.'[66] Or, in the words of Amédée Hallier, the

search for God is a common task, and 'men are instruments for the sanc-
tification of their fellows.'[67]   This is precisely Baldwin's view.
The text from Acts which summarizes the common life mentions not
only one heart and one soul, but also common possessions: 'no one
said that any of the things he possessed was his own, but they had
everything in common.' Baldwin discusses this matter at some length
in his consideration of the third form of human *communio* (that of the
religious community), and shows how this too is a reflection and imitation of the nature of charity which is, in turn, God. The nature
of charity, he says, 'is to love and to wish to be loved. Just as it
is impossible for fire not to burn, so it is impossible for charity
not to love.'[68] By nature and by instinct, charity longs to share
things and have them in common, and if these things are of such a
quality that they cannot be shared, charity would rather do without
and give them to the one who needs them. Therefore, says Baldwin, we
find that charity demands two things: a love of communion and sharing
(*amor communionis*) and a communion and sharing of love (*communio
amoris*).[69] This chiasmus which, as Hallet has shown,[70] is much more
than a simple rhetorical device, is central to Baldwin's theology of
the common life.

> If one or the other is absent, then charity is not yet
> blessed, for charity seeks its blessedness only in the
> sharing of the good [it possesses] and the sharing of
> its own self. If we have a common good, but not a com-
> mon love, then charity lacks something which it wishes
> to have. And if there is a common love but not a common
> good, then charity lacks something which it has no wish
> to be without.[71]

Just as this is true of the common life of the Trinity, so it should
be true of the common life on earth, whether in general, in the church,
or in the monastery. God, says Hugh of Fouilloy, is the Omnipotent
Abbot and teaches us by his Word and his example all that we need to
know.[72]
     These ideas also have a long history. Aristotle makes it clear
that true friends should have all things in common and that friendship lies in sharing;[73] and utilizing the ideas of Cicero, Sallust,
and Augustine, Aelred of Rievaulx leaves us in no doubt that spiritual friendship demands community of possessions, thoughts, manners,
morals, and pursuits.[74] Jerome points out that just as the first
Christians possessed Christ in common, it was only right that they
should possess all else in common;[75] Augustine goes further than this:
goodness can only be possessed by being shared, and the more you share
it the more you possess it.

     A man's possession of goodness is in no way diminished

by the arrival, or the continuance, of a sharer in it;
indeed, goodness is a possession enjoyed more widely
by the united affection of partners in that possession
in proportion to the harmony that exists among them.
In fact, anyone who refuses to enjoy this possession in
partnership will not enjoy it at all; and he will find
that he possesses it in ampler measure in proportion to
his ability to love his partner in it.[76]

Community of goods, therefore, applies not only to material things,
but to thoughts, virtues, and spiritual gifts. This is as clear in
Augustine as it is in Aelred and Baldwin.[77] The catalyst which transforms the individual good into the common good is again charity and
its two corollaries: the love of sharing and the sharing of love.
'Different [spiritual] gifts are made common in two ways: when the
gifts given to individuals individually are possessed in common by
communio amoris, and when they are loved in common by *amor communionis*.'[78] The idea, though not the terminology, may again be seen in Augustine
and Aelred: when one and the same charity works in all, *singula erunt
omnium, et omnia singulorum*.[79] In the fellowship (*communicatio*) of
the Holy Spirit, we share our gifts, our hopes, and our sufferings,
and in this same fellowship, says Baldwin, in and through charity/the
Holy Spirit, we also share in the merits of the saints. In the common
life, which is, ideally, the life of every man on earth, what good we
do is for the common benefit, and if it were not for this, we would
have no hope.

> If someone were to be judged on his own merits, as if
> the merits of others, which are shared in common through
> charity (*per communionem caritatis*), were not there to
> give him support, how could he bear the weight of the
> divine judgement? Many and great are our iniquities,
> and the prophet says, 'If you, O Lord, keep count of our
> iniquities, Lord, who shall stand it?' (Ps 130:3).[80]

Our hope, therefore, lies in the merits of the saints, the *communio
sanctorum*, in which the term *communio* bears the same rich significance
that it does throughout the whole of the *De vita coenobitica*.

> I am sure [says the abbot of Ford] that through the
> communion of charity (*per communionem caritatis*) the
> merits of the saints will profit me, and that the
> communion of the saints (*sanctorum communio*) can make
> good my own imperfection and insufficiency...Charity
> extends our hope to the communion of the saints (*com-
> munio sanctorum*), and we can therefore share with them
> their merits and their rewards (*in communione meritorum*

et communione praemiorum).[81]

This last aspect, however, the *communio praemiorum*, is reserved for
the life to come, 'for it is the sharing of glory (*communio gloriae*)
which shall be revealed in us.'[82]
   It follows then that the common life is both a reflection and
an anticipation of the life to come. If the cloister can be called
a paradise (and a multitude of writers were convinced that it could[83]),
it is a *proleptic* paradise, a symbol and image of true Paradise.[84]
Such an idea is perfectly logical: the key to perfect unity is perfect charity, and perfect charity is only possible when *propria voluntas* has been entirely eliminated. Yet *propria voluntas* cannot be
eliminated so long as we have a body, for concupiscence can be diminished in the flesh, but not ended.[85] 'The enemy dies only in the resurrection of the dead.'[86] The perfection of charity, the perfection
of unity, and the perfection of the common life, therefore, are reserved for the future. The common life here is an anticipation and
a preparation for the common life to come, but it achieves its perfection only after we have shuffled off this mortal coil. 'Through
the common life,' says Baldwin, 'we who are set upon earth can begin
to be fashioned in the likeness of the angels of God, for in the eternal life to come, we shall be united with them as their like and
their equals.'[87] The ideal society, wherever and whenever it may be
found, is, like the Jerusalem community, 'une société de charité,'[88]
and the common life is no more and no less than a manifestation of
charity.

> This, therefore, is the law of the common life: unity
> of spirit in the charity of God, the bond of peace in
> the mutual and unfailing charity of all the brethren,
> the sharing of all the goods which should be shared, and
> the total rejection of any idea of personal ownership
> in the way of life of holy religion.[89]

   Such then is Baldwin's theology of the common life. It is a
theology which begins in charity, proceeds from charity, and ends in
charity, and it is time now to consider whether, in this theology of
charity, the abbot of Ford has anything new to say. The first thing
which should be apparent is that there is nothing in what Baldwin says
which cannot be paralleled in the writings of his predecessors (especially Augustine) or of his contemporaries (especially Aelred).
Certain themes may be stated more clearly and more straightforwardly
--the relationship of the Trinitarian *communio* and the human *communio*,
for example--but the themes themselves are not without precedent.
On the other hand, as Hallier points out, we should not be surprised
at this: the medieval monastic writers intended to remain faithful
to tradition and scripture, and Hallier's comments on Aelred may be

applied with equal accuracy to Baldwin. '[His] originality', he
writes, 'is to be sought less in the fundamental ideas, which after
all are common property, than in the sincerity of his expression of
them, in the truth and relative newness of his testimony, and in the
coherence of his doctrinal synthesis.'[90] If we do not bear this in
mind, we arrive at the absurd position of maintaining that Brahms
shows no advance on Boccherini because both use the same diatonic
scale and the same time-signatures, and both, on occasion, write for
the same instruments. Bernard, for example, has a considerable amount
to say on the common life, and there is truth in Leclercq's comment
that 'he was at the source of a literature which treated of the contemplative community.'[91] There is also truth in Charles Dumont's
statement that Aelred 'was more exclusively intent than St Bernard
on forming and leading a contemplative community.'[92] It would be
equally true to say that Baldwin goes further than Aelred, not in the
sense that his ideas differ from those of the latter, but in the sense
that his *De vita coenobitica* presents us with just such a 'doctrinal
synthesis,' an important and accurate epitome of twelfth-century Cistercian thought on the theology of monasticism and the common life.

Baldwin was heir to a very rich tradition with which he was very
well acquainted. We may well criticise him for his gross errors of
judgement when it came to dealing with people (the business of Roger
Norreys is really indefensible), but no one ever doubted his piety
and learning.[93] He had read his sources and heard them read, and as
Leclercq says, he 'assimilated them to his memory and his style; he
has made them his own and has transmitted them to us in an original
and new combination.'[94] What were these sources? The most important
for the *De vita coenobitica*, I would suggest, are Augustine, Aelred,
Bernard, and Benedict,[95] but whereas these represent the direct and
immediate influences on the treatise, the indirect sources are of no
less importance. The whole concept of medieval monasticism, for example, was much affected by Jerome,[96] and Aelred's *De institutione
inclusarum* was deeply influenced by him.[97] Not for nothing was he
called *doctor monachorum*.[98] It is well known, too, that the influence
of Origen was all-pervasive,[99] and that Gregory the Great and Cassian
(and, through Cassian, the fathers of the desert) were unquestionably
of profound significance.[100] It is this fertile tradition to which
Baldwin was heir, and it is the ideas of these fathers which he has
adopted and adapted, and then presented in his own way and in his own
words in the *De vita coenobitica*. The treatise is, as we have said,
an epitome; that is its real importance. If you want to know what
twelfth-century Cistercians thought of the origins, nature, and significance of the common life, read Baldwin. Unlike such other works
as the *De cohabitatione fratrum* of Hugh of Barzelle,[101] we have in
Baldwin's text not just a description, not just an encomium, but a
true theology of the common life. What he says is not new, but the
manner in which he says it, the sincerity of his expression, and the

coherence of his doctrine lead me to suggest that in this work the abbot of Ford has presented us with a significant contribution to the theology of communion and community. His treatise is worth the reading, and there would be no excuse, in any future study of the theology of the monastic life, for relegating him simply to a few footnotes. He may not deserve a whole book, but to my mind there is no doubt that he deserves at least a chapter.

Memorial University of Newfoundland

NOTES

In the following notes, B. de F. = Baudouin de Ford, and B. of F. = Baldwin of Ford.

1. *De vita coenobitica seu communi*, the fifteenth of Baldwin's *Tractatus Diversi*. The text in the Migne Patrology (PL 204: 545-562) is defective, but useable. A much better text is provided by Robert Thomas in his *B. de F., Traités 15-16 (Pain de Cîteaux* [= PC] 40; Chimay, 1975), and this is the edition which has been used throughout this present study. Fr Thomas also provides a sound French translation, and an English translation was made in 1977 by Chrysogonus Waddell ocso and published, with an excellent introduction, in *Liturgy O.C.S.O.* 11 1 (January 1977) 19-65. Another English translation has been prepared by the present writer, and will be published in due course, together with translations of Baldwin's other *Tractates*, by Cistercian Publications.
2. C. Hallet, 'La communion des personnes d'après une oeuvre de B. de F.,' RAM 42 (1966) 405.
3. *Ibid.* 'Nous n'aborderons pas ici le problème des sources de Baudouin, mais nous dégagerons immédiatement du *De vita coenobitica* un résumé de ce qu'il y dit de la communion....'
4. C. Hallet, 'Notes sur le vocabulaire du *De vita coenobitica seu communi* de B. de F.,' *Analecta Cisterciensia* 22 (1966) 272-278, a useful article.
5. Hallet, 'La communion....' 405-422.
6. A. Hallier, *The Monastic Theology of Aelred of Rievaulx*, tr. C. Heaney (CS 2; Shannon, 1969) 164.
7. P. Diemer, 'The Witness of the Early English Cistercians to the

Spirit and Aims of the Founders of the Order of Cîteaux' in M. B. Pennington (ed.), *The Cistercian Spirit: A Symposium* (CS 3; Washington, 1973) 146. See further *ibid.* 159-161.

8. See J. Fourcade's notice of Hallet's 'La communion,' in *Cistercian Studies* 3 (1968) [140] #231, and R. Summers' review of B. of F., *Sacramento del Altar*, ed. Monasterio Ntra. Sra. de los Angeles (Azul, Argentina, 1978) in *Cistercian Studies* 15 (1980) 299.

9. See Thomas' *B. de F., Traités 15-16* 10, 13. In his *Initiation aux auteurs cisterciens* (PC 42; Rochefort, 1978) 26, Thomas refers to the work as the most important of Baldwin's sixteen treatises.

10. The first sermon ends at PL 204: 550C (PC 40:35); the second at 556B (PC 40:61); and the third at 562D (PC 40:91). The doxology in each case is 2 Co 13:13. During the editing process, small amounts of the second and third sermons may possibly have been lost.

11. Bibliothèque Nationale, MS lat. 2601, which appears to be the earliest of the surviving manuscripts which contain the *De Vita Coenobitica*, dates from this period and already presents the Tractate as a single unit (fol. 54-61). This manuscript, in fact, presents its own problems, but none which need concern us here (see P. Guébin, 'Deux sermons inédits de Baldwin, archevêque de Canterbury 1184-1190' in *Journal of Theological Studies* O.S. 13 [1911-12] 571-574). For a full account of the manuscripts of Baldwin's writings, see my forthcoming 'The *Corpus* of the Works of B. of F.'

12. Baldwin, *Tractatus* [=*Tr.*] XV PL 204:545C (PC 40:15).

13. *Ibid.* 546C-D (PC 40:17): 'Vita sane communis quasi quidam splendor est aeterni luminis, quaedam emanatio vitae aeternae, quasi quaedam derivatio de perenni fonte, unde manant aquae vivae salientes in vitam aeternam (Jn 4:14),'

14. See J. Leclercq, 'Saint Bernard of Clairvaux and the Contemplative Community' in M. B. Pennington, ed,, *Contemplative Community: An Interdisciplinary Symposium* (CS 21; Washington, 1972) 81-82.

15. Baldwin, *Tr.* XV PL 204: 546D (PC 40:19): 'Deus vita est, sancta et individua Trinitas una vita est. Non alia vita est Pater, et alia Filius, et alia Spiritus Sanctus; sed hi tres una sunt vita; et, sicut una est eorum communis essentia, communisque natura, ita una est eorum communis vita.'

16. Augustine, *Ep.* 238. ii. 13; PL 33:1043. See further A. Sage, *La vie religieuse selon saint Augustin* (Paris, 1972) 49-50.

17. In Augustine, *Ep.* 238, ii, 13; PL 33:1043; in Baldwin, *Tr.* XV; PL 204:550C foll. (PC 40:37 foll.).

18. Aelred, *Spir amic* I, 53 PL 195:667A-B (CCCM 1:298; CF 5:62): '...et ita omnia ab ipso qui summe et pure unus est quoddam unitatis vestigium sortirentur.'

19. See Aelred, *Inst incl* 27; PL 32:1463 (cap. xxxix) (CCCM 1:659; CF 2:74). Cf. *Spec car* III, 1; PL 195:576D (CCCM 1:105): 'Et quia

in unitate nulla divisio, nulla sit ibi per diversa mentis
effusio, sed sit unum in uno, cum uno, per unum, circa unum,
unum sentiens, unum sapiens....' Aelred here stands firmly in
the wake of Augustine: cf. *Serm.* 103, 4; PL 38:614-615: 'Et
Dominus ad Patrem de suis: Ut sint unum, sicut et nos unum sumus
(Jn 17:22). Et in Actibus Apostolorum: Multitudinis autem cre-
dentium erat anima una et cor unum (Ac 4:32). Ergo magnificate
Dominum mecum, et exaltemus nomen eius in unum (Ps 33:4). Quia
unum est necessarium, unum illud supernum, unum ubi Pater et
Filius et Spiritus sanctus sunt unum...Ad hoc unum non nos per-
ducit, nisi multi habeamus cor unum.'

20. See *Tr.* XV; PL 204:546C (PC 40:17).
21. Bernard, *Csi* V, 19; PL 182:799-800 (SBOp 3:483; CF 37:164):
'...Porro haec et quaecumque alia dici una possunt, summae
illius unitatis imitatione, non comparatione, una appellari
vera sobriaque probat consideratio.'
22. See *ibid.*: 'Verum haec omnia quid ad illud summum atque, ut ita
dicam, unice unum....' See also SC 71, 9; PL 183:1125C-D (SBOp
2:220; CF 40:55-56): the unity of a community is not the same
as the unity of the Trinity, for 'that unity, which is not the
result of any unifying act, but which exists from eternity, is
unique and supreme (*singularis ac summa*).' According to the PL
text, in *Tr.* XV; PL 204:558D, Baldwin also refers to *unica unitas*,
but Thomas (PC 40:77) reads *una unitas*. Until I have re-examined
the manuscripts, I cannot be sure which of these readings is to
be preferred.
23. See T. Connor, 'The Theology of Contemplative Community' in Pennington, ed., *Contemplative Community*, 226.
24. Baldwin, *Tr.* XV; PL 204:550A (PC 40:33): 'Hujus vitae communis,
quae in Deo est, et Dei est, et Deus est, quaedam repraesentatio
est communis vita angelorum, quam in summa pace conciliat Spiritus
sanctus, sicut amor, et nexus, et communio.'
25. *Ibid.* 550A (PC 40:35): 'omnes idem volunt et idem nolunt.' *Idem
velle et idem nolle* is a proverbial expression which, according
to Sallust, Cataline used to rouse his fellow-conspirators to
revolt (see Sallust, *Catalina* 20, 4). As R. McGushin remarks,
it was 'a widely canvassed concept and it appears in a variety
of forms' (R. McGushin, *C. Sallustius Crispus, Bellum Catalinae:
A Commentary* [Leiden, 1977] 139). Aelred uses it in his *Spir
amic* I, 40; PL 195:665D (CCCM 1:296; CF 5:59).
26. See Baldwin, *Tr.* XV; PL 204:550A-B (PC 40:35). Part of this
description appears word for word in *Tr.* IV; PL 204:434D (PC
36:44) in a section which closely parallels the present discussion. For the same sort of thought, cf. Augustine, *De moribus
ecclesiae catholicae* I, xxxi, 67; PL 32:1338. Baldwin's description of the common life of the angels has also been influenced by
Paul's letter to the Philippians 2:2.

27. See *Tr.* XV; PL 204:550B-C (PC 40:35).
28. *Ibid.*
29. See K. S. Frank, *Angelikos Bios. Begriffsanalytische und begriffsgeschichtliche Untersuchungen zum 'engelgleichen Leben' im frühen Mönchtum* (Münster, 1964), and J. Leclercq, *The Life of Perfection: Points of View on the Essence of the Religious State*, tr. L. J. Doyle (Collegeville, 1961) 15-42. Most monastic writers lay stress on the way in which monks imitate the angelic virtues (e.g. 'Puritas angelica, munditia, castitas, caritas, pax et veritas, et omnes illae virtutes de quibus dicitur: Benedicite Domino omnes virtutes eius (Ps 102:21)' [Peter of Celle, *De disciplina claustrali* ix; PL 202:1115B-C (SCh 240: 185)]). Baldwin, however, concentrates on the angelic concord and unanimity and the way in which they do all things in common (cf. Aelred, *Sermo* 23 [= *De Omnibus Sanctis, Sermo* 2]; PL 195: 347C-348A. See further C. Dumont, 'Personalism in Community' in *Cistercian Studies* 12 (1977) 255-256).
30. This was certainly true for the Cistercians (particularly Aelred), but certain other orders--the Carthusians, for example-- had a less comprehensive view (see D. Knowles, *The Monastic Order in England* [Cambridge, 1950] 259, 376-377). Further on Aelred's view, see Dumont, 'Personalism in Community,' 263; the same author's 'Seeking God in Community according to St Aelred' in Pennington, ed., *Contemplative Community* 123-124; and his 'Aelred de Rievaulx' in *Théologie de la vie monastique: Études sur la Tradition patristique* [= TVM] (Paris, 1961) 534-536. If one does not accept this view, one teeters on the brink of Donatism.
31. Not everyone did like it. Sulpicius Severus and a Gallic friend had been listening to hair-raising tales of Egyptian asceticism, when Sulpicius turned to his friend and asked him how *he* would like a bunch of herbs and half a barley-cake as breakfast for five men. His friend, we are told, took the joke in good part, but said to Sulpicius, 'It's cruel (*inhumanus*) of you to try and force us Gauls to live after the example of the angels' (Sulpicius, *Dialogi* I, iv; PL 20:187B). We might also note that Baldwin (and others) leave us in no doubt that the regular clergy are certainly bound by the same exalted angelic ethics: see *Tr.* XII; PL 204: 531A-D (PC 39:120-124). Cf. Adam of Perseigne, *Ep.* XIV, 148; SCh 66:220-222; CF 21:182 (this letter is not to be found among the collection in PL 211) for the same idea.
32. See Chrysostom, *Adversus oppugnatores vitae monasticae* III, 14; PL 47:372-375. 'Teipsum prorsus fallis,' he says, 'si alia putas a saeculari, alia a monacho exigi' (372).
33. *Tr.* XV; PL 204:545B (PC 40:17).
34. See Leclercq, *Life of Perfection*, 63-80.
35. Guerric, *In natali apostolorum Petri et Pauli, sermo* 1, 3; PL 185:178A (SCh 202:370; CF 32:148-149).

36. *Tr.* XV; PL 204:560A (PC 40:79). Cf. also the text cited at
     n. 24 above.
37. See *ibid.* 557B (PC 40:65).
38. See Augustine, *De Trinitate* V, 12; PL 42:919 and XV, 37; PL 42:
     1086. See further F. Cavallera, 'La doctrine de saint Augustin
     sur l'Esprit-saint à propos du *De Trinitate*,' Part I, RTAM 2
     (1930) 369, 374, 380, 383, and 386.
39. See the whole of Part I of Cavallera's article (RTAM 2 [1930]
     365-387) for all these terms with references and illustrative
     texts.
40. See Augustine, *De Trinitate* VI, 7; PL 42:928 and Cavallera, 383.
41. See Cavallera, 380, 382-386. The concept is so well known that
     further references are unnecessary.
42. Augustine, *In Joannis Evangelium, Tractatus* 39, 4; PL 35:1684.
     Cf. *Collatio cum Maximino* 12; PL 42:715, translated in F. Martin,
     'Monastic Community and the Summary Statements in Acts,' in Pen-
     nington, ed., *Contemplative Community*, 36. The importance of
     Rm 5:5 for Augustine has been studied by A. M. la Bonnardière
     in 'Le verset paulinien Rom. V, 5 dans l'oeuvre de saint Augustin'
     in *Augustinus Magister: Congrès international augustinien, Paris,
     21-24 Septembre 1954* (Paris, 1954) 2:657-665.
43. See my 'The Ascetic Spirituality of B. of F.' in *Cîteaux* 31 (1980)
     239-245.
44. *Tr.* XV; PL 204:547B (PC 40:21): '...Caritas autem, quae per gra-
     tiam in nobis est, aliquo modo repraesentat nobis, qualis sit
     illa incomprehensibilis caritas, quae Deus est, cujus natura sive
     caritas, sive benignitas est.' In speaking of the nature of God,
     or of God the Holy Spirit, as *benignitas*, Baldwin is echoing a
     standard and wide-spread medieval idea. For further examples in
     Augustine, Bernard of Clairvaux, Adam Scot, Abelard, William of
     St Thierry, Thomas of Perseigne, and the Victorines, see my 'The
     Commentary on the Song of Songs of Thomas the Cistercian and His
     Conception of the Image of God,' *Cîteaux* 28 (1977) 13. See also
     Aelred, *Iesu* III, 25; PL 184:865B (CCCM 1:272; CF 2:32).
45. *Tr.* XIV; PL 204:543C (PC 39:200).
46. See Baldwin, *Tr.* XV; PL 204:556C-557A (PC 40:63-65). Cf. Augustine,
     Enarratio in Psalmum 130, 6; PL 37:1707.
47. See Baldwin, *Tr.* IV; PL 204:433C-435C (PC 36:38-48). Cf. Aelred,
     Oner 32; PL 195:496C-D. This is an old and fairly obvious analogy.
     Jerome, for example, makes it clear that it can be applied both
     to the individual and the community: see P. Antin, *Recueil sur
     saint Jerome* (Brussels, 1968) 117, 191-192. One of the most
     curious and striking analogies for this idea of 'unity in commun-
     ity' is to be found in Gilbert of Hoyland's exegesis of the pome-
     granate in *In Cantica, sermo* 35, 7; PL 184:187A-D (CF 26:432-433).
48. For examples from Augustine, Jerome, Richard of St Victor, and
     Thomas of Perseigne (PL 206:832A), see my 'Love and Charity in
     the Commentary on the Song of Songs of Thomas the Cistercian' in

Cîteaux 28 (1977) 262, and for examples from Augustine, Bernard,
Aelred, and Peter of Celle, see *Pierre de Celle, L'École du
cloître*, ed./tr. G. de Martel (SCh 240; Paris, 1977) 181-182 n. 1.

49. Cf. Martin, 'Monastic Community' in Pennington, ed., *Contemplative
Community*, 13: 'Yves Congar once remarked, "the texts of Acts 4:32
and 2:42-47, dominate and inspire all beginnings or reforms of
the religious life".'

50. See M. Verheijen, 'Saint Augustin' in TVM, 204-205, who also provides a full list of references. Cf. also Sage, *La vie religieuse*
59: 'Toutes les prescriptions de la *Règle de saint Augustin* se
résument dans l'*anima una et cor unum in Deum.*'

51. See William of St Thierry, *Vita Bern* III, 15; PL 185:235D.

52. See Baldwin, *Tr.* XV; PL 204: 553A (PC 40:47). See also n. 89
below.

53. See *ibid.* 546C (17).

54. For a comprehensive list of references to the concept of the
cloister as a *schola*, see de Martel's edition of *Pierre de Celle,
L'École du cloître*, 120-121 n. 2.

55. *Tr.* XV; PL 204:557C-D (PC 40:67-69). See also my 'Ascetic Spirituality of B. of F.' 242-243.

56. See *Sermo* 60, xi, 11; PL 38:408 in which Augustine expounds on
the principle 'Deus egere voluit in pauperibus.'

57. Aelred, *In Pentecostem, sermo* 2; *Sermones Inediti B. Aelredi
Abbatis Rievallensis*, ed. C. H. Talbot (Rome, 1952) 108: 'Deus,
itaque, licet sit sufficiens bonum sibi, abundantiam tamen bonitatis sue extendit creaturam, sibi detrahens et utilitatem omnibus conferens. Sed quia anima rationalis deo nil conferre potuit,
creati sunt eiusdem nature plures, ut in hac etiam parte similitudo
divine bonitatis, que refunderet in multos, mutuis beneficiis
appareret.' Cf. also *Spec car* III, xxii, 52; PL 195:596A (CCCM
1:129-130): 'Verum in Dei dilectione nobis non ipsi consulimus.
Deus enim noster est, et bonorum nostrorum non indiget: in mutua
autem dilectione quoniam mutuo indigemus, necesse est ut nobis in-
vicem consulamus.'

58. Christopher Smart, *Jubilate Agno*. Most cat *compendia* contain the
relevant extract. See, for example, G. MacBeth and M. Booth, eds.,
The Book of Cats (Penguin Books, 1979) 103.

59. See *Tr.* V; PL 204:447A (PC 36:118).

60. *Ibid.* 447B (120). We might note that for Baldwin, as for all the
Cistercian abbots, charity for one's neighbor in no way implies
a blindness to his faults. On the contrary, *discretio* is as important here as it is elsewhere (see my 'Ascetic Spirituality
of B. of F.', 232), and it is this which is at the root of Baldwin's startling pronouncement that it is better to hate your
neighbor well than to love him wickedly (see *Tr.* XV; PL 204:
554A [PC 40:51]). I presume that his inspiration for this surprising statement is either Augustine, *In Joannis Evangelium*,

Tractatus 51, 10; PL 35:1767, or Aelred, *Spec car* III, xxvi, 61; PL 195:599D (CCCM 1:134), or both.

61. See Augustine, *Enarratio in Psalmum 132*, 6; PL 37:1732-1733.
62. Baldwin, *Tr.* V; PL 204:447A (PC 36:118): 'Ergo malorum societas fugienda est, animo semper, sed non corpore semper; semper morum dissimilitudine, sed non semper corporali separatione.' This is also Bernard's teaching: see B. K. Lackner, 'The Monastic Life according to St Bernard' in J. R. Sommerfeldt, ed., *Studies in Medieval Cistercian History II* (CS 24; Kalamazoo, 1976) 52. References and illustrative texts are provided there. See also P. Deseille, 'Théologie de la vie monastique selon saint Bernard' in TVM, 513-514.
63. See Guerric, Adv 4, 2; PL 185:22D (SCh 166:136-138). Baldwin also quotes Qo 4:10 in showing how the nature of love is to share 'both its good and itself' (see *Tr.* XV; PL 204: 548A [PC 40:25]).
64. Bernard, PP 1, 4; PL 183:407C (SBOp 5:190): 'Sociabiliter, ut studeas amari et amare.' See generally J. Leclercq, 'La communauté formatrice selon S. Bernard' in *Collectanea Cisterciensia* 42 (1980) 3-21, especially 20-21.
65. See, for example, Hallier's discussion in his *Monastic Theology of Aelred of Rievaulx* 135-147, especially 138. 'Every human being accomplishes his return to God and effects the restoration of the divine image in himself within this community...The *transitus* is a community enterprise' (138). By God's dispensation, says Aelred, each of us needs the other, and what we do not have in ourselves, we have in the other, 'ut sic servetur humilitas, augeatur charitas, unitas cognoscatur' (*In natali Sancti Benedicti, sermo 7*; PL 195:249B).
66. C. Dumont, 'Aelred of Rievaulx's *Spiritual Friendship*' in J. R. Sommerfeldt, ed., *Cistercian Ideals and Reality* (CS 60; Kalamazoo, 1978) 191.
67. Hallier, *Monastic Theology of Aelred of Rievaulx*, 138, 141.
68. See *Tr.* XV; PL 204:547C (PC 40:21).
69. See *ibid.* 548A-B (25) and *passim*. See also my 'Ascetic Spirituality of B. of F.', 240-241. Richard of St Victor also discusses a *communio dilectionis* in the Trinity (see his *De Trinitate* III, xi; PL 196:922D [SCh 63:190]), and throughout the whole of this third book of the text he is obviously thinking along lines similar to Baldwin (there is an English translation of Book III by G. A. Zinn in his *Richard of St Victor: The Twelve Patriarchs, The Mystical Ark, Book Three of the Trinity* [New York, 1979] 371-397). Baldwin's terminology, however, appears to be his own, and his approach is quite distinct from that of Richard.
70. See Hallet, 'Notes sur le vocabulaire,' 272-274.
71. Baldwin, *Tr.* XV; PL 204:548B (PC 40:25). Gilbert of Hoyland also lays emphasis on charity's love for what is common: see

his *In Cantica, sermo* 19, 4; PL 184:99A-D (CF 20:242-243).

72. Hugh of Fouilloy, *De claustro animae* I, *prologus*; PL 176:1019B:
    'Summi quoque abbatis, scilicet Christi, pacem quam ibi habet cum
    subjectis, hic hortatur cum fratribus exhibendam'; IV, xliii;
    1181C: 'Inventor siquidem nostri ordinis missus fuit a claustro
    summi Abbatis, a sinu videlicet Dei Patris....'

73. See F. Martin, 'Monastic Community' in Pennington, ed., *Contem-
    plative Community*, 25, citing the eighth book of the *Nicomachean
    Ethics.*

74. See Aelred, *Spir amic* I, 46; PL 195:666B-C (CCCM 1:297; CF 5:61):
    'Amicitia itaque spiritalis inter bonos, vitae, morum, studiorum-
    que similitudine parturitur, quae est in rebus humanis atque
    divinis cum benevolentia et caritate consensio.' For a discussion
    of Aelred's sources, see Douglas Roby's introduction to the CF
    translation of *Spir amic*; CF 5:29-35. See also n. 25 above.

75. See Antin, *Recueil*, 109 n. 59, who quotes the relevant text.

76. Augustine, *De civitate Dei* XV, 5; PL 41:441 quoted in the trans-
    lation of Henry Bettenson, Augustine, *City of God* (Penguin Books,
    1972) 601. See further my 'Ascetic Spirituality of B. of F.',
    240.

77. In Augustine, see *In Joannis Evangelium, Tractatus* 32, 8; PL
    35:1646: Augustine lists all the spiritual gifts mentioned in
    1 Co 12:8-10 and continues: 'Multa enim dantur ad manifestationem,
    sed tu forsitan eorum omnium quae dixi nihil habes. Si amas,
    non nihil habes: si enim amas unitatem, etiam tibi habet quis-
    quis in illa habet aliquid. Tolle invidiam, et tuum est quod
    habeo; tolle invidiam, et meum est quod habes.' In Aelred, see
    the texts cited by Dumont in his 'Personalism in Community,'
    256-258, especially *In natali Sancti Benedicti, sermo* III; PL
    195:249A (= *Sermo* 7): '...sed sint omnibus omnia communia. Quod
    non tantum intelligendum est, fratres, de cuculla et tunica;
    sed multo magis de virtutibus et spiritualibus donis' (see Du-
    mont, 256-257). In Baldwin, see *Tr.* XV; PL 204:559D (PC 40:77),
    and 561B (85) quoted at n. 78 below.

78. *Ibid.* 'Duobus modis divisiones gratiarum ad communionem reducuntur,
    cum dona quae singulis sigillatim dantur, per communionem amoris
    communiter habentur, et cum per amorem communionis communiter
    amantur.'

79. See Aelred, *Anima* III, 47; CCCM 1:752. Aelred is here inspired
    by Augustine, *In Joannis Evangelium, Tractatus* 68, 1; PL 35:1814.
    See also *ibid.* 67, 2; PL 35:1812: 'atque ita Deus erit omnia in
    omnibus, ut quoniam Deus charitas est, per charitatem fiat ut
    quod habent singuli, commune sit omnibus. Sic enim quisque etiam
    ipse habet, cum amat in altero quod ipse non habet. Non erit
    itaque aliqua invidia imparis claritatis, quoniam regnabit in
    omnibus unitas charitatis.' Aelred takes this idea to its logical

conclusion: in a society truly united in charity 'sicut unusquisque de propria, sic et de alterius felicitate laetetur; et ita singulorum beatitudo omnium sit, et omnium beatitudinem universitas singulorum' (*Spir amic* III, 79; PL 195:690C [CCCM 1:333; CF 5:111]).

80. *Tr.* XV; PL 204:561D-562A (PC 40:87-89).

81. *Ibid.*; 562B-C (89-91). How do we love the saints? 'We love them most of all...if we recall their merits and consider their faith, charity, devotion, and patience, and are thereby stirred to rival [their achievements] and inflamed to imitate their virtues' (*ibid.* 561D [87]).

82. *Ibid.* 562C (91).

83. See Leclercq, *Life of Perfection*, 119-125, with illustrative texts from Jerome, Damian, Anselm of Canterbury, Denis the Carthusian, Bernard of Clairvaux, Nicholas of Clairvaux, and others. We may compare William of St Thierry, *Ep frat* I, iv, 10; PL 184:314A-B (SCh 223:168; CF 12:20), in which the author associates *cella* 'cell' and *coelum* 'heaven' both phonologically and etymologically.

84. Paul Meyvaert quotes a nice passage from the *Rationale Divinorum Officiorum* of the thirteenth-century writer William Durandus: 'Just as the Church building symbolises the Church Triumphant, so is the *claustrum* a symbol of the heavenly paradise, a paradise where all will live together with one heart, rooted in the Love and Will of God, where all possessions will be held in common, where love will make each one possess in another whatever he may lack in himself. This image of Paradise is given by those who dwell within the cloister' ('The Medieval Monastic *Claustrum*' in *Gesta* 12 [1973] 58).

85. See Augustine, *Sermo* 151, 5; PL 38:817. This is a standard Augustinian idea. For a more detailed discussion of *propria voluntas* and its conquest in Baldwin's thought, see my 'Ascetic Spirituality of B. of F.,' *passim*.

86. Augustine, *Enarratio in Psalmum* 148, 4; PL 37:1940.

87. See n. 53 above.

88. See J. Leclercq, 'Le monachisme clunisien' in TVM 451.

89. *Tr.* XV; PL 204: 556B (PC 40:61): 'Haec est ergo lex vitae communis, unitas spiritus in caritate Dei, vinculum pacis in mutua et continua caritate fratrum omnium, communio in omnibus bonis communicandis, omni occasione habendae proprietatis a sanctae religionis proposito procul relegata.'

90. Hallier, *Monastic Theology of Aelred of Rievaulx*, 165.

91. Leclercq, 'St Bernard of Clairvaux and the Contemplative Community' in Pennington, ed., *Contemplative Community*, 112.

92. Dumont, 'Seeking God in Community according to St Aelred' in *ibid.* 116.

93. See my 'B. of F. and Twelfth-Century Theology,' in E. R. Elder (ed.), *Noble Piety and Reformed Monasticism: Studies in Medieval*

Cistercian History VII, (CS 65; Kalamazoo, 1981) *passim*, and
'Ascetic Spirituality of B. of F.,' 227-228. For a discussion
of the career of the despicable Roger Norreys, see Knowles,
Monastic Order in England 331-345.

94. See Leclercq's introduction to John Morson's edition of *B. de F.*,
Le sacrement de l'autel; (SCh 93; Paris, 1963) 44.

95. For further discussion of Baldwin's sources, both named and un-
named, see my 'B. of F. and Twelfth-Century Theology,' 141-142.

96. A great deal of work in this area has been done by Paul Antin.
See especially his *Recueil*, chapters VII, VIII, IX (= TVM 191-
199), X, XXII, XXIII, and XXIV.

97. See, for example, the introduction to M. P. Macpherson's translation of *A Rule of Life for a Recluse* in Aelred of Rievaulx,
Treatises, The Pastoral Prayer (CF 2; Spencer, 1971) 44 n. 4.
Much more could be said on this matter, but this is not the place
to say it.

98. See *De gestis episcoporum Antisiodorensium*; PL 138:293D cited by
Antin in his *Recueil* 291 n. 1. In *ibid.* 140 (= TVM 194) Antin
again refers to Jerome as 'ce docteur du monachisme.'

99. See H. Crouzel, 'Origène, précurseur du monachisme' in TVM 15-
38. This is a useful and accurate summary of the question and
contains all necessary references to the standard secondary
materials.

100. Again, for summaries and further bibliographical references, see
A. de Vogüé, 'Monachisme et église dans la pensée de Cassien' in
TVM 213-240, and R. Gillet, 'Spiritualité et place du moine dans
l'église selon saint Grégoire le Grand' in TVM 323-351. According
to Aelred, the ideas of all these early fathers are to be found
in the *Rule of St Benedict*: 'In Regula [sancti Benedicti] reful-
get aurum beatissimi Augustini, argentum Hieronymi, bis tinctus
coccus Gregorii, sed et sententiae sanctorum Patrum, quasi lapi-
des pretiosi, quibus omnibus hoc coeleste aedificium decoratur'
(*In natali Sancti Benedicti, sermo* III; PL 195:248A [= *Sermo* 7]).

101. See J. Morson, 'The *De Cohabitatione Fratrum* of Hugh of Barzelle'
in *Studia Anselmiana* 4, *Analecta Monastica* 4 (1957) 119-140.

SINGULARITY AND SIMPLICITY IN GILBERT OF HOYLAND (d. 1172)

Lawrence C. Braceland, SJ

I N CISTERCIAN AUTHORS of the twelfth century, *singularity* and *simplicity* are frequent and evocative words and ideas. This paper will consider the use of *singularity* and of *simplicity* in *one* of those authors, Gilbert of Hoyland.

Singularity versus Community

In Gilbert, *singular* and *singularity* are in contrast with *common* and *community*. In effect, *singularity* and *community* help to define each other.[1] In three passages, *singularity* is distinguished first from charity, then from *community*, and finally from subordination, *common* life and *common* property:

'At the pool in the Gospel', writes Gilbert on Jn 5:2-9, 'one man used to be healed after the movement of the water, but in that one man was the symbol of charity, not of *singularity*.'[2] Again, Gilbert writes about Mary Magdalen on the first Easter: suddenly Mary 'hears his word: "Do not touch me!" (Jn 20:17). What one woman could not do, many could do, those to whom he said: "Hail!" and they approached and embraced his feet (Mt 28:9). What *singularity* cannot embrace, *community* does embrace.'[3] In a passage on the prodigal son, Gilbert expands on withdrawal from *community*: 'Beware, brethren, lest in any of you there exist the evil-heartedness of *singularity*, of withdrawal from the *community* of your brothers and the watchfulness of your spiritual father. Beware lest any of you who have made profession of *common life*, fall into this very pattern of withdrawal and of private property.'[4]

On the periphery versus 'in the center'

Singularity is on the periphery, while *community* is 'in the center'. Commenting on Ps 67:14, 'if you sleep in the midst of the chosen', Gilbert remarked:

one who desires nothing for himself *in a singular way* and loves nothing in himself *in a singular way*, places himself 'in the middle', as it were, amid different shares of undifferentiated glory. One who indiscriminately accepts for himself the goods of others and shares his own gifts with others, does he not appear to you to be well placed in the midst and not drawn further away into some faction?[5]

On a similar verse of the Canticle: 'he inlaid the center with charity', Gilbert comments:

> Charity does not think of private gain; it rejoices in
> what is in the center and *common* to all...Christ is *com-*
> *mon* to all, for he is the Mediator and therefore things
> which are not in the center but confine themselves to
> a part, are not his...Do not imprison within the narrow
> limits of your heart a generosity which is *common* to all.
> Do you see how charity is the special emblem of disciple-
> ship in Christ and the singular mark of his teaching?[6]

On another verse of the Canticle, the locks of the bride are believers in unity and in *community*. Gilbert applies the locks first to
one soul individually and then collectively to the *community*. Here
is his transition:

> Why are we applying this text to one soul individually?
> Let us extend our interpretation to the condition of the
> Church, for more pleasant is what applies *in common*. In
> Scripture nothing is more pleasing to the Bridegroom than
> *the community*, or rather the unity of believers (Eph 4:13)
> and the embrace of the Church.[7]

Gilbert is not content to point out the differences between *singularity* and *community*, nor to list and discuss the many kinds of disaffection from the *community*, from *acedia* to *tedium*. Far from ignoring those who are disaffected from the *community*, he tries to understand and to help:

> Unhappy surely is the man who although placed amid the
> lilies, amid the lilies of a *holy community*, where on all
> sides various virtues yield their fragrance, has not
> learned to perceive any sweet perfume, anything resem-
> bling lilies....Would that in this Lebanon of ours, in
> this *holy community* of monks, which both our profession
> and our way of life make charming and chaste, in our
> Lebanon, I say, would that one could discern neither the
> peak of Amana nor the crests of Senir and Hermon.[8]

The people on these three mountains Gilbert characterizes as follows:
those on Amana are vain or fretful people; on Senir, a shaggy and
hairy race; on Hermon, full of hostility and disaffection, indeed anathematized:

> Such a one is not of God's household, not a fellow citi-
> zen, not even a resident alien or a guest...[9] Even now,

good Jesus, if a son of our mother be dead--I mean a son
of this *holy community*, of this widow with whom, so to
speak, you lodge--do you restore him to life...Lead him
to the softer bed of a better hope, by which he may draw
near to God....Then is restored to his mother, the son
she had lost before, while she did not retain his affection but wept over his dead devotion. He returns to us
renewed, after you have clothed him with yourself.[10]

In the striking image of the pomegranate in the Canticle, a good
summary of the place of the *individual in community*, Gilbert comments:

The parable of the pomegranate regards ourselves, for by
rule we live together in *communities* and are united in
one Order like seeds beneath one rind. Yes, may we imitate these seeds, resembling them not only by unanimity
in union of hearts but also by the embrace, as it were,
of our Order...Let us also learn to differ from one another in number, not in spirit. Seeds neither quarrel with
one another, nor grumble about the rind, nor try to break
through the rind...In this Order of ours, brothers, as if
in the rind of a pomegranate, does not the color of Christ's
passion glow red by our imitation? Yes, like the seeds of
this fruit are they who consider it second nature to be
united under the rind of regular discipline and regard themselves not as constrained but as protected. Let there be no
love of property, no love of private ownership, and then
you appear as a seed of this fruit....
However many *communities* of an Order you may see, regard all as so many pomegranates which have issued from
the fountain of baptism. Yes, as we read in Acts, 'the
believers had one heart and one soul' (Ac 4:32). From believers as from the seeds of so many congregations living
in an orderly way and in unity of spirit, pomegranates
have developed. Those first *communities* of believers were
not yet bound by the institute of any Order but by the impulse of love. To dwell in unity they considered not only
useful, not only good, but also pleasant....[11]

Simplicity versus Duplicity

Simplicity is opposed to *duplicity*. The *simplicity* of silence
mutes the excessive noise in the soul and attunes the soul to the
wonderful *simplicity* of the word of God, which is made welcome by
every soul of *simple* faith. This rare virtue of *simplicity* is pictured both as the eye which is *simple* and as the eyes of a dove.

Simplicity is a reflection of and a participation in the divine *Simplicity*.12
    Without using either word, *simple* or *simplicity*, in a treatise sent to Roger of Byland, Gilbert comments at length on what he calls *our rusticity*.13 In summing up, he refers to Cistercians 'among whom linger traces of what men call our ancient rustic behavior.'14 In a sermon addressed to nuns but applicable also to monks, Gilbert comments on one attitude of Christ, especially to those who have embraced the cistercian vocation. He lists first the *simplicity of silence*: 'Christ has a greater horror of harsh manners and sharp tongues than of the pricks of thorns, especially in people who have been called to the *simplicity of silence*, to the commerce of charity, to the repose of leisure, to the school of humility, to a vow of obedience and to the bond of unity.'15 Gilbert cautions a promising cleric named Adam from excusing himself from entry into religion on the score of

> devotion to empty literature,...lest distorted by the subtleties of Aristotle you find fault with our *silence and our simplicity*. Yet in *silence* and *in simplicity* especially is the occasion granted us, 'in contemplating face to face the glory of the Lord, to be transformed into the same image from splendor to splendor as it were by the Spirit of the Lord' (2 Co 3:18). Does our silence seem to you inactive and artless, wherein the activity described for you above is our preoccupation? wherein is taught and practised the art of advancing towards God as it were in a straight line?16

    This *simplicity of silence* mutes the excessive noise in the soul and tunes in the *wonderful simplicity* of the word of God. Gilbert began the first draft of his commentary on the Canticle by reflecting on the *wonderful simplicity* of this verse: 'In my little bed by night I sought him whom my soul loves. I sought him and did not find him' (Sg 3:1). As earlier authors had done, Gilbert uses both the nut and the honeycomb to distinguish between the literal and the spiritual senses of Scripture:

> O how much sweetness exists in the kernel, if so much is tasted in the shell. Mysteries lie hidden to be dug out with effort, but the charm of the words is on the surface, offered gratuitously, slipping without effort into pure souls. Now we do not pay so much attention to the mysteries as to disregard the melody, for these are songs and prefer to be sung rather than debated. I know not whether they can be analyzed more clearly than when they are sung.

Indeed they are honeycombs. When they are analyzed they
are seen by the eye, but when they are sung they are sa-
vored by the tongue. In very different ways does the
taste of the honeycomb tickle the palate and the sight
of the honeycomb greet the eye.[17]

Later Gilbert would comment on the charm of the words in another
verse of the Canticle: 'henna with nard, nard and saffron, calamus
and cinnamon' (sg 4:12):

These words could have been enough to arouse your aesthetic sense. Indeed their *simplicity* is enough for this
sense, yet not enough for the understanding. We must
humor the understanding, which longs to feed on the truth
in our sensations. The refrain of these musical words
rings pleasantly in the ear: ...Perish the thought that
their meaning is not more pleasing.[18]

The Simplicity of Faith

At least three times Gilbert refers to Jesus' distinction between what is hidden 'from the wise and prudent but revealed to lit-
tles ones' (Mt 11:25),[19] but in these references he omits the words
simple and *simplicity*. In six other passages, however, he speaks of
simple faith and the *simplicity of faith*: the first two passages emphasize the object of belief or a creed, while the next four emphasize the act of belief or *fiducia*:

Each and every article of *simple faith*, presented with some
tasty seasoning of explanation, begets in the hearer the
sweetest of affections and transports of the mind.[20]

The Lord drinks wine with milk, because he tempers and
sweetens lofty meanings and surpassing contemplations with
the *simplicity of faith and morals*. He loves the fervor of
zeal, provided milk is at hand to nourish the little ones.[21]

A good sobriety is *simplicity of faith*, for the gaze of the
beholders can endure it and be encouraged by it. Happy the
one who in descending is welcomed on this level of faith
and who in ascending begins on this level.[22]

The *simplicity of such faith* [in the Passion] has less understanding but a great incentive to admiration and love. Here
is a scene accessible to all, which gives birth to the sweetest of transports.[23]

It is a most beautiful realm for contemplation, where a *simple*

consideration of the faith sprinkles the dew of heavenly
and fragrant affections and breathes in the grace of eternal
light.[24]

In our text (Sg 4:1), those dove-like eyes are within, where
simplicity of faith purifies the *heart* and gives light to the
eyes of the *heart*, where not only the eye but the whole inner
self of the *heart* is said to be hidden.[25]

The *simplicity of silence*, then, allows us to absorb the *simplicity*
of the word with the *simplicity of faith*, that is, with our belief in
what has been revealed.

The Virtue of Simplicity

In his striking sermon from which the last quotation was taken,
Gilbert admits that the *virtue of simplicity is rare*. In that sermon, he recounts how the Bridegroom, in sketching the features of his
bride, wisely begins with her eyes, for 'if the *eye be simple*, the
whole body will be full of light' (Mt 6:22-3). The bridegroom compares
her eyes to those of doves, and shows that his beloved is *simple as a*
dove according to Matthew (Mt 10:16):

> the simple's   f   's intention throws light on the whole
> body of one's work and insures that deeds which of them-
> selves could shine before men, would shine before God (Mt
> 5:16, Mk 1:10, Jn 1:32)...Good then is a *simple eye*, for
> it has no share of darkness and makes bright the whole body
> of man's behavior.[26]...In the eyes of the bride, however,
> both are commended: *simplicity and spirituality*. There-
> fore hers are called the eyes of doves.[27] A wrong inten-
> tion and an unfavorable interpretation--each is malicious,
> each is venomous, each false, having nothing in *common*
> with the nature of doves. The eyes of doves are those
> which neither wish to be deceived nor know how to deceive.
> Do you not know that your Bridegroom is Truth? How will
> he say to you, my dove, my beloved! (Sg 2:13-14), when you
> do not rejoice in *simplicity? Simplicity* is the beloved
> of *Truth*; therefore Truth consorts with the *simple* (Pr 3:32).
> In our text the Bridegroom praises the *simplicity* of his be-
> loved with the words: 'yours are the eyes of doves'. Wide-
> eyed *simplicity* is good, for it closes the eyes to pre-
> tense, yet is not blind to the truth.[28]

Gilbert indicates that Christ attributes to the beauty of the
bride, her prudence, not of the flesh but of the spirit: 'Such prudence is pictured in the eyes of doves, since her prudence reflects

simplicity and spirituality, because in the figure of a dove the holy
Spirit is usually understood. Such *simplicity* is not wont to be empty,
for much hidden grace lies concealed within.[29] Gilbert confesses his
ignorance of the specific meaning of the words, *'dove-like simplicity*,
apart from what lies hidden within'. He suggests, however, that he
could recommend this *devout simplicity*, and exhort one to emulate it,
because it contains and perhaps bestows so inexplicable and gentle a
mystery.[30] He then invites his brethren to embrace *holy simplicity*,
repose of mind, pure meditations, free prayer, for in such vessels
and so to speak, in the ark of holy meditation and in the interior urn
of prayer, there is set for us a divine nourishment and that portion
of glory of which we read: 'I shall be filled when your glory appears'
(Ps 16:15 Vulgate).[31]

Simplicity which is in Christ versus duplicity

Gilbert opposes to duplicity that simplicity which is in Christ.
Choosing his most frequent scriptural quotation, he says that *that
simplicity* is good, 'where you who cling to Christ are one spirit with
him' (1 Co 6:17). He continues:

> *Simplicity* exists where *unity* exists. *Simplicity* exists,
> if you live no longer, but Christ lives in you (Ga 2:20),
> if the wisdom of God consumes you, if spiritual joy ab-
> sorbs you and seeps into your inmost marrow. And where
> is such *simplicity* save in his little bed?[32]

'I am afraid', Gilbert again quotes Paul, 'that as the serpent se-
duced Eve, so *your ideas* may be led astray from the simplicity which
is in Christ' (2 Co 11:3). Quoting the same text of Paul, Gilbert
writes to Brother William, who intends to leave for the court of a
duke: 'yet I have anxieties: lest *your affections* be corrupted and
fall from that *simplicity which is in Christ.*'[33] Again he writes,
either apologetically or with tongue in cheek, to Brother Richard,
probably the abbot of Fountains Abbey: 'I have been covered with confusion, for beneath the wool of your *simplicity* I have woven the
flax of my *insincerity*. Perhaps for the bruises of my *duplicity*,
you have sent me twin chalices.'[34]

Cloaks of various kinds are a sign of *duplicity* and therefore
opposed to *simplicity*: 'when the cloak of blemished stripes is removed and *naked simplicity* takes its place, when behavior has been
changed for the better by her ministry, then understandably the
bride is being welcomed for her crown.'[35] Gilbert comments on three
further cloaks suggested by the text: 'the watchman took away my
cloak' (Sg 5:8).

The city watchmen [the angels] took away the cloak in

which as a penalty Adam was wrapped, when stripped of the
splendor of his former *simplicity*. They took away the co-
verlets of fantasies by which he was interiorly impeded.
They took away the cloak, the veil of symbols, and introduced him to the truth. The *simple truth*, revealed and
manifest, begets the fervor of love.[36]

The city watchmen [his superiors] filched my cloak, the
cloak of simplicity, the cloak of light, the amice of
gladness, the vestment of burning affection. How often
was I wont to be wholly wrapped in such cloaks, to be
kept warm in saffron!...The comfortable cloaks I boasted
of, they took away and invested me in others that were a
burden, [the pallium of office].[37]

Because the watchmen took away the cloak of the bride (Sg
5:8), she is revealed to herself in *pure and naked simplicity* and with her affections free for the engagements
of love...If you do not absolutely relinquish your office,
why do you not at least relinquish your worries for a while?
We do not withdraw you from your interests, but we wish you
to reduce their intensity.[38]

To illustrate how the eye of the lover should be fixed on the Beloved,
Gilbert uses a metaphor from archery:

Those who want a sharper view, cock one eye for a more re-
liable view in a direct line. Your eye is one if it is
pure; it is one if it is not directed to many objects; it
is one if somehow it is *simplified* and focused upon and
directed to one object, not split, not wandering, not divided among many objects. Your eye is one if you always
view and focus on one object and on that alone. In our
text, if it is the eye of love, it is one.[39]

The archer cocks one eye to focus an eye of love on the Beloved. The
simple eye brightens the whole body of one's behavior. The bride's
eyes, however, are compared to those of a dove, to show that she is
simple as a dove, but her eyes are mentioned in the plural, because
in her are commended both *simplicity and spirituality*. *Simplicity*
means truth and unity and love.

Simplicity, a divine attribute

The *simplicity* of the bride is a reflection of and a participation in the *simplicity* of the Bridegroom. Gilbert distinguishes be-

tween the head and the locks of the Bridegroom, that is, the Godhead
and the divine attributes (Sg 5:12):

> The Godhead, then, take as the head, the attributes as
> its locks. For the Godhead in itself is *one and simple*,
> but so far as it affects its subjects and impresses its
> image on them individually, the Godhead receives many
> titles of different meaning.[40]

Gilbert reflects on God's attributes seen in his creatures, (Rm 1:20):

> His invisible attributes are visible to the eye of reason
> in the things he has made...How am I not refreshed by what
> bears some pledge, shows some sign, recalls some memory,
> suggests some knowledge of my Love? But again, how do I
> not suffer disappointment, as I reflect that I am being
> cozened by an image, delayed by a shadow, and that I do
> not possess the *naked and simple reality?* 'I will go about
> the city', because in its wide expanse, so fair, I am every-
> where encouraged but nowhere renewed.[41]

In his fourth treatise, Gilbert compares creatures with their Creator:

> Granted that all creatures in the universe are fair to be-
> hold and fashioned in unity and suited to our needs and
> powerful in their effect, still what are they all in com-
> parison with the immense and *simple* and eternal unity of
> the divine essence, in comparison with the beauty of di-
> vine wisdom, the depth of divine love and the might of di-
> vine power?[42]

In his second epistle, Gilbert invites Adam, a scholar, to become a
Cistercian and a teacher of theology:

> O would that some day I might listen to you discoursing
> in the house of the Lord, explaining the mystic and mys-
> terious meanings of the texts, cupping and delicately
> sharing with us some drops of the majesty, the eternity,
> the immensity, the *simplicity* of the divine Essence!
> There nothing is minimal, because this Essence is *simple;*
> nothing is multiple, because this Essence is without
> measure; but the whole is infinite, neither by succession
> in time nor by extension of mass in space, but by essen-
> tial force and power.[43]

In attempting to solve a textual problem referred to him by a friend,
Gilbert comments in his fifth and unfinished treatise: 'Indeed every-

thing which is with the Father of Lights must be considered *simple*
and uniform, not multiple.'[44] Several times he reflects on *divine
Simplicity* and the Incarnation:

> Wonderful in itself is the *divine Simplicity*, but if I may
> so express it, this new blending [in the Incarnation] is
> more wonderful because it is newer. I cannot marvel enough
> at the art of this union, nor, I think, can the angels. In-
> deed they have greater reason to wonder, for to them the
> pure *Simplicity* of the divine nature, made itself known with
> greater clarity. That *Simplicity* is pure beyond comparison
> and therefore makes this union more wonderful.[45]

Again Gilbert writes to a friend about the Incarnation:

> Good is the mixture where grace blends with truth, know-
> ledge with wisdom, the human with the divine. What be-
> longs to Divinity is pure through and through, where
> nothing is either composed of parts or materially subor-
> dinate or formally affected. Therefore nothing is diverse,
> whether created simultaneously or treated successively,
> but all things which in us and according to us are separ-
> ate in name and in notion, here contrary ' are indictin-
> guishable and essential *simplicity*, a blending which
> nothing can divide. These then are the really *pure and
> simple* attributes of Divinity, but they are blended with
> human attributes into the unity of the Person through the
> mystery of the Incarnation.[46]

Gilbert discourses about heaven, probably to Roger of Byland: 'There
we shall enjoy a continuous and unfaltering everlastingness, though
not that absolute *simplicity* conformed to the unity of God. All
other than God, though they be everlasting, are in no way simple.'[47]
Gilbert comments on the heavenly vision of God and of the God-Man:

> Joyous contemplation it is in the family of heaven to gaze
> upon *simplicity* of essence, serenity of mind and the sweet-
> ness of mutual love. Joyous contemplation it is to gaze
> upon everlasting existence, purity of understanding, depth
> of knowledge, and also upon humility in obedience, tran-
> quillity in diligence, ease in achievement.[48]

Finally Gilbert advises a return from heavenly banquets to the blended cup of the Incarnation:

> Therefore, excluded from those banquets, let us return to
> his breasts, from the banquets of contemplation to the

breasts and to the clusters; from that undiluted and festive *simplicity* to this blended cup which Wisdom mixed
for us in that mixing bowl wherein dwells all the full-
ness of divinity.[49]

Summary

In Gilbert, then, *singularity* is opposed to community. *Singularity* is a withdrawal from common life, from the union of individuals in *community*, where the seeds are united under the red rind of
the pomegranate. *Simplicity* is opposed to *duplicity*. The *simplicity
of silence* mutes the excessive noises in the soul and attunes the
soul to the wonderful *simplicity* of the word of God, which is welcomed by every soul of *simple faith*. This rare virtue of *simplicity*
is pictured both as the eye which is *simple* and as the eyes of a
dove. *Simplicity* is a reflection of and a participation in the divine *Simplicity*.

NÓTES

1. Here I prescind from Gilbert's use of *singular* as 'special' or
    'unique', as in Sermon 19:4-5; PL 184:99B-D; CF 20:242-3, and
    from *singular* as opposed to 'plural' or 'multiple', as in S5:3;
    PL 184, 33D; CF 14, p. 88. Hereafter only the column in Migne
    184, will be given; the following abbreviations are adopted here:
    E = Epistles; S = Sermons on the Song of Songs; T = Treatises.
2. S47:2; 246C; CF 26:561: *in illo signata est charitas, non singula-
    ritas.*
3. T 2:1; 259A; CF 34:16: *quod non potest singularitas, obtinet com-
    munitas, obtinet caritas.*
4. Ms. Bodley 87, f. 93r, CF 34:150, 152: *Videte, fratres, ne sit in
    aliquo vestrum cor malum* [*sic*] *singularitatis, discedendi a con-
    sortio fratrum, a spiritualis patris custodia. Videte ne quis
    vestrum, qui communem estis professi vitam, in hoc ipsum incidat
    separationis et proprietatis exemplum.*
5. CF 34:137.
6. S19:4-5, 99B-D; CF 20:242-3: *singulare exemplum*, i.e. special or
    unique.
7. S30:5; 158C; CF 20:365.
8. S28:1; 145B; CF 20:342, and S29:7; 153C; CF 20:356.
9. S29:7; 153C; CF 20:356.
10. S16:8; 86A-C; CF 20:213.

11. S35:7; 187BC; CF 26:432-3.
12. Fr Chrysogonus Waddell suggested that a series of monographs on *simplicity* in cistercian authors of the twelfth century 'would be a valuable contribution in the field of cistercian studies' (CS 61, pp. 11-12). When his article on 'Simplicity and Ordinariness' was translated into French for an issue of Collectanea on 'La simplicité cistercienne', the issue was introduced by a summary of a sermon from Gilbert of Hoyland, (S22:3, in *Coll.* 41 (1979) p. 2). With Fr Waddell, let me acknowledge a debt to a few of many authors: Jean Leclercq, 'Un plaidoyer pour l'unité' in ASOC 9 (1953), fasc. 1-2, pp. 199-201. See Thomas Merton's enviable article, 'St. Bernard on Interior Simplicity', in CS 9 (1980) pp. 107-157, and the entire issue of *Coll.* on Cistercian Simplicity, tome 41, no. 1 (1979) pp. 1-119.
13. T 7^2:4; 283A-C; CF 34:70-71.
14. T 7^2:11; 287D; CF 34:78: *apud quos antiquae, ut aiunt, rusticitatis resedere vestigia.*
15. S20:7; 107A; CF 20:256-7.
16. E 2:4; 292D-293A; CF 34:96-7.
17. *Mira simplicitas,* paragraph 1; ms Bodley 24; CF 26:577.
18. S36:2; 188CD; CF 26:436-7.
19. S18:5 and 6; S20:4; 95B, 96A, 105A; CF 20:232, 234, 253.
20. S6:6; 42A; CF 14:103.
21. S41:2; 215A; CF 26:493.
22. S20:2; 103B; CF 20:250.
23. S20:5; 105B; CF 20:254.
24. S27:6; 144B; CF 20:337.
25. Ac 15:9, Eph 1:18, 1 P 3:4; S22:4; 116C; CF 20:278.
26. S22:2; 114D-115A; CF 20:275.
27. S22:2; 115B; CF 20:275.
28. S22:3; 115CD; CF 20:276.
29. S22:3; 116B; CF 20:277.
30. *dulce mysterium,* S22:5; 117B; CF 20:279.
31. S20:7; 118B; CF 20:280-81.
32. S16:5; 84C; CF 20:210; on *simplicity and unity of spirit,* see also S23:8; 124B; CF 20:293.
33. E 3:2; 294C; CF 34:100.
34. E 1:2; 290BC; CF 34:89.
35. S29:8; 154C; CF 20:358.
36. S45:5; 239AB; CF 26:544.
37. S45:6; 240AB; CF 26:545; see also S45:6; 239D; CF 26:544-5.
38. S45:8; 241B; CF 26:547.
39. S30:3; 156C; CF 20:364; see also 156D.
40. S43:3; 227A; CF 26:519.
41. S4:8; 31C; CF 14:82.
42. T 4:1; 266C; CF 34:34.

43. E 2:3; 292B; CF 34:94.
44. T 5:2; 271C; CF 34:44; see also T 6:2; 273A; CF 34:49.
45. S21:3; 111A; CF 20:266.
46. T 6:4; 273D; CF 34:50.
47. T 1:8; 257A; CF 34:11.
48. S7:6; 46B; CF 14:113.
49. T 6:9; 276A; CF 34:54.

A PRODIGAL WRITES HOME:
AELRED OF RIEVAULX'S *De institutione inclusarum*

Marsha D. Stuckey

ELRED OF RIEVAULX'S *De institutione inclusarum* begins with
an explicit statement of its audience and purpose: 'For many
years now, my sister, you have been asking me for a rule to
guide you in the life you have embraced for the sake of Christ,
to provide spiritual directives and formulate the basic practices of
religious life....I shall do as you ask then, and endeavor to draw up
a definite rule for you, selecting from among the various regulations
of the Fathers those that appear most useful in forming the exterior
man. I shall add some details suited to your particular circumstances
of time and place, and, wherever it seems helpful, blend the spiritual
with the corporal.'[1]
   Aelred is writing a work of instruction for anchoresses, those
who have chosen to devote their lives in solitude to Christ. His introduction makes that clear, and what follows is precisely what one
would expect: rules for eating, sleeping, praying, working, speech,
and silence, a discussion of virtues central to the anchoritic life,
and three meditations to assist the anchoress in contemplation. The
central metaphor of the work is the spiritual marriage of the contemplative to Christ; she is urged to remain pure in expectation of and
preparation for her bridegroom's embrace. The mystical foretastes
of that embrace in this life and its enjoyment in that to come are
the rewards of the anchoress's calling.
   Chastity, which allows and merits the bridegroom's embrace, is
the central and defining virtue of the anchoress's life. It is a
gift from God and a sign of his special grace to her; at the same
time it invites and wins Christ's love. This paradox is more than
an apparent one: the anchoress must constantly keep in mind both elements, remembering that the virtue is not of her own doing and that
she is yet responsible for maintaining herself chaste if she is to
merit the keeping of the love that God gave freely. At the same
time--the circle continues--if she remains pure that too is God's
doing, his grace to her. Much of Aelred's direction to his sister
centers in chastity as the outward sign of God's love and of lust
as the sign of man's flight from that love.
   The work fits firmly into the genre of spiritual instruction
and holds a secure place in the history of devotion through its influence on Bonaventure's *Tree of Life* and Ignatius of Loyola's *Spiritual Exercises*. It is also one of the most valuable historical documents on the anchoritic life and has provided the model (and sometimes
the very words) for other English anchoritic works.[2]

Certain as are all such definitions of the nature and influence
of Aelred's treatise, a repeated reading of the text yields a rather
different understanding of its dramatic and dynamic core and even,
perhaps, of its audience. According to that understanding, the work
is not centrally for or about the seeker after God's love, not about
the anchoress who is chosen for and maintained in purity by God's
mercy. Rather, it focuses on the sinner, the one who flees God's
love but who comes at the Last Judgment into the company of the blessed through God's tireless pursuit and love. The central theme, then,
is God's grace seen in Jesus' parable of the prodigal son: always
available to the child who does not flee from the father's love, but
extended with special joy and abundance to the wanderer who returns
in need of forgiveness. Aelred presents himself as the exemplum of
this understanding, as he uses his sister as the model of the chaste
seeker after God, and it is the extended autobiographical portion of
the treatise which best enunciates it.[3]

De institutione inclusarum consists of two large portions. The
first gives direction for the outer, quotidian life of the anchoress;
the second guides her inner life of virtue and meditation. At the
end of this second portion come three meditations on things past,
present, and future. Aelred develops the theme of God's mercy toward
those who do not seek it exclusively in the inner life portion of the
treatise, primarily within the three meditations. In the first and
third meditations the anchoress audience of the work is asked to participate imaginatively. The second of the three, meditation on things
present, is quite different from the others, not only in its non-
biblical content, but in its demand that the contemplative who reads
the work attend and understand rather than participate. She is not
an actor in this meditation, and her role is intellectual rather than
affective or imaginative.

This meditation is overwhelmingly confessional in content and
is greatly influenced by Augustine's *Confessions*. The subject is
Aelred's own sinful youth. The central themes of the meditation are
those of the treatise itself. Its purpose, however confessional its
content, is still direction, as Aelred twice states: 'But now let my
life serve to bring out all that God has done for your soul,' and
'Let me serve then to show you how much he bestowed on you in keeping
you unharmed.'[4] And just as the defining virtue of the anchoress's
life is chastity, the sin which characterized Aelred's youth was lust.
Speaking almost in the words of Augustine, Aelred says:

> With my wretchedness then in the loss of my chastity
> compare your own happiness in the protection accorded
> to your virginity by God's grace....Your chastity re-
> mained inviolate, while I freely abandoned myself to
> all that is base, accumulating material for fire to
> burn me, for corruption to stifle me, for worms to
> gnaw me.[5]

Two points stand out at this stage of the narrative: Aelred turned from goodness to wickedness, and God's love allowed him to go on, unrestrained, while keeping the sister in purity. Aelred recalls, however, that even as God allowed him to wander unchecked, he protected the sinner from those who would have destroyed him:

> He showed wonderful patience in bearing with my sins.
> Otherwise earth would have gaped open to swallow me,
> heaven's thunderbolts would have struck me down, rivers
> would have drowned me. For how should creation endure
> such great wrong done to its Creator if its wrath were
> not held in check by that same Creator, who does not
> desire the death of the sinner but rather that he be con-
> verted and live?[6]

Finally, he insists on God's pursuit of him, his drawing him back to himself:

> How generous was his grace in following me when I fled,
> in allaying my fears, restoring me to hope as often as I
> was in despair, overwhelming my ingratitude with his
> kindnesses? I had grown accustomed to filthy pleasures
> and he drew me to himself and led me on by the taste of
> interior sweetness. He struck off the unbreakable shack-
> les of bad habit. He rescued me from the world and wel-
> comed me with kindness.[7]

God's love toward the sinner shows itself sometimes as anger, some-times as silence, sometimes as restraint, but finally, always, as salvation.

Although Aelred is careful throughout this section to emphasize that his experience represents merely a different manifestation of God's grace from that which his sister has known, that its wonder lies primarily in his total lack of deserving and--what is more--de-sire for it, and although his ostensible purpose in telling this story is to give evidence to the sister that God has blessed her more richly than him, he apparently realizes at this point that the emphasis on God's love for the sinner has been so great that the sis-ter may see no difference between their benefits. He says, 'In what then, you ask, have you received less than me?'[8] To attempt to rec-tify the error he has made through over-enthusiastic description of God's grace to him, he tells a short parable taken from Gregory the Great's Homily 37 on the Gospels:

> O sister, how much more happy is the man whose ship, full
> of merchandise and loaded with riches, is brought to a

safe homecoming by favorable winds than he who suffers
shipwreck and barely escapes death with the loss of all?
So you exult in these riches which God's grace has preserved for you, while I have the utmost difficulty in
repairing what has been broken, recovering what has been
lost, mending what has been torn.[9]

Aelred's answer to the problem posed by the parable would probably satisfy the sister-anchoress as little as it does the modern
reader: human understanding says that it is the man who 'barely escapes death with the loss of all' who thanks God, who recognizes
the grace which brought him through everything to a life made new
by the near-loss of the old. This is the true resolution to the
parable, and it summarizes the central statement of the meditation:
God's grace comes equally to saint and sinner, in this case, to
sister and brother, to safe traveller and castaway. The neverending surprise of his grace to the shipwrecked remains fixed in human understanding as remarkable precisely because it is unlooked for,
wondrous in a way that the grace of safe travel is not.
    It is probably precisely this wondrous, surprising element of
God's grace that brings Aelred again and again to dwell on it. He
clearly did not set out to write a confessional treatise hidden under cover of direction for anchoresses; his intent is all too clearly expressed and consistently adhered to. Yet he seems unable to
resist constantly renewed joy at God's grace to the sinner. Knowing
and repeatedly saying that the anchoress's virtue is not of her own
merit but of God's grace, he, like the anchoress perfected in virtue
herself, occasionally forgets it, or perhaps loses interest in it.
What amazes him is God's grace to those who reject it.
    Aelred centers his emphasis on this theme in the second medi-
tation, but it occurs as well in the first meditation, where it is
more remarkable because less intentional. This meditation is ideally
suited to an exploration of the theme; its subject is the Incarnation,
the central theological statement of God's outreach to sinful men.
In the gospel narrative which forms this meditation Christ does only
one miracle and little teaching; he does, however, come into contact
with sinners, and in recounting those brief encounters Aelred enunciates God's unremitting love for the wayward.
    Twice in this first meditation Jesus forgives the sin of one
who has not asked forgiveness, and each time Aelred calls attention
to Christ's mercy and to the sinner's lack of merit. The first instance concerns the woman taken in adultery (John 8:3-11). Aelred
tells the familiar story, contrasting Jesus' responses to the just
men who brought her before him and to her:

    But when the words struck them all with terror and drove
    them out of the temple, imagine how kind were his eyes

as he turned to her, how gentle and tender was the voice
with which he pronounced his sentence of absolution.

Further, the author adds:

Happy was the woman [*Felix...mulier*], I feel inclined
to say, in this adultery, forgiven as she was for the
past and assured for the future.[10]

Immediately after this scene comes the washing of Jesus' feet, probably by the same woman. Aelred's epithet for her this time is
'that most blessed sinner,' *illa beatissima peccatrice*.[11] There is
no suggestion that the woman has asked forgiveness nor that she is
less guilty than she is accused of being, only that she is happy in
Christ's blessing.

Again, when the paralytic is let down through the roof for Jesus' healing, Jesus forgives his sin; the bodily healing is clearly
secondary, as it is in the account in Mark 2:3-12. Here again Aelred
calls attention to the special blessing granted the man by the epithet
with which he refers to him: 'That happy man,' *felix*.[12] But in this
case Aelred insists on the man's lack of desert, lack even of desire
for forgiveness:

That happy man received forgiveness of his sins without
having asked for it, without any preliminary confession,
without having earned it by any satisfaction, without any
contrition that might seem to call for it. It was bodily
health he asked for, not that of the soul, yet he received
health of both body and soul.[13]

Those who love Jesus and are loved by him also appear in great
numbers in this meditation. Aelred insists on Jesus' special love
for these followers and friends, but he reserves the epithets of
special blessedness for sinners forgiven by Jesus.

In the third meditation the two threads come together. There,
as in Matthew's account of the Last Judgment, the blessed and the
damned stand together before the throne, and the damned are described
in much the same words as those in which Aelred previously described
his own prospective tortures:

Not so is it with the wicked, not so. Evil spirits with
the instruments of hell drag them from the body as from a
fetid tomb and cast them, defiled with lust, wrapped up
in covetousness, into fire to burn. They commit them to
worms to be gnawed, deliver them up to be stifled by eternal stench. Indeed the expectation of the just is gladness, while the hope of the godless shall perish.[14]

Aelred is not among these, as are not, one assumes, the woman taken in adultery and the former paralytic. They stand among the company of the blessed, among whom there is no distinction. God's grace, which manifested itself in preserving the chastity of the sister and calling back the unchaste brother, reconciles all his chosen ones to him. This is the final miracle, leaving no place for differences of quantity or quality of grace. Unlike Dante's paradise, Aelred's hereafter has no tiers, no separation between the blessed and the blessed.

Aelred never abandons his intention of directing the anchoress toward love of God and acknowledgment of his mercy. He uses the confessional portion of the work precisely as Christians through the centuries have used Augustine's *Confessions*--to point up God's mercy to the greatest of sinners as a reminder of his mercy to those who might come to think that they earned his love through their virtue, that they did it all themselves. In fact, Aelred warns his sister against back-sliding, against a failure to struggle always toward greater purity. After expressing his own need to 'repair what has been broken,' he adds:

> Yet in this respect I would have you emulate me. How you
> would have to blush if after all my sins I were found
> equal to you in the next life. The glory of virginity is
> often tarnished by vices which make their way in later on,
> while the reformation of a man's life and the replacement
> of vices by virtues can cancel the infamy of his former
> behavior.[15]

He makes the same point in the first meditation after the story of the paralytic, saying:

> But we do not read that the paralytic had performed any
> of these preliminaries [acts of devotion and penance],
> and yet we read that he was found worthy to receive
> forgiveness of his sins. This is the power of Christ's
> unutterable mercy, and as it is blasphemous to deny it,
> so it is the height of folly to presume on it. He can
> say and do to anyone he wills the same as he said and did
> to the paralytic: 'Your sins are forgiven,' but anyone
> who expects this will be said to him without any toil or
> contrition or confession or even prayer on his part will
> never be forgiven his sins.[16]

Aelred's constant memory of his own experience of God's unde-served forgiveness leads him ever and again to turn his attention to the sinner. The danger for the sister is precisely that of the elder brother in the parable of the prodigal son: she may forget her unceasing blessings and complain at God's grace to her brother. To her God must reply, 'You are ever with me, and all that I have is yours.' But for the wanderer Aelred recalls the words: 'This your brother was dead and is alive again, and was lost, and is found' (Luke 15:31-32). The emotional and dynamic theme for Aelred, and for all non-anchorites who read this work, is that promise which precedes the same parable in the gospel of Luke: 'Joy shall be in heaven over one sinner who repents more than over ninety-nine righteous persons who need no repentance' (Luke 15:7).

University of Michigan

NOTES

1. *Inst.* 11. 1-16; p. 43. All citations of *De institutione inclusarum* refer to the line numbers of C. H. Talbot's edition in CCCM 1: ??? ?? . 1 *????* ?:1?? ?1?ιρ ?????ρ?? ?? ?????l?ti?? ???? from M. R. Macpherson's translation of the treatise in *Aelred of Rievaulx: Treatises I and Pastoral Prayer*, CF 2, pp. 43-102 and are located by their page numbers in that volume.

2. While the extent of *De institutione inclusarum*'s influence on the English *Ancren Riwle* is still only casually assumed or disputed, the work appears almost without change in Richard Rolle's fourteenth century *Rule for Hermits*; it certainly played an important part in the development of English anchoritism and mysticism. For a discussion of the influence of Aelred on the *Ancren Riwle*, see Hope Emily Allen, 'On the Author of the *Ancren Riwle*,' *PMLA* 44 (September 1929) 546, and C. H. Talbot's introduction to his edition of *De institutione inclusarum* in ASOC 7, p. 170.

3. This treatise, or portions of it, was long attributed to both Augustine and Anselm. Oddly, the second meditation, that which most closely resembles Augustine's *Confessions*, was consistently omitted from the texts of *De institutione inclusarum* ascribed to Augustine. Migne, who includes the work among Augustine's (while recognizing in a note the true author and printing the meditations among Anselm's *Meditationes* as well), has a text lacking the entire confessional portion of the second meditation. One of the two Middle English translations, in Oxford MS Bodley 423, also omits this portion of the second meditation. Such a textual history may help to explain the limited attention in the past to

the confessional theme and emphasis of the work. The Bodley 423 translation and a discussion of the complicated history of ascription both appear in my edition of the two Middle English translations of Aelred's treatise. Stuckey, Marsha D., 'An Edition of Two Middle English Translations of Aelred's *De institutione inclusarum*,' Ph.D. dissertation, University of Michigan, 1981.

4. 1267-8, 1275-7; p. 93.
5. 1278-83; pp. 93-4. Pierre Courcelle cites the passage which follows this in *Inst.* as part of his evidence for the influence of Augustine's *Confessions* on Aelred's writings in 'Ailred de Rievaulx à l'école des "Confessions,"' *Revue des études Augustiniennes* 3 (1957) 164. Walter Daniel, Aelred's twelfth century biographer, records that Aelred's favorite reading was the Gospel of John and the *Confessions*; in *De institutione inclusarum* the Augustinian influence is most clear in this second meditation, which is throughout largely reminiscent of Book II of the *Confessions*.
6. 1305-10; pp. 94-5.
7. 1311-16; p. 95.
8. 1326; p. 95.
9. PL 40:981. This passage is printed in the appendix to Augustine's works, but a footnote assigns it to Gregory.
10. 976-81; p. 83.
11. 988; p. 83.
12. 1006; p. 84.
13. 1006-9; p. 84.
14. 1402-7; p. 98.
15. 1333-7; pp. 95-6.
16. 1021-8; p. 85.

EARLY CISTERCIAN EXPANSION IN PROVENCE: THE ABBEYS
OF AIGUEBELLE, BONNEVAUX, LÉONCEL, AND VALCROISSANT

Constance Hoffman Berman

HE CISTERCIANS EXPANDED FROM BURGUNDY into Provence in 1119.
That move was brought about by Guy de Bourgogne, archbishop
of Vienne, who became Pope Calixtus II that same year. Two
years earlier, he had begun negotiations with Cîteaux for the
foundation of a daughter-house in his diocese. The result was the
1119 foundation of Bonnevaux, twenty-five kilometers east of Vienne.
This Cistercian abbey founded many daughter-houses and produced a
number of twelfth-century saints: John, its first abbot, who became
bishop of Valence in 1141; Peter, who eventually became archbishop
of Tarentaise; Amedeus of Hauterive, who became bishop of Lausanne;
and Hugh, its sixth abbot.[1]

Bonnevaux's daughter-abbeys were: Mazan, founded in the Viva-
rais west of the Rhone in 1123; Montpeyroux in the Auvergne proper,
founded in 1126; Tamié in Savoy, founded in 1134; Léoncel, which was
founded in the diocese of Valence in 1137 (and which will be discussed
in more detail below); Valmagne, near Montpellier, originally a foundation by Cadouin and reputed to have been made under the patronage
of the Trencavel family incorporated by the Cistercians as a daughter
of Bonnevaux in 1155; Ulmet, later moved to Sauveréal near Arles,
founded in 1173 and transferred in the thirteenth century; Valbénoît,
founded in the Forez west of Lyon in 1184; and Valcroissant, in the
diocese of Die, founded in 1188.[2]

Bonnevaux's eldest daughter-house, Mazan, in turn founded yet
other Cistercian houses in southern France: le Thoronet in Provence
in 1136; Sénanque in the Vaucluse in 1148; Silvanès and Bonneval in
the Rouergue in 1136 and 1147 respectively.[3] At the same time the
Cistercian filiation of Morimond was gaining ground in the region
south of Lyon. Morimond founded two houses in the area: Aiguebelle,
in the diocese of Saint-Paul-Trois-Châteaux (today Valence), founded
near Montélimar in 1137, and once again a Cistercian house today; and
Franquevaux, founded near Nîmes in 1143. Morimond also incorporated
the house of Silvacane in 1147; this abbey, originally founded by the
monks of Saint-Victor of Marseille in the eleventh century,[4] in turn
founded the Cistercian abbey of Val-Sainte in the diocese of Apt in
1188.[5]

This paper will concentrate on the Cistercian foundations in the
geographical regions known as the Viennois and Valentinois, areas
which the Empire and the counts of Toulouse controlled during the
twelfth and thirteenth centuries. There, roughly between the heights
of Grenoble and the valley of the Rhone, were sited the abbeys of Bonnevaux and Aiguebelle, daughters of Cîteaux and Morimond respectively,

and the two abbeys of Léoncel and Valcroissant, founded by Bonnevaux. Also in that region were the Cistercian nuns of Bonlieu, dependent on Aiguebelle until the end of the fourteenth century.
Although it was believed until recently that the abbey of Aiguebelle stemmed from the incorporation of a Cluniac house located at
Montjoyer, historians now agree that documents for Montjoyer were
simply forgeries created to promote the noble claims of a local family. Therefore, the foundation stone, dated 1137, is the earliest
surviving authentic record for this house.[6] All four houses then
were genuine foundations, made probably by Cistercian monks sent out
from Burgundy. Indeed, with the exception of Silvacane, there is no
evidence that Cistercian abbeys in Provence were preceded by earlier
(often eremitical) religious groups as have elsewhere been noted.

This does not mean that these four monasteries derived no benefit from previously existing religious communities. The records
show that the monks of Bonnevaux were in 1167 granted the Cluniac
priory or monastery of Artasium located in the parish of Maceoneya
and absorbed its properties; similarly, Léoncel incorporated the semi-
eremitical community of Parsdei in 1194.[7] Somewhat later, in 1400,
the properties of the Cistercian nuns at Bonlieu, governed by Aiguebelle, were assigned to the monks of Valcroissant, because of the
poverty of those monks. The nuns were dispersed, and Bonlieu was un-
doubtedly reduced to a grange; there is no support for claims that it
became a Cistercian men's house.[8]

Surviving charters do not abound for these abbeys, but there are
two surviving cartularies which were published in the nineteenth century.[9] Léoncel's cartulary is generally more useful than that of Bonnevaux for the former contains full texts of the original acts and important papal bulls and safeguards giving precise lists of its properties.[10] The cartulary of Bonnevaux tends to report acts in abridged
form, particularly in sections describing land conveyed. These acts
are, however, more informative on recruitment of new members, on
the establishment of anniversaries for donors, and on the departures
for Crusades and pilgrimages which often motivated donations.[11] Despite their limitations, these two cartularies, in concert with a few
surviving acts for Aiguebelle and Valcroissant, illuminate the early
Cistercian patrimony of the region.[12] They reflect the efforts by
the white monks there to provide the material base and the rights and
privileges from which to derive a livelihood.

The pattern which emerges in a study of these four Cistercian
houses is in many ways similar to that discovered in earlier research
conducted on the Cistercian foundations of the southwestern regions
of what is today France.[13] Although there were some potential assarts
in the Alps and the possibility of drainage in marshes along the major
rivers, most reclamation and resettlement had already taken place by
the time the Cistercians arrived in the region.[14] There is no indication that large tracts of uncleared and unsettled forest were given

to the new order.[15]   Rights in the Alps tended to be exclusively for
pasture.[16]   Moreover, although there are documents conveying ditches
and water-channels to the monks, these were not intended for drainage, but instead, for the flooding and irrigation of meadows to produce more abundant hay.[17]   For drainage activities there are no documents (such as those found for the Hospitallers) which record receipt
of marshes, islands, and riverine areas by the Cistercians.[18]   What
is found in the charters of these Cistercian abbeys is not the acquisition of boundless waste, but the receipt by donation or purchase
of established fields and farms: of *condaminae, culturae,* and peasant
mansi.[19]   Indeed, in one document conveying such settled property,
the monks of Valcroissant were forbidden by the deacon and canons of
the church of Die from 'cutting, or uprooting, or otherwise destroy-
ing, or from making assarts in the forest,' in which the abbey of Valcroissant was located.[20]

That this was the case--that these Cistercian houses did not
move into the wilderness--may at first sight seem to be contradicted
by a consideration of their sites. Léoncel, in particular, conforms
to traditional notions of the Cistercian foundation in the 'desert',
for it was founded in an elevated valley in a mountainous area of
summer pasture-lands, which even today is reached only by a difficult,
winding road.[21]   Its animals descended from the neighboring heights
into the Rhone valley for protection in the dead of winter.[22]   Bonnevaux was sited in an area near the sources of the Valèze and Varèze
Rivers, in a district with dozens of small lakes or ponds. Valcroissant, although not far from Die, was in a tiny valley oversha-
dowed by peaks rising to well over six thousand feet. In contrast,
Aiguebelle, despite descriptions which locate it in a 'savage canyon',
is actually in an open, gently-sloping valley not far from the Rhone.[23]
Regions in which Cistercian sites often appear today rarely reflect,
however, the state of settlement and cultivation at the moment when
Cistercians first arrived. Early documents provide little evidence
that Cistercian abbeys, and still less their farms and granges, were
actually in uninhabited places. Instead such houses were often in
artificial 'deserts' created by the Cistercians themselves in their
desire for solitude.

The previous settlement of Cistercian lands is evinced by charters in which the prior peasant-occupants are actually named. In the
Bonnevaux cartulary there is a series of acts from 1164 concerning
the conveyance of a *villa* by Drodo of Belvoir. The donor transferred
the inhabitants of that *villa*, 'who are his by law' to another place
(apparently a *villa franca* mentioned elsewhere), and they are assigned
new house sites there. Each of these peasants confirmed the action and ceded to Bonnevaux his rights in his previous tenancy. Thus
we know that Stephan, Andrew, and John, all sons of John Lunel, and
Durannus of Canal and his brothers, and a number of others, had previously occupied the holding acquired by the Cistercians in 1164.[24]

Around the same year the monks of Léoncel, similarly acquired the
territory of Alixan in partnership with the church of St Ruf. After
the property was divided with St Ruf, rents were owed to Léoncel by
a group of inhabitants of Alixan: Maria Grossa, the wife of Peter
of Vienne; Agnes Velleruda; Peter of Columber; Robert Nancos; and
others. In both cases previously occupied land had clearly come
into Cistercian hands.[25] In the case of Alixan the short *censier*
attached to the donation charter shows that peasants continued to
hold tenures from the Cistercians under conditions similar to those
which had pertained under earlier lords.

In numerous cases, Cistercian lands were cleared of previous
tenants, as in the case of the *villa* acquired by Bonnevaux, and the
monks established granges on which the 'classic' method of cistercian agriculture was carried out: the direct management of arable
land by the monks themselves, using the labor of lay-brothers. Because direct cultivation of Cistercian granges was made exempt from
tithes by papal privilege, one can demonstrate the institution of
direct management in any specific place by citing contracts ceding
to the Order the right to tithes on lands under Cistercian management or labor.[26] It also appears that whenever an area was referred
to as 'grange' direct management was in effect there. According to papal privileges and safeguards, Léoncel had at least five
such 'granges' by 1176: at Cumba Calida, at Cognerio, at Pallaranges,
at Lenthio, and at Voulpes.[27] Bonnevaux also held at least one, at
Petraria, by the same date, and Aiguebelle, too, had a grange at
Freissinet, reputedly pillaged and destroyed in 1207.[28] Such granges
were often created by the compacting and simplification of tenures through purchases from all small-claims owners of a number of
adjoining holdings. Such a process is seen, for example, in Bonnevaux's acquisition of properties at Landrins; rights in that territory were conveyed to the abbey in at least seventeen individual
acts.[29]

Rather than bringing new areas under cultivation, early Cistercians in Provence actually brought about a reorganization, in at
least some of their holdings, of traditional patterns of tenure. By
converting and compacting smaller holdings into large granges and
by placing them under direct management, they effected considerable
increases in agricultural surpluses. Such surpluses could be sold
to provide the funds for additional land acquisition, reorganization, and amelioration.[30]

These increases in yields derived first of all from the larger
than usual scale on which Cistercian agriculture would have been
practised and from the natural advantages of longevity and continuity
in planning these institutions enjoyed over individual lay-lords and
peasants. The attempts by Cistercians to acquire adjoining holdings,
and presumably to reduce and remove barriers between them, must also
have contributed both to increased efficiency and to some increase

in available arable land. The Order's policy of acquiring lordship
rights, as well as tithes and other claims by the church, also meant
that crops were less often ravaged or spoiled by bad weather while
still standing in the fields. Cistercians, being their own lords
and their own tithe-collectors, did not have to wait for others to
take their share before removing the harvest from the land. Moreover, the capital available to hire extra laborers in peak seasons
would have made more efficient both harvesting and sowing. Cistercian capital also included livestock which could feed on the fallow
and stubble land, providing fertilization of the soil; and capital
could provide better draft animals, made stronger by adequate nourishment, and could provide iron tools and other equipment. Finally,
because the Cistercians had fewer dependent mouths to feed than had
most peasant families, net yields per unit of labor would have been
higher.[31]

All these benefits were, of course, only reaped to the extent
that traditional agriculture was converted to direct management.
Such reorganization, where it occurred, could have had startling results, particularly in situations in which the old tenurial system
had become so burdensome and complex that it had virtually ceased to
function.[32]

These agricultural innovations, many of them linked to Cistercian capital and the Order's exemption from certain tithes, were remarkable, but even more spectacular was the Order's exploitation of
pastoralism. By the middle of the thirteenth century, or before,
the abbeys of Bonnevaux, Léoncel, and Valcroissant were moving large
numbers of sheep and other animals from winter pastures along the
Rhone to the high Alps for spring and summer feeding.[33] At the same
time, Aiguebelle was taking its flocks into the Massif Centrale,
where its shepherds were in constant conflict with those of Mazan
in the thirteenth century.[34] The numbers of new born lambs which
Cistercian flocks produced were considerable, and disputes arose between various religious corporations over the tithes on those lambs.
For example, in 1254, officials of the churches of St Felix of Valence and St Peter du Bourg-les-Valence were involved in a dispute
over tithes on newborn lambs born in the *decimaria* or tithe
collecting area belonging to St Felix but later in the year moved
to areas under the control of St Peter du Bourg, and *vice versa*.
The animals in question seem to have belonged primarily to Léoncel.[35]

Indications of this pastoralism abound; in at least one case
the numbers of sheep which the abbeys might hold are mentioned.[36]
Not only were rights to pasture itself conveyed, but the Order also
received various exemptions from tolls and other taxes levied on
sheep as they moved from one area to another.[37] Disputes between
one Cistercian house and another, or between the Cistercians and
other religious groups, or between the Cistercians and their lay
neighbors, produced records of arbitrated settlements which describe

areas of exclusive or shared pasture and provisions allowing semi-
annual transit by flocks and herds ascending to or descending from
the *montagnes* or alps, as the summer pasture areas were called.[38]
Some of these documents also reveal the degree to which lay neighbors felt that the Cistercians were over-pasturing.[39]

To some extent the geographical limits of pasturage can be traced.
Léoncel's pasture rights stretched from the vicinity of the confluence of the Isère and the Rhone Rivers (between Romans and Valence)
south to the Drôme and to a distance of at least forty kilometers
east of the Rhone. East of Léoncel's pasture areas would have been
those enjoyed by Valcroissant. Bonnevaux's rights may well have
been more extensive, stretching from the vicinity of Vienne eastwards
to the heights of la Chartreuse just north of Grenoble, where Bonnevaux's claims soon came into conflict with those of the Carthusians.[40]
Aiguebelle's pastoralists, in contrast to those of the other three
houses, seem to have looked west to the valleys of the Massif Centrale.[41]

Much earlier than Cistercian houses further west, the abbeys of
Provence introduced a 'commercial' element into their pastoralism.
At a very early date they began to acquire permission to include
'alien beasts' in the flocks they introduced into various areas of
pasture.[42] These alien beasts were, of course, animals belonging to
lay neighbors, or perhaps to very small religious corporations, which
could benefit from interbreeding and pasturing with Cistercian flocks.
The cartulary of Léoncel mentions the inclusion of such animals in
Cistercian flocks and herds under an arrangement known as *ad medium
crescementum*, which seems to mean that the monks would receive half
of the new born animals in return for their guardianship and provi-
sion of pasture, water, and salt.[43] This was in 1284, when in regions
further west the Cistercians were only beginning to practise transhumance with their own animals.[44] Clearly the abbeys of the Viennois
and Valentinois, if not those throughout Provence (a question still
to be studied), were in advance of Cistercians further west in ex-
ploiting pastoral opportunities to the full.

In this region, as in other areas of Cistercian foundations recently studied, the white monks provided themselves with a livelihood
through two major means--the reorganization of existing arable land
into 'granges' over which direct management might be instituted, and
the exploitation of the possibilities of transhumant pastoralism which
maximized the use of abundant grass at various seasons at different
elevations. In this region east of the Rhone pastoralism was exploited far more extensively and much earlier than it was the Rouergue and
regions further west. Perhaps it is not surprising then, to find that
the abbeys in Provence placed less emphasis on acquisition of granges
and on such related properties as mills.[45] It is a fitting reminder
of the importance of transhumance in the economies of Bonnevaux, Léoncel, and Valcroissant in particular, that we find Léoncel's monks

themselves, after 1194, at least in theory, making yearly migrations from the mountains. In that year, in the agreement for incorporation of the house of Parsdei, the monks of Léoncel promised to reside at Parsdei for several winter months each year.[46] Like their shepherds, the monks of Léoncel followed their sheep into the warmer valley lands during the worst seasons of the year. This too may be an unusual innovation for a Cistercian house at the beginning of the thirteenth century.

The Catholic University of America

Table

Solidi Expended for Land Purchases, by Decades

	Bonnevaux	Léoncel
undated	18,974	--
1120-9	100	--
1130-9	--	--
1140-9	1,557	--
1150-9	1,216	--
1160-9	10,316	1,800
1170-9	4,394	1,710
1180-9	1,400	1,958
1190-9	1,293	2,480
1200-9	125	130
1210-9	--	610
1220-9	--	1,790
1230-9	--	2,039
1240-9	220	3,844
1250-9	5	2,387
1260-9	--	3,970
1270-9	--	60
1280-9	--	868
1290-9	--	255
Totals	39,600	23,901

NOTES

The author would like to acknowledge help given in conversations with Father J. Ambrose Raftis and Professor Giles Constable as well as in the written comments of Brother M. Jean de la Croix-Bouton of the abbey of Aiguebelle.

1. J.-M. Canivez, 'Bonnevaux,' *Dictionnaire d'Histoire et de Géographie Écclésiastiques (DHGE)*, 9: cols. 1074-6.
2. Marie-Odile Lenglet, 'Un Problème d'histoire monastique: la fondation de l'abbaye de Mazan,' *Cîteaux* 21 (1970) 5-22.
3. Ibid.
4. Laurent H. Cottineau, *Répertoire topo-bibliographique des abbayes et prieurés* 3 vols. (Macon, 1939-70) cols. 33-4, 1211, 3037-8, 3264-5.
5. Paul Pontus, *Silvacane Abbaye* (Caisse Nationale des Monuments Historiques, 1966).
6. J. Sautel, 'Aiguebelle,' DHGE 1: 1122-1131, but see also the publications of documents for Aiguebelle listed in note 12.
7. *Cartulaire de l'abbaye Notre-Dame de Bonnevaux au diocèse de Vienne, ordre de Cîteaux (publié d'après le manuscrit des Archives Nationales)*, ed. Ulysse Chevalier (Grenoble: Allier, 1889), no. 118 (1167), in which Stephan, abbot of Cluny gave rights in the monastery of A. (Artas?) to Bonnevaux; and *Cartulaire de l'abbaye Notre-Dame de Léoncel au diocèse de Die, ordre de Cîteaux*, ed. abbé C.-U.-J. Chevalier, vol. 1 (Montélimar: Bourron, 1869), no. 53 (1194), hereafter cited as *Léoncel*. Bonnevaux documents are also published in *Cartulaire de l'abbaye N.-D. de Bonnevaux au diocèse de Vienne, ordre de Cîteaux, publié par un moine de Tamié* (N.-D. de Tamié, Savoy, 1942), referenced as *Bonnevaux T.*
8. J.-M. Canivez, 'Bonlieu,' (DHGE 9: 1007) maintains that it was reduced to a grange, but Anselme Dimier in *Recueil de plans d'églises cisterciennes*, Vol 1 (Aiguebelle, 1949), follows the older tradition that it was a foundation of 'moniales, puis hommes en 1400.' A recent article entitled 'Cîteaux dans la Drome,' appearing as number 93 in *Revue Drômoise*, has reopened the controversy about the transfer of this convent to the monks.
9. As listed in note 7 above.
10. *Léoncel*, no. 25 (1176), lists five granges and seven other properties (mostly expanses of pasture); *Léoncel*, no 29 (1178) adds the cellars of St Julian: *Léoncel*, no. 65 (1201) lists four granges, the cellars, and four areas of pasture.
11. Twenty-five contracts dated between 1160 and 1190 promise future admission to a donor or mention that the gift is given at the time of his entrace into Bonnevaux. A number of gifts were made by those about to depart on Crusades, or to establish anniver-

saries: see *Bonnevaux*, nos. 3 (1120), 157 (1150s), 279 (1161), 65 (1197), *etc.*

12. Acts for Aiguebelle and Valcroissant are published in *Chartes et documents de l'abbaye de Notre-Dame d'Aiguebelle* (Paris: C.N.R.S., 1954, and Lyon: Audin, 1969), and Jules Chevalier, *L'Abbaye de Notre-Dame de Valcroissant de l'ordre de Cîteaux au diocèse de Die* (Grenoble: Pinel Frères, 1897). There may be additional unpublished acts for Valcroissant in the Bibliothèque de Grenoble.

13. See my 'The Cistercians in the County of Toulouse: 1132-1249: the Order's Foundations and Land Acquisitions,' Ph. D. dissertation, University of Wisconsin--Madison, 1978.

14. The empty (*apstae*) farms and *medium vestum* contracts (used for resettlement) which are mentioned in earlier Benedictine cartularies are not found in the Cistercian documents, although there is some reference to *medium fenum* (regarding the creation of new meadows) and *medium crescementum* (the division of newborn lambs between owners of the sheep and those who provide pasture); on the earlier documents see Stephen Weinberger, 'Peasant Households in Provence: ca. 800-1100', *Speculum* 48 (1973) 247-257. See also, *Bonnevaux*, no. 267 (1164-7), and *Léoncel*, no. 252 (1284).

15. Forest rights given to the Cistercians were limited to such various usages as gathering firewood and pasturage, or to the occasional grant of wood for building materials. See *Bonnevaux*, nos. 177 and 181 (n.d.), and *Léoncel*, nos., 150 (1247), 192 (1259), 203 (1261), 232 (1269), 252 (1284), and 275 (1296).

16. *Léoncel*, nos. 23 (1173), 24 (1174), 27 (1178), 42 (1191), *etc.*, and *Bonnevaux* nos. 429 (c. 1130), and 430 (1185), *etc.*

17. *Bonnevaux*, nos. 212 and 215 (n.d.), *etc.*, and the division of water for irrigation of meadows (*de divisionem aquarum ad prata irriganda*) between Bonnevaux and six laymen, three of whom got water from Thursday through Sunday, while Bonnevaux and the other three got it from Sunday through Wednesday, in *Bonnevaux*, no. 288 (n.d.).

18. Compare the charters of the Hospital at Arles in *Cartulaire de Trinquetaille*, ed. P.-A. Amargier (Aix: Publications Universitaires, 1972), nos. 42 (1191), 49 (1196), 51 (1196), *etc.*

19. *Léoncel*, nos., 41 (1178-91), 37 (1188), 48 (1192), 49 (1193), 67 (1202), 71 (1209), 91 (1223); *Bonnevaux*, nos. 429 (c.1130), 246 (c.1147), 239 (1147), 52 (1164-7), 54 & 56 (1164); *Aiguebelle* nos. 19 (1174), and 65 (1238), *etc.*

20. *Valcroissant*, p. 157: 'Nullatenus debent extirpare vel rumpare vel alio modo destruere nemore, que tempore dicte concessionis et statuti census erant propria Dyensi ecclesie et ecclesie Valliscrescentis, vel aliquam partem dictarum nemorum, faciendo mortalia vel esarta, vel ex alia quacumque causa'.

21. Pictures of the site are found in M.-A. Dimier, Jean Porcher, *et. al.*, *L'Art Cistercien: France* (Paris: Zodiaque, 1962) 160ff.

22. *Léoncel*, nos. 24 (1174), 68 (1204), 134 (1244), *etc.*

23. Sautel, 'Aiguebelle', 1124.

24. *Bonnevaux*, nos. 54, 56, 57, 58 (1164).

25. *Léoncel*, no. 11 (1163-5).

26. For example, tithes on Bonnevaux's labor at St. Maurice and at Landrins are mentioned in *Bonnevaux*, nos. 312 (1151-7), 264 (1163), 291 (1169), and 199 (n.d.).

27. *Léoncel*, nos. 13 (1165), 25 (1176), and 29 (1178).

28. *Bonnevaux*, nos. 376 (1167-94) and 324 (1169), and *Aiguebelle*, no. 40 (1207).

29. *Bonnevaux*, nos. 201 (1141), 198 (n.d.), 200 (n.d.), 230 (n.d.), *etc,*, or see the evidence of consolidation in *Léoncel*, no. 208 (1262).

30. These surpluses help explain the large sums shown in the table.

31. Richard Roehl, 'Plan and Reality in a Medieval Monastic Economy: The Cistercians', in Howard L. Adelson, ed., *Studies in Medieval and Renaissance History* 9 (Lincoln: Univ. of Nebraska Press, 1972) 83-113, was perhaps the first to discuss dependent costs for the Order.

32. In situations, for instance, when lordship or tithes were divided into tiny portions, as is found for the Rouergat house of Bonnecombe. See my 'Administrative Records for the Cistercian Grange: the Evidence of the Cartularies of Bonnecombe,' *Cîteaux: Commentarii Cistercienses* 30 (1979) 201-220.

33. *Bonnevaux*, nos. 429 (c. 1130), 431 (1222), and 430 (1185), and *Léoncel*, nos. 23 (1173), 24 (1174), 27 (1178), 34 (1185), 35 (1185), 42 (1191), 50 (1193), 60 (1196), *etc.*

34. *Aiguebelle*, nos. 44 (1215), 47 (1217), 49 (1219), 54 (1229), and 58 (1235).

35. *Léoncel*, no. 178 (1254).

36. *Léoncel*, no. 26 (1163-9) gives pasture in the territory of Turre for 1200 sheep.

37. *Léoncel*, nos. 4 (c. 1140), 5 (n.d.), 6 (n.d.), 10 (1163), 36 (1185).

38. *Aiguebelle*, nos. 48 (1219), 49 (1219), and 53 (1228), *Léoncel*, nos. 17 (1169), 44 (1190-2), 62 (1196), and *Bonnevaux*, nos. 430 (1185), 402 (1193), *etc.*

39. *Léoncel*, no. 79 (1216).

40. *Bonnevaux*, no. 430 (1185).

41. *Aiguebelle*, no. 49 (1219), *etc.*

42. The prohibition of animals *in gardia* in *Léoncel*, no. 100 (1228) suggests that this was already the practice, but see also *Léoncel*, nos. 222 (1265) and 252 (1284) in which outsiders' animals are definitely included.

43. *Léoncel*, no. 252 (1284).
44. Compare the evidence presented for the Rouergue by Jacques Bousquet, 'Les Origines de la Transhumance en Rouergue', *L'Aubrac: Etude Ethnologique, Linguistique, Argonomique, et Economique d'un établissement humain*, vol. 2 (Paris: C.N.R.S., 1971) 217-55.
45. Although Léoncel probably had more than the five granges mentioned above, it certainly did not have as many as Grandselve, near Toulouse, with eleven, or Bonneval, Bonnefont, and Boulbonne, all with nine. There is no indication that these abbeys had the extensive milling facilities which were found further west where some houses had as many as sixteen mills. See Berman, *Cistercians in Toulouse*, Tables 8 and 15.
46. *Léoncel*, no. 53 (1194). The convent was to abide at Parsdei from the feast of St Andrew until at least Easter.

PAPAL MINISTRY: A SOURCE OF THEOLOGY,
BERNARD OF CLAIRVAUX'S LETTERS

Richard Ver Bust

ATHEOLOGY OF PAPAL MINISTRY as proposed by Bernard of Clairvaux in his letters was a theology developed through a lifetime of experience and thought, and one which culminated in
his great work, *De consideratione*. His letters, while they
do not have the exclusive concern of *De consideratione*, still are
fruitful for the insight they provide into Bernard's awareness and
understanding of the role of the pope in the Church. The letters
which the Abbot of Clairvaux wrote to popes, bishops, lay leaders and
and christian communities were composed for specific historical situations and they give a glimpse into his grasp of the Church's problems and the theological mind of a person who was deeply involved in
ecclesiastical politics of his day. *De consideratione* can be seen
in this context as his mature thought rather than an isolated response
to a unique opportunity.

Bernard, after becoming abbot of the new foundation at Clairvaux, found that many people from many stations in life sought both
his advice and his help. In time, the ever-expanding influence and
reputation of Abbot Bernard grew. His wisdom and insights were of
ten sought. Sometimes the advice was sought personally and directly.
At other times people wrote to him and he responded.
His replies and words of advice filled many pages even in an age
when communication was often not easy. Bernard himself, on the other
hand, often initiated the contact because it concerned a problem within the Church. Few problems were too small to attract his interest
and concern. Bernard felt strongly about the Church and the many issues of his time. He wrote fearlessly to people in high positions
and no one was exempt from his stinging criticisms and rebukes. He
once wrote to Haimeric, Cardinal Deacon and Chancellor of the Holy
See, that 'nothing that concerns God is a matter of indifference to
me'.[1] This statement attempted to answer those who might have wondered why this young abbot did not simply attend to his own affairs. It
was written quite early in Bernard's career, between 1126-1128, and,
interestingly, it was written not about a specific personal problem
but in regard to a circumstance concerning the Church in Rheims.

Bernard's letters are documents of great historical value for
the history and problems of the contemporary Church. Further, they
are a valuable tool for discerning his own theology as well as the
thinking of his contemporaries, especially if we assume that Bernard
judged that the recipients understood what he was trying to say.

It must be remembered that the letter in his time was a specific
literary form. It had a long tradition in monastic communities and

fit well within the context of monastic life regulated by the Rule.
Silence in the spoken word allowed for the expression of the written
word. Writing a letter in that culture and circumstance was an
event, just as was receiving a letter, a gift that had real value.
Everyone realized the expense and work involved, and thus even personal letters had an almost public quality. It was expected that others
would read them, and that the letters would be exchanged. Thus, the
audience was always much wider than the recipient to whom the letter
was addressed; both the writer and the reader expected this. The
writer, knowing he would reach a greater audience, assumed his letters needed great care in preparation. Letters needed to be of a
high literary quality. Rules of composition had developed even for
ordinary correspondence, and they regulated not only the form but
the style, so the letter would be ornamented and expressed in rhyth-
mical language. Bernard revealed a great deal of himself and his
thinking in his letters, and gave us as well an insight into his times.
The letters could contain exhortation or doctrinal consultation, they
might set out points of controversy, express friendship, or discuss
business.

The letters which will be specifically discussed in this paper
are those which are helpful in discerning Bernard's theology of papal
ministry. All the letters, in a sense, bear on this ecclesiology,
but some letters more directly bear on the role of the pope. Often
these letters are addressed to those men who served as popes in Bernard's active lifetime, but they also include letters to persons or
communities in which this role was discussed.

One of the Abbot's earliest letters was addressed to Pope Honorius II (1124-1130). In this letter (46) Bernard discussed a particular problem of disagreement between Stephen of Senlis, Bishop of
Paris, and Louis VI, King of France, in which many bishops and abbots,
including Bernard, had already become involved. Louis had persuaded
Honorius II to intervene. In his letter to Honorius, Bernard recognized the authority of the pope to intervene, but also critically eval-
uated the results, especially the subversion of the authority of bishops. Bernard expressed his respect for the pope, his rights, and his
authority, and in this he clearly showed himself to be no 'spiritual-
ist' in the sense of refusing to recognize all authority other than
personal holiness. He wrote:

> The humility, or rather the constancy of the bishops, had
> bent the anger of the king, when, lo and behold, the su-
> preme authority of the supreme pontiff intervening over-
> threw constancy, and, alas, erected pride.[2]

Bernard certainly shows a certain forthrightness in writing
to the pope. He shows respect yet not only a willingness but a
right to criticize, and in that sense the passage communicates the

presuppositions of Bernard's notion of papacy. He clearly recognized
the authority of the pope but also the right of members of the Church
to speak out when need demanded. It shows Bernard as one who sensed
a need for an authority which must not domineer but carefully weigh
the consequences of intervening. In this letter the abbot spoke out
against what he felt to be inappropriate use of authority and balanced
respect and criticism.

Bernard demonstrated his ecclesiology in another letter (49),
when in writing Honorius he used the scriptural image of the Church
as Bride and referred to the pope as the guardian of the Bride and
friend to the Bridegroom:

> We, who live in monasteries, compelled to be there because
> of our sins, constantly pray for you and for the Church of
> God committed to you, and we rejoice with both the Bride
> of the Lord about such faithful care and with the friend of
> the Bridegroom about such fruitful work.[3]

Referring to his own life in the monastery and to the prayers
that monks offer for the pope because of his special relationship
to the Church, Bernard recognized that the pope's function was that
of guardianship. The pope must labor as friend of the Bridegroom for
the well-being of the Bride.

Later, in a letter to Pope Innocent II (156), Bernard further expressed his thoughts about the ministry of the pope. He borrowed from
the Old Testament without directly quoting it when he wrote about the
need to care for widows and orphans. The care of these people had once
been the task of the king in Israel and now it had passed to the Church,
especially to the person of the pope. Bernard wrote, 'How long will
the misery of the Church of Orleans strike in vain the entrails of the
Father of Orphans and the Judge of Widows'.[4]

In another letter (158), Pope Innocent was asked by Bernard to be
an effective judge. The judgments of the pope, as the pope should realize, Bernard admonished, would frequently set precedent and therefore have much broader and far-reaching effects than application to
the particular case. Papal judgment, Bernard suggested, should be
such 'that it may be advantageous to the Church and that its salutary
effect in this time may influence and be recognized by future generations'.[5] Bernard indicated that he knew the potential power and authority of these judgments and wanted the pope to realize their influence in the universal Church.

In a letter written to Pope Innocent about 1139 he asked the
Pope to minister by healing. 'What therefore remains except that the
apostolic hand be held out to the injured Church, applying to her
wounds healing care and poultices?'[6] In this letter (318) Bernard
clearly described a particular function of the pope as a unifier and
as such a healer of the divisions within the churches of God. The

abbot vividly and expressively used terms of physical healing such
as poultices to explain spiritual healing. In this way Bernard marked out as most important to any pope a ministry of healing and recon-
ciliation. He related this ministry to the pope's succession to the
role of shepherd-apostle. A shepherd must not only defend; he must
also lead, help, and heal. Bernard saw and expressed a multiple ministry. He was asking not just for a good man or even a good pope;
he was explaining the functions of the ministry that the role itself
demanded.

    Bernard also saw what the effects of a misuse of power and a
lack of true ministry would be. He wrote to Innocent about the problem of a multiplicity of legal appeals and the resulting denigration
of the rightful authority and ministry of the local bishop. He wrote:

> All those who have faithfully the care of the people are
> saying that justice in the Church is perishing. The keys
> of the Church are being abolished, all episcopal author-
> ity is being cheapened when none of the bishops is able
> to avenge promptly the offences given to God, and they
> are not allowed to punish unlawfulness even in their own
> dioceses. They must refer the matter to you and the Ro-
> man Curia. They say you destroy what they have done well
> and you establish what they have rightly destroyed.[7]

Bernard did not deny, but in fact recognized the right to appeal.
On the other hand, he also recognized the abuses of appeal and saw
that they might lead to the breakdown of authentic authority, especially on lower levels. He continued in the same letter:

> Our friends are confused, the faithful are insulted,
> bishops everywhere are placed in disgrace and contempt,
> for while their just judgments are despised, much of
> your authority is also diminished.[8]

    There was a danger that by its constant use of appeal, the papacy
might belittle the legitimate role and ministry of the bishop. Bernard
insisted that if the pope failed to recognize the bishops' specific
authority, and if as a result they could not exercise it fruitfully,
then papal authority itself would be placed in jeopardy. There was
an essential link between the authority of bishop and of pope.
    Bernard portrayed in his theology of ministry a necessary inter-
relationship between papal and episcopal authority. These ministries
were tied closely together and must be held in balance. Each had its
own rights and purpose for existence that did not negate or destroy
the other. In fact, one was dependent upon the other and both must
work together in the full mission of the Church. The abbot,
in these letters, did not play one off against the other. His

ecclesiology rested on the need for both ministries, and each ministry thereby clarified the role of the other.

Bernard also expressed his understanding that the pope had supreme authority within the Church when he wrote:

> It clearly stands out as one of the privileges of the
> Apostolic See that, in the last resort, we look to
> your most powerful, supreme authority and fulness of
> power. Indeed when you rescue the poor man from the
> hand of the strong, it is a singular mark of your pri-
> macy, making it noble and illustrious and giving re-
> nown to your apostolate.[9]

This authority therefore must be exercised for a cause, in Bernard's
view, and that cause was service. The abbot expanded the theology
of previous letters and called service a mark of primacy, tying supreme authority and primacy to the ministry of service. It was not
to be authority for its own sake. This incipient concept is an important one, and one which Bernard used frequently later. He carefully
elaborated on the concept when he wrote in this same letter (198):
'I judge that in your crown there is no more precious jewel than your
zeal with which you are accustomed to strive for the oppressed'.[10]

Finally, in a letter to Pope Eugene III (238), Bernard returned
to his familiar imagery of the friend of the Bridegroom. But he also
added a new dimension, a concern that there be no sense of control
or, rather, ownership:

> It remains, that since this change has happened to you
> that she [the Bride of the Lord] who has been entrusted
> to you, benefit for the better and no longer be called
> Sarai but Sarah. Know what I say: The Lord gives you
> understanding. If you are a friend of the Bridegroom,
> then you should not call his beloved my princess but a
> princess, claiming nothing of her as yours, rather, if
> necessary, to give up your life for her.[11]

This now-familiar biblical image was used by Bernard to express his
conviction that no one has a claim on the Bride, no one has ownership
over the Bride. Bernard did not allow for ownership, rejecting the
idea that Eugene could speak of *my* princess. More clearly than ever
before, he wrote of the service that was part of the ministry of the
pope: 'If Christ sends you, then you should remember that you are
not to be ministered to but have come to minister'.[12] This was Bernard's clearest statement of a ministry and a theology of service.
To add to its emphasis, he used scripture, quoting freely: 'The successor of Paul truly ought to say with Paul: "We come not that we
should rule over your faith but because we are helpers of your joy."'[13]

Bernard used the word dominion or *dominium* to indicate, not an exercise of ownership or lordship, but Eugene's role as a helper in joy.
A helper is one who aids and cares for another. Bernard, continuing
in this same context but now quoting Peter, wrote: 'Let the heir of
Peter say with Peter: "not dominating the household of God, but being
an example for the flock of God"'.[14] Lord and example are placed in
contrast. In imitation of Peter, Eugene was to be not a lord, but an
example. Thus, the abbot joined together two biblical images of the
household and flock and applied them both to the Church.

Eugene, as bishop of Rome, was a successor of these two biblical leaders, Peter and Paul, and should therefore know the consequences of their injunctions, Bernard thought:

> So the Bride no longer a servant but free and beautiful
> shall be delivered by you into the desired embraces of
> her most handsome Bridegroom. From whom else can she
> look forward to the freedom to which she is entitled
> if you seek as your own, the inheritance of Christ,
> which you learned before not to hold as your own, not
> even your body.[15]

Bernard believed that the Bride must be free even in relationship to
the friend of the Bridegroom. The Bride was not his servant; he was
her servant who must deliver her to the Bridegroom. The Bride must
never be used for the friend's own benefit or profit. Bernard recalled that Eugene in his monastic training had learned not to be posses-
sive, not even of himself, but to be truly poor in spirit.

The letters of Bernard were written for a specific historical situation and were often an emotional reaction to that situation. They
exhibit a preaching style even though cast in the literary form of a
letter. They are biblical and patristic in language and terminology.
While Bernard shows he was aware of emerging thought he remains basically conservative. Yet he does not simply repeat biblical images and
patristic phrases. They are part of his total language and he uses
them to express his thoughts. They are a tool for getting at the ecclesiology out of which he was working.

The letters of Bernard contain many of the ideas which he was
able to develop more extensively in *De consideratione*, which was specifically dedicated to expounding the meaning of papal ministry. The
patterns which began to emerge in the letters are important to an understanding of the more theoretical *De consideratione*, which, in a
sense, the letters represent his practice.

The themes which emerge from the letters are significant in relationship to the *De consideratione* and include: the relationship of the
pope to the whole of the Church but in particular to the bishops; appeals and their effect on authority, both papal and episcopal; the
nature of authority in terms of service; poverty of spirit in a posi-

tion of power, wealth and glory; the nature of papal ministry in terms of service, healing, unity and care; the role of a prophet who challenges the institution and is at the same time its leader. The historical progression of the letters shows how Bernard himself was able to take a basic position and, with growing awareness, reshape and refashion it. What need demanded shaped his thought. Yet there is always a consistency in his basic ecclesiology and the presuppositions out of which he acted and wrote. They lead logically to the theory expressed in *De consideratione*. They were not intended to express a coherent, systematic sense of theology. Yet taken as a whole, the letters are not only useful in providing an insight into the theology that Bernard proposed in *De consideratione*, but in their own right they express what a lived and practised theology must be.

St Norbert College
De Pere, Wisconsin

NOTES

1. Letter 21; SBOp 7 (Rome, 1974): 70 (1126-1128).
2. Letter 46; 135 (about 1129).
3. Letter 49; 140 (about 1129 or 1130). Bernard offered support to Henry, archbishop of Sens.
4. Letter 156; 363 (1134-1135). Bernard expressed his thoughts about the election of a certain Philip to the See of Tours.
5. Letter 158; 363. This letter dates from about 1133 and in general concerns the policy of church reform developed by the murdered Master Thomas, the Prior of St Victor's in Paris.
6. Letter 318; 251 (1139). This letter was occasioned by a controversy between the people and the Chapter of the Cathedral of Rheims.
7. Letter 178; 397 (1136). The letter was about another disputed episcopal election.
8. Letter 178; 397.
9. Letter 198; 54-55 (1141). Bernard supported a cistercian daughter house of Clairvaux at Besançon in a dispute with Peter, the Dean of that city.
10. Letter 198; 54-55.
11. Letter 238; 116-117. Bernard strongly urged Eugene to reform the Church. He added the sense of the reform of the whole Bride to a theology of reform which traditionally was more personal and individual.
12. Letter 238; 116-117.
13. Letter 238; 116-117.
14. Letter 238; 116-117.
15. Letter 238; 116-117.

SAINT BERNARD OF CLAIRVAUX: FRIEND OR FOE OF THE ARTS?

M. Kilian Hufgard, OSU

UNTIL QUITE RECENTLY, most art historians have ignored all of Bernard's writings except a few paragraphs extracted from his *Apologia*,[1] and their conclusions on the saint's artistic opinions have put him in a very unfavorable light. If these excerpts taken from the *Apologia* are more carefully reviewed in context together with other of Bernard's writings, a more positive aesthetic concept can be discovered.

Saint Bernard wrote the *Apologia* in the year 1125 as a protest against extravagances at Cluny and as a plea for mutual charity among monastic orders. It was written in response to an urgent request from Bernard's good friend, the Benedictine Abbot, William of Saint Thierry. In his *Apologia* Bernard rebukes the monks of Cluny in these words:

.., as one monk to another, may I ask the question which a heathen poet put to his fellows. 'Tell me, O priests,' he said, 'why is there gold in the holy place?'[2] I shall put the question slightly differently. I am more interested in the sense of the text than in its precise words. 'Tell me, O poor men,' this is my question, 'tell me, O poor men-- if you are really poor men--why is there gold in the holy place?'[3]

If the entire *Apologia* and others of Bernard's works are studied carefully, it becomes clear that his intention is not so much to despoil churches or to condemn beauty or works of art, as it is to question the propriety and the approval of superfluities in monastic life --a life professing poverty and charity.

Etienne Gilson, in analyzing Bernard's aesthetics, holds that the saint stands upon the *Nosce te ipsum* of the ancients, and remarks that he finds Bernard's terminology to be surprisingly technical and precise.[4] The writings of Bernard, moreover, make it clear that the cistercian Socratic *Nosce te ipsum* is harmonized with and expanded by an Augustinian concept of universal order. A man does not know himself until he knows his proper place in the universal order. A man ought to know his own condition and place; he needs to know what he owes to things above and beneath him and to himself; he ought to understand what he has been made, how he should conduct himself, what he should do and not do--in this, for man, consists self-knowledge.[5]

Even though Saint Bernard, like Saint Augustine, emphasizes the necessity of universal order and its concrete expression through measure and number and weight, 'number is not an arid mathematical abstraction but rather an intelligible ingredient entering into the

ontological structure of the object.'[6] Bernard, like Augustine, finds
order in the very nature of a thing. A thing is in order when it comes
into being in response to a human need. This order is principally determined by a thing's purpose or propriety. Order implies the presence
of the essential, the absence of the unnecessary, the superfluous.

An individual's dwelling place and environment, the things he
makes and the things he delights in are conditioned by what he understands himself to be. An individual's idea of man and universal order
therefore determines his concept of 1) the origin, 2) the nature, and
3) the value of works of art.

In the cistercian monastery, the *Nosce te ipsum* discipline, the
attempt to harmonize the inner man with external reality, was put into
practice. Bernard encouraged his disciples in their search for self-
knowledge to ponder three questions with regard to the things which
composed the great world about them: 1) what are they? 2) how are they
disposed? and 3) for what purpose have they been made? The saint himself did this and reveals a profound personal discovery when he writes:

> The existing universe speaks to our minds [1] of the in-
> comprehensible *power* which could produce things so many,
> so great, so multiform, and so magnificent. [2] In the
> disposition of its parts there is revealed to us an incom-
> parable *wisdom* whereby some bodies are placed above, others
> below, others in the centre, in a most orderly collocation.
> But [3] if you reflect on the end for which the world was
> made, you will discover such *beneficent kindness*, such kind
> beneficence as ought to overwhelm with gratitude even the
> most ungrateful by reason of the multitude and the magni-
> tude of its useful effects.[7]

Bernard discovered that creation bears the image of its Triune
God--the image of *power, wisdom,* and *love.* This is the ultimate ontological as well as mystical lesson to be learned, to be understood.

Bernard reminds us that all things are for men's profit. The presence of goodness in the simplest, most insignificant thing can be the
source of an aesthetic experience for the disciplined soul capable of
intuitively grasping the wisdom, power, and love shining forth from
the ontological structure of a being. Bernard explains this truth as
follows:

> Thus the Creator has manifested the infinitude of his power
> in producing all things from nothing, He has manifested the
> infinitude of his wisdom in disposing all things in beauti-
> ful order, and the infinitude of his goodness in ordaining
> all things to our profit. He hath made all things for his
> own sake, because all have proceeded from his own gratuitous
> goodness; and he hath made all things for his elect, because

all are destined for their utility; so that the divine
goodness is the efficient cause, and man's profit the
final. They...are spiritual men who 'use this world as
if they used it not' (Cor. 7:31) and seek God in simplicity of heart' (Wisdom 1:1) with but little curiosity to
know about the revolution of the spheres.
        I rejoice to know, dearest brethren, that you belong
to...the school of the Holy Ghost, where you are being
taught 'goodness and discipline and knowledge' (Ps 119:66),
so that each one of you can say with the Psalmist, 'I have
understood more than all my teachers' (Ps 119:99).[8]

Man himself is reflected in this universal order: he is, could
be, should be, a being of power, intelligence and good will. Moreover, he too can discover a truly human way of working--a way of cre-
ating new beings for sustaining himself in existence. Working along
the same course of 1) power or skill, 2) wisdom or right reason, and
3) good will or beneficence, the human artist is qualified and free to
create original works of his own, free to exercise his art. Works of
art are no different in their essential causes than are works of nature.[9]
        Bernard's aesthetics and mystical theology are of one piece. Gil-
son discerned that Bernard's mystical theology is basically the science
of a way of life[10]--the life lived in the cistercian *schola caritatis*.
Charity is or should be both the first and final cause of any creation,
human or divine. Charity or the desire for goodness ought, first of
all, to serve the manifold needs of our fellowmen. Propriety--a harmony between an individual's or a society's way of life, and the works
of art it produces and which serve it, is the desired end.[11]
        Twelfth-century cistercian architecture has been recognized by
eminent experts of our day as the 'Architecture of Truth'.[12] From the
spiritual and elementary material necessities of cistercian monasticism,
architectural forms evolved which 'for vigour and boldness of design,
for excellence of proportion, and for simplicity, elegance, and purity
of treatment...are unsurpassed by buildings of any age or country....'[13]
Like a living organism, a cistercian architectural complex grows out of
the insights of the cistercian school of simplicity and love.
        Should charity or good will be neglected, curiosity, and cupidity
tend to exude the superfluous. Superfluities in Bernard's theory are
unnatural--not a part of man's nature. Before the transgression, Adam
lived by a preventive law of simplicity; he was forbidden superfluities.
In eating of the forbidden fruit, our first parents violated the law
of charity. Through Adam's fall, man lost his native simplicity. Curiosity changed charity into cupidity.[14] Bernard reminds monks that:

        From the beginning, my brethren, God has shown his predi-
        lection for order, and nothing out of order has ever been

acceptable to Him Whose very Essence is order. Hence it
is that not only has He, as Creator 'ordered all things in
measure and number and weight,' (Wisd. 11:21) but He also
prescribed an order to be observed by man, and gave him a
precept, saying to Adam, 'Of every tree of paradise thou
shalt eat; but of the tree of knowledge of good and evil
thou shalt not eat.' A most easy commandment surely, and
a most ample liberty. Nevertheless, man refused to observe
the order thus established, but transgressed the limits appointed him.[15]

Bernard asks the abbots and monks of Cluny if they are motivated by
charity or cupidity:

> These are only small things; I am coming to things of
> greater moment. I merely mention these minor details
> because they happen to be rather common. I shall say
> nothing about the soaring heights and extravagant lengths
> and unnecessary widths of the churches, nothing about
> their expensive decorations and their novel images, which
> catch the attention of those who go in to pray, and dry
> up their devotion.
>   Let me speak plainly. Cupidity, which is a form of
> idolatry, is the cause of all this. It is for no useful
> purpose that we do it, but to attract gifts. You want to
> know how? Listen to the marvels of it all. It is pos-
> sible to spend money in such a way that it increases; it
> is an investment which grows, and pouring it out only
> brings in more. The very sight of such sumptuous and
> exquisite baubles is sufficient to inspire men to make
> offerings, though not to say their prayers. In this way,
> riches attract riches, and money produces more money.[16]

The end products of cupidity are unreasonable and ridiculous, as Bernard's words further demonstrate as he calls attention to the decora-
tions of Cluny's *cloister*:

> What excuse can there be for these ridiculous monstrosities
> in the cloisters where the monks do their reading, extra-
> ordinary things at once beautiful and ugly? Here we find
> filthy monkeys and fierce lions, fearful centaurs, harpies
> and striped tigers, soldiers at war, and hunters blowing
> their horns. Here is one head with many bodies, there is
> one body with many heads. Over there is a beast with a
> serpent for its tail, a fish with an animal's head, and a
> creature that is horse in front and goat behind, and a
> second beast with horns and the rear of a horse. All round

there is such an amazing variety of shapes that one could
easily prefer to take one's reading from the walls instead
of from a book. One could spend the whole day gazing fascinated at these things, one by one, instead of meditating
on the law of God. Good Lord, even if the foolishness of
it all occasion no shame, at least one might balk at the
expense.[17]

The unreasonable extravagances of cluniac monasteries violate
charity. Bernard views the bad example given there as a disregard
for the common good, and he continues his admonition:

Do you think such appurtenances are meant to stir penitents
to compunction, or rather to make sight-seers agog? Oh,
vanity of vanities, whose vanity is rivalled only by its
insanity! The walls of the Church are aglow, but the poor
of the Church go hungry. The stones of the Church are covered with gold, while its children are left naked. The food
of the poor is taken to feed the eyes of the rich, and amuse-
ment is provided for the curious, while the needy have not
even the necessities of life.[18]

Against the vanities and excesses of Cluny, Bernard places the
cistercian ideal of simplicity and charity. Charity is exercised by
means of the *voluntas communis*. Man is a free creature, lord of the
inferior appetite which was made subject to him. It is chiefly on
account of his freedom that man is a noble creature, simple and up-
right, made to the image of God, and capable of entering into society
with God and man. Gilson notes that the *voluntas communis*, the common will, is nothing else than charity:[19] '...an altruistic will is
a will dominated by charity.'[20] The contrary, *voluntas propria*, is
self-willed, self-seeking. 'But as for the man who does not renounce
his own will, how can *he* compassionate his brother, since he only
knows how to feel for himself?'[21]

The undisciplined forms and embellishments at Cluny, as these are
pictured in the *Apologia*--extravagant, luxurious, lavish, costly, showy,
ostentatious, immense, immoderate, superfluous, curious, precious, glit-
tering, ridiculous, novel, spectacular--were to Bernard's eye contrary
to the spirit of the common will and to the common good. They are not
in keeping with the life of monks who profess charity and poverty, the
love of God and neighbor. The abbot of Clairvaux was keenly sensitive
to the welfare of all his fellowmen, whatever their social level.

As head of a very large community of monks and as founder of many
affiliated monasteries, Bernard was experientially aware of the manifold necessities of mankind. He knew, for instance, the problems confronting a builder--problems 'admitting of few short cuts, if any at
all';[22] he knew the detailed planning and the hard labor required to

house a large group of men and believed these perennial necessities ought to stimulate the creativity of men.

Saint Bernard's experience with the exacting requirements of architecture is realistically illustrated by the story of the building of the second monastery at Clairvaux. A reduction of the history of the event, as it is related by Saint Bernard's biographer, Ernald, follows:

> When the excitement of the welcome was over, the prior, Geoffrey de la Roche [future Bishop of Langres], and [Bernard's] own brother Gerard, with other officers, came to speak to the abbot on a matter of importance. Notwithstanding the numerous colonies sent out--two every year on an average--the community had grown so large that the accommodation of the abbey was insufficient. There was hardly room enough in the church for all the professed religious, so that the novices were excluded from the choir at the hours of the cannonical office. They proposed, therefore, the building of a new and more spacious monastery. Further down the valley, at a convenient distance from the river Aube, they had discovered a very suitable site, with plenty of space not alone for all the necessary edifices, but even for gardens, granges, shrubberies and vineyards. If there were no woods to serve as a natural enclosure, as in the present site, at least there was an abundance of stones wherewith to build walls. The saint at first was strongly opposed to the design. 'You know,' he answered, 'what labour and expense it cost us to build this monastery and to construct the canals which convey the water from the river. Now, if we abandon these, worldings will take scandal: they will say that we are either light-minded and inconstant, or that we have more wealth than we know what to do with--how far this is from the truth I need not say...' 'What you say would be reasonable,' they replied, 'if God ceased to inspire vocations as soon as the monastery was filled. But as the case is, we must either shut the gate against postulants that flock hither daily or else provide more accommodation. Surely the Lord desires that we should receive those whom He sends us. And shall we incur his displeasure through a cowardly lack of confidence?' The holy abbot hearing this was delighted at their faith and charity and willingly gave his consent.[23]

The sequel to the above discloses some of the many problems which challenged the builders of twelfth-century cistercian monasteries and something, too, of the spirit which animated their activities:

As soon as the news spread abroad that the monks of Clairvaux were about to build a new monastery, all the neighbour-
ing bishops and nobles [and tradesmen] vied with one another
in assisting the work....[Although the expense was great,
workmen were quickly gathered for the project.] Much of
the work was done by the religious themselves: they felled
trees, squared stones, [constructed walls], dug canals,
built waterfalls [for the mills....The walls were completed
with unusual speed including a very spacious enclosure
around the entire monastery. The building arose, and within a very short time a newly-born edifice advanced and increased in size as if it possessed a living and pulsing
soul.]24

Restrictions do not curtail the artist's production or stifle
his creativity. As the story of the new monastery indicates, they
can have the opposite effect. Bernard has this to say about the elementary needs of humankind:

Nor is this way of necessity a straight and simple way,
but very round about, with many twists and turns and
admitting of few short cuts, if any at all. What man is
not aware how manifold and multiform are our human necessities? Who shall be able to enumerate them all? Experience
is our best instructor in this matter, because, as the
Prophet Isaiah bears witness, 'vexation alone shall give
understanding.'25

In this same sermon on Psalm 90, Bernard compares the ways of necessity and cupidity:

By this each of us is taught how much need he has to cry
to the Lord, not, 'Deliver me from my *necessity*,' but with
the Psalmist, 'Deliver me from my *necessities*.' Nor is
it alone out of the way of necessity we desire to be led,
but also out of the way of cupidity, as many of us, I mean,
as do not turn a deaf ear to the admonitions of the Wise
Man. What does he say? 'Turn away from thy own will'; and
again, 'Go not after thy lusts.' Indeed of the two evils,
it were better to walk in the way of necessity than in that
of cupidity. The former way has been described as manifold; but more manifold still is the latter, yea, it is
manifold beyond all measure.26

In the vain display of Cluniac embellishments, Bernard sees men
being drawn into the unending ways of cupidity, to the superfluous
and extravagant forms of art, 'which seem good to men, but the end

thereof is without end, because they lead down into hell's abyss.'[27]

Cluniac extravagance is contrary (1) to the *Nosce te ipsum* principle, (2) to the theory of universal order, (3) to the *schola caritatis* discipline, and (4) to the way of simplicity and necessity. In fact, in Bernard's thinking, it is contrary to the true nature of man. It is a wasteful example of the way of *cupiditas* and is of no real value to mankind.

As long as a man lives on this earth, physical and spiritual necessities will vex and challenge him to produce works of art--housing, clothing, utensils of all kinds, images, songs. These are so vast in scope that in his effort to furnish them, the human maker need never be idle nor without incentive to skillfully create works of art. He is, in fact, 'drawn' and 'driven' by necessity to produce them.

Ultimately, Bernard would have men, especially monks, pass beyond the way of necessity into the realm of contemplation. But even the mystic knows that as long as man remains in the body and on the earth, he must be served by the works of men. Recognizing and accepting this inescapable fact, Bernard makes it a part of his philosophy and of his prayer:

> Give me a man who loves God before all things and with his whole being, self and neighbor in proportion to their love of God,...In like manner let him deal with the other things of God too with an ordered love,,,,let him pay but passing attention to things that pass, as existing need demands.... Give me such a man, I repeat, and I shall boldly proclaim him wise, because he appreciates things for what they really are, because he can truthfully and confidently boast and say: 'he set love in order in me' (Sg 2:4)....O Wisdom reaching mightily from end to end in establishing and controlling things, (Wis 8:1) and arranging all things sweetly by enriching the affections and setting them in order! Guide our actions as your eternal truth requires, that each of us may confidently boast in you and say: 'he set love in order in me' (Sg 2:4). For you are the strength of God and the Wisdom of God (1 Cor 1:24), Christ the Church's bridegroom, our Lord and God who is blessed for ever (Rom 1:25). Amen.[28]

Near the beginning of this paper a statement was made: An individual's idea of man and universal order determines his concept of 1) the origin, 2) the nature, and 3) the value of works of art. The words of Saint Bernard suggest the following conclusions: 1) art, in the sense of creativity, has its genesis in the necessities of mankind; 2) a work of art may be defined as that which is produced according to a love for and knowledge of human nature and craftsmanship; and 3) once the artist relates his work to the necessities of man and society, he is free to apply his devotion and skill to the work at hand. He will assist men in the solving of their most vital problem: to live a temporal life here on earth as it should be lived and, by this very means, to prepare an 'eternal dwelling place' hereafter.

Ursuline College
Pepper Pike, Ohio

NOTES

1. Translated in *Bernard of Clairvaux: Treatises I*, CF 1 (Cistercian Publications, 1970).
2. Perseus, *Satires*, II, 69, cited in CF 1: p. 64, n. 161.
3. CF 1: 64.
4. Etienne Gilson, *The Mystical Theology of Saint Bernard*, trans. A.H.C. Downes (New York: Sheed and Ward, 1940) p. 157 and passim, E. Gilson, *The Spirit of Medieval Philosophy*, trans. A.H.C. Downes (New York: Charles Scribner's Sons, p. 215. In the latter, see also the whole of chap. xi, 'Self-Knowledge and Christian Socratism,' pp. 209-228. See also, *Bernard of Clairvaux: On the Song of Songs*, vol. 2 (CF 7) Sermons 35, 36, 37.
5. Gilson, *The Spirit*. Gilson takes this statement from Hugh of St Victor's *de Sacramentis*, I, 6, 15.
6. Emmanuel Chapman, *Saint Augustine's Philosophy of Beauty* (New York: Sheed and Ward, 1939) p. 14.
7. Pent. 3; I have used as my text *St Bernard's Sermons for the Seasons & Principal Festivals of the Year*, translated by a priest of Mount Melleray (Westminster, Maryland: The Carroll Press, 1950), 2: 309. Bernard repeats this same truth many times. (This translation will hereafter be cited as *Sermons for the Seasons*).
8. Pent 3; *Sermons for the Seasons*, 2: 309-311. Cf. CF 4: 27-29.
9. Pasc 2; *Sermons for the Seasons*, 2: 192-193. Pent 2; *Sermons for the Seasons*, 2: 302-305.
10. Gilson, *The Mystical Theology*, pp. viii, 46.
11. CF 7: 174-179. See also *Bernard of Clairvaux, Treatises II*, CF 13: 114-117. Cf. Bernard's lament for his brother, Gerald: CF 7: 65-66.
12. François Cali, *Architecture of Truth*, trans. Rayner Heppenstall, Photography by Lucien Herve, preface by Le Corbusier (New York, George Braziller, Inc., n.d.). Otto von Simson in his *Gothic Cathedral*, pp. 47-8 has the following: 'Bernard's most remarkable and in fact epoch-making artistic contribution, however,

lies in the field of architecture'.
13. Edmund Sharpe, *The Architecture of the Cistercians* (London: E. and F. Spon, 1875), p. 27.
14. CF 13: 96-97.
15. Circ 2; *Sermons for the Seasons*, 1: 430.
16. CF 1: 63, 65.
17. CF 1: 66.
18. CF 1: 65-66.
19. Gilson, *The Mystical Theology*, 55. Pasc 2; *Sermons for the Seasons*, 2: 192-3.
20. Pasc 2; *Sermons for the Seasons*, 2: 193.
21. Ibid.
22. QH 11; *Sermons for the Seasons*, 1: 234-35. In these pages, Bernard discusses 'the ways of the children of Adam [which] lie in necessity and cupidity'.
23. *Vita prima*, II, 5, 29-30; PL 185: 284C-285B. I have used the translation of Ailbe J. Luddy, O. Cist., *Life and Teaching of St Bernard* (Dublin: M. H. Gill & Sons, 1950) 302-303.
24. *Vita prima*, II, 5, 30-31; PL 185: 285CD; Luddy's translation, pp. 303-304.
25. QH 11; *Sermons for the Seasons*, 1: 234-35.
26. Ibid.
27. Ibid.
28. SC 50:7; CF 31: 36-7.

THE VOCABULARY OF CONTEMPLATION IN AELRED OF RIEVAULX'
ON JESUS AT THE AGE OF TWELVE, A RULE OF LIFE FOR A RECLUSE,
AND *ON SPIRITUAL FRIENDSHIP*

John R. Sommerfeldt

AMEDÉE HALLIER'S fundamental book on Aelred of Rievaulx appeared in English in 1969 under the title *The Monastic Theology of Aelred of Rievaulx: An Experiential Theology.*[1] The index to that work contains a heading 'The vocabulary of experience'. This is followed by 'Mystical experience', and the reference is to page 131. The pages referred to under 'The vocabulary of experience' are penetrating and instructive. Page 131, however, contains no explicit reference to 'mystical' experience. And this is probably just as well, for the word 'mystical' is seldom found in Aelred's writings—only once in those I have examined so far.[2] And, for Aelred, 'mystical' surely did not have the connotation of a totally transcendent experience of God that it often does today.

On that same page, Hallier's book contains a statement which is surely true, yet which needs stating and restating. Hallier writes:

> There are various degrees and forms of spiritual experience. A real encounter with God can be experienced without its being marked by any sign of unusual intensity. On the other hand, there are some states that human language is incapable of describing. In this case nothing is more grateful than silence.

This last sentence may be what the indexer had in mind as 'mystical experience'.

The application of twentieth-century terminology to twelfth-century concepts understandably breeds confusion. In this paper, I shall attempt to avoid this; but, in so doing, I owe it to you to define with what kinds of contemplation I shall be concerned—with what 'degrees and forms of spiritual experience', to use Hallier's phrase. I shall use the word 'contemplation' when referring to the total and transcendent experience of God today often called 'mystical'. As you will see, I shall be led unavoidably by this concern to consider the activity most often today called 'meditation', but for which Aelred had many words, including 'contemplation'.[3] 'Meditation' here means a spiritual activity involving human effort, especially that of the intellect, even though that activity—or the fruits of that activity—may be inspired.[4]

If the study of Aelred's vocabulary of contemplation were simply a matter of calculating the number of times Aelred used *contemplatio* (or its verbal or adjectival equivalents), this would be an even shorter paper than it is. But medieval authors, especially twelfth-century monastic authors, used *contemplatio* in different ways at different times--or, to say it another way, in different contexts. Aelred's fellow Cistercian, Bernard of Clairvaux, used different words at different times to describe his contemplative experience, and was fully conscious of his variant usages.[5]

The contemplative experience--indeed, any experience--is of its nature ineffable; as Aelred says: 'Neither mind nor tongue can convey its utter delight'.[6] Thus we must expect the contemplative to use poetic language when he attempts to convey the nature of his experience. With Aelred--as with many, if not all, spiritual writers--the recurring imagery is that of the senses: taste, sight, hearing, and touch (the last often expressed through the metaphors of the kiss and the embrace).

Each of these words--'see', for example--has a range of potential meanings from the most literal to the most figurative. 'See' may refer to the act of vision, to the understanding of a concept, to a poetic description of the most exalted experience of ultimate Reality. Obviously, it is not sufficient to assign a specific meaning to a word without regard for the context in which it appears. Just as the Old Testament word *torah*, though commonly translated 'law', has meanings '...which range from specific rituals for so-called leprosy (Lev. xiii 59, xiv 2, 54, 57) to general precepts and sayings...' to a name for a hortatory poem,[7] so in Aelred 'contemplation' and 'seeing' can mean many things in different places, and '...the meaning...must be determined in each case by the context'.[8] Hallier has shown that this is the case with works like 'image' and 'likeness';[9] I shall begin my study with a few references to sense imagery.

On Jesus at the Age of Twelve
and *A Rule of Life for a Recluse*

Aelred begins his treatise on *Jesus at the Age of Twelve* (I, 2) with the wish that '...Jesus himself would deign to communicate to me...so that I might be able to impart to you what I knew and tasted'.[10] The translation seems tame when compared to the Latin *gustata eructare*.[11] One of Aelred's sermons has a similar image: '*Ille solus potest eructare, qui novit gustare*'[12]--mildly translated as 'he alone can impart what he knows to taste'.[13] Is this tasting a matter of contemplation or meditation? The context--a meditation on the meaning of Luke 18:16--makes the answer obvious, especially as the sentence quoted has the rhetorical form of a prayer to Mary.[14]

A more common image in Aelred is sight. In his *Rule of Life for*

a Recluse, there is a long series of words which evoke visual imagery, though the verb used is not always the same.

> At the river Jordan you will see (*videas*) the Father
> in the voice, the Son in his human form, the Holy
> Spirit in the dove.[15]

> And see (*vide*) how death is the beginning of
> eternal happiness, the goal of all your labors,
> the destroyer of vice.[16]

> But now turn your gaze (*intuere*) to the terror of
> that day when the powers of heaven will be moved,
> the elements dissolved in the heat of fire, when
> hell will gape open and all that is hidden will be
> laid bare.[17]

> Now turn your eyes (*retorque oculos*) to the right
> and look at (*adverte*) those with whom he will place
> you by glorifying you.[18]

The context shows clearly that what is demanded here is activity,
the activity I have called meditation. And the imperative form of
most of the verbs cited underscores my contention that Aelred was
indeed calling for activity.

At the end of Aelred's *Rule of Life for a Recluse*, there is
a passage which begins with the activity of seeking--the verb is
quaeramus--but which seems to go beyond human initiative, though
the image continues to be visual. Aelred writes:

> What is there further for us to seek? To be sure,
> what surpasses all these things, that is, the sight
> (*visio*), the knowledge (*cognitio*), and the love
> (*dilectio*) of the Creator. He will be seen (*vide-
> bitur*) in himself, he will be seen in all his crea-
> tures, ruling everything without anxiety, upholding
> everything without toil, giving himself and, so to
> speak, distributing himself to one and all according
> to their capacity without any lessening or division
> of himself. That loveable face, so longed for, upon
> which the angels yearn to gaze (I Pet 1:12) will be
> seen (*videbitur*). Who can say anything of its beauty,
> of its light, of its sweetness? The Father will be
> seen (*videbitur*) in the Son, the Son in the Father,
> the Holy Spirit in both. He will be seen (*videbitur*)
> not as a confused reflection in a mirror, but face to
> face (1 Cor 13:12). For he will be seen (*videbitur*)
> as he is, fulfilling that promise which tells us:
> 'He who loves me will be loved by my Father, and I

shall love him and show myself to him' (Jn 14:21).[19]

This is an attractive passage, one which seems to point to a contemplative experience in its imagery, in its scriptural references, and in its ineffability. But, as a matter of fact, it points beyond the contemplative experience to the Beatific Vision, as the context makes clear. The vision to which Aelred refers here is not a foreshadowing of eternity in contemplation, but the experience foreshadowed. Aelred continues in the same place:

> From this vision (*visione*) will proceed that knowledge (*cognitio*) of which he says again: 'This is eternal life, that they should know you, the one God, and him whom you sent, Jesus Christ' (Jn 17:3).[20]

The conclusion of the treatise, which follows this passage, combines repeated use of the noun *meditatio* with a quotation from the *Song of Songs* often used by twelfth-century monastic writers as a poetic vehicle to express their contemplative experience.[21] This would be a curious combination if the passage just quoted were not a reference to the Beatific Vision. Aelred writes:

> These, sister, are some seeds of spiritual meditation (*meditationum spiritualium*) which I have made it my business to sow for you concerning the memory of Christ's boons in the past and the expectation of what lies in the future, to the end that from them a rich crop of the love of God may spring up and grow to maturity. Meditation (*meditatio*) will arouse affection (*affectum*), affection (*affectus*) will give birth to desire, desire will stir up tears, so that your tears may be bread for you day and night (Ps 41:4) until you appear in his sight (*conspectu*), are embraced by him,[22] and say to him what is written in the *Song of Songs*: 'My Beloved to me and I to him' (Sg 2:16).[23]

Aelred, I am forced to conclude, simply does not mention the possibility of the contemplative experience to his sister, the recluse. The route laid out in the *Rule* passes from meditation to Beatific Vision, with no foretaste of that Vision in contemplation.

This view is supported, I think, by the vocabulary of the entire treatise. Aelred repeatedly urges the recluse to meditation, sometimes using the noun *meditatio*, sometimes the verb *meditare*. 'She (the recluse) should spend the interval between vigils and lauds in prayer and meditation (*meditationi*)'.[24] Aelred points to Jesus' desert experience and his fasting and comments: 'This was

done for you and in your stead; meditate (*meditare*) on the way in
which it was done and imitate what was done'.[25]
There seems to be no indication that Aelred meant by meditation
anything beyond the usual monastic practice involving the exercise
of the intellect. When the recluse is urged '...not to omit the Magi
and their gift from your meditation (*meditatione*)...,'[26] she is to
'turn it over mentally' (*mente pertracta*) as she did in considering
the shepherd's vigil.[27] When thinking of Paradise, she is to 'turn
all this over' (*revolve*) in her mind, so that her spirit may go out
wholly to the Lord.[28] This passage is followed by the admonition to

> Imagine (*cogita*) now that you are standing before Christ's
> judgement seat between these two companies and have not
> been assigned to one or the other. Turn your eyes
> (*deflecte nunc oculos*) to the left of the Judge and gaze
> on that wretched multitude.[29]

We have returned to visual imagery.
But let us return to the words 'meditation' and 'meditate'.
Aelred's treatise on *Jesus at the Age of Twelve* provides a classical
description of that process, that activity. Aelred writes of Jesus'
experience in the Temple and of Mary's reflection on it:

> But what is the meaning of the Evangelist's state-
> ment that 'they (the elders) did not understand what
> he had said to them' (Lk 2:50)? It does not, I
> think, apply to Mary, for, from the moment the Holy
> Spirit came upon her and the power of the Most High
> overshadowed her (Lk 1:35), she could not be ignor-
> ant of any purpose in her Son. But while the rest
> did not understand what he (Jesus) had said, Mary,
> knowing and understanding, kept all things in her
> heart and pondered over them (*conferens*) in her
> heart (Lk 2:51). She kept them in her memory, she
> pondered them in meditation, and she compared them
> with the other things she had seen and heard of him.[30]

The phrase I have translated 'pondered them in meditation' is *meditatione ruminabat*, not the Vulgate *conferens*. Mary is here made
the archetypal monastic meditator who 'chews her cud' in meditation.
Aelred used other verbs--and images--in describing what I judge
to be meditation, not contemplation. The verbs are easier to in-
terpret, as they most often indicate activity.[31] Even image verbs
as evocative of contemplation as 'kiss' and 'embrace', by their imperative form in the *Rule* and *On Jesus at the Age of Twelve* indicate the action of meditation, not the reception of contemplation:

Next with all your devotion accompany (*prosequere*)
the Mother as she makes her way to Bethlehem.
Taking shelter with her, be present (*assiste*) and
help (*obsequere*) her as she gives birth, and, when
the infant is laid in the manger (Lk 2:7), break
into words of exultant joy (Ps 41:5) together with
Isaiah and cry: 'A child has been born to us, a son
is given to us, (Is 9:6). Embrace (*amplectare*)
that sweet crib, let love overcome your reluctance,
affection drive out fear. Put your lips to those
most sacred feet, kiss (*oscula*) them again and
again.[32]

A list of references to kisses and embraces could be made,[33] but
such a list might well be misleading. It is in the context of the
words that their meaning for our problem is discerned. This is as
true of this tactile image as it is of visual or saporous imagery.
We shall, however, return to kisses and embraces later.

It is surely necessary to see if Aelred uses the words 'contemplate' and 'contemplation' in the treatises under consideration.
He does indeed, and often; and this leads us to examine the context
of this usage to determine what Aelred meant by 'contemplation'.
The *Rule for a Recluse* uses the verbal form of the word, but always
as an equivalent for meditate. For example, Aelred writes:

Further, do you not think you will gain some devotion
by contemplating (*contempleris*) him (Jesus) at Nazareth as a boy among boys, obedient to his mother and
helping his foster-father with his work?[34]

The activity involved in this sort of 'contemplation' is underscored
by parallelism of the verb in the very next sentence:

Consider (*quaeseris*) him too at the age of twelve
going up with his parents and staying in the city
while all they unawares began their return.[35]

The third book of Aelred's *On Jesus at the Age of Twelve* is
particularly rich in references to 'contemplation' in various
usages and imaginal contexts. But the *Leitmotiv* is established at
the very beginning of this book, labeled in the critical edition as
Secundum moralem sensum. Aelred writes:

Now I must come back to you, my dearest son, who have
resolved to model yourself on Christ and follow closely
in Jesus' footsteps. I hope to be able to explain
your progress to you through this passage from the

Gospel, so that you may read in these pages what you
are experiencing (*experiris*)³⁶ with interior joy in
yourself. For you have, I think, made the passage
from the poverty of Bethlehem to the wealth of Nazareth, and, arriving at the age of twelve, you have
gone up from the flowers of Nazareth to the fruits of
Jerusalem. Thus you are able to study hidden things
not so much in books as in your own experience.³⁷

This last sentence deserves quotation in the Latin where it is the
concluding phrase of the previous sentence and reads: '...*ut non
tam in codicibus, quam in propriis moribus mystica valeas lecti-
tare*'. The word *mystica* stands out immediately and intriguingly,
but it has little to do with our word 'mystical'. We must take
Aelred seriously here when he sets out on an exegetical quest--on
the third of his exegetical quests in the treatise: this one a
quest for the *mystica*, the hidden (or, if you will, secret) things
contained in the accounts of Jesus' boyhood related in the gospel
of Luke.

Aelred's words seem to me to be particularly appropriate to
this quest. His reader, Ivo, is sufficiently advanced in the spiritual life that he need no longer rely on the words, the literal
sense of scripture, contained in books. Ivo has had sufficient
spiritual experience that he can see the mystical things, the mys-
teries, the hidden or secret meaning of Scripture. Ivo has reached
the age of twelve, the fruits of Jerusalem. Aelred continues:

For as Bethlehem, where Christ was born little and
poor, is the beginning of a good life, and Nazareth,
where he was brought up, is the practice of virtue,
so Jerusalem, to which he went up at the age of
twelve, is the contemplation of heavenly secrets.³⁸

Ivo's life and Aelred's exegetical insights now lead us to Jerusalem where '...*caelestium secretorum est contemplatio*'.

What is the nature of the contemplation which knows the secrets
of heaven? Many of the images Aelred uses to describe the contemplation at Jerusalem are familiar. The passage which follows immediately contains both saporous and visual images:

At Bethlehem the soul becomes poor, at Nazareth it
grows rich, at Jerusalem it abounds in delights.
It becomes poor by perfect renunciation of the
world; it grows rich by perfecting the virtues; it
abounds in delights through the sweetness of spiritual tastes (*spiritualium saporum*). The ascent must
be made from the valley of tears, amid the difficulties

of temptation, through the plains of spiritual exercise, to the heights of luminous contemplation
(*luminosae contemplationis*).[39]

The editor of the English translation of the treatise, Basil Pennington, suggests this passage introduces a '...quite traditional
yet very personal description of the three ages of spiritual growth'.[40]
And I agree. The third, and highest, age of spiritual growth is clearly contemplation. Is this 'contemplation' 'meditation', or is it an
ecstatic state of union with God?

The 'third' stage of spiritual growth is also the twelfth year,
the year of Jerusalem, the year of contemplation. Let us hear Aelred
describe the preceding years which lead to contemplation; of particular interest here are years six and seven:

> If the spirit of understanding (*spiritus intellectus*)
> grants him meditation (*meditationem*) on the holy law,
> happy progress will bring him to the age of six. Seven
> years of age is brought by the spirit of wisdom (*spi-
> ritus sapientiae*), which proceeds from meditation
> (*meditatione*) on divine law....[41]

Understanding makes possible meditation, which in turn brings
forth wisdom. This wisdom, Aelred continues, leads to the virtues
of years eight, nine, ten, and eleven, which are temperance, prudence,
justice, and strength. Thus, through the age of twelve, the soul is
still in the second stage, the stage of Nazareth. And this second
stage includes the gift and activity of meditation.

We may thus expect the twelfth year, the year of Jerusalem, to
transcend meditation. Again, let us hear Aelred:

> The twelfth year follows, that is, the light of contem-
> plation (*contemplationis*). This raises the ardent soul
> to the heavenly Jerusalem itself, unlocks heaven, opens
> the gates of paradise, and reveals to the gaze of the
> pure mind (*purae mentis oculis exhibet contemplandum*)
> the Bridegroom himself who, looking out, as it were,
> through the lattice-work (Sg 2:9), is more comely
> than the sons of men (Ps 44:3). And thus the soul de-
> serves to hear (*audire*) those sweetest of words: 'You
> are wholly beautiful, my friend, and there is no spot
> in you' (Sg 4:7). For she has been cleansed (*evolans*)
> from the defilement of the passions and has escaped
> the snares of business. The memory of past things has
> been banished. The images of outward things (*imagin-
> ibus exteriorum*) have disappeared, and with ardent
> longing she raises the face of her heart in all its

beauty to look on him whom she loves. And therefore
she deserves to hear: 'You are wholly beautiful....'[42]

The striking parallels between this passage and Bernard's *Sermon
Twenty-three on the Song of Songs*, in which Bernard both acknowledges and describes his contemplative experience,[43] strengthens
my conviction that Aelred's twelfth year is a year of contemplative
experience of God.
     Aelred continues his description of the twelfth year:

> Further, 'Winter has passed away, the rains have abated
> and gone. Flowers have appeared' (Sg 2:11f.). These
> sweet-smelling flowers are the virtues, new as yet
> though they be, happily springing up in the field of
> the heart that is making good progress after the win-
> ter of persecutions and the rains of temptations. De-
> lighted at once with their beauty and their fragrance
> Christ invites the soul to come up on high from
> below....[44]

If the previous eleven years of the soul's life have called for
activity, including the activity of meditation, the virtues which
result do not demand contemplation, but lead to the invitation of
Christ to 'come up higher'. The initiative in contemplation is
God's, not man's.
     Aelred continues by another image. The soul feels the 'whis-
per of a gentle breeze' which 'raises the soul in contemplation
(*contemplantem*) up to the very gates of the heavenly Jerusalem.
Then (the Bridegroom)...invites to kisses: "Rise up, hasten, my
friend, and come"' (Sg 2:9f.).[45]

> Then, entering Jerusalem, the soul passes 'into the
> place of the majestic tabernacle, as far as the house
> of God, with cries of exultation and thanksgiving'
> (Ps 41:5). Then there are embraces, then there are
> kisses, then 'I have found him whom my soul loves, I
> have held him fast, and I shall not let him go' (Sg
> 3:4), then she abounds in delights and enjoys good
> things in Jerusalem, celebrating a feast day with
> joy and exultation.[46]

Like Bernard,[47] Aelred complains that the contemplative experience comes both rarely and lasts but a short time. *'Sed heu,
heu, rara hora et parva mora'.*[48]
     But if contemplation comes but rarely, this does not prevent
Aelred from using the words 'contemplation' and 'contemplate' almost immediately in contexts which show he once again returns to
the meaning 'meditation'.[49] Aelred tells us why:

There are many kinds of contemplations (*Sunt
enim multa genera contemplationum*) and spiritual
visions, but all of them, in my opinion, may be
seen to belong either to God's power or his wisdom
or his goodness.[50]

Following this, Aelred launches into a meditative description of
three days in the life of Christ in which 'contemplation' (*contem-
plari*) is equated with looking 'with the eyes of an enlightened
mind' (*oculis illuminatae mentis aspexeris*) and even with consideration (*considerare*) and meditation (*meditatione*).[51] Aelred has come
full circle, and so have we.

On Spiritual Friendship

As I have said, a common image for contemplation is that of
sight. But if visual imagery is important in Aelred's *Rule for a
Recluse*, it is entirely missing in the *Spiritual Friendship*. Aelred
uses the verb *videre* and its derivatives some forty-six times in the
Spiritual Friendship.[52] But what does Aelred see here when he 'sees'?
The answer is disappointing to one seeking contemplative imagery: Aelred uses 'see' three times in the most literal sense;[53] the remaining forty-three uses ascend only to the next level of meaning. To
see most often means 'see' in the intellectual sense, as when we say
'Do you see what I mean?' We do invariably see what Aelred means,
but this does not advance our quest one iota.
       The same is true of the verb 'to hear'. Of the eight times in
which hearing is mentioned,[54] none contains aural imagery of an experience more transcendent than that of everyday understanding, and
half the examples refer only to simple auditory activity. This is
a similar lack of saporous imagery. *Sapere*, and its derivatives
sapidum, sapiens, sapienter, are used some thirteen times,[55] but always in the usual senses, ranging from simple 'taste' to 'relish'
to 'wise' or 'wisely'.
       The more generic words referring to sense, *experior* and *sentire*,
leave us equally empty-handed. Aelred uses *experior* three times,[56]
with the commonplace meaning 'experience'. *Sentire* and its derivatives are used much more often, twenty-one times,[57] but all save one
of them refer to feeling, sense, opinion, and, in one case, intelligence in the sense of sharpness.[58]
       The importance of seeing and understanding the meaning of each
of Aelred's words in its context may be illustrated by one instance
of the uses of *sentire*. A recent rereading of *Spiritual Friendship*
caused me to pause over a phrase in Book II, 67. The words *sublimia
sentire* seemed to leap out of the page at me. was this an unexpected case of an exalted experience? Not for Aelred, it seems. The
context leads, I think, to a prosaic rendering of the sentence in

which the phrase occurs as: 'How shameful it would be for anyone to
regard his friend as he regards himself, since each ought to feel
himself humble and his friend exalted'. So much for *sublimia sen-*
tire.

But Aelred seems to go beyond the usual use of *sentire* in a
passage which occurs in the penultimate section of the last book
of *Spiritual Friendship*.[59] The passage is worth quoting at some
length. Aelred is speaking of the prayer of friends for one another.

> And thus a friend praying to Christ on behalf of his
> friend, and, for his friend's sake, desiring to be
> heard by Christ, directs his attention with diligence
> and longing to Christ. Then it sometimes happens
> that suddenly and imperceptibly one love passes over
> into another, and touching in the friend the sweet-
> ness of Christ himself, he begins to taste how sweet
> and how delightful he is.

Here we have a combination of the two sense images of taste[60] and
feel. The sweetness and delight felt and tasted by the friend
through his friend is expressed in paraphrases of psalms 33 (34)
and 99 (100). This does not quench the fire in the passage. But
is that fire the transcendent, ineffable fire of the contemplative experience? A striking parallel exists: Bernard described
the onset of his contemplative experience as sudden and impercep-
tible.[61] Aelred's passage is attractive, but by itself it is not
enough to let us conclude that his feeling and tasting are metaphors for a contemplative experience of God. I shall, however,
return to this passage later to set it in its larger context.

It is surely necessary to see if Aelred does address contemplation directly and not simply through the imagery of the senses.
Aelred uses the word 'contemplation' four times in the *Spiritual*
Friendship. In three of these cases he clearly refers to the sort
of mental and spiritual activity I have called meditation.[62] In
Book II, 63, he speaks of '...the sacred bond of friendship between David and Jonathan, which was consecrated not through hope
of future advantage but through the contemplation of virtue...'
(*virtutis contemplatio*). The phrase recalls Cicero,[63] but evokes
no suspicion of transcendent experience. Indeed, the usual hierarchy of latin words Aelred uses to describe meditation and con-
templation--*contemplatio, consideratio, meditatio*--generally under-
goes a shift toward the prosaic in the *Spiritual Friendship*. *Con-*
templatio almost always indicates 'meditation'; *consideratio* (in
its verbal form) means simply 'consider'.[64] *'Diligentius proinde*
haec quinque consideremus...'[65] indicates, I think, mental activity which requires little or no inspiration. *Meditatio* occurs

only twice, and signifies only a most prosaic sort of mental reflection.[66]

But in one case Aelred's use of 'contemplation' seems to go beyond meditation. In Book II, 57, Aelred writes:

> Such a reward friendship will certainly be for those cultivating it, when wholly transported (*translata*) into God, it immerses in contemplation of him (*in eius contemplatione*) those whom it has united.

The notion of being wholly transported, of being immersed, surely evokes a sense of transcendence, of a direct experience of ultimate Reality. But some nagging doubts remain. Could it be that it is friendship rather than the friend that is transported, that is immersed? I think not. But even if that were true, the passage could still refer to what I have called contemplation. Some ambivalence remains, however. As we have seen, a similarily attractive passage occurs in Aelred's *Rule for a Recluse*, a passage which seems to point to a contemplative experience in its imagery, in its scriptural references, and in its ineffability.[67] But, as we have also seen, it points beyond contemplative experience to the Beatific Vision. Is it possible that our 'contemplative' passage in *Spiritual Friendship* is, in the same way, not a foreshadowing of eternity in contemplation, but the experience foreshadowed? I think it less likely here than in the *Rule*, for friendship is usually thought of as a this-worldly relationship. But, failing a clear confirmation of contemplation elsewhere in Aelred's *Spiritual Friendship*, I should hesitate to take my stand on this passage alone.

The same is true of Aelred's extended treatment of kisses in Book II, 20-27. Aelred begins this central passage of his treatise by describing the ascent of the soul to God through friendship.

> In friendship are joined honesty and delight, truth and joy, sweetness and good-will, affection and action. All these begin in Christ, advance through Christ, and are perfected in Christ. Therefore, not too steep or unnatural does the ascent appear from Christ, the inspiration of the love by which we love our friend, to Christ giving himself as our friend for us to love, so that delight may follow upon delight, sweetness upon sweetness, affection upon affection. And so, friend cleaving to friend in the spirit of Christ, is made with him one heart and one soul.[68] Thus, mounting aloft through degrees of love to friendship with Christ, he is made one spirit with him in one kiss.[69] Aspiring to this kiss, the saintly soul cries out: 'Let him kiss me with the kiss of his mouth'.[70]

This passage is provocative, not only because of the union motif,
but because that union is expressed in the language of the *Song
of Songs*, the favorite vehicle of twelfth-century contemplatives
in describing their experience.

Aelred goes on to describe a hierarchy of kisses--corporeal,
spiritual, and intellectual. But 'intellectual' does not mean to
Aelred what it means to us, for the intellectual kiss is accomplished '...through the Spirit of God by the infusion of grace'.[71]
In what does this gift consist? Aelred describes it:

> The soul, therefore, accustomed to this kiss and not
> doubting that all this sweetness comes from Christ,
> reflects within itself, so to speak, and says, 'Oh,
> if only he had come!' The soul sighs for the kiss of
> grace and with the greatest desire exclaims: 'Let him
> kiss me with the kiss of his mouth'. So that now,
> after all earthly temptations have been tempered, and
> all thoughts and desires which savor of the world
> have been quieted, the soul takes delight in the kiss
> of Christ alone and rests in his embrace, exalting and
> exclaiming: 'His left hand is under my head, and his
> right hand shall embrace me'.[72]

This way in which Aelred uses the quotation from the *Song of
Songs* (2:6), his emphasis on transcendence, and his exaltative
language convince me that Aelred here attempts to convey to us
some sense of his contemplative experience, an experience rooted
in friendship and consummated in the embrace of Christ. Could
Aelred here be describing the Beatific Vision? It is possible,
but I think not. My conviction rests on the passage surrounding
Aelred's only other uses of the word 'embrace' in the *Spiritual
Friendship*.

In Book III, 127, almost at the end of the treatise, Aelred
interrupts his own 'nuts and bolts' description of how to gain
and maintain friendship by declaiming this poetic passage:

> What more is there to say? Was it not a foretaste
> of blessedness thus to love and be loved (by my
> friend), thus to help and be helped; and in this
> way from the sweetness of fraternal love to wing
> one's flight aloft to that more sublime splendor
> of divine love, and by the ladder of love now to
> mount to the embrace of Christ himself; and again
> to descend to the love of neighbor there pleasantly
> to rest?

This is a telling passage, for the descent to love of neighbor

which follows the embrace of Christ clearly indicates that the union
experienced can be enjoyed in this life, not only in the next.

Earlier I promised to return to the passage in which Aelred
describes how love for a friend can lead the soul to Christ and
enable her to taste the sweetness and feel the delight of Christ's
touch.[73] The very last sentence of Aelred's treatise continues
from that description. In it Aelred uses the word 'embrace' twice
again:

> Thus, ascending from that holy love with which he em-
> braces his friend to that with which he embraces
> Christ, he will joyfully partake in the abundance of
> the spiritual fruit of friendship, awaiting the full-
> ness of all things in the life to come. Then, with
> the dispelling of all anxiety by reason of which we
> now fear and are solicitious for one another, with
> the removal of all adversity which it now behooves
> us to bear for one another, and, above all, with the
> destruction of the sting of death itself,[74] whose
> pangs now often trouble us and force us to grieve
> for one another, with salvation secured, we shall
> rejoice in the eternal possession of supreme goodness.
> And then this friendship, to which here we admit but
> few, will be poured out on all and by all will be
> poured on God, and God shall be 'all in all'.[75]

Aelred's friendship leads to eternal union with God and friend in
the next life; but, he tells us, it can be foreshadowed in this
life by the contemplative embrace of Christ.

I began this paper with a reference to Hallier's *The Monastic
Theology of Aelred of Rievaulx*. A quotation from the forward to
that great book shall serve as my conclusion. In it, Jean Leclercq
writes:

> One cannot but admire the importance that is rightly
> given to terminology. How many treasures are waiting
> to be found in these writers if only we pay attention
> to the words they were fond of using: For they did
> not use these words haphazardly....When, with the help
> of instructive comparisons, we have grasped the meaning
> of some key word, this will then frequently suffice to
> cast light on an entire passage. When the full mean-
> ing of such a word has been comprehended, we shall
> find delight in recognizing it in other contexts, dis-
> covering echoes of it, enjoying all its overtones.[76]

The University of Dallas

NOTES

1. Trans. Columban Heaney; CS 2; Shannon, Ireland.
2. Iesu, III, 19; *Opera omnia* (edd. A. Hoste and C. H. Talbot; CC, *Continuatio medievalis*, I; Tvrnholti, 1971) p. 266, l. 9.
3. When Aelred uses the words 'contemplate' or 'contemplation', he often means 'meditate' or 'meditation'. This is true of all six uses in the *Rule of Life for a Recluse*: Inst incl 15 (*Opera*, p. 482, l. 651), 29 (p. 663, l. 899), 30 (p. 664, l. 953), 31 (p. 667, l. 1059), 31 (p. 671, l. 1174), 33 (p. 678, l. 1426). Of the eighteen uses of the various forms of *contemplare* and *contemplatio* in *On Jesus at the Age of Twelve*, four indicate meditation: Iesu III, 25 (*Opera*, p. 272, ll. 212-13); III, 25 (p. 272, ll. 214-15); III, 30 (p. 276, ll. 349-50); III, 31 (p. 278, ll. 390-91). In five cases (III, 23, p. 270, l. 150; III, 24, p. 271, l. 197; III, 25, p. 271, l. 199; III, 28, p. 274, l. 281; III, 29, p. 275, l. 314), Aelred describes a progression from meditation to contemplation, but uses the word 'contemplation' to include both meanings. For example, in III, 28 (p. 274, l. 281), Aelred speaks of the soul's progress through three 'days': the first, consideration of God's power; the second, admiration of his wisdom; the third, 'a sweet foretaste of his goodness and kindness'. In one case (I, 6, p. 254, l. 140), *contemplare* means 'contemplation' in a very literal sense, meaning 'look at' or 'watch'.
4. When Aelred uses the various forms of *meditare* or *meditatio* in Iesu or Inst incl, he always means the activity of pondering prayerfully. Iesu, I, 1 (p. 249, l. 3); I, 9 (p. 257, ll. 234-35); III, 20 (p. 267, l. 48); III, 20 (p. 267, l. 51); III, 24 (p. 271, l. 183); III, 26 (p. 273, l. 234); III, 30 (p. 276, ll. 355-56); III, 32 (p. 278, l. 400). Inst incl, 20 (p. 654, l. 611); 20 (p. 654, l. 612); 22 (p. 655, l. 638); 29 (p. 662, l. 884); 29 (p. 662, l. 885); 30 (p. 664, l. 932); 31 (p. 665, ll. 970-71); 33 (p. 682, l. 1533); 33 (p. 681, l. 1521); 33 (p. 681, l. 1523). Aelred also uses 'consider' (*considerare*) and 'consideration' (*consideratio*) to mean 'meditate' or 'reflect'. Iesu, III, 20 (p. 266, l. 35); III, 25 (p. 272, l. 223); III, 28 (p. 274, l. 289); III, 31 (p. 277, l. 376). Inst incl, 29 (p. 662, l. 887); 31 (p. 670, l. 1165).
5. See, for example, Csi, II, ii, 5; SBOp 3:414.
6. *Sermones inediti* (ed. C. H. Talbot; *Series S. Ordinis Cisterciensis*, I; Rome, 1952) p. 140.
7. E. A. Speiser, 'Introduction' to *Genesis* (*The Anchor Bible*, 1; Garden City, 1964) p. xviii.
8. Hallier, p. 9.
9. Hallier, pp. 3-24.
10. The translation is from *Treatises; The Pastoral Prayer* (CF 2;

Spencer, Massachusetts, 1971) p. 5. Although I have consulted
the translations in this volume, I have not always followed
them.

11. *Opera*, p. 250, 1. 50. Other uses of taste imagery are in Iesu,
I, 3 (p. 252, 1. 85); I, 8 (p. 256, 1. 216); II, 12 (p. 259, 1.
30); II, 12 (p. 259, 1. 31). Curiously, there are no uses of
this image in the Inst incl.

12. *First Sermon for the Feast of Pentecost; Sermones inediti*, p. 106.

13. CF 2, p. 5, n. 10.

14. On Aelred's use of taste imagery, see Odo Brooke, 'Monastic
Theology and St Aelred', in his *Studies in Monastic Theology*
(CS 37; Kalamazoo, Michigan, 1980) p. 221.

15. Inst incl, 31; *Opera*, p. 665, 1. 964.

16. Inst incl, 33; p. 677, 1. 1387.

17. Inst incl, 33; p. 678, 1. 1414.

18. Inst incl, 33; p. 679, 1. 1439. Aelred would have us 'turn our
eyes' also in Inst incl, 29 (p. 662, 11. 888-90); 33 (p. 678,
1. 1425).

19. Inst incl, 33; p. 681, 11. 1499-1508. The Inst incl uses forms
of the verb *videre* and the noun *visio* some forty-nine times;
usually the meaning is either literal or intellectual (as in
'it would seem' or 'do you see?'). In one case (11, p. 647,
1. 361) *visio* refers to the Beatific Vision. Iesu uses *videre*
or *visio* some fourteen times; of these, two (III, 21, p. 268,
1. 88; III, 22, p. 269, 11. 120-21) refer to contemplation.
In Iesu, Aelred refers to eyes some six times; in two cases
(I, 1, p. 250, 1. 24; III, 25, p. 272, 1. 226) the reference is
to meditation: for example, 'bring before your mind's eye'
(III, 25). In one case (III, 29, p. 276, 1. 331) the meaning
is contemplation: '...*oculis mentis in ipsa caeli secreta
radium porrexit...*'.

20. Inst incl, 33; p. 681, 11. 1510-12.

21. Perhaps the most thorough use of this vehicle is in Bernard of
Clairvaux' eighty-six sermons *In Cantica Canticorum*; SBOp 1
and 2.

22. Curiously enough, the embrace is ignored by the CF 2 translator.

23. Inst incl, 33; *Opera*, p. 681, 11. 1519-27.

24. Inst incl, 11; p. 648, 11. 381-82.

25. Inst incl, 31; p. 665, 11. 970-71.

26. Inst incl, 30; p. 664, 1. 932.

27. Inst incl, 29; p. 664, 1. 928.

28. Inst incl, 32; p. 676, 1. 1354.

29. Inst incl, 33; p. 678, 1. 1425.

30. Iesu, I, 9; p. 257, 11. 234-35.

31. For example, *rimantur* (examine diligently) in Iesu, III, 28;
Opera, p. 275, 1. 302.

32. Inst incl, 29; *Opera*, pp. 663-64, 11. 921-27.

33. There are eighteen instances of *oscula* and *amplexus*, and their
    verbal equivalents, in Iesu. Of these, six are literal: I, 5,
    p. 253, 1. 130; I, 5, p. 253, 1. 134; I, 5, p. 253, 1. 138; I,
    8, p. 256, 1. 209 (twice); I, 8, p. 256, 1. 217. Eight uses
    are meant figuratively: III, 26, p. 273, 11. 241, 242, 246,
    249; III, 27, p. 274, 1. 267. There are four cases in which
    the reference is to contemplation: III, 22, p. 269, 1. 136;
    III, 22, p. 270, 1. 139 (twice); III, 24, p. 271, 1. 191. Of
    the some seventeen uses of 'kiss' and 'embrace' in Inst incl,
    eleven are meant to be taken literally: 4, p. 640, 1. 89; 4,
    p. 640, 1. 120; 19, p. 654, 1. 592 (twice); 26, p. 658, 1.
    750; 28, p. 661, 1. 837; 30, p. 664, 11. 939-40; 31, p. 669,
    1. 1113; 31, p. 671, 1. 1193; 31, p. 672, 1. 1229; 33, p. 681,
    1. 1526. Six take place in meditation: 29, p. 663, 1. 919; 29,
    p. 663, 1. 925; 29, p. 664, 1. 927; 31, p. 665, 1. 989; 31,
    p. 666, 1. 1002; 31, p. 667, 1. 1058.
34. Inst incl, 30; p. 664, 11. 952-55.
35. Inst incl, 31; p. 664, 11. 956-58.
36. *Experientiae* occurs in Iesu, III, 28, p. 275, 1. 299. Aelred
    also begins the *Rule* with a reference to experience: Inst incl,
    1, p. 637, 11. 8-9. *Experientia* (in the sense of knowledge by
    meditation) appears in Inst incl, 29, p. 662, 1. 886.
37. Iesu, III, 19; *Opera*, pp. 265-66, 11. 1-9.
38. Iesu, III, 19; p. 266, 11. 9-13.
39. *Ibid.*, 11. 14-19.
40. CF 2, p. 25, n. 1.
41. Iesu, III, 20; *Opera*, p. 267, 11. 47-51.
42. Iesu, III, 20; pp. 267-68, 11. 62-73.
43. Especially 11-16; SBOp 1:145-50.
44. Iesu, III, 20; *Opera*, p. 268, 11. 73-79.
45. Iesu, III, 22; p. 269, 11. 129-36.
46. Iesu, III, 22; p. 270, 11. 137-42.
47. SC 23, 15; SBOp 1:148.
48. Iesu, III, 23; *Opera*, p. 270, 11. 148-49.
49. Iesu, III, 24; p. 271.
50. Iesu, III, 25; pp. 271-72, 11. 199-201.
51. Iesu, III, 25-26; pp. 272-73.
52. Spir amic, *prologus*: 3; I:4, 6, 10 (twice), 14, 17, 19, 20,
    21 (twice), 25, 41, 47, 51, 55 (twice), 68; II: 4, 5, 26, 49
    (quoting Cicero), 51; III: 3, 16, 18 (twice), 20, 21, 29, 30,
    52, 62, 69, 72, 88, 93, 99, 100, 102, 107, 109 (twice), 111
    (twice), 122, 131.
53. Spir amic, III: 29, 30, 131.
54. Spir amic, I: 7; III: 16, 22, 36, 47, 102, 105 (*aures*), 121.
55. Spir amic, I: 52, 62, 63 (five times), 64, 66 (twice), 68; II:
    3, 5, 8, 18, 26; III: 48.
56. Spir amic, I: 33, 36; II: 9.

57. Spir amic, I: 20, 37, 45, 52, 58, 59, 60; II: 19, 28, 67; III: 1, 7, 22, 65, 70, 76, 80, 82, 89, 93, 133.
58. Spir amic, III: 1.
59. Spir amic, III: 133.
60. There are three instances of *gustare* in the *Spiritual Friendship*: I: 23, 58; III: 133.
61. *In Cantica Canticorum, sermo 74*, 5; SBOp 2:242.
62. Spir amic, II: 63; III: 32, 130.
63. *De amicitia*, 30.
64. Spir amic, III: 23, 90.
65. Spir amic, III: 23.
66. Spir amic, *prologus*, 8; I: 26.
67. Inst incl, 33; *Opera omnia*, 681; see above pp. 74-75.
68. Ac 4:32.
69. 1 Co 6:17; compare the antiphon for second vespers in the office for Saint Gertrude.
70. Sg 1:1.
71. Spir amic, II: 24.
72. Spir amic, II: 27.
73. See above, p. 82.
74. 1 Co 15:54f.
75. 1 Co 15:28.
76. Hallier, p. xvi.

GETTING THINGS THE WRONG WAY ROUND:
COMPOSITION AND TRANSPOSITION IN AELRED OF RIEVAULX'S
De institutione inclusarum

Marsha Dutton-Stuckey

MEDIEVAL AND CHURCH historians who explore the historical context and quotidian details of the anchorite's life find their information in three primary sources: the ninth century Latin *Regula Solitariorum* of Grimlaic, the thirteenth century English *Ancren Riwle*, and the twelfth century Anglo-Latin treatise on the contemplative life by Aelred of Rievaulx, *De institutione inclusarum*. Aelred's treatise, especially its first portion, consistently provides much of the standard historical information about early English anchoritism.

Such an approach to *De institutione inclusarum*, however, leaves the second and larger portion of the work almost untouched. Here Aelred discusses the three virtues inherent in the life of the anchoress--chastity, humility, and charity--and presents three meditations to encourage 'the sweet love of Jesus...to grow in (her) affections' (11. 883-84).[1] Students of medieval devotional writing focus on this portion of the work, examining its affective and mystical core and citing it as an important influence on such later writers on contemplation as Ignatius, Bonaventure, Richard Rolle, and Julian of Norwich.

De institutione inclusarum's appeal for scholars in different disciplines is evident. That an internal disjunction and apparent lack of coherence between its parts underlies the breadth of that appeal is somewhat less obvious. Indeed, the treatise is so complete and satisfying in its applicability to all facets of the anchoress' life that no one has ever challenged even its summary and totally inaccurate description by Aelred's twelfth-century biographer, Walter Daniel, who calls it 'a book...in which (Aelred) traced the course of this kind of profession from the ardour of the entrance into the same to its perfection'.[2]

Daniel's description prefigures precisely the approach to the text taken by successive centuries of readers and scholars; he describes the handbook on the anchoritic life that one wants to have read rather than the one Aelred in fact wrote. The reader's expectations smooth the seam between the two parts of the work, provide unity and coherence in one work where Aelred, it appears, wrote two. This coherence, though is finally more apparent than real; it is primarily a child of the reader's desire rather than of the author's conception.

The two portions of Aelred's treatise on the contemplative life are both well known. The first is a short manual of direction for the daily life of the anchoress (the 'exterior man', as Aelred says), and the second is a considerably longer work of spiritual guidance. The two parts fit together well in content and rhetorical ordering, and the audience is much the same in each--new young contemplatives whose individual circumstances Aelred does not know. (The sister whose urging he acknowledges at the beginning of the first portion and whom he occasionally addresses in both is explicitly defined as one for whom his recommendations are unnecessary and inappropriate.) The apparent unity of the work does not, then, lend itself to easy attack.

The introductory paragraphs to the first part of the treatise, however, suggest that Aelred did not originally conceive his work as comprising both kinds of direction. They begin by acknowledging his sister's desire for his guidance, then promise,

> I shall do as you ask then, and endeavor to draw
> up a definite rule for you, selecting from the
> various regulations on the Fathers those that ap-
> pear most useful in forming the exterior man. I
> shall add some details suited to your particular
> circumstances of time and place, and wherever
> it seems helpful, blend the spiritual with the
> corporal (*Prologue*, ll. 11-16).[3]

These words are an entirely appropriate introduction to this manual on the daily life of the anchoress. They establish a personal reason for writing and a personal audience for the work, and they de- fine its subject. The text that follows justifies the introductory words, addressing the sister occasionally and advising on such dis- parate subjects of interest to the new anchoress as gossip, gift- receiving, servants, almsgiving, silence, prayer, food, and cloth- ing. Included here and there in the midst of these topics is some blending of the spiritual--a first identification of the contempla- tive as the bride of Christ, an explanation of the spiritual values of and reasons for fasting during Lent, a promise that amidst her silence and solitude she will be with Christ.

The work does what Aelred initially said it would do and then ends decisively with these words:

> All this that concerns external behavior I have
> written, my dearest sister, at your insistence.
> Bearing in mind not so much the fervor of the
> days of old as the tepidity of our own times,
> I have offered you a rule of life which, while
> tempered to the needs of the weak, allows the
> strong every opportunity of advancing to great-
> er perfection (ll. 434-38).[4]

Again he establishes his personal audience and her role in prompt-
ing the work; again he explicitly defines its contents and purposes:
to give guidance for the behavior of the anchoress in the life she
has chosen. The handbook is finished.

This clear ending, however, barely strikes readers as an ending
at all, because they can see the work continuing on into a text almost three times as long as that which has gone before; in C. H. Talbot's edition 454 lines contain the portion on the exterior life,
1100 that on the inner. In fact, the ending to the first portion
is so easily overlooked and so intrusive if noted that one of the
two Middle English translations of the work, Bodleian Library ms.
423, blurs the separation between the two parts and interpolates
a transition between them, as Aelred does not:

> Loo, sustir, now I haue write the a forme of
> lyuynge touchinge thy conuersacioun after
> thin outwarde lyuinge. Now shal I write the
> a forme of lyuynge touchinge thin ynner con-
> uersacion, bi the helpe of Iesu and thy
> deuoute prayers.[5]

Evidence indicating that the fifteenth-century English translator
worked in slavish obedience to his Latin source suggests that this
pedestrian and non-Aelredian transition arose within a Latin manuscript tradition no longer extant.[6]

While a disregarding of the conclusion to the handbook on the
quotidian life of the recluse is not surprising in light of the
clear continuation of the text after it, the introduction to the
portion following should strike readers as surprising and unlikely,
should indicate that something strange is happening. For after 435
lines of specific direction and occasionally personal address or al-
lusion ('as to the quality and quantity of your food and drink, it
is surely unnecessary to impose any rule upon you, my sister. From
your very childhood until now, when age is taking its toll of your
body, you have scarcely taken enough food to keep yourself alive'
(ll. 388-391)[7], Aelred suddenly launches into a formal exordium:

> But now, whoever you may be who have given up
> the world to choose this life of solitude, de-
> siring to be hidden and unseen, to be dead as
> it were to the world and buried with Christ in
> his tomb, listen to my words and understand
> (ll. 439-42).[8]

The formality, the extreme impersonality of this passage, the ortho-
dox definition of the anchoress' task, the abandonment of the pre-
tense that the author writes only at a sister's urging, in exchange

for a statement of authorial initiative, the intrusion of these
words on a listener not at the moment expecting or desiring them
--all of these elements are new. This passage is not simply the
beginning of chapter two, it is not a promise to continue the direction for the outer life of the anchoress. It is a new beginning,
a formal introduction that anyone would recognize as such were there
no other text before it.

It is probably the reader's instinctive response to visual
signals that inhibits his recognition of the abruptness of the exordium's appearance at this point in the text. Just as a letter
written over several days' time appears to its reader as one letter,
not several, because it comes in one envelope, its sections follow
one another on matching stationery without significant break, and
one greeting and signature enclose the whole, so Aelred's two treatises, both concerning the same general subject, appear one and whole
because they stand in undivided manuscript or printed pages, usually
follow one *incipit*, and close with one *explicit*. In fact, the Cistercian Fathers translation of *De institutione inclusarum* reinforces
the reader's automatic expectation of one unified work by preceding
the exordium with a heading, 'The Inner Man', to match that before
the other portion, 'The Outer Man', and by appending a footnote to
the second heading: 'In the manuscripts Aelred's letter to his sister is not divided into parts. However, it is clear from the final
paragraph that he himself saw it clearly as made up of three sections
which we...have presented here as three distinct parts'.⁹

The text that follows the exordium is also not a continuation
of what has gone before, although it sometimes restates points already covered in the treatise on the outer life. Indeed, it is
partly the occasional repetition of previously stated direction
that gives a sense of unity to the whole. When the reader thinks
'Ah, I've heard that before', he naturally assumes that Aelred
thought the point important enough to say twice, or perhaps that he
forgot having already said it. For example, the passage which immediately follows the exordium concerns 'why you should prefer solitude to the company of men' (ll. 443-44).¹⁰ The fact that the handbook on the exterior life also began with this topic, 'You must first
understand the reasons that motivated the monks of old when they instituted and adopted this form of life' (ll. 1-2),¹¹ gives a ring of
familiarity and security to the announcement of the topic here,
and there is of course no reason that Aelred should not begin each
section with the same concern, especially as he gives quite different reasons in the two places.

Another, more striking, repetition has to do with almsgiving.
In the handbook, discussing the proper response of the anchoress to
those who beg outside her cell, Aelred advises:

> Her cell is not to be besieged by beggars, nor
> by orphans and widows crying for alms....I tell

you, if you have more food and more clothes
than you need for yourself, you are no nun.
So what have you to give away? The recluse
is advised, then, should she earn by her own
labor more than is necessary for her mainten-
ance, to hand it over to some trustworthy
person who will distribute it to the poor
(11. 75-85).[12]

In the treatise on the contemplative life, he says the same thing
at much greater length:

The giving of alms belongs to those who have
earthly possessions or who have been entrusted
with the administration of church property....
For since no one gives you anything to distribute in alms, from what source will you come
to possess anything you might give away? If
your work yields something, give it away not
by your own hand but by that of some other
person. If your food comes from others what
right have you to give away what belongs to
them...? (11. 812-46).[13]

Not only does this passage essentially repeat the earlier advice on the same subject, but it does not really fit here, in the
portion of the work dealing with the contemplative life of the anchoress, within the discussion of charity as one of the three defining virtues of the anchoress' life. It certainly makes sense;
it can easily be explained, but it does not belong. And it does
not belong precisely because it does belong in the other portion,
in that which discusses the daily behavior and experience of the
anchoress.
     Another such misplaced passage discusses the apparel of the
anchoress' altar. Again, one would expect such a passage to be
included among the directions for times and kinds of prayer, which
Aelred gives in the behavioral handbook. Its inclusion here indicates that he had no place better to put it while composing, especially as the transition into the subject is abrupt and peculiar:
'Let it be in these that you glory and find your happiness; within, not without, in true virtues, not in paintings and statues.
Your altar should be covered with white linen cloths' (11. 714-16).[14]
The passage can be made to fit, one has no trouble justifying its
presence, but on what basis would an author--especially one so
concerned with structural resonance of idea as Aelred--actually
choose to place it at this point in his treatise?
     Shortly thereafter, prompted in fact by this piece of advice,

appears the famous set piece comparing the preparation of flax for
linen to the preparation of the Christian soul for chastity. This
extended metaphor is appropriate at this point in the treatise, but
it is not satisfyingly incorporated into the texture of the whole;
it lacks the resonance, the echoes of words and images that so char-
acterize the treatise on the contemplative life. For example, fire
and water, which appear with specific and consistent metaphoric content elsewhere in the treatise, are here only signs, similes rather
than symbols. One has the sense, again, that Aelred wanted badly to
include this analogy in his work but at the time of writing had no
place so appropriate for it as the handbook of rules for behavior
would have offered.

The treatise on the contemplative life ends with a fitting summary of its contents and purposes:

> There, sister, are some seeds of spiritual medi-
> tation which I have made it my business to sow
> for you concerning the memory of Christ's boons
> in the past, the experience of things present
> and the expectation of what lies in the future,
> to the end that from them a rich crop of the
> love of God may spring up and grow to maturity.
> Meditation will arouse the affections, the af-
> fections will give birth to desire, desire will
> stir up tears so that your tears may be bread
> for you day and night until you appear in his
> sight and say to him what is written in the Song
> of Songs: 'My beloved is mine and I am his' (11.
> 1527).[15]

This conclusion, like that to the handbook on the exterior life, implies that the work it summarizes is complete in itself, concerning
only the spiritual life of prayer, meditation, and contemplation of
the anchoress, who has chosen 'to be...buried with Christ in his
tomb'. The purpose of this work is not 'to draw up a definite rule'
or even to 'blend the spiritual with the corporal', but specifically
to sow the seed of 'a rich crop of the love of God'.

Besides the two enclosing sets of defining words of introduction
and conclusion for the two parts of *De institutione inclusarum*, additional internal evidence argues that the two pieces of the treatise
do not really fit together: the tone differs greatly between the two,
the constant autobiographical presence of the author in the portion
on the contemplative life is entirely lacking from that on the exterior life, and the organizational subtleties and skills that char-
acterize the contemplative portion of the work are notably absent
from the handbook. Careful syntactic and structural analysis of the
two portions would surely yield valuable insight on this point.

The conclusion that Aelred originally composed two separate
treatises on the anchoritic life, at different times, for different
purposes, and even for different audiences, and then combined them
into one connected whole opens another question: In what order did
he write them?

The exordium to the contemplative portion of the treatise suggests that Aelred undertook to write a devotional work appropriate
for anyone who had undertaken the life of an anchorite. This work,
which greatly resembles several others among his writings, cites the
example of two young men attempting to maintain chastity, concentrates on Aelred's own struggles toward perfection, and provides not
only direction for anchoritic virtues, but also meditations to be
used in contemplation. Indeed, the work is widely applicable to different sorts of contemplatives, lay or ordained, cenobites as well
as anchorites. The treatise is characteristically Aelredian in its
careful logical and rhetorical development, its combination of the
affective with the intellectual, its thematic patterns of vocabulary
and imagery.

The passages already cited as out of place in the contemplative
treatise and as repeating instructions adequately given in the handbook on the exterior life seem also to argue that the contemplative
treatise was written first, probably before the author had any clear
intention of writing a work of direction for the quotidian life of
the anchoress. Had he already put such direction where it properly
belonged, in a handbook on the daily behavior and concerns of the
anchoress, he would hardly have needed to insert it in a treatise
which had no logical place or clear need for it. Surely both the
coverings for the altar and the analogy of pure linen with the chaste
soul might better have been presented within the instructions for
the times, reasons, and contents of prayers in the anchorite's life
than within the passage arguing that the true matters of concern for
the anchoress are those lying within her.

Three extant Latin manuscripts support the assertion that the
treatise on the contemplative life of the anchoress was written
first and circulated alone, however briefly. C. H. Talbot's list
of the ten extant Latin manuscripts of *De institutione inclusarum*
includes three which contain only portions from the second half of
the treatise. All three of these--British Library ms. Royal 8 D III,
Oxford ms. Bodley 36, and Oxford ms. Hatton 101--date from the thirteenth century.[16]

Further, one of the two extant Middle English translations of
the treatise, that which appears in the fourteenth-century Vernon
manuscript (Bodleian ms. English Poetry a. 1) as its preface, begins with the exordium. It contains no reference to any omitted
earlier portion, and its own *incipit* ('*Informacio Alredi, abbatis
monasterii de Rieualle, ad sororem suam inclusam, translata de latino
in anglicum per Thomam*') implies that what follows is considered

complete by the translator or scribe. Certain passages within this
translation suggest that its source may have been closer to Aelred's
original text than any Latin text now extant; its evidence on this
question may be taken to be significant.[17]

An independent circulation of the contemplative portion of *De
institutione inclusarum* could help to explain the long-time ascription of the three meditations to Anselm;[18] excerpting that unit, so
much like Anselm's meditations, from a smaller treatise without the
personalization that begins Aelred's work would have been easier
than taking it from the longer work, and Aelred's authorship might
more easily have genuinely not been recognized. One of the three
partial manuscripts, Oxford ms. Hatton 101, contains only the three
meditations, that is, only the portion elsewhere attributed to Anselm.

The combination of internal and external evidence suggests, then,
that the two portions of the treatise may have been composed in the
following manner: Aelred first wrote a highly structured treatise of
spiritual guidance and affective meditation for contemplatives. While
writing this painstakingly planned work, he found himself frequently
confronted by concerns and crises arising within English anchoritism
as scandals erupted, as monasteries of nuns asked his intervention
and advice,[19] as nuns in those houses left the community to take up
the life of reclusion and requested spiritual guidance from him.
At first he incorporated his thoughts and direction on these subjects
within the treatise at hand, occasionally disrupting his plan for the
treatise in order to advise regarding the ailing and altar apparel.
As time more on however, he found himself increasingly unwilling to
interrupt the structure and contents of his intensely confessional
guide to contemplation for the mundane concerns of daily life in an
anchorhold.

Not able to put these matters entirely away, he perhaps kept a
list of topics to be treated when time allowed. A sentence that appears at a crucial point within the treatise appears to support this
understanding of Aelred's nagging concern for these topics while writing the longer work. In it he accomplishes the transition from the
three virtues intrinsic to the life of the recluse by stating (for
a second time) the two divisions of charity, love of God and love of
neighbor, and, having already dealt at some length with love of neighbor, turns to the two elements in the love of God: 'interior dispositions and performance of works. The latter consists in the practice
of the virtues, the former in the sweetness tasted by the spirit' (ll.
878-80).[20] All that follows in the treatise has to do with interior
dispositions: the three meditations are provided 'in order that the
sweet love of Jesus may grow in your affections' (ll. 883-84).[21] Similarly, what has preceded this paragraph in the contemplative work
constitutes the performance of works, 'the practice of virtues'.

However, between his definition of the two elements of the love
of God and his meditations to encourage the love of Jesus, Aelred in

one sentence defines even more explicitly what he understands to
comprise the latter element: 'The practice of the virtues is a
matter of a rule of life, fasts, vigils, work, reading, prayer,
poverty, and such like, while the affections are nourished by whole-
some meditation' (11. 880-83).[22] This summary definition is striking
in its resemblance to the contents of the handbook on the exterior
life of the anchoress, which provides direction for all the items
listed here except vigils. While the passage is not conclusive--
one might argue that Aelred intentionally here summarizes an already
composed work on charity as exemplified in the daily life of the
anchoress--this list would seem to indicate a concern for matters
to be dealt with at some other time.

    When Aelred had completed his writing of the contemplative trea-
tise, then, he turned at last to his list and quickly wrote a short
handbook, a collection of chapters on those matters that concerned
him most in the daily life of the anchoress, perhaps in the very order in which he had previously listed them for himself. For that
reason a great many of the topics discussed here are warnings--against
gossip, against giving alms and receiving guests, against accepting
gifts and letters, against money-making, against all kinds of sensual
temptation ranging from the caresses of school children to gentle attention and words from a man. He included some casually compiled and
terribly dull horariums, largely from the Rule of Benedict, and jotted
some brief suggestions regarding food, clothing, and servants.

    Quite simply, compelled by external requests and an internal
sense of duty, Aelred wrote a 'spin-off'. But because he was much
less interested in the details on the anchoress' daily life than
in those of the spiritual journey, this shorter work is characterized
by a formlessness and lack of logical order, evidence of an eagerness
to say quickly what had to be said in order to be quit of the subject.
While this brief manual must certainly have aided the new recluse in
need of rules to live by, it is rather clearly from the point of view
of the author and modern reader something to be endured, and a seasoned
contemplative would in any age find it largely useless. It is interesting to readers now as a historical datum, but it is, by and large,
not of enduring spiritual significance.

    Once the 'spin-off' was written, Aelred attached it to the
earlier treatise, in front of what he surely regarded as his real work.
Rhetorically that was where it belonged--details of food and clothing
must clearly precede the rising movement toward the heavenly Jerusalem that ends the treatise. He even wrote a new ending for the new
two-part work:

        You have now what you asked for: rules for bodily
        observances by which a recluse may govern the be-
        havior of the outward man; directions for cleans-
        ing the inner man from vices and adorning him with

virtues; a threefold meditation to enable you
to stir up the love of God in yourself, feed
it and keep it burning' (11. 1528-36).[23]

Here for the only time in the work he used the phrase *interiorem
hominem* to match the *exterioris hominis* of the handbook; here for
the only time he indicated his sister's desire for something other
than 'bodily observances'; here he treated his discussion of the
virtues as a section separate from the meditations, although in the
text itself he explicitly defined the three meditations as part of
and furtherance for his discussion of the love of God. (One might
wonder, in fact, whether some later scribe, overlooking Aelred's
clear transition from charity as a virtue to charity as an affection as well as his conclusion to the handbook and introduction to
a work on contemplation might have composed and inserted this three-
part summary himself, but such a thought may indicate only scholarly
wishful thinking.) Aside from writing this three-part ending, as
one must assume he did, Aelred did nothing to smooth the seam between the two portions of the text, and it turns out that there was
little need: in the eight hundred years between his composition and
transposition and today no one has noticed either the seam or the
two similarly patterned pieces of fabric which it joins.

    There is much to be said against this theory. The weight of
tradition, the very fact that the work reads easily as one text
and that it has long been read, is perhaps the most compelling
one. The address to the sister-audience in both portions of the
received text, the fact that most surviving manuscripts contain
both portions with no notable separation between them (and that
even those that contain only the contemplative treatise are not
uniform in how much of it they contain), the use of spousal imagery
for the contemplative in both portions, the treatise's concluding
paragraph cited above, clearly showing authorial intention that the
whole be seen as one work, all speak for one unified treatise for
the enclosed contemplative. Even the repetitions here cited as in-
trusions into the contemplative treatise and early indications of
Aelred's compulsion to speak on external matters to anchoresses
could be taken to show a continuing and centralized concern for the
anchoresses' 'external man' even as he composed direction for her
spiritual life to accompany the handbook already written. While
none of these objections may be dismissed out of hand, sufficient
evidence exists at least to demand a re-evaluation of the received
text in the terms outlined above.

    Many benefits would accrue from considering the two pieces as
two treatises, written for separate purposes and distinct audiences.[24]
Scholarly evaluation of two works rather than one would allow both
the inadequacies of the shorter and the delights of the longer their
deserts. The unity of the contemplative treatise could be studied

without anxiety about the remarkable disunity of the handbook or,
because of it, of the combined text. It would at last be possible
to note that the first portion is not, in fact, up to Aelred's usual
standards and to inquire both into his reasons for writing it and
the identity or circumstances of his audience.

More important, such a separation of the two would allow Aelred's
contemplative masterpiece to take its rightful place in the history
of English contemplative writing, not to be known merely as an example of rules for recluses[25] or as a possible source for later literary lights, but as the earliest, most elegant, and most truly contemplative of the English works in that tradition. Its historic merging
with the lesser work has diminished it, distracted readers from its
power and purpose. This treatise, which begins 'Now, whoever you
may be...listen to my words and understand', which ends 'My beloved
is mine and I am his', and whose substantive core is 'the unity which
is found only in the One, by the One, with the One',[26] is itself complete, unified, and one.

The University of Michigan

NOTES

1. All quotations from *De institutione inclusarum* will be cited
   within the text according to their location within the standard
   edition of the work, C. H. Talbot, 'The "De Institutis Inclusarum"
   of Aelred of Rievaulx', *ASOC* 7 (1951) 12-217. The translations
   themselves are taken from the translation of M. P. Macpherson,
   'The Rule of Life for a Recluse', in *The Works of Aelred of
   Rievaulx I: Treatises and Pastoral Prayer*, CF 2 (Spencer, Mass:
   Cistercian Publications, 1971) pp. 43-102. The location of the
   translated passages will be given in the notes, as here, p. 79.
2. Maurice Powicke, ed., *The Life of Aelred of Rievaulx by Walter
   Daniel* (Oxford: Oxford University Press, 1950) p. 41.
3. CF 2: 43-4.
4. CF 2: 61.
5. Marsha Dutton Stuckey, ed., 'An Edition of Two Middle English
   Translations of Aelred's *De Institutione Inclusarum*' (Ph.D. dissertation, University of Michigan, 1981) p. 388, ll. 400-404.
6. Stuckey, pp. 106-107.
7. CF 2: 59.
8. CF 2: 62.
9. *Ibid.*
10. *Ibid.*

11. CF 2: 45.
12. CF 2: 48.
13. CF 2: 77.
14. CF 2: 72.
15. CF 2: 102.
16. Talbot, pp. 175-76.
17. Stuckey, p. 110, ll. 1-3; pp. 80-86.
18. André Wilmart, 'Les Méditations VII et VII attribuées à Saint Anselme', *Revue d'ascetique et de mystique*, 8 (1927) 249-82, and 'La tradition des prières de S. Anselme', *Revue Bénédictine* 36 (1924) 52-71; Talbot, pp. 167-9.
19. E.g., viz. J.-P. Migne, ed., 'De sanctimoniali de Wattun', *PL* 195: 789-96.
20. CF 2: 79.
21. *Ibid.*
22. *Ibid.*
23. CF 2: 102.
24. Professor Ann Warren, of Case Western Reserve University, has suggested to me that the first portion of the work may have been written for lay anchoresses, those never before in religious life, and the second portion for experienced religious long members of monasteries and newly emerged from the cloister to the life of reclusion. Such an idea, while not conclusive, bears further study and has clear relevance to the argument presented here.
25. Macpherson's title for the translation of the work is itself misleading, implying that the work which follows is simply defined as a rule and so ignoring the fact that less than half of the text is devoted to giving direction *per se*.
26. Talbot, ll. 765-72; CF 2: 74.

CAESARIUS OF HEISTERBACH'S *DIALOGUE OF MIRACLES*
REPORT OF THE TRANSLATOR

Renata E. Wolff

CAESARIUS OF HEISTERBACH was a well known author in his life time, though his name appears in no record, not even the charters of Heisterbach, the monastery where he spent forty years of his life. The exact dates of his birth and death, therefore, are not known. He was probably born around 1180, probably in Cologne; and he probably died in Heisterbach around 1240. The sources for his life are entirely his own writings. According to his own account in the *Dialogue*, he became a monk at Heisterbach early in 1199. At the time he was writing the *Dialogue* he was master of novices. Later he became prior. The number of surviving manuscripts containing his work, as well as the early printed editions, prove their enduring popularity.

Some years ago, Professor Wagner of the Freie Universität Berlin started to prepare a new critical edition which I hoped to use as the basis for my translation. He answered my letter telling me not to expect anything soon, for at the time he had already one hundred fifty manuscripts to collate. As far as I know, he has given up; at least he is not listed in *Speculum* any more. Therefore I am using the edition brought out by Joseph Strange in 1851. Last year a newer edition by Alfons Hilka and his collaborators, made in the early 1930's, came to my attention. Volume I contained Caesarius' Homelies, Volume II was supposed to contain the *Dialogue of Miracles*, and Volume III other works. According to tantalizing references in Volume I some of the one hundred fifty MSS were to be listed in Volume II. However, I have not been able to locate this volume and have come to the conclusion that it was never printed because of the outbreak of war in 1939. Therefore, I can say nothing about the manuscript tradition.

The title of Hilka's edition reads *Die Wundergeschichten des Caesarius von Heisterbach*, and of the homilies he gives only excerpts, namely, the stories which Caesarius loved to insert into his sermons to elucidate his religious teaching as well as into the *Dialogue of Miracles*. These are important to folklorists, to local historians of Cologne and its surroundings, and to social and economic historians. The rest of the text, or most of what is strictly religious, monastic, theological, is left out. In a German translation, Selected Stories from the Dialogue of Miracles, by E. Mueller Holm (1910) which was published as part of a series called *Verschollene Meister der Literatur* the text receives the same treatment.

Unbelievable as it is, there has never been a complete translation of the *Dialogue of Miracles* into German. The only more or less complete translation in modern times was made in England in the

1920s by Scott and Bland in a series called the *Broadway Library
of Medieval Literature*. This translation is still useful, despite its quaint language, but both translators were classicists
and tended to use in a classical sense words which by Caesarius'
time had changed their meaning. Now, sixty years later, with the
help of newer and better medieval Latin dictionaries, a medievalist
is undertaking the task of translation and trying to snatch Caesarius from the folklorists and all other interested parties to place
him where he belongs, in monastic literature.

Obviously, Caesarius did not write for the delectation of
folklorists and other lovers of old tales, but for the education
and edification of his novices and fellow monks. He introduces
his *Dialogue* with a biblical reference to the multiplication of the
loaves and fishes. As twelve baskets of leftovers were collected
after this miracle, so he wants to collect bits and pieces of stories to show that miracles did not cease with biblical times but happen still, happen particularly in the Cistercian Order. In his
words:

> Therefore, twelve is the number of the parts in-
> to which I have divided the work. The first
> part deals with entry into the monastery, the
> second with repentance, the third with confes-
> sion, the fourth with temptation, the fifth with
> the demons, the sixth with the virtue of simpli-
> city, the seventh with the Virgin Mary, the
> eighth with various visions, the ninth with the
> Body and Blood of Christ, the tenth with mira-
> cles, the eleventh with death, the twelfth with
> pain or the glory after death.

In his introduction, Caesarius then explains:

> To order the examples better I am introducing two
> persons as participants in a dialogue, a novice
> who asks questions and a monk who answers them.

This dialogue frequently contains questions and answers of a theological and spiritual nature and moves the narrative along. Most translators, being interested in various non-spiritual aspects of the
work, have deemed it a very wooden device and eliminated it. Granted,
it is not very entertaining when the novice is made to say for the
umpteenth time, *Miror, Valde miratus sum,* or *Stupenda sunt ista.* But
just as many times one has the feeling that the questions asked and
the objections raised by the novice in the *Dialogue* are those most
often brought up by Caesarius' real life novices. The dialogue also
allows Caesarius to refer back to earlier chapters with 'I told you

so in part x, chapter y'. Or he mentions a name and says: 'Whom I
mentioned in part s, chapter y'. In the fourth part he puts off
one of the novice's questions with an astonishing line: 'This will
be dealt with in the twelfth part'. Since he could hardly have had
all 746 stories in his head, he must have had an outline or at least
a list of chapter headings before him down to the twelfth and last
part of the book. He repeatedly uses the same examples twice, even
three times. They appear in longer and shorter versions and under
different headings. As he refers his novice back and forth in the
dialogue, so he also refers him to his homilies, some of which he
wrote at the same time and in which he sometimes used the same stories as in the dialogue.
    Back to Caesarius' introduction:

> Many times I have inserted events which happened
> outside of our order, partly because I learned
> them from monks, like the rest of the stories.

The events which happened outside the order make the *Dialogue* a
fascinating book because they come from the daily lives of almost
all classes of society, from popes and emperors down to servants and
peasants. Not to forget the clerics! They eat, drink, and make
merry, they gamble and seduce women. The impression is that they
were frequently men who 'held a living', some kind of benefice, often
from their uncle, the bishop, and that many may never have been in
higher orders. Conversely, Caesarius nearly always makes special
mention if a canon or priest in the *saeculum* is *satis religionis,
vir satis laudabilis vitae,* or *vir bonus.*
    Feudal customs and feudal language pervade the whole scene.
Eventually one comes to realize that the expression *Dominus Noster*
and *Domina Nostra,* Our Lord and Our Lady, which we still use, had
    very different context in the thirteenth century. *Dominus Noster,*
the title given Jesus, is the same as the title given a feudal over-
lord, prince, or king. When the Cistercians spoke of *Domina Nostra*
they addressed their very own feudal suzerain to whom all their
houses belonged. She was a good suzerain too, according to Caesarius,
taking up the cause of her monks with God and men whenever necessary,
not hesitating to kill the enemies of her Order if she could not
bring them to repentance.
    To show what Caesarius meant by an 'event outside our order',
I will give a shortened example. During Lent a woman came to make
her confession. Kneeling down before the priest, she began to recite her good deeds and alms like the pharisee in the Gospel.

> The priest said to her, My good woman (*Domina*),
> why have you come? You wouldn't want to do penance
> for these good works? Why don't you tell me your

sins?' She answered that she was not conscious of
any. The priest then asked her, 'What is your business?' and she told him that she was an ironmonger.
Whereupon the priest replied: 'Don't you sometimes
mix smaller pieces of iron into a bundle of larger
ones and sell them together?' The woman said, yes,
she did. 'See', said the priest, 'that is a mortal
sin because it is fraud'. And he continued, 'Do
you sometimes lie, swear, give false statements,
curse your rivals, envy others who sell more?' She
answered that she often did such things and was good
at them. The pastor told her, 'These are all mortal
sins, so, unless you do appropriate penance, you
will land in hell'. The woman was frightened by these
words, recognized that she had sinned and learned
how she should confess. It was good for her that this
prudent and well-educated priest knew how to break
down her pretensions.

This story is one of a series of examples about good and bad confessors. Though it was far from Caesarius' intention to write social
and economic history, he first mentions a woman in business on her
own and then gives a wonderful tableau of medieval merchandising methods. This is not his only story about merchants and their cheating.
In his introduction, Caesarius goes on to tell his readers:

God is my witness that I have not invented one chapter in this *Dialogue*. For my informants will be
held responsible if perchance other things happened
or they happened in a different way than described.

Alas, there were informants who loved to tell tall tales. Furthermore,
we all know that stories of events told and retold tend to get better
and more elaborate as time goes by.

The names of certain monks recur again and again as sources of
stories. There is *Conradus senex monachus noster*, mentioned another
time as *pene centenarius*. He liked to spin out tales of hellfire and
damnation. The monk Gottschalk of Volmuntstein, a frequent contribu-
tor to Caesarius' store of exempla, believed that a cleric named Phillip was a practitioner of black magic. 'I saw Phillip myself', Caesarius informs his readers. 'He was killed a few years ago, as I think,
by his master and friend, the devil'. Phillip was a marvelous story
teller, who obviously delighted in telling his incredible stories to
a gullible person. They are about a master of the black art at Toledo
and his students, one of whom was carried off to hell, returned looking forever pale, could never smile again, and supposedly became a
Cistercian monk. The guileless monk Gottschalk took this to be gospel

truth. So did Caesarius, because he uses the tales of this clever
cleric, Phillip, to prove the existence of the devil.

Another time, 'a worthy citizen' told Caesarius a story, assur-
ing him that it had actually happened in Mainz. This is a tale to
delight the folklorists who could be wrong, however, in thinking of
it as a folkloristic topic because quite possibly it originated to
fool a trusting soul.

> When a priest was going around the church
> sprinkling the people with holy water, his
> path was crossed by a woman coming in pom-
> pously, looking like a peacock in her vari-
> ous fineries. On her long train- which she
> trailed behind her, he saw a multitude of
> demons. They were small as dormice and
> black as Ethiopians and were laughing and
> clapping their hands and jumping like fishes
> caught in a net. Truly the finery of women
> is the net of the devil.

The story goes on to say that this priest, because he was a good
and a just man, achieved through his prayer that all present could
see this vision. The woman realized that she was made ridiculous
through her pride, went home and changed her clothes.

This story may be pedagogical, even edifying, but it is just
too cute and too neat. Somebody made fun of somebody and not only
of overdressed women. The monks, constantly striving for truthful-
ness in themselves seem to have assumed the same in others—which
made them an all-too-easy target for pranksters. So much for the
honesty of our author and also his credulity. It might be added
here that, while he was certainly truthful, Caesarius was not beyond exaggerating a bit if it made a point and he had a knack of
making ordinary events appear very miraculous.

In his introduction Caesarius dealt with his reasons for the
arrangement of his miracles into distinct parts:

> A person can be seen to enter a monastery with-
> out repentance; therefore, the first part deals
> with entry into the monastery. But since en-
> trance is useless if the sinner does not feel
> repentance, the second place is given to re-
> pentance. Similarly, repentance by itself
> peters out if it is not followed by an open
> confession. So it is fitting to let the part
> about confession follow it. As confession
> rarely is enough to lift the punishment for
> sin, it seems good to continue on to the part
> about giving satisfaction for sins, which I

have found to consist in temptation. Again,
the demons are the perpetrators and instigators
of temptation, therefore the part dealing with
them comes next. Simplicity is the great an-
tidote to temptation, so the part about simplicity has to come after the part about the demons. These six parts pertain to merit, the
other six parts to the reward of merits'.

But Caesarius does not give a similarly reasoned sequence for the
six parts about merits in the second volume in his introduction. To
my knowledge, he was the first Cistercian to impose such a reasoned
order on his collection of exempla. Two other Cistercian authors
whose works I could check, Herbert of Clairvaux and Conrad of Eber-
bach, do not arrange their collections of miracles topically.

I have gone through Caesarius' introduction and his intentions
in writing the *Dialogue of Miracles*. When did he write it? Karl
Langosch dates the *Dialogue* to approximately 1219-23. Since Caesarius freely mentions names and events, the dating of the *Dialogue* can
be done from internal evidence. He wrote during the reigns of the
Emperor Frederic II (1212-50), and of King Phillipe Augustus of
France (1180-1223), who figures in quite a few stories as a kind of
ideal king. The time of composition can be further narrowed down
through frequent mention of Archbishop Engilbert of Cologne, who
was elected in 1216 and murdered in 1225. Caesarius always wrote
about him as the archbishop, which means the earliest date at which
he could have begun work on the *Dialogue* would be 1216. Langosch
points out that the death of King Phillipe is not mentioned, therefore the *Dialogue* must have been finished by 1223. The murder of
the archbishop is mentioned, but in a homily, not in the *Dialogue*.
Among datable events in the first volume are a reference to Landgrave
Hermann of Thuringia (1217) 'who died two years ago' in Part I, Chapter 37, and of the Emperor Otto of Poitou (1218) 'who died two years
ago' in Part IV, Chapter 15. Two years after the Landgrave died, in
1219, Caesarius was near the end of the first part, then, and in 1220,
when Otto died, he was working on the fourth part. I have to reserve judgement about the date of completion until I have translated the second volume.

Now I will give a quick overview of the six parts of the first
volume of the *Dialogue of Miracles* and their content.

The first part, *De conversione*, is rendered in the earlier English translation 'Of Conversion', while in a German one it reads: *Vom
Eintritt ins Kloster*. My translation follows the German usage. It
might be added here that Caesarius uses *monasterium, coenobium, con-
ventum*, even *cella* very nearly interchangeably. All the parts start
with an introductory chapter of theological content, except the first,
which starts with a thoroughly condensed history of the Order down

to the founding of Heisterbach. When Caesarius lists the many reasons for which people come to a monastery, it is clear that many have
little to do with the modern sense of conversion. Here is Caesarius'
list of reasons: some come through a direct call from God, others
by the instigation of the devil; some come out of irresponsibility,
but the greater number come through other monks, either by words of
encouragement or through prayers and good example; a large number
come out of necessity, like sickness, poverty, captivity, shame
over some horrible deed, danger to life, the terror of hell, and,
the last of all reasons mentioned, a longing for heaven. Caesarius
gives one or more examples for all these categories. I would say
that some of these categories are so strange that he probably made
them up to fit the stories he had collected. Here are shortened examples:

> We can read in the life of Saint Bernard how
> Master Stephen de Vitry once came to Clairvaux.
> He was a man of great learning and was thought
> to have come for the grace of becoming a monk.
> At his arrival the whole valley was overjoyed
> ....But Blessed Bernard burst out: 'The devil
> brought him here! He came alone and alone he
> will leave!'

For, according to this story, Stephen had come to take back into
the world some novices who had been his students. But the devil,
through the mouth of Stephen, did not succeed in seducing his former students to leave and, as the saint prophesied, Stephen returned
to the world alone. To translate the title of this chapter 'Of the
Conversion of Doctor Stephen de Vitry' seems to miss the point.
     Caesarius tells us how another person entered the monastery
with the idea of robbing it and spent his year of probation waiting
and scheming, while the conscientiousness of the sacristan prevent-
ed him from stealing some altar plate. Finally the man was made a
monk and now follows the conversion: By the grace of God he wants
to stay, confesses all, and progresses so quickly in his new life
that he is soon made prior. He himself was fond of repeating the
story of how and why he became a monk.
     The story of Stephen de Vitry shows Caesarius' attitude toward
novices who left. They are apostates. They go to hell. His novice
remarks at one point that this contradicts the rule of St Benedict,
who says that they are free to leave. Caesarius' explanation is a
bit lame.

> Our Holy Father Benedict chose between two evils,
> namely novices leaving during their time of
> probation rather than monks after the day of

their profession. He called them free from the
place, but not free from the vow. Persons of
the world (*saeculum*) who in words only have made
a commitment into the hands of the abbot (*qui solo
verbo votum fecerant inter manus abbatis*) are
not free to follow a worldly life or contract a
marriage. Concerning the needs of a novice, the
Lord Pope will give a dispensation so he can
change to a milder order, but he does not per-
mit him to return to a worldly life.

There is a contradiction between the Rule and the Cistercian practice as described here. It seems the key words are *qui votum fecer-
unt inter manus abbatis*, at other times it is *abbato se reddidit*,
which lead me to think that some feudal notions are here at work
and have superseded the Rule.
     Repentance, the second part, is the shortest in the whole *Dia-
logue*. Caesarius seems to have faced a dilemma. If someone entered
a monastery, there was another member of the community with a story
to tell of how and why he or she got there. But, as Caesarius points
out, contrition is in the heart; it is often known only to God, unless the repentant sinner gives public testimony. Caesarius seems
to have had some trouble finding enough examples for this part.
     He begins with some nice stories concerning repentance, then
goes into stories concerning the gift of tears. Through a story
about a cleric seducing a Jewish girl and repenting, he gets off
his subject with stories concerning the conversion of Jews, until
he is recalled to it by his novice. Then he goes into a long vision
about the civil wars in the empire, the calamities of Cologne and
of the Holy Land, and the coming of Antichrist. This ends again
with the novice saying, 'Please get back to the subject'. Caesarius
complies by giving stories about repentant moneylenders. The Latin
word for moneylender is *Usurarius* and it is generally translated as
'usurer'. But if Caesarius meant a usurer in the modern sense, one
who charges exorbitant interest, he would have told us so in one of
his graphic descriptions. The context of his stories and the dic-
tionary agree that *usurarius* is quite simply a moneylender.
     Caesarius explains very ingeniously why moneylending is such
a grave sin.

There is no other sin from which there is no
rest. Lending money never ceases from its sin-
ning. Even though the money's owner is sleeping, the money itself never sleeps but keeps
on growing and accumulating. It is hard to
amend, because God does not forgive a sin unless restitution has been made. Fornicator,
adulterer, perjurer, blasphemer, as soon as

one of these people is torn loose from his
sins, he receives God's forgiveness. The moneylender, however, assuming that his sin grieves
him, receives no forgiveness as long as he
holds the interest when he might return it. Now
the novice interjects: 'What if he already spent
this interest, or has given it to his children
and has nothing left but his rightful possessions?'
And the monk answers: 'Then he has to sell them
and restore what he has robbed'.

In other words, he has to return the interest. It is clear that
moneylending at interest is Caesarius' concern, showing that *usurarius* at this time meant a person giving a loan for interest.

One story concerns a rich Parisian moneylender, who first con-
sults Bishop Maurice (de Sully) on how he should make good his
crimes. The bishop advises him to give his money to the building
of Notre Dame in which he was at the time heavily engaged. The
moneylender, knowing this, is not quite satisfied with this advice
and goes to Master Peter, the Chanter, who advises him to have a
crier go throughout the city announcing that he is prepared to make
restitution to everybody. This done, the moneylender returns to
Peter, telling him that even after conscientious restitution he has
a lot of goods left. The Chanter then tells him: 'Now it is safe to
give alms'. Up to this point the story seems reasonably historical.
What comes at the end sounds like a pious addition by the abbot
from whom Caesarius got his story.

The abbot had heard that, on the advice of the
Chanter, this moneylender went through the streets
of the city naked except for his underpants while
a servant drove him with a rod, saying: 'Behold
the man whom the prince honored for his money and
who held the sons of noblemen for surety'.

Another moneylender who repented on his deathbed told the abbot, his confessor and advisor, to bring wagons to carry away his
goods to the rightful owners, for, '...he had two chests full of gold
and silver, many pawns like weapons, books, and jewelry, and owned
much grain and vine and an infinite number of cattle'. Overall, the
stress of the chapter is that sins can be forgiven through repentance. As Caesarius says:

If the Lord would strike down instantly all sinners while they sin, he would not have such a
multitude of believers.

Part three, Confession, starts with the usual theological instruction and it is truly amazing how little it differs from the good
old Baltimore Catechism. The first stories concern mostly Cistercians and how a confession made to anybody but the right person, the
abbot or prior, is quite invalid.

One of the interesting stories in this part concerns the secrecy
of the confessional, though this term is not used. A monk in confession told his abbot that he was not a priest, but he refused to stop
saying mass. The abbot begged him with tears, admonished, commanded
him to stop such blasphemy, but without success for the monk was
afraid of a formal accusation if he stopped and was found out. The
abbot then brought the case up at the next general chapter, asking
what a confessor should do in such a case, whether he could reveal
name or deed. Neither the abbot of Cîteaux, nor the other abbots
dared to decide, so they submitted the case to Pope Innocent.

> The pope convoked his cardinals and learned men
> and asked every one singly for his opinion of the
> case. Almost all agreed that a confession should
> not be revealed. The pope replied: 'But I say,
> that in such a case it is to be revealed, because
> such a confession is not a confession but a blas-
> phemy and insanity through which danger might be-
> fall the whole church'.

Caesarius concludes by stressing that a confessor's lot is not always easy! This is one of the examples, like the one about the
woman ironmonger, which were supposed to teach what good confessors do right and bad confessors do wrong. The general idea Caesarius tried to emphasize was that a good and proper confession wipes
out all sin.

'Temptation is the life of the monk', says Caesarius, and
launches himself into the longest part by far of the whole *Dialogue*,
containing over one hundred stories. He tries to structure this
part by subdividing it into a very complete catalogue of vices, giving examples for temptations through each one of them, showing how
people can be overcome by multifarious temptations and fall into
sin and perdition to a point where the novice remarks that he now
would like to hear about people who overcame their temptations and
won their spiritual battles. Caesarius then includes a series of
stories about hospitality and giving to the poor, which is the an-
tidote to the vice of avarice. He stresses the idea that the more
you give, the more you will have and applies this rule to monastic
communities as well as individuals.

Attempted suicide provides the topic of several exempla, and
is said to be caused by the sin of sloth. The stories are a bit

sad for the modern reader who realizes that these suicidal characters were probably suffering from real depressions and not from the
vice of sloth.

But let me tell a really cut story 'from the inside' concerning
the temptations awaiting Henry, a Cistercian who was made bishop
of Albano and cardinal and sent by the pope to preach the crusade.

> One day, as he and his companions were riding along
> together, the cardinal said, 'Who of you will give
> us some good story?' To this one of them replied,
> 'He will', pointing to a laybrother. Right away the
> cardinal ordered him to give them some words of ex-
> hortation. The brother first tried to excuse him-
> self, since a brother should not talk to educated
> monks, but finally he began: 'When we have died and
> are led to heaven, our Holy Father Benedict will
> meet us. When he sees the monks in their hoods he
> will let us in with joy. But when he sees a bishop
> and cardinal, he will be surprised at his garments
> and say: "And who are you?" and the bishop will
> answer: "I am a Cistercian monk". The saint will
> reply: "Not possible! A monk does not wear horns".
> Then, when this has been sufficiently explained,
> judgement will finally be announced like this: St
> Benedict will say to the doorkeepers: "Lay him down
> and cut open his belly. When you find there un-
> seasoned food, beans, peas, and lentils which are
> the foods of the monks who live according to the
> rule, then he can be admitted with the monks. But if
> you find fishes, fat things and worldly food well
> prepared, he shall remain outside"'. The laybrother
> turned to the cardinal and said: 'What is he going
> to say in that hour, poor man?' Hearing the story,
> the cardinal laughed and he praised it.

Another story about temptations mentions, quite incidentally,
that Heisterbach owned two crosses. One cross of black wood came
from Apulia, the other one had recently been given and came from
Constantinople.

The Demons are dealt with in the fifth part from which I
have already given examples. This part contains also a series of
stories about heretics, a short account of the Albigensian crusade,
and the fullest account anywhere, according to Grundmann, of the
burning at Paris of heretical masters who had been pupils of Amaury
of Bene and of the resulting condemnation of books in 1210.

Here is an example of another good story 'from the outside'.
A man wanted to jump from a very high churchsteeple for money. Some

sensible burghers tried to talk him out of it, but this forerunner
of Evil Knievel insisted on trying it. Caesarius describes how a
great mass of people came together in the market place while others
looked out windows as the man climbed up the steeple. He had put
on a very wide cloak to carry him on the air. 'He jumped, but he
could not get up. Finally the people lifted him up and found him
dead. He had burst asunder', says Caesarius, because he had trusted the devil to carry him down and the devil had deceived him. This
malice of the devil is explained as envy of man, who is capable of
being saved.

The last part treats the virtue of simplicity. It contains
many charming and truly edifying stories. Though Caesarius makes
a point about the difference between a simple person and a simpleton,
he himself has more than a little trouble with the distinction, particularly in the mini-life devoted to his teacher he included in
this part, whom he really paints as a complete simpleton. This part
also contains stories which do not really belong to the subject,
stories about perpetrators of deception and treachery who die in
unexpected ways to show that'all punishment comes from God, that
God punishes in accordance with the method and the degree of guilt'.
Here too the novice recalls Caesarius to the subject: 'Do please
give less attention to the vice of duplicity and return to the stories about simplicity'.

I will close by letting Caesarius himself have the last word
with one of several stories concerning simple people and their
projects.

> At Himmerod a simple laybrother was tempted
> quite severely. While he stood at prayer, he
> used the following words: 'Lord, if you don't
> free me from this temptation, I will go to
> your mother and complain about you!' The good
> Lord, the teacher of simplicity and lover of
> humility, as if he was afraid to be accused in
> front of his mother, anticipated the complaint
> of the brother and quickly mitigated the temp-
> tation. Another laybrother who was standing
> behind him and heard this prayer started to
> laugh, and it was he who told it to the others
> for their edification.

Freeport, Illinois

ACEDIA IN THE WRITINGS OF GILBERT OF HOYLAND (d. 1172)

Lawrence C. Braceland, S.J.

G ILBERT OF HOYLAND wrote in the twelfth century for fervent souls in cloister. In the first sentence of his commentary on the Song of Songs, he shows his concern for the changing affections of lovers, for their consolation and their desolation. 'The affections of lovers are subject to change'...for now, according to our longing, we enjoy the Beloved, but again, contrary to our longing, we are bereft of him. It was no surprise to Gilbert that not only young but also experienced monks should feel listless, frustrated, melancholic, or depressed, even bored to death with the regular round of daily discipline. If you have not lived in *acedia*, that is, in listlessness or frustration, then you may have lived in a neighboring province with relatives of *acedia*: sadness and tedium, disgust and disdain, idleness and depression. Your consolation may have changed into desolation and bordered on despair. When your affections might well be called disaffections, you might like to revisit a concerned spiritual father, the Cistercian Gilbert of Hoyland.

These reflections on Gilbert's writing, thanks to a travel grant from the University of Manitoba, were communicated at Kalamazoo, in 1982, at the International Congress on Medieval Studies and the Annual Meeting of the Medieval Academy of America. At a special convocation, Western Michigan University honored Professor Morton W. Bloomfield, distinguished among other things for his authorship of *The Seven Deadly Sins*, one of which is *acedia*.[1] With a whimsical adaptation of a text from the Song of Songs: *Ego sum flos agri*, Professor Bloomfield was hilariously introduced by Professor Siegfried Wenzel, the author of *The Sin of Sloth: Acedia in Medieval Thought and Literature*.[2] In that context I was pleased to expand this footnote from an article by Professor Wenzel: 'Gilbert of Hoiland...uses *acedia* occasionally (PL 184. 153D; 163C) but not where he speaks of *siccitas* or *sterilitas* (35-36; 38; 185)'.[3]

As Gilbert's comments on the virtues emphasize the role of the affections, so his comments on temptations to vice could be summed up under the title 'disaffection'. His approach is that of a spiritual father and a prose-poet rather than that of an analytical philosopher. How invaluable are both! Gilbert does not seem to have made a catalogue of sins. Indeed, for him, the seven deadly sins seem neither seven, nor deadly, nor sins, a comment which would surprise neither Professor Bloomfield nor Professor Wenzel. Let us examine first the disaffection of *acedia* in the two passages referred to by Professor Wenzel, and then relatives of *acedia* in five other passages: *tristitia* and *taedium*, *fastidium*, *otiositas*, *ira* and other kith and kin.

In Sermon 28, Gilbert comments on a verse from the Canticle (Sg 4:7-8): 'Come from Lebanon, my bride,...Come from the peak of Amana and the crests of Senir and Hermon, from the lairs of lions and the mountains of leopards'.[4] For Gilbert, Mt Lebanon, the mountain of myrrh, means the monastery with its monks. He contrasts it with three other mountains, Amana, Senir and Hermon, the homes of wild beasts, the lairs of lions and the dens of leopards; these leopards are translated 'pards', because in Gilbert they have stripes rather than spots. 'The use of animals to represent sins was given authority by Jerome in his Commentary on Isaiah, XI.6-9'.[5] Gilbert understands Mt Amana as a 'vain' or a 'fretful' people, Mt Senir as a 'shaggy' people, while Mt Hermon means 'anathema'. He wished that one could not discern 'in this Lebanon of ours, this holy community of monks, which both our profession and our way of life makes charming and chaste', either the peak of Amana or the crests of Senir and Hermon. He sees these peaks in the man who is proud and vain, irascible and cantankerous, idle and frustrated.

> When you see in an assembly and congregation
> of saints someone exalting himself, puffed up
> with the wisdom of the flesh, vain in his
> boasting (that is, proud and vain), irascible
> and cantankerous (*tumidum et turbidum*), fret-
> ful in the emptiness of idleness (*anxium vani-
> tate otiositatis*)--for idleness breeds frus-
> tration (*otium acediam parit*)--when you see
> such a man, what else are you discerning but
> the peak of Amana with Mt Lebanon?[6]

The pride and vainglory mentioned here, Gilbert expands in the first part of Treatise Seven, where he includes his apostrophe to Satan, the prince of pride. Though Cassian had written that idleness is born of *acedia*, Gilbert says the opposite: *otium*, by which he here means *otiositas*--idleness, begets *acedia*--listlessness/frustration.[7] He adds that 'nothing is more empty than idleness, nothing is more fretful than frustration' (*nil anxius acedia*), a statement which is reminiscent of Cassian's remark that what the Greeks call *acedia*, we call tedium or anxiety of heart.[8] Gilbert continues: 'nothing is more cantankerous than irascibility (*nil tumore turbatius*), for where there is frustration, there is irascibility (*ubi enim acedia, ibi tumor*)'.

Gilbert expands on the disorder following upon this disaffection. 'Where there is cantankerousness, there nothing is gentle, nothing composed, nothing orderly (*ubi turbatio, ibi nil lene, nihil compositum, nihil ordinatum*), but everything bristles (*totum horridum*); a person bristles like the fretful porcupine'. 'Someone of

such a character is devoid of tact, without affection, full of hostility and disaffection, indeed anathematized, which is the meaning
of Mt Hermon (*sine foedere, sine affectione, inimici sensus et alien-
ati, imo anathematizati, quod Hermon significat*)'.
How should one treat a person so alienated? Should one give
in to despair, which in Cassian's list of vices is the last child of
tristitia--sadness/melancholy? Gilbert continues:

> Such a one is not of God's household, not a
> fellow-citizen, not even a resident-alien or
> a guest, and therefore no grace, no devotion
> pays him a visit. The Bridegroom does not
> turn aside to visit him even in passing nor
> to stay with him as a guest. But there dwell
> with him 'pards', demons of striped and turn-
> coat hides, and with him lions make their
> lairs. They do not go out of their way to
> hasten past him, but they hold him fast and
> bed down with him. Such characters, however,
> should not be abandoned in despair, for many
> of this sort are predestined to be ornaments
> of the Bridegroom.[9]

In the second passage on *acedia*, in Sermon 31, Gilbert comments
on the verse: 'How beautiful are your breasts, Sister, better than
wine are your breasts' (Sg 4:10). To preachers he recommends the
model and devices of women, who cultivate and develop physical beauty and have mastered that art. He cautions preachers against stumb-
ling into banalities (*in vana devolvi*), 'while they seek words of solace beyond what is right'.

> While they wish to cheer up an audience bored
> to death by long silence (*auditores longo per-
> taesos silentio*), and glum from listlessness
> (*et quasi quadam subtristes acedia exhilarare
> volunt*), through the wantonness of a capri-
> cious tongue they run on from useful comment
> to buffoonery and either before or after they
> sow some grains of wheat, they sow a great
> deal of cockle....The word of God is not to
> be adulterated or corrupted by any alien in-
> gredient. Let it be satisfied with its own
> breasts, those of the two Testaments. Let
> these, learnt by heart, cling to your bosom;
> let them provide you with discourse full, as
> it were, with the milk of consolation; let
> them provide what others may imbibe.[10]

With word-play, quotation, metaphor and comparison, Gilbert returns to his emphasis on affection and disaffection.

Let the Scriptures burst from the very roots of your bosom, that your message may not be affected but uttered with pure, heartfelt affection. As Horace says: 'if you wish me to weep, first show me your tears' (*Ars Poetica*, 102-3). Let the affection of compassion and thanksgiving be born within you, but let it flow through the words of sacred Scripture as through breasts, to nourish your hearers....Breasts of grace, breasts of consolation, are better than the wine of austerity and harshness, because they are more affective, better able to change sad and exasperated feelings (*tristes et exasperatos affectus*), and to strengthen weak and tender feelings....Today who is tossed about in bitterness and disorder (*Hodie quis amarus et turbidus fluit?*). Do not despair, offer your breasts, provide milk; perhaps tomorrow he himself will flow with milk.[11]

So far we have seen Gilbert use *acedia*--listlessness, dejection with pride, vainglory, anxiety, idleness, distress, anger and disaffection, but especially with *tristitia*--sadness/moroseness, and *taedium*--tedium or ennui. Elsewhere Gilbert does not use *acedia*. Instead he uses *tristitia* and *taedium* with *fastidium*, *amaritudo* or *amaritudo cordis*--bitterness of taste or bitterness of heart, and *turbatio*--distress or confusion. This list is not complete. Such passages cluster together especially in Sermons 38-40, on the following verse of the Canticle: 'Begone, O North Wind, and come, O South Wind, blow through my garden and let its perfumes fill the air' (Sg 4:16).

As the north wind of adversity blew without respite in the time of the conflict between Thomas Becket and Henry II, Gilbert himself seems to have come close to despair. 'Where no ray of good counsel breaks through, where even a shadow of fair hope does not appear, there one plays the role not of anxiety (*sollicitudo*) but of grief (*moeror*)'. In addition to the exterior hardships which affect all his monks, Gilbert as abbot felt anxiety of mind from a harsher north wind: 'From all sides troubles, murmuring, reproaches (*incommoda, murmura, probra*) blow upon us. Distracted and hampered (*distractus et constrictus*) amid such sorrow, the spirit cannot welcome the gentle breezes of the south wind'. Gilbert then focuses on the inner disaffection which concerns us here. 'Those whom outward anxiety cannot affect, inner anxiety afflicts with boredom (*taedium*)'.

He adds that 'joys once festive turn to disdain (*fastidium*) and that 'sadness (*tristitia*) transforms the cheerful face of the mind'. His questions suggest how universal the problem is, one which affects not only novices but also veterans, as he says elsewhere: 'Who is the man whom boredom (*taedium*) does not weary at times and sadness (*tristitia*) exasperate?' So no one should be surprised, when trouble comes knocking on everyone's door. Affection and disaffection are not subject to reason:

> Even when no reason is apparent, trouble intrudes (*turbatio*). Since its source is not evident, it poses a threat. A man is angry at the anger he suffers without reason, and he loathes the emotion without knowing its source (*Irascitur homo irae quam irrationabiliter patitur et cujus detestatur motum nescit exortum*). Of itself such an emotion tends towards evil but it often ends in good. It does not reach the goal to which it tends but 'God provides a way out even from trial' (1 Co 10:13). When God wishes, he introduces the north wind; when God wishes, he commands: 'North wind, begone'.[12]

Here Gilbert introduces a series of distinctions which he considers helpful for the future and worth remembering:

> If in the meantime you complain of the annoyance (*molestia*) of the north wind, know that thanks to such experience you are given a reminder and a warning. You are reminded to be aware of the nearness of the north wind, but warned to avoid its chill. It is not in your power to escape its neighborhood as long as you dwell on the northern slopes, but you can escape its violence. While we are here, the north wind is always our neighbor. It is not always violent, but after we have wheeled through the north, we often take back by the south. Even when you do not feel its assault, be on guard against its proximity ...Yes, utter boredom and bitterness of heart (*vehemens taedium et amaritudo cordis*) exercise the virtues without destroying them. This whirlwind attacks your holy resolve without blowing it away; it checks your happiness; it does not blow your constancy away.[13]

Concerning the embattled spirit wrestling with the north wind,

Glibert introduces a series of paradoxes to ponder over:

> The spirit is affected by boredom (*taedium*) but
> it is not overwhelmed. The spirit is saddened
> (*tristatur*) but wrestles with its sadness (*tris-
> titia*). Virtue thus troubled is not less brave
> but less happy. What has the spirit in common
> with the vice with which it brawls, against
> which it makes war? The spirit is not respon-
> sible for the disgust (*fastidium*) it feels,
> since it never came to terms with this disgust
> (*fastidium*), feeling its batteries aimed at vir-
> tue.[14]

Gilbert has not yet finished his paradoxes about the spirit's battle
against the north wind, and here he illustrates from sailing and
fishing off the Wash or in the inland waterways of Lincolnshire:

> The spirit attacked by boredom knows with what
> boredom (*taedium*) it endures being bored with
> the good life. How it disdains the disdain
> (*fastidit fastidium*)! With what bitterness it
> wrestles against bitterness (*amaritudo*), against
> that violent bitterness which intrudes uninvit-
> ed into the unchanging round of regular disci-
> pline! The spirit by choice veers towards the
> south wind and behold! the north wind relent-
> lessly interferes, despite the vigorous opposi-
> tion of the spirit. It is hard to hold out
> against the frosty face of the north wind, and
> it is not in our power to break its hold. The
> spirit is worn out both by its boredom (*taedium*)
> and by loathing for this boredom (*hujus taedii
> odio*). Both feelings are repugnant: to have no
> taste for what you have chosen, and to experience
> what you loathe. Each is a trial: to protect
> discipline and to put lethargy to rout (*propul-
> sare desidium*).[15]

As a relief from boredom, Gilbert often praised the rhythm, the
ebb and flow, the alternating duties of monastic life. There is also relief in the alternation of the north and south winds. But when
the north wind prevails for so long that boredom (*taedium*) becomes
lethargy (*desidium*), Gilbert again has recourse to prayer, which
he begins with his favorite invocation:

> How do you tolerate for so long, good Jesus, so

much harassment (*vexatio*) of your beloved bride?
Unwillingly she suffers lethargy (*desidium*) and
pursues it to punish it in herself as if it were
deliberate. She scarcely endures her inability
to delight at will in you, who are her only
good. She blames herself for what she suffers
unwillingly. One comes riding on the north
wind to goad her, but his goad spurs the bride
to prayer. Chafed by this goad she casts herself on her knees, though previously she had
made ready for his embraces. Protect your bride,
good Jesus, from these evil days.[16]

In Sermon 39, Gilbert continues his comment on the north and
south winds. Again beginning with his favorite invocation, he returns to the disaffection of boredom and sadness:

Execute your command, good Jesus; dispatch the
south wind from heaven and conduct it into
your garden, into the soul of your bride. By
this gentle breeze dispel boredom (*taedium*),
dispel sadness (*tristitiam*) from her feelings.
For each is a misery and each resembles the
north wind. Each fetters the mind, as it were,
and bars access to the current of pure joy.[17]

In an important and consoling passage, Gilbert distinguishes
freedom to will the good freely, from freedom to will the good with
affection or affectively. Gilbert has been discussing at some length
the freedom of the will and distinguishes a 'freedom of our state,
a freedom of disposition and a freedom of affection'.

Let this much be said of the freedom by which
we will the good, that it is from grace. But
another freedom exists none the less through
grace, by which we not only will rightly but
also will goodness itself affectively. Feelings have nothing to do with our liberty of
choice. Yet the freedom of a good will is
not wholly free, if it is without affection.
But when the south wind blows, at once the
perfume of affections fills the air. No pressure is exerted to elicit them; they flow
freely. Frequently a kind of boredom and
sadness (*taedium quoddam et tristitia*) accompany a holy will. But sweet affections do not
share the journey with boredom and sadness.[18]

Gilbert has a further pertinent passage in Sermon 40, where
he comments on the verse: 'I have drunk my wine with my milk' (Sg
5:1). Here he keeps before the eyes of his monks both the Passion
and the Resurrection of Christ as an example and a promise:

> If for your food you have been given gall, if
> in your thirst you have drunk vinegar, remem-
> ber that Jesus suffered the like. These he
> tasted on the cross but did not drink, so sug-
> gesting the swift passage of bitterness (*amari-*
> *tudo*). But now he drinks wine with his milk.
> No longer is he distressed (*non turbatur*) at
> the tomb of Lazarus. No longer is he sad unto
> death (*non tristatur usque ad mortem*). He does
> not drink vinegar and gall at the point of
> death. That distress, sadness and boredom
> (*turbatio illa, tristitia, taedium*) inherited
> for a time from the old man in the economy of
> salvation have passed into the new sweetness
> of milk.[19]

In an earlier sermon addressed to nuns, Gilbert had given some
arresting advice, first on the perfume of virtue and secondly on
being a carriage of the Lord, a match for the carriage of Solomon.
Again he warns against the temptations of sadness and tedium:

> Now if yours is the fragrance of virginity, of
> persistent prayer, of fast and abstinence, yours
> is a good fragrance, the fragrance of balsam.
> But if you still suffer from the malady of im-
> patience, if gossip, fickle resolution, deter-
> mination to do your own will, moroseness or te-
> dium (*tristitia, taedium*)--if any of these is
> reported in you, your perfume is still mixed and
> you do not breathe forth the fragrance of pure
> balsam.[20]

Gilbert distinguishes the act from the habit of sin:

> It is well with the person who immediately
> brushes aside any drop of sadness (*quid triste*)
> which may appear by chance or on a sudden.
> 'For in many ways we all offend', says James
> (Jm 3:2). From a sudden fall, immediately
> corrected, no odor is noticeable; malodor comes
> rather from a vice in which one persists. Per-
> ilous and poisonous is the mixture when some

vice is disguised as a virtue; even an angel of
Satan 'appears as an angel of light' (2 Co 11:14),
and, as it were, makes poison smell like balsam.
Satan is a compounder of perfumes; buy no oil
from him. Indeed he is not so much a compounder as a confounder of ointments![21]

Earlier in the same sermon, the nuns are invited, not without
humor, to become happy carriages of the Lord:

That person also is a carriage who carries Christ
not only on the lips but also in the body. 'Glorify and carry Christ in your body', says Paul (1
Co 6:20). Paul wishes Christ to be carried by
you, but proudly, not with tedium, not with com-
plaint, not with indignation and a wavering resolution (*non cum taedio, non cum murmure, non
cum indignatione et fluctuante proposito*). Paul
wants Christ carried, not dragged. For to anyone
who drags him, Christ is burdensome, chastity is
a burden, humiliation is a burden, obedience is
an onus, poverty is squalid.[22]

Gilbert confirms his point with a play on words and a humorous application of scriptural texts; his human hay-rick is a memorable
metaphor from the fields:

You are a misshapen porter, if such is your de-
portment! Faith seems to you a heavy rod and
piety cumbersome. You cannot say: 'My Beloved
is a sachet of myrrh for me' (Sg 1:12). So your
faith seems to you like a cart-load of hay,
for under its weight you creak and groan and
complain, 'as a wagon creaks when loaded with
hay' (Am 2:3). Christ is not a load of hay
but a flower and a fruit and the tree of life,
a tree which gives fruit in due season (Gn 2:9,
Rm 11:20, Qo 24:17, Sg 5:15) and are you unwilling to wait?[23]

In the previous sermon to the same nuns, Gilbert gives advice
on how to treat those who are spiritually weak unto death. He had
said negatively: do not despair of them. Now he advises positively
with the adaptation of a scriptural passage: they must be cherished
in the bosom of the Order, as the widow cherished her son, until
Christ, the new Elisha, comes to raise a dead brother to life:

Even now, good Jesus, if a son of our mother be
dead--I mean a son of this holy community, this
widow with whom, so to speak, you lodge--do you
restore him to life. That son is dead who is
crushed by the weight either of tedium or of
despair (*vel taedii vel desperationis*), who possesses no lively devotion, no fervor of spirit,
who although he does not abandon the precepts
of the Law and hides himself in the lap of the
Rule, none the less languishes in a cold and
moribund affection (*frigido et moribundo languet
affectu*), and feels no sweetness in our holy
work. The sorrowful countenance of the whole
Order disheartens him (*tristis exanimat facies*).
He must be cherished in the soft and womanly
bosom of his mother, that he may not become re-
bellious (*exasperatus*) and 'be swallowed up by
excessive sorrow' (*abundantiore tristitia ab-
sorbeatur*, 2 Co 2:7). He should not be found
outside the embrace of his mother's bosom, lest
perhaps the true Elijah should fail to take him
to his upper room. Consider those whom Christ
raises to life. Everywhere he grants this
gift thanks to the tears of women. So at the
prayers of her parents he raised their daughter.[24]

Gilbert not only warns against despair, but also counsels affection, prayer, and preparation for healing and resurrection:

Raise also this dead brother of ours, good Jesus,
from his mother's bosom. This outward observance of our Rule leads no one to perfection.
Lead him to the softer bed of a better hope, by
which he may draw near to God. Let him experience what he is awaiting, 'for good is the
Lord' to those who wait for him, 'to the soul
which seeks him' (Lm 3:25). This experience of
an hour brings gladness to the labors of many
seasons. Then is restored to his mother the
son she had lost before, while she did not retain his affection (*non teneret ejus affectum*)
but wept over his dead devotion. He returns
to us renewed, after you have clothed him with
yourself. You stretch yourself over him like
this, that you may cover what is repulsive and
clothe what is naked. Good is the use of this

little bed, (that is, contemplation), which
in a brief hour injects a lively eagerness
for the seasons to come. There is greater
grace in the little bed of Solomon, for in it
the bride, leaving her mother according to the
flesh, clings to her Beloved in an everlasting bond and becomes one spirit with him.[25]

Gilbert recognizes that feelings are facts. In themselves they
are neither right nor wrong, though in their causes and effects
they may be so. If one ever feels listless, frustrated, bored to
death, melancholic or depressed, then one can say: I too have lived
in *acedia*, in listlessness/frustration. For Gilbert, 'to love' is
to make a decision. In his school of love, this decision is the
sun surrounded by the rays of affection in a bright sky or misted
over with clouds of disaffection swept in by the north wind. Disaffection or emotional/psychic/spiritual distress is no respecter of
persons; it attacks not only novices but also the mature and the
veterans. The symptoms of distress listed in modern manuals were
anticipated by Gilbert: irritability and tension, restlessness and
depression, lack of energy and motivation, poor concentration, ener-
vation, feelings of worthlessness and/or temptations to dispatch
oneself to a better life. Gilbert counsels both patient and guide
to be on guard against all the disaffections which lead to despair.
The north wind and circumstances beyond our control cannot prevent
our willing the good freely, but can prevent our willing the good
affectively. In disaffection, the nun and the monk do require the
sympathy and encouragement of others, especially of the healers,
the guides, the prayerful and the lovers in a community.
    In his seventh treatise, written to Roger of Byland, Gilbert
warns against ambition and pride, but also advises his friend Roger
not to resign as abbot of Byland. For Gilbert, ambition is the
root of bitterness; ambition sprouts above ground and entangles
and poisons many. Gilbert recalls that 'a sprig of pride could
spring up in paradise, though there it could not last, for "every
plant not planted by my Father will be uprooted"' (Mt 15:13). In
the translation of Gilbert's works, I included a translation of a
vocation letter of Roger to his friend G., edited by Dr C. H. Talbot. Following Dr Talbot's lead, I erroneously attributed this
letter, *Lac Parvulorum*, to Roger of Byland rather than to Roger of
Ford; following the lead of Fr Edmond Mikkers, I erroneously iden-
tified Roger's correspondent, *dilectissimo suo G.*, as Roger of Byland's friend, Gilbert of Hoyland, rather than Roger of Ford's
friend, Galienus the poet.[26] If Professor Bloomfield was rightly
honored as *flos agri*, I would be rightly dishonored as *zizania campi*.
'Behold the day!...Pride has budded' (Ezk 7:10). Happily I recall
a reflection of Professor Bloomfield: 'Hamartiology is still, as

Professor Lovejoy wrote me many years ago, "an important, though
relatively neglected, subdivision in the history of ideas"'.[27]

St Paul's College
University of Manitoba

NOTES

1. Morton W. Bloomfield, *The Seven Deadly Sins*. (East Lansing:
   Michigan State University Press, 1952, reprint of 1967, with
   bibliography pp. 257-306).
2. Siegfried Wenzel, *The Sin of Sloth: Acedia in Medieval Thought
   and Literature*. (Chapel Hill: University of North Carolina
   Press, 1960, reprint of 1967, with printed sources and manuscripts cited pp. 253-260).
3. '*Acedia* 700-1200' by Siegfried Wenzel, in *Traditio* 22 (1966)
   pp. 73-102; see page 89, n. 54.
4. Sermon 29:7; PL 184:153C-154B; CF 20: 356-57.
5. Bloomfield, p. 351, n. 156; pp. 28-29 and note 243 on p. 328;
   p. 51 and note 59 on p. 344. Gilbert wrote to Brother William:
   'search diligently for a copy of Jerome on Isaiah for me, so
   that when I send for it, you may have it at hand' (Ep 3:6).
   There Jerome comments on the pard of Isaiah 11:6: *et pardus
   qui prius non mutabat varietates suas* (Jr 13:23), *lotus in
   fonte Domini, accubuit cum haedo* (Is 11:6), *non qui a sinistris
   est* (Mt 25:33), *sed qui immolatur in Pascha Domini* (PL 24:151C).
6. Sermon 29:7; PL 184: 153C; Cf 20: 356.
7. Cassianus, *Collationes*, Liber V, caput XVI, ed. Petschenig,
   CSEL 23, (Vienna 1886, reprint of 1966) pp. 142-3: *de acedia
   otiositas, somnolentia, importunitas, inquietudo, pervagatio,
   instabilitas mentis et corporis, uerbositas, curiositas*; in the
   previous line Cassian had given his list of the children of sadness: *de tristitia rancor, pusillanimitas, amaritudo, desperatio.*
   Gregory the Great lists the following offspring of *tristitia:
   malitia, rancor, pusillanimitas, desperatio, torpor circa prae-
   cepta, vagatio mentis erga illicita, instabilitas mentis et
   corporis verbositas, curiositas*; see Wenzel, *The Sin of Sloth*,
   pp. 23 ff.
8. Cassianus, *De Instutis Coenobiorum, Liber X, caput I*, ed. Petschenig, CSEL 17 (Vienna, 1888) p. 173. *Sextum nobis certamen est
   quod Graeci* ἀκηδίαν *vocant, quam nos taedium siue anxietatem
   cordis possumus nuncupari.* E. Vansteenberghe, *Paresse*, in DTC,
   XI[2] (Paris, 1932), cc. 2023-30, clearly distinguishes *acedia*
   from laziness: G. Bardy, *acedia*, in DSp 1 (Paris, 1937), cc.

166-69, gives a helpful survey with special attention to spiritual authors. Jean Vuong-Dinh-Lam, 'Les observances Monastique: instruments de vie spirituelle', in COCR 26 (1964) pp. 196-99, sets disaffection into the context of the observance of the Rule.

9. Sermon 29:7; PL 184: 153C-154B; CF 20: 356-57.
10. Sermon 31:4; 163C; CF 20: 378.
11. Sermon 31:4-5; 163D-164B; CF: 378-79.
12. Sermon 38:5; 202B; CF 26: 463.
13. Sermon 38:5-6; 202CD; CF 26: 463-64.
14. Sermon 38:6; 202D; CF 26: 464.
15. Sermon 38:6; 202D-203A; CF 26: 464.
16. Sermon 38:7; 203AB; CF 26: 464-65.
17. Sermon 39:1; 203C; CF 26: 467.
18. Sermon 39:5; 206B; CF 26: 472.
19. Sermon 40:9; 213C; CF 26: 287.
20. Sermon 17:6; 90C; CF 20: 223.
21. Sermon 17:6; 90C; CF 20: 223.
22. Sermon 17:2; 88B; CF 20: 219.
23. Sermon 17:2; 88C; CF 20: 220.
24. Sermon 16:8; 86AB; CF 20: 213.
25. Sermon 16:8; 86BC; CF 20: 213-14.
26. 'A Letter of Roger, Abbot of Byland' by C. H. Talbot, in ASOC 7 (1951) 218-231. In 'Gilbertus de Hoylandia' (*Citeaux* 14 (1963) p. 273, n. 93) Fr E. Mikkers, accepted the authorship of Roger of Byland, adding: '*Ex alia parte scimus Rogerium etiam scripsisse epistolam dilectissimo suo G., qui fere certo Gilbertus de Hoylandia dicendus est*'. I could not detect Dr Talbot's retractation in this footnote to an article by Dr Holdsworth: 'Dr Talbot pointed out to me that the Tournai MS contained a letter which he had earlier published as by Roger of Byland...'; see C. J. Holdsworth, 'John of Ford and English Cistercian Writing 1167-1214', in *Transactions of the Royal Historical Society*, Fifth Series, Vol. 11 (1961) pp. 125 and 126 with note 5. Likewise I did not detect Dr Talbot's retractation in his article, 'The English Cistercians and the Universities', in *Studia Monastica 4* (1962) p. 199, n. 17, which states that a collection of Roger of Ford's letters 'was preserved until 1940 in Ms. Tournai 154 and one was published by myself from Cambridge Pembroke Coll. Ms 134, fos. 169v-170 in A.S.O.C. VII, 1951, 218-231'. I failed to detect that Ms. Tournai 154 should have read Ms. 134, and that Cambridge Pembroke Coll. Ms. 134 should have read Ms. 154. In a recent article, 'Roger of Byland, Gilbert of Hoyland and the *Lac Parvulorum*', Dr Talbot demolished his own argument for the authorship of Roger of Byland in favor of the authorship of Roger of Ford, and demolished all argument for Gilbert of Hoyland as Roger's correspondent, in favor of Galienus the poet; see *Studia Monastica 22* (1980) pp. 83-88; the argument for Roger of

Ford's authorship of *Lac Parvulorum* rests not on ms. Tournai
134, which was destroyed in 1940, but on the catalogue listing
of P. Faider-P. Van Sint Jan, *Catalogue des Manuscrits Con-
servés à Tournai* (Gemblous 1950) pp. 150-53.

27. *The Seven Deadly Sins*, p. ix.

THE LETTERS OF NICOLAS OF CLAIRVAUX

Luanne Meagher, OSB

NICOLAS OF CLAIRVAUX, a secretary to St Bernard, abbot of
Clairvaux, composed various letters of his own, which this
paper will survey. Though we will deal primarily with
Nicolas' letters, we must also go to other twelfth-century
documents to see the true Nicolas, for there is no complete, up-to-
date account of that monk elsewhere, and--as yet--no translation of
his letters in print. Valuable material may be found in Constable's
second volume of *The Letters of Peter the Venerable*,[1] in several
articles by John F. Benton of the California Institute of Techno-
logy,[2] and a few by the benedictine scholar, Jean Leclercq.[3]

First, let me review the main facts of Nicolas' life, without
an understanding of which many of his letters will be incomprehen-
sible. He was born in France in the early part of the twelfth century and educated at the benedictine monastery of Montiéramey, where
he later became a monk. Early in his early monastic life, he became chaplain for Bishop Hato of Troyes, a city ten miles from his
monastery, and held this position until Hato retired to Cluny in
1145 or 1146. During this period, too, Nicolas spent some time in
Rome, apparently on business. An encounter with Bernard may have
influenced Nicolas in his later decision to enter Clairvaux, as he
did, quite probably in 1146, remaining there until he fled that
house in 1152.

The letters are of value, I think, in giving a glimpse of
monastic life, in showing us the interests and thoughts of a twelfth
century monk, and in illustrating contrast between the newly-founded
cistercian house of Clairvaux and the older benedictine monastery
of Cluny.

In greater part, the letters were assembled by Nicolas himself
and dedicated to Henry, brother of King Louis VII, and to Gerard
of Pérrone, another of Bernard's secretaries. They were first published in Paris in 1610, by Jean Picard. This text was republished
in Lyons in 1677, and reprinted by Migne with the addition of two
letters. Since Picard had access to a manuscript or manuscripts now
lost, his text is believed to have the value of an original. There
are other manuscripts containing a limited number of letters: a Paris
manuscript with letters 28-49; MS Phillipps 1719 with letters 3-42
in succession and five others; a Dijon MS with letters 7 and 15; a
British Museum Harley MS, published by Jean Leclercq; a Vatican MS
with Nicolas' Letter to Pope Adrian IV; a MS in the Biblical Museum
at Troyes; a Letter 35, reproduced by Leclercq in the *Cistercienses*,[4]
MS Jesus 46 with one letter at Cambridge (England); Le Haye MS,
Bibliothèque Royale; and Florence, Laurentianum, Strozzi 28, the

last two manuscripts containing the same letter.
   Nicolas was not a distinguished writer. His passion for improv-
ing his style led him to a repetition of clichés and commonplace
quotations. There is some plagiarism, especially in his sermons,
though he attempts to excuse this by saying that he borrowed only
in *paucis locis*. He succeeded in writing Bernard's letters, probably because Bernard dictated most of them to him. When he was left
to his own resources, his writing was turgid, involved, and often
difficult to comprehend. He seems to have prided himself on his
literary ability, though he makes an occasional effort to depre-
ciate himself, as in Letter 1 where he says that 'his thoughts are
sometimes expressed in a hidden way, sometimes more distinctly'.[5]
In the same letter he says: 'I am not an orator, but a simple home-
abiding man, rather a country farmer, who trims sycamore trees'--
true enough of the prophet Amos, but mock-humility in Nicolas.
   Nicolas' letters do not enable us to build up a complete biography of the man, though they do help us to follow his career in
a general way. As a young monk, he was clearly a favorite of his
abbot. He writes:

> I was young in age, heartless, a weakling in
> spirit, fickle in word, indiscreet in works,
> vicious in tongue, and proud in knowledge....
> How often did I sit at his table when he was
> present and presiding, nor was I so much as
> associate and fellow-servant as master....At
> my wish a table companion and a feast were
> provided, for he knew that I was accustomed to
> splendid banquets. He arranged for me what-
> ever delicacies there were, and placed them
> before me, though he himself fasted while I
> feasted....He would do wholly whatever I wished,
> and he assigned to himself any act that would
> distinguish me.[6]

Apparently this was done to avoid envy on the part of the other
monks. I suspect that few young monks have been coddled in this
way in the Middle Ages or today.
   In the meantime, Nicolas was considering a transfer to Clairvaux, and says that it was the fear of God that prevailed on him
and influenced his decision to transfer from a cluniac house to the
Cistercians. This word got out. The abbot of Mortiéramy was probably the last to hear of it (as sometimes happens in monasteries).
When he did, he convened the monks, together with Nicolas, and
found that the rumor was true.

   At once, his face changed, and with deep sighs,

his grief overflowed into streams of tears.
He begged prayerfully. Using precepts, he
urged me to reconsider.[7]

But Nicolas was as a man 'not hearing'. The bonds of a sincere affection had been broken. Nicolas betook himself to the abbey church,
where he prayed fervently; in his mind he reviewed his relation with
the abbot who, he says, 'had preferred him to all the rest'. He considered himself an Absalom, and says that in spirit he would

Grovel at his feet, cling to his knees, hold
his hands tight, hang on to his neck, and kiss
his dear and friendly face if only I would hear
the pardon of my sins and a peaceful dismissal.[8]

But regardless of his feelings and his regret at causing sorrow to
his abbot, his determination to leave for Clairvaux remained un-
changed.
     He initiated his transfer to that house by writing to Fromont,
the guestmaster, telling him of his sufferings:

If you are willing to listen to me, briefly hear
what the situation is. Who will give water to
my head and a fountain of tears to my eyes, for
I am forced to live without you (i.e., the monks
of Clairvaux)....Suggest to the fathers and to
our brothers that they bring me out of this
prison, that they take me into the place of the
admirable tabernacle, into the house of God
that I may not die in the bitterness of my
soul. If I were able to be here any longer,
death would be preferable to life.[9]

Nicolas, with several of his brother monks, then attempted to leave
Montiéramey for Clairvaux. Of this flight he writes:

Who will tell of how we slipped away from their
hands (the abbot and monks) without garments,
without money, without servants, and with difficulty we got to Aripatorium.[10]

From there, they fled to Clairvaux, where they were reclaimed by
Nicolas' abbot and forced to return home. Nicolas was grief-
stricken over his own failure and the suffering of his fellow-monks.
He says:

They are afflicted with death all day long, and I

cannot lessen their sufferings even for an hour.[11]

In a letter to the monks and prior of Clairvaux, he relates his misery:

> I who sit in darkness and do not see the light
> of heaven, the light of Clairvaux....I say be-
> fore God that if all the kingdoms of the world
> and their glory were conferred upon me, it were
> as nothing, if I could not be with you in that
> place. Clairvaux is in my affection, Clairvaux
> is in my feelings, Clairvaux is in my presence,
> Clairvaux is in my memory, Clairvaux is in my
> mouth, Clairvaux is in my heart, and inflames
> my soul with tender thoughts...if there is any
> devotion, any affection and love, have pity on
> me, have pity on me, and take me out of this
> prison-house, for without you, everywhere is a
> prison.[12]

Nicolas got to Clairvaux, probably in 1146, and soon became a full-
time secretary to Bernard. He was happy to have a little scriptor-
ium of his own (the other scribes worked in a common room in which
architectural drawings of Clairvaux at that time show space for
'''). His room he described in some detail, indicating that it
was surrounded on the right by the monks' cloister, on the left by
the infirmary and the ambulatory for the sick. Though walled off
on all sides, it opened into the novices' cells. He expressed his
satisfaction with it, saying:

> Do not think my little nook is to be despised,
> for it is desirable for its effect, delightful
> to see and a place to recline when one wishes
> to withdraw.[13]

Nicolas also mentions that it was full of books, giving rise to the
impression that he may also have been Clairvaux's librarian.

Bernard had a voluminous correspondence, which must have kept
his secretary busy. Nicolas complained of being overburdened with
work while the other monks had time for meditation and prayer. Yet
Nicolas still found time to write his own letters, especially to his
friends, to the 'high and mighty' he had known earlier, and he entered heartily into the task of appealing for vocations to Clairvaux,
often encouraging monks to enter or to return.

To a certain Theobald who had entered Clairvaux about the same
time Nicolas did, but had left for Cluny, Nicolas wrote:

> I grieve over you and that grief is always in
> my sight....You were a man in a position of
> honor, well-on in age, well-disposed toward
> letters, very useful and a delightful associ-
> ate.[14]

He spoke of their close friendship, and of how 'they had fled the
shadows of Cluny to the purity of the Cistercians'. He then drew
an interesting comparison of life at those houses:

> If that former place (Cluny) had been without
> fault, surely we would not have sought out a
> second place (Clairvaux)....For in gold and
> purple, in food and drink, and in various ablu-
> tions, they brought in every rite of divine
> worship....Where there is more gold, there is
> believed to be more merit; where there are more
> coverlets, more moral living; where there is
> more sumptuous food and elegant garments, there
> is more perfect observance of commands....[15]

As to their decisions, he says:

> You left them (Cluniacs), you advanced to those
> (Cistercians), but you have returned to them,
> and your return is a detestable act. Leaving,
> you left a scandal; returning, you have multi-
> plied it....Perhaps you may say: 'the tunic
> pricked me, the food annoyed me, the heat over-
> came me, the vigils wore me out, the silence
> crucified me, and meditation left me dizzy'.[16]

Nicolas ends this five-page letter with the exhortation: 'Pick up
your heart, my beloved, and come to a man of God'--to Bernard, of
course.
    In a letter which is lengthy, wandering, replete with scrip-
tural quotations and figurative allusions, he pleads that Walter, a
noble youth, ought to be ashamed 'to be devoted to his stinking limbs
and his own flesh'. Should he return, Nicolas promises: 'how willingly would I share with you cold bread, cooked with the fat of wheat
in the heavenly Jerusalem'.[17]
    Continuing his efforts to secure vocations for Clairvaux, he
wrote to Peter, deacon of Trier, reminding him of his past, urging
his conversion, as he says:

> I say to you, Peter, that tonight before the
> rooster crows, who awakens the whole world

with his strident music, you sleep too much,
you are too much given to lethargy'.[18]

Philip, archdeacon at Liège, was reminded of their friendship
at Rome, in younger days, when 'they passed over and climbed slip-
pery mountains' and 'watched by night in the hills of the Tivoli
mountains'. Referring to the same time in an earlier letter, Nicolas threw light on his own character by saying:

> Entering and leaving in the clothing of the
> humility of Christ, I leaped into a whirlwind
> of pleasure; I appeared as a monk without a
> rule, a priest without reverence. Going in
> curiosity to the Roman curia, and returning,
> I made a great name for myself'.[19]

Elsewhere, he admitted that he was never a monk at heart. But still
he encouraged vocations to Clairvaux, or congratulated newcomers,
as he did one Garner, who left Cluny, apparently with the approba-
tion of his abbot, Peter the Venerable, to come to Clairvaux.

A letter to Henry, brother of King Louis VII, who had been a
monk at Clairvaux expresses Nicolas' concern:

> After your departure, joy left me, and my
> soul time li ' l , i ̖ ̠ l̠ iɔi wu̠ ɔ llɔ ̠tɬuɳɡ̠, for
> half of my soul was deserting me, and the bet-
> ter portion right before my face. When you
> mounted your horse, adorned with rustic trap-
> pings, I began to be astonished and violently
> disturbed. I wondered that you were so de-
> parting, you who a little earlier, aflame in
> scarlet, shining in gold, brilliant in silk,
> whom a horse, nay horses, had preceded and
> followed.[21]

Nicolas went on to express his feelings at being deprived of Henry's
companionship in a lengthy lament, and closed his letter with these
words:

> The Lord knows that I write these last words
> with tears. Return, return, my beloved, re-
> turn that we may look at you. Return because
> of my grief, return because of Andrew, and our
> community which awaits you as an angel of God!.[22]

But Henry did not return. Instead he becomes bishop of Beauvais,
(his election having already been assured at the time he left

Clairvaux), and later archbishop of Rheims. His illness, the alleged reason for leaving monastic life, was apparently not too serious to impede ecclesiastical preferment, and may have been the kind that afflicted others who pleaded it and returned to secular life from monasteries.

Friendship played an important part in Nicolas' life as it did in that of other twelfth-century persons. Peter the Venerable spoke of it as 'a port in storm', a 'well-favored wine', 'a silver cord' or 'fair weather'. Nicolas' philosophy about it found expression when he said" 'The absence of friends were intolerable were it not for the remedy of letters'.[23] As an example of this, we may cite a paragraph from his letter to the cantor of Grandisylva, a dependency of Clairvaux:

> He who knows the hidden thoughts of the heart
> knows how much I love you in the bosom of
> Jesus Christ. For your memory has rushed
> deeply into my heart; it has taken possession
> of it rather completely. It possesses it
> permanently and lives with it alive. Who
> will grant that I will never abandon your
> memory, never be separated from it....[24]

The letter was written for another, but it expresses his own feelings.

This preoccupation with love and friendship runs through a number of other letters, though equally frequent are letters he wrote that are purely eulogistic or flattering--hog-wash, one of my Sister-colleagues, an English teacher, called them. To an archdeacon, probably one Gebuinus, he wrote:

> It is daring and presumptious of me to write
> to you because of my poor understanding and
> blunt style which stand in awe of your wisdom
> and revere your eloquence....Your polished
> tongue, your pleasant countenance, your rhetor-
> ical style, pleasing to your friends and not
> unpleasant to your enemies, has overcome infeli-
> citous envy with a more felicitous glory. The
> Giver of gifts has given you two talents, and
> that lavishly. He has endowed you with a two-
> fold spirit, the spirit of subtle intelligence
> and the spirit of discretion....[25]

To Bishop Amadeus of Lausanne he wrote in somewhat the same strain:

> ...I have seen you noble without pride, power-
> ful without envy, religious without being

superstitious, well-lettered without being
proud, serious without folly, facetious without study, and constant without being bitter....[26]

The purpose of this type of letter is difficult to discern unless
it is simply taken as an expression of Nicolas' desire to remain
on good terms with 'the high and mighty'.

One sometimes wonders why Nicolas wrote so little of monastic
life in terms of spirituality or theology. One lengthy letter, to
Peter, abbot of Celle, was a reply to that abbot's discourse on the
Trinity. Yet Nicolas' letter is pedantic and involved. When I fin-
ished translating it, I found myself in the same mood as Graham
Greene's character, Morin, who says:

> A man can accept anything to do with God until
> scholars begin to go into details and the im-
> plications. A man can accept the Trinity but
> the arguments that follow--no, no, that's the
> rub.[27]

Still, Nicolas spoke with admiration of the prayer life of his fellow-monks at Clairvaux:

> I have seen them standing as a guard of the
> Lord ~~ontime by~~ ~~antic nights~~, clothed
> with breast plates of justice and the helmet
> of salvation, having the shield of faith, and
> the sword of the spirit, which is the word of
> God. With the eyes of faith, I saw men of one
> way of life dwell in a house, rise at night to
> praise the name of the Lord, to proclaim it
> evening, morning and noonday, and to announce
> his glory and to devote all their zeal to the
> round of divine service'.[28]

Nicolas also expressed deep sympathy for the monks during the cus-
tomary period of blood-letting,[29] when in spite of weakness, they
continued unabated in their strenuous life of work and prayer.

Nicolas' letters show, too, that he borrowed books from Cluny,
specifically, the history of Alexander the Great, and Augustine's
treatise *Contra Julianum*.[30] We also think that Henry of Champagne
aided Nicolas in his acquisition of books.[31] It may well be that
Nicolas did for the library at Clairvaux what Lupus of Ferrières
had done for his monastery in the ninth century. And it is to be
noted that when Nicolas left Clairvaux for good, he took books with
him.

An unusual letter, written with a touch of humor and an unusual

use of Sacred Scripture belongs to the Phillipps collection (1719)
at Berlin. Professor Benton suggests that it may have been written
to Bishop Aline of Auxerre (1152-1167) who had once been a monk at
Clairvaux.[32] Having spent some time at Auxerre on business for
Bernard, as a letter to Peter the Venerable indicates,[33] Nicolas
uses a more familiar tone in the letter than he otherwise would in
writing to a bishop. The letter reads:

> To the bishop of Auxerre: his Nicolas assures
> his devotion.
> To use the words of the gospel: 'they have no
> more wine'. Send me not 'the wine of perdition'
> but 'the wine which gladdens the hearts of men',
> whose excellence, color, sweet flavor and pleas-
> ant odor bear witness to its quality. It is in
> these three elements that its perfection is
> manifested, and 'the rope with the three threads
> does not break easily'.
>
> Send me the wine, the barrel and the cart, since
> you have given me this hope because you promised
> it to me. But if the cart poses a problem (and
> I'm afraid it does), send it rather than have
> me lose the wine.
>
> ...Command that the barrel be clean so that so
> noble a drink may not be spoiled by the coarse-
> ness of the wood. Send one separately for the
> abbot (probably of Montiéramey) and one for me,
> 'for Jews do not associate with Samaritans'.[34]

The letter probably belongs to the period after Nicolas left Clairvaux, for Nicolas would hardly be asking for wine for Bernard,
having gone out from Clairvaux in disfavor.

Nicolas' friendship with Peter the Venerable, abbot of Cluny,
remained very close, but there were times when apparently Bernard
was not happy at having his secretary off visiting Cluny. In the
fall of 1150, Peter wrote to Bernard asking that Nicolas come and
stay until Christmas, a visit which never materialized because
Nicolas was ill at the time. Later, Peter wrote Bernard asking
that Nicolas come for Easter, reminding Bernard that he had given
up several of his monks to Clairvaux, and also that the two of them
had discussed Nicolas' visits when Bernard had been at Cluny at
some time; Bernard had then asked Peter frankly: Why do you want
Nicolas? Peter admits he had given him an evasive answer, not the
one in his heart. We do not know whether the Easter visit took
place even though Peter petitioned Bernard, the Prior Philip, the
cellarer Gaucher, and Nicolas himself.

Nicolas' tendency to be a little deceptive appears in several
of his letters, especially in one he wrote Peter about the Easter
visit. He suggested to Peter that he send copies of his letters to
Bernard secretly to himself, and added:

> I know my lord abbot told you not to ask for me
> unless it were necessary...but it is necessary,
> and very necessary to see you. Order that I
> may come.[35]

That was probably Nicolas' last letter to Peter the Venerable, for
Nicolas seems to have left Clairvaux in May of 1152. Peter's last
letter to him had been written in May of that year. In the previous
September Bernard had written to Pope Eugene III, a former Cistercian
monk, to reveal his worries about his secretary. He wrote, para-
phrasing 1 Cor 11:26:

> I am in peril from false brethren, and many
> forged letters under my forged seal have come
> into the hands of many men, and it is said,
> what I fear more, that this falseness may
> even have reached you. I have therefore thrown
> away that (old seal), and am using a new one....[36]

After Nicolas' departure, Bernard wrote again to Eugene III with
much more vehemence:

> That man Nicolas had gone out from us, because
> he was not of us (1 Jn 2:19); but he has left
> foul traces behind him (*Aeneid*, III, 244). I had
> for a long time known the man for what he was,
> but I waited either for God to convert him or
> for him to betray himself like Judas, which is
> what happened. For when he left there were
> found upon him, besides books, money, and much
> gold, three seals: one his own, one the prior's,
> and the third one mine, and that not the old one
> but the new one, which I was recently forced to
> change on account of his deceits and secret
> frauds. I remember writing to you about this,
> naming no names, but saying that I was in peril
> from false brethren. Who can say to how many
> people he has written in my name whatever he
> wanted, without my knowing....It has been partly
> proved and partly confessed that he wrote
> falsely to you not just once but on several
> occasions. I shall not sully my lips or your

ears with his base deeds, with which the earth
is polluted and which have become a byword
among all men. If he comes to you (for he
boasted of this and relied on having friends
in the curia) remember Arnold of Brescia,
since here is a man worse than Arnold. No
man more richly deserves perpetual imprison-
ment; nothing is more fitting for him than
perpetual silence.[37]

In earlier letters to the pope, Bernard had spoken of Nicolas
with genuine affection and trust; he had used similar language in
his letters to the papal chamberlain, Haimeric; in a letter to Peter
the Venerable, he had called him 'our common son'. No more. His
favorite secretary had failed him.
It may be well to remember that Bernard was not well at this
time, for his life was drawing to a close. Jean Leclercq thinks
that he was unnecessarily severe, saying that Bernard expelled Nicolas 'with an energy one would have to call excessive'.[38] Harsher
than Bernard was the great scholar Mabillon, who in his work on St
Bernard spoke of Nicolas as a 'hypocrite, a cheat and a liar', and
added: 'How far the inconsiderate and confiding kindness of his pa-
trons conduced to spoil a clever, conceited, ambitious young man,
is more than I can pretend to say'.[39]
Bernard's biographer, Vacandard, spoke of Nicolas as having
practically disappeared from history after his expulsion.[40] Not so!
Recent research, especially by John Benton, disproves this statement.
Nicolas may have gone to Montiéramey after leaving Clairvaux, but
within a year or two he was found, as might be expected, 'in high
places', first in Rome in the service of Cardinal Rolando Bandinelli,
the future pope Alexander III. Through the cardinal, a close friend
of Pope Adrian IV, Nicolas secured the attention and favor of that
pope, and from him received some sort of pardon, as a letter to
Adrian indicates. In it, Nicolas wrote:

I will never forget your mercies, O most blessed
Father, for with these you have given me life.
I had been turned over to oblivion as one dead
at heart. You recalled me from being dead and
buried....[41]

Nicolas gave the pope certain sermons of Bernard as a gift, and then
asked to return to France:

Send me back to the land of my birth that I,
poor, may die among the poor and attain the
reward of poverty which is the kingdom of
heaven.[42]

But that Nicolas' last years were spent in poverty is doubtful. By 1158 he was back at Montiéramey, his first monastic home, and in 1160 he was prior at the small dependency of Montiéramey, Saint Jean-en-Châtel near Troyes. There he lived until his death some time between 1175 and 1178.

Professor Benton has shown in an article on the court of Champagne--to which I am indebted for the details that follow--that during this time Nicolas worked closely with his old friend, Count Henry of Champagne. Apparently he was often at Henry's court as a literary counselor, for he witnessed at least six charters for the Count. Henry proved a generous patron, making substantial donations either directly to Nicolas or to his monastery. Among these were an income from a house in the market place in Troyes in 1160, and later the income from two houses at Bar-sur-Aube. As a canon of the church of Saint-Etienne-de-Troyes, Nicolas also received 100 sous annually--a fair income for a monk who had written Adrian IV that he wanted to go back to France to die poor and to receive the reward of poverty. Henry's continued interest and affection, however, relieved him of any financial worries he might have had as prior at St Jean-en-Châtel.

There is a bit of irony in the fact that Nicolas' last days were spent at the little monastic house of St Jean-en-Châtel. Montiéramey had not been big enough for him when he was at the height of his powers. Moving to Clairvaux, he was content at first to be Bernard's secretary, to act in his stead in certain matters. the temptation to usurp Bernard's power, by using his seal unlawfully, overcame this ambitious monk and brought about his downfall as a Cistercian and as an intimate of the 'high and mighty'.

St Paul's Priory
St Paul, Minnesota

NOTES

1. Giles Constable, *The Letters of Peter the Venerable*, 2 vol. (Cambridge: Harvard University Press, 1967).
2. John F. Benton, 'Nicolas de Clairvaux à la recherche du vin d'Auxerre', *Annales de Bourgogne* 34: pp. 252-55. Idem., 'An Abusive Letter of Nicolas of Clairvaux', *Medieval Studies* 33 (1971) 365-70. Idem., 'The Court of Champagne as a Literary Center', *Speculum* 36 (1961) 551-57.
3. Jean Leclercq, 'Les Collections de Sermones de Nicolas de Clairvaux', *Revue Benedictine* 66 (1956). Idem., *Recueil d'etudes sur saint Bernard et le texte de ses ecrits* (Rome: Storia e letterature, 1962, 1966, 1969). Idem., *Etudes sur Saint Bernard et le Texte de ses ecrits,* Analecta Sacri Ordinis Cistercienses 9 (1953) 62-3.
4. For material on the MSS in this paragraph I am indebted for the most part to a personal type-sheet, kindly supplied by John F. Benton.
5. Letter 1; PL 196: 1503-4.
6. The numbering of the Letters is that followed in Migne, PL 196: 1503-1654, in the section entitled, *Nicolai Claravallensis Epistolae.*
7. Letter 40; PL 196: 1636.
8. Ibid.
9. Letter 46; PL 196: 1647.
10. The town, *Aripatorium*, seems to have disappeared from history, for today it is unknown. The reference is in Letter 45; PL 196: 1645.
11. Ibid.
12. Letter 7; PL 196: 1601.
13. Letter 35; PL 196: 1626.
14. Letter 8; PL 196: 1603.
15. Ibid.
16. Ibid.
17. Letter 16; PL 196: 1610.
18. Letter 17; PL 196: 1613.
19. Letter 45; PL 196: 1645.
20. In a letter quoted by Leclercq, *Recueil*, p. 61, Nicolas says: 'Though I wore the insignia of a monk, not even for one day was I a monk'. Elsewhere he refers to his dissolute early life, especially when he was in Rome.
21. Letter 39; PL 169: 1575.
22. Ibid.
23. Letter 35; PL 169: 1626.
24. Letter 50; PL 169: 1649.
25. Letter 5; PL 169: 1598.
26. Letter 34; PL 169: 1625.

27. Graham Greene, 'The Birth of a Catholic Writer', *Commonweal*,
     Jan. 16, 1981, p. 13. Also in 'A Visit to Morin', a short
     story in Greene's *A Sense of Reality* (New York: Viking, 1963).
28. Letter 45; PL 196: 1645.
29. Constable notes that the practice of bloodletting was widespread
     in medieval monasteries. (2: p. 249). In *The Monastic Consti-
     tutions of Lanfrance*, edited by David Knowles (London: Thomas
     Nelson & Sons Ltd., 1951) there is a rather complete account of
     bloodletting. Permission had to be obtained by the monk each
     time, and a certain ritual accompanied the practice (pp. 93-4).
     The need for the bloodletting may have been due to physical
     weakness brought on by an unbalanced or insufficient diet. It
     was usually followed by a diet of richer and more plentiful
     food. The time might be chosen by the individual, and could
     be as seldom as five times a year. (152-3)
30. In Letter 176, Peter the Venerable asks Nicolas to bring these
     two books with him when he comes to Cluny. (See Constable,
     Letters 1: p. 437).
31. This statement is an inference from the relationship of author
     and patron established between Henry, Count of Champagne, and
     Nicolas. Benton says: ('The Court of Champagne as a Literary
     Center', *Speculum* 36: 557) that Nicolas dedicated some of his
     works to the Count, who rewarded him with liberality.
32. See *Annales de Bourgogne* 34: 254.
33. Letter 55; PL 169: 1651. Bernard also refers to Nicolas being
     away at Auxerre in a letter to Peter the Venerable (Constable,
     Letters 2: 324).
34. Phillipps MS 1719; translated from the French in *Annales de
     Bourgogne* 34; 253-4.
35. Letter 55; PL 169: 1651.
36. Bernard, Letter 284; PL 182: 490-1.
37. Bernard, Letter 298; PL 182: 500-1.
38. Jean Leclercq, *Revue Benedictine* 66; 290-1.
39. Joannes Mabillon, *Opera Omnia Sancti Bernardi*, 1, 4th ed.
     (Paris: Gaume Fratres, 1839) 1629-30; translation by Constable,
     Letters 2: 329.
40. L'Abbé Elphège Vacandard, *Vie de Saint Bernard*, 2, 4th ed.
     (Paris: J. Bagalda, 1910) 513.
41. MS Vat. Lat. 5055. The Latin text is published with notes by
     Jean Leclercq in *Etudes*, 63-64.
42. Ibid.
43. *Speculum* (Oct. 1961) 551 7.

Abbreviations

Adv	Guerric of Igny, *Sermo(nes) in adventu Domini* (Sermons for Advent)
Anima	Aelred of Rievaulx, *De anima* (Dialogue on the Soul)
ASOC	*Analecta Sacri Ordinis Cisterciensis=Analecta Cisterciensia*
CCCM	Corpus Christianorum Continuatio Medievalis
CF	The Cistercian Fathers Series, Cistercian Publications
Circ	*Sermo in circumcisione domini* (Sermon on the feast of the Circumcision)
CS	The Cistercian Studies Series
CSt	*Cistercian Studies*
Csi	Bernard of Clairvaux, *De consideratione* (On Consideration)
DHGE	*Dictionnaire d'histoire et de géographie écclesiastique*, Paris, 1912.
Ep(p)	Epistola(e) (Letter[s])
Ep frat	William of St Thierry, *Epistola ad fratres de Monte Dei* (The Golden Epistle)
Inst incl	Aelred of Rievaulx, *De institutione inclusarum* (Rule for a Recluse)
Jesu	Aelred of Rievaulx, *De Jesu puero duodenni* (On Jesus at the Age of Twelve)
Oner	Aelred of Rievaulx, *Sermones de oneribus* (Sermons on Isaiah)
Pasc	*Sermo in die Paschae* (Easter Sermon)
Pent	*Sermo in die Sancto pentecostes* (Sermon for Pentecost)
PP	Bernard of Clairvaux, *Sermon in festo SS. Apostolorum Petri et Pauli* (Sermon for the Feast of SS Peter and Paul)
QH	*Sermo super psalmum Qui habitat* (Lenten Sermons on the Psalm 'He who dwells')
RTAM	*Recherches de théologie ancienne et médiéval*
SBOp	*Sancti Bernardi Opera*, edited J. Leclercq, H. M. Rochais, and C. H. Talbot. Rome, 1957–77.
SC	Bernard of Clairvaux, *Sermones in Cantica canticorum* (Sermons on the Song of Songs)
Spir amic	Aelred of Rievaulx, *De spirituali amicitia* (Spiritual Friendship)
TVM	*Theologie de la vie monastique:* Etudes sur la tradition patristique. Paris, 1961.
Vita Bern	William of St Thierry et al., *Vita prima Bernardi* (The First Life of St Bernard of Clairvaux)

CISTERCIAN PUBLICATIONS INC.

Titles Listing

THE CISTERCIAN FATHERS SERIES

THE WORKS OF BERNARD OF CLAIRVAUX

THE WORKS OF WILLIAM OF SAINT THIERRY

THE WORKS OF AELRED OF RIEVAULX

THE WORKS OF GILBERT OF HOYLAND

OTHER EARLY CISTERCIAN WRITERS

THE CISTERCIAN STUDIES SERIES

EARLY MONASTIC TEXTS

Evagrius Ponticus—Praktikos and
  Chapter on Prayer   CS 4
The Rule of the Master   CS 6
Dorotheos of Gaza—Discourses and
  Sayings   CS 33
Pachomian Koinonia I:
  The Lives   CS 45

CHRISTIAN SPIRITUALITY

The Spirituality of Western Christen-
  dom   CS 30
Russian Mystics
  (Sergius Bolshakoff)   CS 26
In Quest of the Absolute: The Life
  and Works of Jules Monchanin
  (J. G. Weber)   CS 51
The Name of Jesus
  (Irénée Hausherr)   CS 44
Gregory of Nyssa: The Life of Moses
                                       CS 31
Entirely for God: A Life of Cyprian
  Tansi (Elizabeth Isichei)   CS 43

MONASTIC STUDIES

The Abbot in Monastic Tradition
  (Pierre Salmon)   CS 14
Why Monks?
  (François Vandenbroucke)   CS 17
Silence in the Rule of St Benedict
  (Ambrose Wathen)   CS 22
One Yet Two: Monastic Tradition
  East and West   CS 29
Community and Abbot in the Rule
  of St Benedict I
  (Adalbert de Vogüé)   CS 5/1
Consider Your Call
  (Daniel Rees)   CS 20
Households of God
  (David Parry)   CS 39
The Rule of Iosif of
  Volokolamsk   CS 36

CISTERCIAN STUDIES

The Cistercian Spirit
  (M. Basil Pennington, ed.)   CS 3
The Eleventh-Century Background of
  Cîteaux
  (Bede K. Lackner)   CS 8
Contemplative Community
  (M. Basil Pennington, ed.)   CS 21
Cistercian Sign Language
  (Robert Barakat)   CS 11
Saint Bernard of Clairvaux: Essays
  Commemorating the Eighth Cen-
  tenary of his Canonization
                                       CS 28
William of St. Thierry: The Man &
  His Work
  (J. M. Déchanet)   CS 10

The Monastic Theology of Aelred
  of Rievaulx
  (Amédée Hallier)   CS 2
Christ the Way: The Christology of
  Guerric of Igny
  (John Morson)   CS 25
The Golden Chain: The Theological
  Anthropology of Isaac of Stella
  (Bernard McGinn)   CS 15
Studies in Medieval Cistercian
  History I   CS 13
Studies in Medieval Cistercian
  History II   CS 24
Cistercian Ideals and Reality
  (Studies III)   CS 60
Simplicity and Ordinariness
  (Studies IV)   CS 61
The Chimaera of His Age: Studies on
  St Bernard (Studies V)   CS 35
Cistercians in the Late Middle Ages
  (Studies VI)   CS 38

STUDIES BY DOM JEAN LECLERCQ

Bernard of Clairvaux and the Cister-
  cian Spirit   CS 16
Aspects of Monasticism   CS 7
The Contemplative Life   CS 19
Bernard of Clairvaux: Studies Pre-
  sented to Jean Leclercq   CS 23

THOMAS MERTON

Thomas Merton on St Bernard
                                       CS 9
The Climate of Monastic Prayer CS 1
Thomas Merton's Shared Contempla-
  tion: A Protestant Perspective
  (Daniel J. Adams)   CS 62
Solitude in the Writings of Thomas
  Merton (Richard Cashen)   CS 40

FAIRACRES PRESS, OXFORD

The Wisdom of the Desert Fathers
The Letters of St Antony the Great
The Letters of Ammonas, Successor
  of St Antony
The Influence of St Bernard
Solitude and Communion
A Study of Wisdom

---

*   out of print

"Poignant, hilarious, and contemplative."

—Cosmopolitan.com

"One of the most impressive aspects of this book is the level of nuance, self-reflection, and humanity that West displays in her analysis of her own writing and her relationships with others.... It's the best kind of memoir, and it shows that Lindy West still has a lot more to say—and that we should all keep listening."

—Bitch Media

"West is utterly candid and totally hilarious...as funny as she is incisive."

—Vogue.com

"With SHRILL West cements her reputation as a woman unafraid to comfort (and confound) her critics. [SHRILL] illustrates just how deeply sexism pervades our society while laughing at the absurdities that sexism somehow normalizes."

—Elle.com

"Lindy West is one of the Great Ladies of the Feminist Internet... 250 pages of pure hilariousness."

—Feministing.com

"Both sharp-toothed and fluid...West is propulsively entertaining."

—Slate

"This is who Lindy West is: a constantly harangued feminist writer ready to transmute your BS into comedy.... You need to read [SHRILL]. It's hilarious, biting, and wise."

—Huffington Post

"Incredible and insightful...What West ultimately strives for is to incrementally make those small changes that can lead to something so much bigger and better for us all."

—Amy Poehler's Smart Girls

"[Lindy is] warm and cutting, vulnerable and funny in equal measures; her sense of self makes you yourself feel seen."

—BuzzFeed

shrill

LINDY WEST

hachette
BOOKS

NEW YORK   BOSTON

Hachette Books
Hachette Book Group
1290 Avenue of the Americas, New York, NY 10104
hachettebooks.com
twitter.com/hachettebooks

Originally published in hardcover in 2016 by Hachette Books, Inc.
First trade paperback edition: March 2017
ISBN 978-0-316-34846-1 (pbk.)

Hachette Books is a division of Hachette Book Group, Inc. The Hachette Books name and logo are trademarks of Hachette Book Group, Inc.

The publisher is not responsible for websites (or their content) that are not owned by the publisher.

The Hachette Speakers Bureau provides a wide range of authors for speaking events. To find out more, go to www.hachettespeakersbureau.com or call (866) 376-6591.

The Library of Congress catalogued the hardcover edition of this book as follows:

Names: West, Lindy.
Title: Shrill : notes from a loud woman / Lindy West.
Description: First edition. | New York : Hachette Books, 2016.
Identifiers: LCCN 2016001577| ISBN 9780316348409 (hardcover) | ISBN 9781478964872 (audio cd) | ISBN 9781478909309 (audio download) | ISBN 9780316348454 (ebook)
Subjects: LCSH: West, Lindy—Humor. | Women journalists—United States—Biography. | Feminists—United States—Biography. | Women—Humor. | Conduct of life—Humor.
Classification: LCC PN4874.W425 A3 2016 | DDC 818/.602—dc23 LC record available at http://lccn.loc.gov/2016001577

Printed in the United States of America

LSC-C

10 9 8

For Dad

Contents

Contents

Introduction

I am writing this two weeks after the 2016 presidential election, and in case you don't remember what that was like, because things have gotten either better or worse— the world feels concussed. Everyone I know is dizzy and afraid. When you ask "How are you?" no one says "Good!" anymore. We say, "Eh, you know." Or worse. I put off going to sleep every night because that instant upon waking, when I momentarily forget that the world is different now and then have to remember, is too painful—a sickly, deep-inside pain, like a cervical biopsy. Snip. As I wrote in *The New York Times* the morning after the election, "It is indistinguishable from fresh, close grief."

Everything is uncertain. We still don't know whether Hillary Clinton will demand an audit of the vote totals in Wisconsin, Pennsylvania, and Michigan. We don't know the extent of vote tampering, and we don't know if we will ever know. We don't know what Russia is doing, or did. We don't know how many of Trump's potentially catastrophic cabinet appointments will stick. We don't know if our representatives will fight for us, or if our phone calls make any difference. We don't know if Trump will be impeached. We don't know if our Muslim, Mexican, black, trans, and disabled loved ones will be safe. We don't know how many teenage girls will die from botched abortions. We don't know if (when) the biosphere will collapse. We don't know if November 8, 2016, was the republic's last fair election. We don't know whether Trump is simply robbing us, or robbing us and seeding a holocaust.

You must know a lot of these things, in the future. I'm envious. It is so horrible to not know. I'm wondering if it's ethical to have a baby anymore. I wanted a baby. I hope you and your family are okay.

I wrote this book during the prenatal glimmerings of the 2016 election—when Donald Trump was still a joke and it felt like progress was winning. I called the book *Shrill* because of Hillary Clinton. I knew that the backlash to her campaign, particularly if she secured the nomination, would be brutal and violent and degrading and insultingly fixated on aesthetics (our culture's only comfortable metric for women's success): She's old, she's unfuckable, "I just don't like her voice." "Shrill" is a gendered insult; calling a man "shrill" makes as much sense as calling a smell "tall." To be shrill is to reach above your station; to abandon your duty to soothe and please; in short, to be heard.

I expected this election to be bad. I know from expe-

rience that shrill bitches get punished. I did not antic-
ipate that millions of Americans would be so repulsed
by the hubris of female ambition that they would elect a
self-professed sexual predator with zero qualifications and
fewer scruples. But I should have anticipated it. They'd
been warning me for years.

When I started writing about Internet trolling in 2012
or so, I knew that it was important, but I couldn't quite see
why. I couldn't make out the shape of the monster yet. I
watched as, gradually, the seemingly disparate groups of
angry men who had been hounding me and my colleagues
online for half a decade, many of which I write about
in this book—Men's Rights Advocates, pickup artists,
GamerGaters, 4channers, rightwing talk-radio toadies,
rape apologists, the anti-PC brigade—coalesced behind
the euphemism *alt-right* and, later, presidential candidate
Donald Trump. Of course, it made perfect sense—Trump
was a Twitter troll himself, and he promised to "Make
America Great Again," that is, drag us back a half century
to a time when black men didn't tell white men what to
do and girls kept their mouths shut about rape. I watched
as Trump was elected president, thanks to strategic voter
suppression, the Electoral College, and the white supremacy in my nation's DNA. I watched as neo-Nazis held a
conference in a federal building a few blocks from the
White House and the Ku Klux Klan planned a "victory
parade" and the media and "nice" centrist white folks got
busy normalizing it all.

I write in this book that "Internet trolling is not random—it is a sentient, directed, strong-armed goon of the status quo," and "Internet trolling is a force with a political agenda," but I didn't foresee how literally that would manifest. I had long insisted that Internet trolls were a symptom of the slow death and rising panic of male privilege—one last, snarling grasp at power by white men who could feel diversity winning and their supremacy waning. I should have expected that when the establishment grasps, it grasps hard.

Internet trolling wasn't just a symptom, it was a canary. Trolls tested the boundaries of how far society would allow racism, misogyny, and transphobia to be normalized. Would anyone do anything? Would anyone take action? Would anyone powerful take this seriously? The answer turned out to be no. Those of us on the receiving end begged for help, and were told to grow a thicker skin, because the Internet "isn't real life." Until, surprise, the Internet became president, and we as a society were so inured to hate speech—our boundaries had been so thoroughly obliterated and "political correctness" so stigmatized—that we had no defense.

There are a few simple directives that I tried to lay out in this book: Do a good job. Be vulnerable. Make things. Choose to be kind. That notion of choice—of choosing what kind of person you want to be—is more important now than ever. If our country isn't going to take care of everyone, we must take care of the people left behind.

The day after the election, I wrote:

We have been weathering this hurricane wall of doubt and violence for so long, and now, more crystalline than ever, we have an enemy and a mandate. We have the smirking apotheosis of our oppression sliming, paw-first, toward our genitals. We have the popular vote. We have proof, in exit polls, that white women will pawn their humanity for the safety of white supremacy. We have abortion pills to stockpile and neighbors to protect and children to teach. We have the right woman to find. We have local elections in a year.

The fact that we lost doesn't make us wrong; the fact that they don't believe in us doesn't make us disappear.

Progress is still winning. Be brave, and be shrill.

Lindy West
November 22, 2016

Lady Kluck

Why is, "What do you want to be when you grow up?" the go-to small talk we make with children? "Hello, child. As I have run out of compliments to pay you on your doodling, can you tell me what sort of niche you plan to carve out for yourself in the howling existential morass of uncertainty known as the future? Also, has anyone given you a heads-up that everyone you love will die someday?" That's like waking a dog up with an air horn and telling it that it's president now. "I don't know, Uncle Jeff. I'm still kind of working on figuring out how to handle these weird popsicles with the two sticks."

There was a time, I am told, when I was very small, that I had a ready response to the question. The answer was ballerina, or, for a minute, veterinarian, as I had been erroneously led to believe that "veterinarian" was the grown-up term for "professional animal-petter." I would later learn, crestfallen and appalled, that it's more a term for "touching poo all the time featuring intermittent cat murder," so the plan was abandoned. (The fact that ANY kid wants to be a veterinarian is bananas, by the way—whoever does veterinary medicine's PR among preschool-aged children should be working in the fucking White House.)

That period—when I was wholly myself, effortlessly certain, my identity still undistorted by the magnetic fields of culture—was so long ago that it's beyond readily accessible memory. I do not recall being that person. For as long as I can recall, anytime I met a new adult—who would inevitably get nervous (because what is a child and how do you talk to it?) and fumble for that same hacky stock question—my imagination would come up empty. Doctor? Too gross. Fireman? Too hard. Princess? Those are fictional, right? Astronaut? LOL.

While we're interrogating childhood clichés, who decided that "astronaut" would be a great dream job for a kid? It's like 97 percent math, 1 percent breathing some Russian dude's farts, 1 percent dying, and 1 percent eating awesome powdered ice cream. If you're the very luckiest kind of astronaut ever, your big payoff is that you get to visit a barren airless wasteland for five minutes, do some more math, and then go home—ice cream not guaranteed. Anyway, loophole: I can already buy astronaut ice cream at the Science Center, no math or dying required. Lindy, 1; astronauts nada. (Unless you get points for debilitating low bone density, in which case...I concede.)

Not that it mattered anyway. Astronaut was never on the table. (Good luck convincing a fat kid that they should pursue a career in floating.) Thanks to a glut of cultural messaging, I knew very clearly what I was not: small, thin, pretty, girlish, normal, weightless, Winona Ryder. But there was precious little media telling me what I was, what I could be. For me, "What do you want to be when you grow up?" was subsumed by a far more pressing question: "What are you?"

I'd squint into the future and come up blank.

What do you want to be when you grow up?

I can't tell. Static? A snow field? A bedsheet? Sour cream?...Is sour cream a job?

As a kid, I never saw anyone remotely like myself on TV. Or in the movies, or in video games, or at the children's theater, or in books, or anywhere at all in my field of vision. There simply were no young, funny, capable, strong, good fat girls. A fat man can be Tony Soprano; he can be Dan from *Roseanne* (still my number one celeb crush); he can be John Candy, funny without being a human sight gag—but fat women were sexless mothers, pathetic punch lines, or gruesome villains. Don't believe me? It's cool—I wrote it down.

Here is a complete list of fat female role models available in my youth.

Lady Kluck

Lady Kluck was a loud, fat chicken woman who took care of Maid Marian (and, presumably, may have wet-nursed her with chicken milk!?) in Disney's *Robin Hood*. Kluck was so fat, in fact, that she was nearly the size of an adult male bear. Being a four-hundred-pound chicken, she wasn't afraid to throw down in a fight with a lion and a gay snake* (even though the lion was her boss! #LeanIn), and she had monstro jugs, but in a maternal, sexless way, which is a total rip-off. Like, she doesn't even get to have a plus-sized fuckfest with Baloo!†

---

* "Gay snake" felt kind of weird, so I texted my friend Guy Branum.

> **ME:** Is it problematic to refer to Sir Hiss as a gay snake?
> **GUY:** He's super gay. He exists in the tradition of insidious gay dandies.
> **ME:** That's still fucked up, though. Is Prince John gay? Wait, is Jafar gay???
> **GUY:** Jafar is super gay. Prince John is effete and incompetent. Scar is gay.
> **ME:** Those are all the exact same character! They even have the same voice! Disney is the worst.
> **GUY:** Pop culture is the worst. Disney only uses character tropes we've seen before. We gays are unnatural and preoccupied with power. A common theme here is conniving outsiders trying to steal the game—manipulate the system to gain power/protection the non-noble way. Grima Wormtongue, all Jews, gays, women who gossip or do anything but be pretty and passive.
> **ME:** I'm so grossed out by how aggressively Disney trains children to defend traditional straight "alpha male" authority.
> **GUY:** It's changing.
> **ME:** We are fun at parties.

† I know that this bear's name is technically Little John. But Little John is clearly a character being played by a bear actor named Baloo, who also played himself in *The Jungle Book* and, decades later yet seem-

(It's weird that motherhood is coded as sexless, by the way. I know most of America is clueless about the female reproductive system, but if there's one thing most babies have in common it's that your dad goofed in your mom.)

Baloo Dressed as a Sexy Fortune-Teller

In order to assist Robin Hood in ripping off Prince John's bejeweled decadence caravan, Baloo adorns himself with scarves and rags and golden bangles and whirls around like an impish sirocco, utterly beguiling PJ's guard rhinos and incapacitating them with boners. Baloo dressed as a sexy fortune-teller luxuriates in every curve of his huge, sensuous bear butt; self-consciousness is not in his vocabulary. He knows he looks good. The most depressing thing I realized while making this list is that Baloo dressed as a sexy fortune-teller is the single-most positive role model of my youth.

The Queen of Hearts

I do not even know this bitch's deal. In *Alice in Wonderland*, her only personality trait is "likes the color red," she doesn't seem to do any governing aside from executing minors for losing at croquet, and she is married to a one-foot-tall baby

---

ingly un-aged, in *Tale Spin*. (Sub-theory: Baloo is the thirteenth Doctor.) I'm calling the bear Baloo and this conversation is over.

with a mustache. She is, now that I think about it, the perfect feminazi caricature: fat, loud, irrational, violent, overbearing, constantly hitting a hedgehog with a flamingo. Oh, shit. She taught me everything I know.

That Sexual Tree from *The Last Unicorn*

This fine lady was just minding her biz, being a big purple tree, when Schmendrick the garbage sorcerer came along and accidentally witchy-pooed her into a libidinous granny. Then he's all mad when she nearly smothers him twixt her massive oaken cans! Hey, man, if you didn't want to get motorboated to death by a fat tree, you should have picked something thinner and hotter to transform into your girlfriend. Like a spaghetti noodle, or clarinet.

The sex-tree that launched a thousand confusing fetishes taught me that fat women's sexuality isn't just ludicrous, it's also suffocating, disgusting, and squelchy.

Miss Piggy

I am deeply torn on Piggy. For a lot of fat women, Piggy is it. She is powerful and uncompromising, assertive in her sexuality, and wholly self-possessed, with an ostentatious glamour usually denied anyone over a size 4. Her being a literal pig affords fat fans the opportunity to reclaim that barb with defiant irony—she invented glorifying obesity.

But also, you guys, Miss Piggy is kind of a rapist? Maybe

if you love Kermie so much you should respect his bodily autonomy. The dude is physically running away from you.

Marla Hooch

A League of Their Own is a classic family comedy that mines the age-old question: What if women...could do things? Specifically, the women of *A League of Their Own* are doing baseball, and Marla Hooch is the most baseball-doingest woman of them all! She can hit homies and run bases and throw the ball far, all while maintaining a positive attitude and dodging jets of Tom Hanks's hot urine! The only problem is that she is not max bangable like the other baseball women—she has a jukebox-like body and makes turtle-face any time she is addressed—which, if you think about it, makes her not that good at baseball after all. Fortunately, at the end, she meets a man who is ALSO a jukebox turtle-face, and they get married in a condescending-ass ceremony that's like "Awwwww, look, the uglies thinks it's people!" (Presumably they also like each other's personali—What? Doesn't matter? Quarantine the less attractive? 'K!!!)

The thing about Marla Hooch is that the actress who plays her is just a totally nice-looking regular woman. I always think of this thing Rachel Dratch said in her memoir: "I am offered solely the parts that I like to refer to as The Unfuckables. In reality, if you saw me walking down the street, you wouldn't point at me and recoil and throw up and hide behind a shrub." Hollywood's beauty standards are so wacko that they trick you into thinking anyone who isn't Geena Davis is literally a toilet.

The Neighbor with the Arm Flab from
The Adventures of Pete & Pete

Big Pete and Little Pete spent an entire episode fixated on the jiggling of an elderly neighbor's arm fat. Next, I didn't wear a tank top for twenty years.

Ursula the Sea Witch

The whole thing with Ariel's voice and Prince Ambien Overdose is just an act of civil disobedience. What Ursula really wants is to bring down the regime of King Triton* so she and her eel bros don't have to live in a dank hole

---

* I HAVE SOME QUESTIONS ABOUT KING TRITON. Specifically, King, why are you elderly but with the body of a teenage Beastmaster? How do you maintain those monster pecs? Do they have endocrinologists under the sea? Because I am scheduling you some bloodwork. While we're on the subject, a question for the world at large: What is the point of sexualizing a fish-person? It's not like you could really have sex with King Triton, because FISH PENIS. I don't think fish even have penises anyway. Don't they just have, like, floppy anal fins that squirt out ambient sperms in the hope that lady-fishes will swim through their oops-cloud? *Is that really what you want from your love-making,* ladies!? To inadvertently swim through a miasma of fin-jizz and then call it a night? A merman is only a hottie with a naughty body *if you are half attracted to fish.* In conclusion, IT'S A FUCKING FISH-MAN TRYING TO DRAG YOU TO THE OCEAN FLOOR,

tending their garden of misery slime for the rest of their lives. It's the same thing with *The Lion King*—why should the hyenas have a shitty life? History is written by the victors, so forgive me if I don't trust some P90X sea king's smear campaign against the radical fatty in the next grotto.

Morla the Aged One from *The NeverEnding Story*

A depressed turtle who's so fat and dirty, people literally get her confused with a mountain.

Auntie Shrew

I guess it's forgivable that one of the secondary antagonists of *The Secret of NIMH* is a shrieking shrew of a woman who is also a literal shrew named Auntie Shrew, because the hero of the movie is also a lady and she is strong and brave. But, like, seriously? Auntie Shrew? Thanks for giving her a pinwheel of snaggle-fangs to go with the cornucopia of misogynist stereotypes she calls a personality.

Mrs. Potts

Question: How come, when they turn back into humans at the end of *Beauty and the Beast*, Chip is a four-year-old

---

WHERE IT PLANS TO USE YOUR DEAD BODY SEXUALLY. KILL IT. IT HAS A FORK.

boy, but his mother, Mrs. Potts, is like 107? Perhaps you're thinking, "Lindy, you are remembering it wrong. That kindly, white-haired, snowman-shaped Mrs. Doubtfire situation must be Chip's grandmother." Not so, champ! She's his mom. Look it up. She gave birth to him four years ago. Also, where the hell is Chip's dad? Could you imagine being a 103-year-old single mom?

As soon you become a mother, apparently, you are instantly interchangeable with the oldest woman in the world, and/or sixteen ounces of boiling brown water with a hat on it. Take a sec and contrast Mrs. Potts's literally spherical body with the cut-diamond abs of King Triton, father of seven.

The Trunchbull from *Matilda*

Sure, the Trunchbull is a bitter, intractable, sadistic she-monster who doesn't even feel a shred of fat solidarity with Bruce Bogtrotter (seriously, Trunch?), but can you imagine being the Trunchbull? And growing up with Miss Effing Honey? The world is not kind to big, ugly women. Sometimes bitterness is the only defense.

That's it.

Taken in aggregate, here is what I learned in my childhood about my personal and professional potential:

I could not claim any sexual agency unless I forced

myself upon a genteel frog; or unless, as part of a jewel caper, I was trying to seduce a base, horny fool such as a working-class rhinoceros; and if I insisted on broadcasting my sexuality anyway, I would be exiled to a sea cave to live eternally in a dank garden of worms, hoping that a gullible hot chick might come along once in a while so I could grift her out of her sexy voice. Even in those rare scenarios, my sexuality would still be a joke, an oddity, or a menace. I could potentially find chaste, comical romance, provided I located a chubby simpleton who looked suspiciously like myself without a hair bow, and the rest of humanity would breathe a secret sigh of relief that the two of us were removing ourselves from the broader gene pool. Or I could succumb to the lifetime of grinding pain and resentment and transform into a hideous beast who makes herself feel better by locking helpless children in the knife closet.

Mother or monster. Okay, little girl—choose.

Bones

I've always been a great big person. In the months after I was born, the doctor was so alarmed by the circumference of my head that she insisted my parents bring me back, over and over, to be weighed and measured and held up for scrutiny next to the "normal" babies. My head was "off the charts," she said. Science literally had not produced a chart expansive enough to account for my monster dome. "Off the charts" became a West family joke over the years—I always deflected, saying it was because of my giant brain—but I absorbed the message nonetheless. I was too big, from birth. Abnormally big. Medical-anomaly big. Unchartably big.

There were people-sized people, and then there was me.

So, what do you do when you're too big, in a world where bigness is cast not only as aesthetically objectionable, but also as a moral failing? You fold yourself up like origami, you make yourself smaller in other ways, you take up less space with your personality, since you can't with your body. You diet. You starve, you run till you taste blood in your throat, you count out your almonds, you try to buy back your humanity with pounds of flesh.

I got good at being small early on—socially, if not physically. In public, until I was eight, I would speak only to my mother, and even then, only in whispers, pressing my face into her leg. I retreated into fantasy novels, movies, computer games, and, eventually, comedy—places where I could feel safe, assume any personality, fit into any space. I preferred tracing to drawing. Drawing was too bold an act of creation, too presumptuous.

In third grade I was at a birthday party with a bunch of friends, playing in the backyard, and someone suggested we line up in two groups—the girls who were over one hundred pounds and the girls who were still under. There were only two of us in the fat group. We all looked at each other, not sure what to do next. No one was quite sophisticated enough to make a value judgment based on size yet, but we knew it meant something.

My dad was friends with Bob Dorough, an old jazz guy who wrote all the songs for *Multiplication Rock*, *Schoolhouse Rock*'s math-themed sibling. He's that breezy, froggy voice on "Three Is a Magic Number"—you'd recognize it. "A man and a woman had a little baby, yes, they did. They had three-ee-ee in the family..." Bob signed a vinyl copy of *Multiplication Rock* for me when I was two or three years old. "Dear Lindy," it said, "get big!" I hid that record, as a teenager, afraid that people would see the inscription and think, "She took *that* a little too seriously."

I dislike "big" as a euphemism, maybe because it's the one chosen most often by people who mean well, who love me and are trying to be gentle with my feelings. I don't want the people who love me to avoid the reality of my body. I don't want them to feel uncomfortable with its size and shape, to tacitly endorse the idea that fat is shameful, to pretend I'm something I'm not out of deference to a system that hates me. I don't want to be gentled, like I'm something wild and alarming. (If I'm going to be wild and alarming, I'll do it on my terms.) I don't want them to think that I need a euphemism at all.

"Big" is a word we use to cajole a child: "Be a big girl!" "Act like the big kids!" Having it applied to you as an adult is a cloaked reminder of what people really think, of the way we infantilize and desexualize fat people. (Desexualization is just another form of sexualization. Telling fat women they're sexless is still putting women in their sexual place.) Fat people are helpless babies enslaved to their most capricious cravings. Fat people do not know what's best for them. Fat people need to be guided and scolded like children. Having that awkward, babyish word dragging on you every day of your life, from childhood into maturity, well, maybe it's no wonder that I prefer hot chocolate to whiskey and substitute Harry Potter audiobooks for therapy.

Every cell in my body would rather be "fat" than "big." Grown-ups speak the truth.

Please don't forget: I am my body. When my body gets smaller, it is still me. When my body gets bigger, it is still me. There is not a thin woman inside me, awaiting excavation. I am one piece. I am also not a uterus riding around in a meat incubator. There is no substantive difference between the repulsive campaign to separate women's bodies from their reproductive systems—perpetuating the lie that abortion and birth control are not healthcare—and the repulsive campaign to convince women that they and their body size are separate, alienated entities. Both say, "Your body is not yours." Both demand, "Beg for your humanity." Both insist, "Your autonomy is conditional." This is why fat is a feminist issue.

All my life people have told me that my body doesn't belong to me.

As a teenager, I was walking down the street in Seattle's International District, when an old woman rushed up to me and pushed a business card into my hand. The card was covered in characters I couldn't read, but at the bottom it was translated: "WEIGHT LOSS/FAT BURN." I tried to hand it back, "Oh, no thank you," but the woman gestured up and down at my body, up and down. "Too fat," she said. "You call."

In my early twenties, I was working a summer job as a cashier at an "upscale general store and gift shop" (or, as it was known around my house, the Bourgeois Splendor

Ceramic Bird Emporium & Money Fire), when a tan, wiry man in his sixties strode up to my register. I remember him looking like the infamous Silver Lake Walking Man, if anyone remembers him, or if Jack LaLanne fucked a tanning bed and a Benjamin Button came out.

"Do you want to lose some weight?" he asked, with no introduction.

I laughed uncomfortably, hoping he'd go away: "Ha ha, doesn't everyone? Ha ha."

He pushed a brochure for some smoothie cleanse pyramid scheme over the counter at me. I glanced at it and pushed it back. "Oh, no thank you."

He pushed it toward me again, more aggressively. "Take it. Believe me, you need it."

"I'm not interested," I insisted.

He glared for a moment, then said, "So you're fine looking like that and getting the cancer?"

My ears roared. "That's rude," was all I could manage. I was still small then, inside. He laughed and walked out.

Over time, the knowledge that I was too big made my life smaller and smaller. I insisted that shoes and accessories were just "my thing," because my friends didn't realize that I couldn't shop for clothes at a regular store and I was too mortified to explain it to them. I backed out of dinner plans if I remembered the restaurant had particularly narrow aisles or rickety chairs. I ordered salad even if everyone else was having fish and chips. I pretended to hate skiing because my giant men's ski pants made me look like a smokestack and I was terrified my bulk would tip me off the chairlift. I stayed home as my friends went hiking, biking, sailing, climbing, diving, exploring—I was sure I couldn't keep up, and what if we got into a scrape? They couldn't boost me up a cliff or lower me down an embankment or squeeze me through a tight fissure or hoist me from the hot jaws of a bear. I never revealed a single crush, convinced that the idea of my disgusting body as a sexual being would send people—even people who loved me—into fits of projectile vomiting (or worse, pity). I didn't go swimming for a fucking decade.

As I imperceptibly rounded the corner into adulthood—fourteen, fifteen, sixteen, seventeen—I watched my friends elongate and arch into these effortless, exquisite things. I waited. I remained a stump. I wasn't jealous, exactly; I loved them, but I felt cheated.

We each get just a few years to be perfect. That's what I'd been sold. To be young and smooth and decorative and collectible. I was missing my window, I could feel it pulling at my navel (my obsessively hidden, hated navel), and I scrabbled, desperate and frantic. Deep down, in my honest places, I knew it was already gone—I had stretch marks and cellulite long before twenty—but they tell you that if you hate yourself hard enough, you can grab just a tail feather or two of perfection. Chasing perfection was your duty and your birthright, as a woman, and I would never know what it was like—this thing, this most important thing for girls.

I missed it. I failed. I wasn't a woman. You only get one life. I missed it.

There is a certain kind of woman. She is graceful. She is slim. Yes, she would like to go kayaking with you. On her frame, angular but soft, a baggy T-shirt is coded as "low-maintenance," not "sloppy"; a ponytail is "sleek," not "tennis ball on top of a mini-fridge." Not only can she pull off ugly clothes, like sports sandals, or "boyfriend jeans," they somehow make her beauty thrum even more clearly. She is thrifted J.Crew. She can put her feet up on a chair and draw her knees to her chest. She can hold an ocean in her clavicle.

People go on and on about boobs and butts and teeny waists, but the clavicle is the true benchmark of female desirability. It is a fetish item. Without visible clavicles you might as well be a meatloaf in the sexual marketplace. And I don't mean Meatloaf the person, who has probably gotten laid lotsa times despite the fact that his clavicle is buried so deep as to be mere urban legend, because our culture does not have a creepy sexual fixation on the bones of meaty men.

Only women. Show us your bones, they say. If only you were nothing but bones.

America's monomaniacal fixation on female thinness isn't a distant abstraction, something to be pulled apart by academics in women's studies classrooms or leveraged for traffic in shallow "body-positive" listicles ("Check Out These Eleven Fat Chicks Who You Somehow Still Kind of

Want to Bang—Number Seven Is Almost Like a Regular Woman!")—it is a constant, pervasive taint that warps every single woman's life. And, by extension, it is in the amniotic fluid of every major cultural shift.

Women matter. Women are half of us. When you raise every woman to believe that we are insignificant, that we are broken, that we are sick, that the only cure is starvation and restraint and smallness; when you pit women against one another, keep us shackled by shame and hunger, obsessing over our flaws rather than our power and potential; when you leverage all of that to sap our money and our time—that moves the rudder of the world. It steers humanity toward conservatism and walls and the narrow interests of men, and it keeps us adrift in waters where women's safety and humanity are secondary to men's pleasure and convenience.

I watched my friends become slender and beautiful, I watched them get picked and wear J.Crew and step into small boats without fear, but I also watched them starve and harm themselves, get lost and sink. They were picked by bad people, people who hurt them on purpose, eroded their confidence, and kept them trapped in an endless chase. The real scam is that being bones isn't enough either. The game is rigged. There is no perfection.

I listened to Howard Stern every morning in college. I loved Howard. I still do, though I had to achingly bow out as my feminism solidified. (In a certain light, feminism is just the long, slow realization that the stuff you love hates you.) When I say I used to listen to Stern, a lot of people look at me like I said I used to eat cat meat, but what they don't understand is that *The Howard Stern Show* is on the air for hours and hours every day. Yes, there is gleeful, persistent misogyny, but the bulk of it, back when I was a daily obsessive, at least, was Howard seeking validation for his neuroses; Robin cackling about her runner's diarrhea; Artie detailing the leviathan sandwich he'd eaten yesterday in a heroin stupor, then weeping over his debasement; Howard wheedling truth out of cagey celebrities like a surgeon; Howard buoying the news with supernatural comic timing; a Sagrada Familia of inside jokes and references and memories and love and people's lives willingly gutted and splayed open and dissected every day for the sake of good radio. It was magnificent entertainment. It felt like a family.

Except, for female listeners, membership in that family came at a price. Howard would do this thing (the thing, I think, that most non-listeners associate with the show) where hot chicks could turn up at the studio and he would look them over like a fucking horse vet—running his hands over their withers and flanks, inspecting their bite and the sway of their back, honking their massive horse jugs—and tell them, in intricate detail, what was wrong with their bodies. There was literally always something. If they were 110 pounds, they could stand to be 100. If they were 90, gross. ("Why'd you do that to your body, sweetie?") If they were a C cup, they'd be hotter as a DD. They should stop working out so much—those legs are too muscular. Their 29-inch waist was subpar—come back when it's a 26.

Then there was me: 225, 40-inch waist, no idea what bra size because I'd never bothered to buy a nice one because who would see it? Frumpy, miserable, cylindrical. The distance between my failure of a body and perfection stretched away beyond the horizon. According to Howard, even girls who were there weren't there.

If you want to be a part of this community that you love, I realized this family that keeps you sane in a shitty, boring world, this million-dollar enterprise that you fund with your consumer clout, just as much as male listeners do—you have to participate, with a smile, in your own disintegration. You have to swallow, every day, that you are a secondary being whose worth is measured by an arbitrary, impossible standard, administered by men.

When I was twenty-two, and all I wanted was to blend in, that rejection was crushing and hopeless and lonely. Years later, when I was finally ready to stand out, the realization that the mainstream didn't want me was freeing and galvanizing. It gave me something to fight for. It taught me that women are an army.

When I look at photographs of my twenty-two-year-old self, so convinced of her own defectiveness, I see a perfectly normal girl and I think about aliens. If an alien came to earth—a gaseous orb or a polyamorous cat person or whatever—it wouldn't even be able to tell the difference between me and Angelina Jolie, let alone rank us by hotness. It'd be like, "Uh, yeah, so those ones have the under-the-face fat sacks, and the other kind has that dangly pants nose. Fuck, these things are gross. I can't wait to get back to the omnidirectional orgy gardens of Vlaxnoid 7."*

The "perfect body" is a lie. I believed in it for a long time, and I let it shape my life, and shrink it—my real life, populated by my real body. Don't let fiction tell you what to do.

In the omnidirectional orgy gardens of Vlaxnoid 7, no one cares about your arm flab.

---

* This is also the rationale that I use to feel better every time there's a "horse meat in your IKEA meatballs" scandal. Do you think an alien could tell the difference between a horse and a cow? Please.

Are You There, Margaret? It's Me, a Person Who Is Not a Complete Freak

The first time I was informed that my natural body was gross and bad I was at a friend's house. We were eight or nine, still young enough to call it "playing" instead of "hanging out," and my friend looked down at my shins shining with long, iridescent blond hairs. "Oh," she said with recently learned disgust, "you don't shave your legs?" I went home and told my mom I needed a razor. I can still see her face.

"You know," she said, equal parts pleading and guilt-tripping, "your grandmother never shaved her legs, and I always wished I hadn't either. Her leg hair was so soft. You can't get that back."

"Mom, it's fine," I groaned. I'm sure I was short with her. I didn't want to be doing this either.

I was never one of those kids who couldn't wait to grow up. Childhood was a solid scam! I had these people who bought and cooked my food, washed and folded all my clothes, gave me Christmas presents, took me on trips, kept the house clean, read out loud to me until I fell asleep, found me fascinating, and spent pretty much all their time constructing a warm, loving, safe bubble around me that gave order and character to life. Now that I'm a grown-up, what do I have to show for it? Audiobooks, taxes, dirty hardwood floors, a messed-up foot, and negative a hundred dollars? A realistic ad campaign for adulthood would never sell: Do you like candy for dinner? *And plantar fasciitis?*

Childhood suited me—I was a lucky kid, and my life was simple, it was fun—so I dug in my heels as hard as I could against every portent of growing up, puberty most of all. I was still pretty weirded out from the time my babysitter let me watch *Animal House* in fourth grade, specifically the part in which a woman apparently extrudes huge wads of white tissue from her chest cavity (is that what boobs do!?); and I wasn't entirely sold on having a vagina at that point, so I sure as shit wasn't ready for it to transform into a chocolate fountain (SORRY) and turn my pants into a crime scene once a month. What a stupid thing for a vagina to do! And I had to run a terrifying pink knife all over my legs and armpits once a week to get rid of perfectly innocuous little blond hairs that, as far as I could tell, served no purpose to begin with. Why did I grow them if I just had to scrape them off? Why have a vagina if it was just going to embarrass me?

"Puberty" was a fancy word for your genitals stabbing you in the back.

When you're a little kid, everyone talks about your period like it's going to be a party bus to WOOOOOOOOOO! Mountain. It's all romantic metaphors about "blossoming gardens" and "unfurling crotch orchids," and kids buy into it because they don't know what a euphemism is because they're eleven. But it's also a profoundly secret thing—a confidence for closed-door meetings between women. Those two contradictory approaches (periods are the best! and we must never ever speak of them), made me feel like I was the only not-brainwashed one in a culty dystopian novel. "Oh, yes, you can't imagine the joy readings in your subjectivity port when the Administration gifts you your woman's flow! SPEAKING OF THE FLOW OUT-SIDE OF THE MENARCHE BUNKER WILL RESULT IN DEACTIVATION."

Girls in the '70s were the cultiest—they couldn't wait to get their periods and incessantly wrote books about it. "Oh, I hope I get it today! I just have to bleed stinkily out of my vagina before that cow Francine." The reality, of course, is that when you hit puberty you don't magically blossom into a woman—you're still the same tiny fool you were at puberty-minus-one, only now once a month hot brown blood just glops and glops out of your private area like a broken Slurpee machine. Forever. Or, at least, until you're inconceivably elderly, in an eleven-year-old's estimation. Don't worry, to deal, you just have to cork up your hole with this thing that's like a severed toe made out of cotton (and if you don't swap it out often enough, your legs fall off and you die). Or you wear a diaper. Or, if you have a super-chunky flow, you do both so you don't get stigmata on your pants in front of [hot eighth-grade boy I'm still too bashful to mention]. Also, your uterus is knives and you poop a bunch and you're hormonal and you get acne. Have fun in sixth grade, Margaret.

Personally, I couldn't handle that dark knowledge at all. So, before I hit puberty (and, let's be honest, for like fifteen years afterwards), I treated my reproductive system like it was the Nothing from *The NeverEnding Story*: "When you look at it, it's as if you were blind." I mean, I washed the parts and stuff, but I had no use for it—and the only thing I really knew was that it was eventually going to screw me over and ruin this sunny, golden childhood biz I had going on. More like vagin-UUUUUUUGGGHHHHHHHH.

If Google had existed when I was eleven, my search history would have looked something like this:

> *how much comes out*
> *how many cups come out*
> *how to stop period*
> *cancel your period*

people with no period
spells to delay period
magic to stop period
blood magic
witchcraft
witches
the witches
roald dahl
new roald dahl books
free roald dahl books for kids

(Priorities.)

My mom—probably sensing my anxiety—dragged me to a mother-daughter puberty class called Growing Up Female*—four hours on a sunny Saturday, trapped in my elementary school library talking about penises

---

* There was a part of "Growing Up Female" where everyone was supposed to write their most embarrassing questions on little note cards and the pube instructor would answer them anonymously in front of the class. I don't remember what my question was, but I do remember that when I went up to put it in the pile, I recognized my mom's handwriting on the top card. "Please talk about inverted nipples," it said, succinctly. In the pantheon of Worst Ways to Learn You Have One Weird Nipple, this ranks just above skywriting but just below Guy Fieri naming a dish after it (Lindy West's Great American Triple-Bangin' Weird Nip Diesel Dip). Also, it was a totally unnecessary horror, as my inverted nipple eventually became an extroverted nipple ALL ON ITS OWN. It's even considering going to some open mics. Seriously, you should come.

and nipples with my mom. Strangely enough, this did not make my eventual pubin'-out process less awkward.

I don't want to give you guys TMI, but let's just say that my "Aunt Period Blood" eventually did come to town. When it arrived, my avoidance was so finely calibrated that I blocked out the memory almost completely. I think, though I don't know for sure, that I was swimming in the ocean near my uncle's house: a wide, shallow inlet where the flats bake in the sun until the tide pours in, and then the hot mud turns the whole bay to bathwater. I can recall quick flashes of confusion and panic, guiltily unspooling toilet paper in an unfamiliar bathroom by that strange, sticky beach.

I did not want to talk about it. I avoided talking about it so assiduously that—for years—I invariably failed to tell my menopausal mom when we'd run out of stuffin' corks and diaper nuggets (#copyrighted), forcing her to run to the grocery store at inhumane hours while I squeezed out silent, single tears in the car. (If this had been a Roald Dahl book, she would have developed clairvoyance and summoned the 'pons by telekinesis and/or delivery giant. Thanks for nothing, regular human mom.*)

This avoidance (and my life) reached an all-time nadir one morning when my mom didn't have time to make it to the store and back before work, so I was forced to

---

* "Nothing" except for the unconditional love and support and meticulous care to make sure that I faced the world fully informed about my body and reproductive health! I forgive you for not being a real witch.

go to school wearing a menstrual pad belt that had been in our first aid drawer since approximately 1861. If you've never seen one of these things, because you haven't been to THE ANTIQUITIES MUSEUM, it is a literal belt that goes around your waist, with two straps that dangle down your front and back cracks, ice cold metal clips holding a small throw pillow in place over your shame canyon. I wish I could tell you I only had to go through that once before I learned my lesson.

One time, I noticed that the little waxy strips you peel off the maxi pad adhesive were printed, over and over, with a slogan: "Kotex Understands." In the worst moments, when my period felt like a death—the death of innocence, the death of safety, the harbinger of a world where I was too fat, too weird, too childish, too ungainly—I'd sit hunched over on the toilet and stare at that slogan, and I'd cry. Kotex understands. Somebody, somewhere, understands.*

Then, each month, once my period was over, I would burrow back into snug denial all over again: pretending my lady-parts didn't exist and that nothing would ever, ever come out of them, to the point where the blood would surprise me all over again, every month.

Twelve years later, I finally said the word "period" out loud in public.

---

* Some forty-seven-year-old advertising copywriter in Culver City named Craig understands.

Part of that anxiety came from the fact that, particularly in my youth, I was a hider, a dissociater, a fantasist. It was easier to bury myself in stories than to deal with the fact that the realities of adulthood were barreling down on me: money and loneliness and self-doubt and death.

Part of that anxiety came from the fact that, as a fat kid, I was already on high alert for humiliation at all times. When your body itself is treated like one big meat-blooper, you don't open yourself up to unnecessary embarrassment. I was a careful, exacting child. I hoarded my dignity. Even now, I watch where I step. I double-fact-check before I publish. I avoid canoes.

The most significant source of my adolescent period anxiety was the fact that, in America in 2016 (and far more so in 1993), acknowledging the completely normal and mundane function of most uteruses is still taboo. The taboo is so strong that it contributes to the widespread stonewalling of women from seats of power—for fear that, as her first act in the White House, Hillary might change Presidents' Day to Brownie Batter Makes the Boo-Hoos Stop Day. The taboo is strong enough that a dude once broke up with me because a surprise period started while we were having sex and the sight of it shattered some pornified illusion he had of women as messless pleasure pillows. The taboo is so strong that while we've all seen swimming pools of blood shed in horror movies and action movies and even on the news, when a woman ran the 2015 London Marathon without a tampon, photos of blood spotting her running gear made the social media rounds to near-universal disgust. The blood is the same—the only difference is where it's coming from. The disgust is at women's natural bodies, not at blood itself.

We can mention periods obliquely, of course, when we want to delegitimize women's real concerns, dismiss their more inconvenient emotions, and perpetuate the myth that having outie junk instead of innie junk (and a male gender identity) makes a person an innately more rational and competent human being. But to suggest that having a period isn't an abomination, but is, in fact, natural and good, or—my god—to actually let people see what period blood looks like? (This is going to blow a lot of you guys' minds, but: It looks like blood.) You might as well suggest replacing the national anthem with Donald Trump harmonizing with an air horn.

Yeah, personally I hate my period and think it's annoying and gross, but it's not more gross than anything else that comes out of a human body. It's not more gross than feces, urine, pus, bile, vomit, or the grossest bodily fluid of them all—in my mother's professional opinion—phlegm. And yet we are not horrified every time we go to the bathroom. We do not stigmatize people with stomach flu. The active ingredient in period stigma is misogyny.

This is just a wacky idea I had, but maybe it's not a coincidence that, in a country where half the population's normal reproductive functions are stigmatized, American uterus- and vagina-havers are still fighting tooth and nail to have those same reproductive systems fully covered by the health insurance that we pay for. Maybe periods wouldn't be so frightening if we didn't refer to them as "red tide" or "shark week" or any other euphemism that evokes neurotoxicity or dismemberment. Maybe if we didn't perpetuate the idea that vaginas are disgusting garbage dumps, government officials wouldn't think of vagina care as literally throwing money away. Maybe if girls felt free to talk about their periods in shouts instead of whispers, as loudly in mixed company as in libraries full of moms, boys wouldn't grow up thinking that vaginas are disgusting and mysterious either. Maybe those parts would seem like things worth taking care of. Maybe women would go to the doctor more. Maybe fewer women would die of cervical and uterine cancer. Maybe everyone would have better sex. Maybe women would finally be considered fully formed human beings, instead of off-brand men with defective genitals.

Maybe I wouldn't have had to grow up feeling like a strip of wax paper was the only "person" who understood me.

I don't remember how I got over it. Just time, I guess. I just waited. Eventually I moved from pads to tampons, and eventually I moved from tampons with applicators to the kind of tampons that you just poke up there with your finger, and eventually I was able to ask a female friend for a tampon without dying inside, and eventually I was able to have a tampon fall out of my purse on a crowded bus and not construct an elaborate ruse to frame the woman next to me, and now I'm just a normal adult with a husband she's not afraid to send to the store for o.b. super-pluses. Ta-daaaah.

The truth is, my discomfort with my period didn't have anything to do with the thing itself (though, to any teenage girls reading this: yes, it is gross; yes, it hurts; no, it's not the end of the world; yes, sometimes it gets on your pants; no, nobody will remember)—it was just part of the lifelong, pervasive alienation from my body that every woman absorbs to some extent. Your body is never yours. Your body is your enemy. Your body is gross. Your body is wrong. Your body is broken. Your body isn't what men like. Your body is less important than a fetus. Your body should be "perfect" or it should be hidden.

Yeah, well, my name is Lindy West and I'm fat and I bleed out of my hole sometimes. My body is mine now. Kotex understands.

How to Stop Being Shy in Eighteen Easy Steps

Don't trust anyone who promises you a new life. Pick-up artists, lifestyle gurus, pyramid-scheme face cream evangelists, Weight Watchers coaches: These people make their living off of your failures. If their products lived up to their promise, they'd be out of a job. That doesn't make the self-help economy inherently sinister or their offerings wholly worthless—it doesn't mean you can't drop five pounds by eating Greek yogurt under the nurturing wing of a woman named Tanya, or lose your virginity thanks to the sage advice of an Uber driver in aviator goggles, or help your cousin's sister-in-law earn her February bonus while adequately moisturizing your face for $24.99—we are all simply trying to get by, after all. It's just that, sadly, there are no magic bullets.* Real change is slow, hard, and imperceptible. It resists deconstruction.

Likewise, lives don't actually have coherent, linear story arcs, but if I had to retroactively tease one essential narrative out of mine, it'd be my transformation from a terror-stricken mouse-person to an unflappable human vuvuzela. I wasn't shy in a cute, normal way as a kid—I was a full-blown Mrs. Piggle-Wiggle plant-radishes-in-my-ears-and-leave-me-in-the-care-of-an-impudent-parrot situation. I was clinically shy. Once, in the first grade, I peed my pants in class because I was too scared to ask the teacher if I could go to the bathroom. When the class bully noticed the puddle between my feet, I pointed at a water pitcher on the other side of the room and whispered that it had spilled. Just in one small, discrete pool under my chair. And also on my sock. And also the pitcher was filled with urine for some reason. Public schools, am I right? (Pretty sure he bought it.)

Just a few decades later, here I am: the Ethel Merman of online fart disclosure. I now get yelled at and made fun of for a living—my two greatest fears rendered utterly toothless, and, even better, monetized. Women ask me: "How did you find your voice? How can I find mine?" and

---

* Except for Lean Cuisine French Bread Pepperoni Pizza, which is an edible poem.

I desperately want to help, but the truth is, I don't know. I used to hate myself; eventually, I didn't anymore. I used to be shy; eventually, I made my living by talking too much.

Every human being is a wet, gassy katamari of triumphs, traumas, scars, coping mechanisms, parental baggage, weird stuff you saw on the Internet too young, pressure from your grandma to take over the bodega when what you really want to do is dance, and all the other fertilizer that makes a smear of DNA grow into a fully formed toxic avenger. Everyone is different, and advice is a game of chance. Why would what changed me change you? How do I know how I changed anyway? And how do you know when you're finished, when you're finally you? How do you clock that moment? Is a pupa a caterpillar or a butterfly?*

It's flattering to believe that we transform ourselves through a set of personal tangibles: Steely resolve and the gentle forbearance of a mysterious young widow who wandered in off the moor, but reality is almost always more mundane. Necessity. Luck. Boredom. Exhaustion. Time. Willpower is real, but it needs the right conditions to thrive.

I can tell you my specifics, though. I can tell you the stepping-stones that I remember along the path from quiet to loud—the moments when I died inside, and then realized that I wasn't actually dead, and then died inside a

---

* RHETORICAL QUESTION—DON'T YOU DARE ANSWER IT.

little bit less the next time, until now, when my wedding photo with the caption "FAT AS HELL" was on the motherfucking cover of a *print newspaper* in England (where Mr. Darcy could see it!!!!!!!!), and my only reaction was a self–high five.

Maybe, if you follow these steps to the letter, you'll end up here too.

Step One: Shoplift One Bean

I was four years old, following my mother around the grocery store. She stopped near the bulk dry goods, and I stuck my hand deep into a bin of beans, cool and smooth. I thought the beans were cute—white with black freckles, like maybe you could plant one and grow a Dalmatian— and there were so many of them, one wouldn't be missed. When we got home, I showed my mother my prize. To my surprise, she was mad at me. It's just one bean, I said. It's not *stealing*.

"What if everyone who came to the grocery store took 'just one bean'? How many beans would the grocery store have left?"

This was an incomplete story problem. How many beans were in the bin? How many people go to the grocery store? How often do they restock the beans? I was going to need some more information.

Instead, she jumped straight to the answer: *zero more beans*. If everyone took just one bean, beans would go extinct and I would tell my grandchildren about the time I ate a Crunchwrap Supreme with the same hushed reverence my dad used when talking about riding the now-extinct Los Angeles Railway from Glendale all the way to Santa Monica. Oh my god, I realized. She was going to make me RETURN THE BEAN.

We drove (*drove*! wasted fossil fuels! we fight wars over those!) back to the store. The teenager mopping the meat section looked up at us.

"Can I help you?"

"My daughter has something she'd like to tell you."

I proffered my Dalmatian egg, rigid with terror and barely audible. "I took this. I'm sorry."

"Oh, uh," he said, glancing at what was, unmistakably, just some fucking bean, "it's okay. It's not a big deal."

"No," my mom corrected. "She needs to learn." I don't know what would constitute adequate compensation for being forcibly dragged into a small child's object lesson about accountability and theft while you were just trying to finish your blood mopping so you could make it to Amber's house party later, but $4.25 an hour wasn't it. He played along anyway.

"Oh. Um. Thanks for being honest? Don't do it again."

"I won't," I whispered. And I never did.*

---

* A few months ago I was at Walgreens with my mom and walked out absentmindedly clutching a pack of Rolaids. In the parking lot I said, "Oh!" and uncurled my fist. She looked at me like, "You know what to do." We went back in.

Step Two: Accidentally Make Fun of Your Mom's Friend's Barren Womb

Third grade. My mom's friend spread her arms for a hug: "Come here, sweetie!" Hopped up on my latest vocab test, I gasped in mock horror, "Are you STERILE!?"

I thought "sterile" meant "germ-free." Turns out, it also means that your uterus doesn't work anymore because you're old and/or the victim of some authoritarian eugenics program and/or just life. She quipped something dry and perfect that I can't remember. Everyone laughed at me and I hid in a small cupboard for one year.

Step Three: Do a Mediocre Oral Presentation on Thelonious Monk

When you grow up with a four-hundred-year-old jazz dad instead of the three-hundred-year-old rock 'n' roll dads all your friends have, sometimes your cultural references are weird and anachronistic. For my seventh-grade Language Arts class, we had to do a fifteen-minute oral presentation on the black artist of our choice, and while 99 percent of kids were like "Whitney Houston!" or "Denzel Washington!" I was all, "Pioneering jazz iconoclast Thelonious Monk, a-doy." Which is actually a pretty cool pick, in retrospect—and even at the time was not inherently embarrassing—but, nevertheless, an oral presentation violated my "never speak audibly to anyone but my mom's leg" policy, so I spent the week leading up to the event in a shivering flop sweat.

As I sat in the back of the class, waiting for my name to be called and trying not to lose consciousness, a wave of sudden, intellectualized calm washed over me—a tipping point so unanticipated that it still feels a hair supernatural. I looked to my left at the kid who'd been carrying around a "pet" light bulb since kindergarten. I looked to my right at the girl I'd once watched eat an entire tube of ChapStick for "lunch dessert." What the fuck was I scared of again? These people? It made no sense. Talking in front of people is the same as any other kind of talking, I realized—and anyway, do you know who's more intimidating than a bunch of booger-encrusted seventh graders? MY MOM. I talked to her all the time. I could do this.

I went up and did my presentation and I wasn't scared at all and the only thing that happened was that people were bored because seventh graders don't care about Thelonious Monk.

Step Four: Get a Show Dog

Mozart was a Tibetan terrier, a fairly uncommon breed—too big to be hilarious but too small to be useful—designed to sit on a mountain and keep a monk company. He had long, white fur, Crohn's disease, and the personality of an Elliott Smith song. We got him when I was in eighth grade, from a woman named Linda, with the caveat that she be allowed to continue showing and breeding him indefinitely. We were forbidden to cut his hair or tamper with his testicles. He was allergic to all common proteins, so my mom would buy whole rabbits from the butcher and cook up mounds of rabbit meat for the dog. For breakfast he had scrambled eggs.

"Hey, Mom, can I have some scrambled eggs?"

"You know how to cook. Mozart doesn't."

At least one weekend a month, Linda would come pick up Sunwind Se-Aires Rinpoche (his show name, in case you thought I wasn't dead fucking serious) and bring him back a few days later covered in ribbons. More often than not, we'd go to the dog show too and cheer him on, and Linda would prod me to become a junior handler.* I thought about it. I really did. A couple of times I even pawed wistfully through pantsuits in the basement of the mall. But there are some lines you just can't cross.

Step Five: Join a Choir with Uniforms that Look Like Menopausal Genie Costumes

Okay, so it was these massive palazzo pants—like polyester JNCO jeans—with a long-sleeved velour shirt, a teal cummerbund, and a felt vest festooned with paisley appliques

---

* Have you ever been around dog show people? One time I overheard a prospective buyer talking to a basenji breeder about the breed's distinctive "yodel." "They don't bark," the breeder said, "but they can make a noise like a woman being raped!"

and rhinestones. The overall effect was "mother-of-the-bride at a genie wedding who hot-glue-gunned her outfit in the parking lot of a Hobby Lobby."

I was in this choir for ten years.*

Step Six: Watch *Trainspotting* with Your Parents

Contrary to all of your body's survival instincts, this is not, in fact, fatal.

Step Seven: Read High Fantasy on the School Bus

Oh, you think you're a badass for leaving the book jacket on *Half-Blood Prince*? You think it makes you a "total nerd" because you're trying to get through *A Clash of Kings* before the next season of *Game of Thrones* comes out? Try reading Robert Jordan on the bus in 1997 with your bass clarinet case wedged between your legs while wearing a Microsoft Bob promotional T-shirt your dad brought home from work. Then try losing your virginity.

---

* Choir actually changed my life and taught me how to dedicate myself to a collective and settle for nothing less than excellence, but, holy god, the outfits were fucked.

Step Eight: Break a Heel on the Stairs in Your College's Humanities Building and Fall Down So Everyone Sees Your Underpants

You know what's a liberating thing to figure out? Everyone's butt looks basically how you think it looks.

Step Nine: Taco the Back Wheel of Your Tiny Friend's Tiny Bicycle in Amsterdam

I TOLD HER IT WOULDN'T WORK.

Step Ten: Neglect to Tell the Heavy Metal Doofus You Lose Your Virginity to that It's Your First Time and Then Bleed All Over His Bed

"Okay, but, having your bed anointed with virgin's blood is like the most metal thing ever, right?"

   "You should go."

Step Eleven: Ignore Several Weeks of Voicemails from Your Landlord

This was back when you had to actually physically call a phone number and type in a code to retrieve your own voicemails, which means I literally never did it. Too bad I missed the heads-up that my landlord would be touring my apartment with two appraisers from the insurance company just as I stepped out of the shower fully nude and singing "Just Around the River-bend" from the soundtrack of Disney's *Pocahontas!* YOU'RE WELCOME FOR THE BONERS, INSURANCE APPRAISERS.

Step Twelve: Have Sex that Is
Not Silent and Still

On November 17, 2010, I received this e-mail from my handsome, gay apartment manager:

> *Hi Lindy,*
>
> *Sorry to have to be the bearer of this type of com-plaint, but it is what it is, and we're both adults.*
> *I have had complaints from tenants regarding "sex noise" coming from your apartment, really late at night. The complaints are about creaking and vocaliza-tions late at night (3am).*
>
> *Thanks,*
> *[REDACTED]*

Well, I am a dead body now, so problem solved.

Step Thirteen: Tip Over a Picnic Table While Eating a Domino's Personal Pan Pizza in the Press Area of a Music Festival

A music festival is a kind of collective hangover in which people who are cooler than you compete to win a special kind of lanyard so they can get into a special tent with unlimited free Gardetto's. The only food available to the non-lanyarded hoi polloi is expensive garbage dispensed resentfully from a shack, which is how I found myself, in 2010, sitting alone at a picnic table in the press area of the Sasquatch! Music Festival, sweatily consuming a $45 Domino's pepperoni personal pan pizza and a Diet Pepsi and hoping nobody noticed me.

Someone was interviewing the band YACHT at the next table, and I was sort of dispassionately staring at my phone, pretending like my friends were texting me even though they weren't because I think they were all back in the free Gardetto's area playing VIP four-square with Santigold or something probably. I watched the woman from YACHT do her interview for a few minutes before I remembered that we'd gone to college together, where, even before experimental pop fame, she'd been an untouchably cool and talented human lanyard who was also beautiful and nice. I chewed my oily pork puck.

A little gust of wind picked up and blew my Domino's napkin off the picnic table and onto the ground.

No big deal. I leaned over, nonchalantly, to pick it up. Gotta have a napkin! Can't be a fat lady eating pizza with red pig-grease all over my face! Unfortunately, due to my intense preoccupation with not drawing attention to myself while eating a Domino's personal pepperoni pan pizza in public at a music festival while fat, I misjudged the flimsy plastic picnic table's center of gravity.

When I leaned over to grab the napkin, the table leaned over too.

I fell in the dirt. The pizza fell on top of me. The Diet Pepsi tipped over and glugged out all over my dress. The table fell on top of the Pepsi on top of the pizza on top of me. The napkin fluttered away. EVERYONE LOOKED AT ME. The music journalists looked at me. The band YACHT looked at me. In an attempt at damage control, I yelled, "I'm really drunk, so it's okay!" which wasn't even true, but apparently it's better to be drunk at ten in the morning than it is to be a human being who weighs something? All that anxiety about trying not to be a gross, gluttonous fat lady eating a "bad" food in public, and I wound up being the fat lady who was so excited about pizza that she threw herself to the ground and rolled around in it like a dog with a raccoon carcass. Nailed it.

Step Fourteen: Get Hired to Write a Press Release for the Band Spoon, Then Write

Something So Weird and Unusable that the Band Spoon Quietly Sends You a Check and Never Speaks to You Again and Hires Someone Normal to Write a Real Press Release

Here is the actual full text that I actually e-mailed to Britt Daniel of the band Spoon:

Some years ago in the past (no one knows how many for sure), a baby was born: his mother's pride, hearty and fat, with eyes like pearls and fists like very small fingered hams. That baby was named David Coverdale of Whitesnake. Meanwhile, on the other side of the world and many, many years later, an even better and newer baby came out. They called that one Britt Daniel of Spoon. The two would never meet.

The son of an itinerant barber-surgeon (his motto: "Oops!") and his raven-haired bride who may or may not have been Cher (she definitely wasn't, say "historians"), Daniel spent his formative years traversing America's heartland, on leech duty in the back of the amputation/ perm wagon. Despite mounting pressure to join the family business—"the Daniel child's bonesaw work truly is a poem!" swooned Itinerant Barber-Surgeon's Evening Standard Digest—*Daniel heard the siren song of song-singing and fled the narrow confines of his itchy-necked, blood-spattered world.*

Little is known of Daniel's whereabouts and associations in these dark interim years (when consulted for comment, David Coverdale of Whitesnake said, "Get away from me, please"), but he emerged in 1994, saw his shadow, and formed the band Spoon, stronger and taller and more full of handsome indie rock and roll than ever before. After the great big success of 2001's Girls Can Tell, *2002's* Kill the Moonlight, *2005's* Gimme Fiction, *and 2007's* Ga Ga Ga Ga Ga, *Daniel—along with Jim Eno (inventor of the bee beard), Eric Harvey (feral child success story), and Rob Pope (white male)—birthed* Transference: *in Daniel's words, Spoon's "orangest" and "most for stoners" album yet.*

Asked about her son's new record, Daniel's mother, who is definitely "not" Cher, quipped: "Too metal!" Reached for comment on whether or not Daniel's non-Cher mother is really qualified to judge the metalness of things, David Coverdale of Whitesnake said, "Seriously, how did you get this number?"

I am so, so sorry, the band Spoon.

Step Fifteen: Get a Job Blogging for a National Publication with Thousands and Thousands of Commenters Who Will Never Be Satisfied No Matter What You Write

At a certain point you just have to be like [jack-off motion] and do you.

Step Sixteen: Ask Pat Mitchell if She Is Marlo Thomas at a Banquet Honoring Pat Mitchell

Hollyweird Fun Fact: Pat Mitchell does not like this at all.

Step Seventeen: Break a Chair While Sitting on the Stage at a Comedy Show

I went to see my friend Hari work out some new jokes at a small black-box theater in Seattle. The ancient theater seats were too narrow for my modern butt, so I moved to an old wooden chair that had been placed on the side of the stage as overflow seating. A few minutes into Hari's set, a loud crack echoed through the theater and I felt the chair begin to collapse under me. I jumped into a kind of emergency squat, which I nonchalantly held until the producer rushed out from backstage and replaced my chair with some sort of steel-reinforced military-grade hydraulic jack.

Step Eighteen: Admit that You Lied Earlier About How Old You Were When You Peed Your Pants in Class

Third grade. It was third grade, okay? Are you happy?

This is the only advice I can offer. Each time something like this happens, take a breath and ask yourself, honestly:

Am I dead? Did I die? Is the world different? Has my soul splintered into a thousand shards and scattered to the winds? I think you'll find, in nearly every case, that you are fine. Life rolls on. No one cares. Very few things—apart from death and crime—have real, irreversible stakes, and when something with real stakes happens, humiliation is the least of your worries.

You gather yourself up, and you pick the pepperoni out of your hair, and you say, "I'm sorry, Pat Mitchell, it was very nice to meet you," and you live, little soldier. You go live.

When Life Gives You Lemons

I don't keep track of my periods and kind of think anyone who does is some sort of neuroscientist, so I have no idea what prompted me to walk over to Walgreens and buy a pregnancy test. Maybe women really do have a weird, spiritual red phone to our magic triangles. I never thought I did, but for whatever reason, that day, I walked around the corner, bought the thing, took it home to my studio apartment, and peed on it. I probably bought some candy and toilet paper too as, like, a decoy, so maybe the Walgreens checker would think the pregnancy test was just a wacky impulse buy on my way to my nightly ritual of wolfing Heath bars while taking a magnum dump.

I always throw a decoy purch' in the cart any time I have to buy something embarrassing like ice cream or vagina plugs. (Obviously, on paper, I disagree with this entire premise—food and hygiene are not "embarrassing"—but being a not-baby is a journey, not a destination.) Like, if I want to eat six Tootsie Pops and a Totino's for dinner, I'll also buy a lemon and a bag of baby carrots to show that I am a virtuous and cosmopolitan duchess who just needs to keep her pantry stocked with party pizza in case any Ninja Turtles stop by. The carrots are for me, Belvedere. Or, if I want to buy the super-economy box of ultra-plus tampons, I'll also snag a thing of Windex and some lunch meat, to distract the cashier from the community theater adaptation of *Carrie* currently entering its third act in my gusset. Maybe I'm just buying these 'pons for my neighbor on my way to slam some turk and polish my miniatures, bro! (IMPORTANT: One must NEVER EVER use tampons and Ben & Jerry's as each other's decoy purchases, as this suggests you are some sort of Bridget Jones situation who needs ice cweam to soothe her menses a-bloo-bloos, which defeats the entire purpose of decoy purchases, Albert Einstein.)

So, peeing on things is weird, right? As a person without a penis, I mean. I could show you the pee-hole on any crotch diagram—I could diagram pee-holes all day (AND I DO)—but in practice, I'm just not... entirely clear on where the pee comes out? It's, sort of, the front area? The foyer? But it's not like there's, like, a nozzle. Trying to pee into a cup is like trying to fill a beer bottle with a Super Soaker from across the room in the dark. On a moonless night. (This is one of those disheartening moments where I'm realizing that I might be The Only One, and I may as well have just announced to you all that I don't know how shoes work. What's the deal with these hard socks??? Right, guys?

.

...

....

...Guys?)

So, I pee on the thing a little bit, and on my hand a lot, and these two little pink lines appear in the line box. The first line is like, "Congratulations, it's urine," and the second line is like, "Congratulations, there's a baby in it!"

This was not at all what I was expecting and also exactly what I was expecting.

My "boyfriend" at the time (let's call him Mike) was an emotionally withholding, conventionally attractive jock whose sole metric for expressing affection was the number of hours he spent sitting platonically next to me in coffee shops and bars without ever, ever touching me. To be fair, by that metric he liked me a lot. Despite having nearly nothing in common (his top interests included cross-country running, fantasy cross-country running [he invented it], New England the place, New England the idea, and going outside on Saint Patrick's Day; mine were candy, naps, hugging, and wizards), we spent a staggering amount of time together—I suppose because we were both lonely and smart, and, on my part, because he was the first human I'd ever met who was interested in touching my butt without keeping me sequestered in a moldy basement, and I was going to hold this relationship together if it killed me.

Mike had only been in "official" relationships with thin women, but all his friends teased him for perpetually hooking up with fat chicks. Every few months he would get wasted and hold my hand, or tell me I was beautiful, and the first time I tried to leave him, he followed me home and said he loved me, weeping, on my doorstep. The next day, I told him I loved him, too, and it was true for both of us, probably, but it was a shallow, watery love—born of repetition and resignation. It condensed on us like dew, only because we waited long enough. But "I have grown accustomed to you because I have no one else" is not the same as "Please tell me more about your thoughts on the upcoming NESCAC cross-country season, my king."

It was no kind of relationship, but, at age twenty-seven, it was still the best relationship I'd ever had, so I set my jaw and attempted to sculpt myself into the kind of golem who was fascinated by the 10k finishing times of someone who still called me his "friend" when he talked to his mom. It wasn't fair to him either—he was clear about his parameters from the beginning (he pretty much told me: "I am emotionally withdrawn and can only offer you two to three big spoons per annum"), but I pressed myself against those parameters and strained and pushed until he and I were both exhausted. I thought, at the time, that love was perseverance.

I'm not sure how I got pregnant—we were careful, mostly—but, I don't know, sometimes people just fuck up. I honestly don't remember. Life is life. If I had carried that pregnancy to term and made a half-Mike/half-me human baby, we may have been bound to each other forever, but we would have split up long before the birth. Some people should not be together, and once the stakes are real and kicking and pressing down on your bladder, you can't just pretend shit's fine anymore. Mike made me feel lonely, and being alone with another person is much worse than being alone all by yourself.

I imagine he would have softened, and loved the baby; we would share custody amicably; maybe I'd move into my parents' basement (it's nice!) and get a job writing technical case studies at Microsoft, my side gig at the time; maybe he'd just throw child support at me and move away, but I doubt it. He was a good guy. It could have been a good life.

He didn't want to be in Seattle, though—New England pulled at his guts like a tractor beam. It was all he talked about: flying down running trails at peak foliage; flirting with Amherst girls in Brattleboro bars; keeping one foot always on base, in his glory days, when he was happy and thrumming with potential. He wanted to get back there. Though it hurt me at the time (why wasn't I as good as running around in circles in Vermont and sharing growlers of IPA with girls named Blair!?), I wanted that for him too.

As for me, I found out I was pregnant with the part-Mike fetus just three months before I figured out how to stop hating my body for good, five months before I got my first e-mail from a fat girl saying my writing had saved her life, six months before I fell in love with my future husband, eight months before I met my stepdaughters, a year before I moved to Los Angeles to see what the world had for me, eighteen months before I started working at *Jezebel,* three years before the first time I went on television, four years and ten months before I got married to the best person I've ever met, and just over five years before I turned in this book manuscript.

Everything happened in those five years after my abortion. I became myself. Not by chance, or because an abortion is some mysterious, empowering feminist bloode-magick rite of passage (as many, many—*too many for a movement ostensibly comprising grown-ups*—anti-choicers have accused me of believing), but simply because it was time. A whole bunch of changes—set into motion years, even decades, back—all came together at once, like the tumblers in a lock clicking into place: my body, my work, my voice, my confidence, my power, my determination to demand a life as potent, vibrant, public, and complex as any man's. My abortion wasn't intrinsically significant, but it was my first big grown-up decision—the first time I asserted, unequivocally, "I know the life that I want and this isn't it"; the moment I stopped being a passenger in my own body and grabbed the rudder.

So, I peed on the thingy and those little pink lines showed up all, "LOL hope u have $600, u fertile betch," and I sat down on my bed and I didn't cry and I said, "Okay, so this is the part of my life when this happens." I didn't tell Mike; I'm not sure why. I have the faintest whiff of a memory that I thought he would be mad at me. Like getting pregnant was my fault—as though my clinginess, my desperate need to be loved, my insistence that we were a "real" couple and not two acquaintances who had grown kind of used to each other, had finally congealed into a hopeful, delusional little bundle and sunk its roots into my uterine wall. A physical manifestation of how pathetic I was. How could I have let that happen? It was so embarrassing. I couldn't tell him. I always felt alone in the relationship anyway; it made sense that I would deal with this alone too.

It didn't occur to me, at the time, that there was anything complicated about obtaining an abortion. This is a trapping of privilege: I grew up middle-class and white in Seattle, I had always had insurance, and, besides, abortion was legal. So, I did what I always did when I needed a common, legal, routine medical procedure—I made an appointment to see my doctor, the same doctor I'd had since I was twelve. She would get this whole implanted embryo mix-up sorted out.

The nurse called my name, showed me in, weighed

me, tutted about it, took my blood pressure, looked surprised (fat people can have normal blood, NANCY), and told me to sit on the paper. I waited. My doctor came in. She's older than me, with dark, tightly curled hair, motherly without being overly familiar. "I think I'm pregnant," I said. "Do you want to be pregnant?" she said. "No," I said. "Well, pee in this cup," she said. I peed all over my hand again. "You're pregnant," she said. I nodded, feeling nothing.

I remember being real proud of my chill 'tude in that moment. I was the Fonz of getting abortions. "So, what's the game plan, Doc?" I asked, popping the collar of my leather jacket like somebody who probably skateboarded here. "Why don't you go ahead and slip me that RU-486 prescriptsch and I'll just [moonwalks toward exam room door while playing the saxophone]."

She stared at me.

"What?" I said, one hundred combs clattering to the floor.

Turns out, THE DOCTOR IS NOT WHERE YOU GET AN ABORTION.

I'd been so sure I could get this taken care of today, handle it today, on my own, and move on with my life— go back to pretending like I had my shit together and my relationship was bearable, even good. Like I was a normal woman that normal men loved. When she told me I had to make an appointment at a different clinic, which probably didn't have any openings for a couple of weeks, and started writing down phone numbers on a Post-it, I crumpled.

"That's stupid," I sobbed, my anxiety getting the better of me. "You're a doctor. This is a doctor's office. Do you not know how to do it?"

"I covered it in medical school, yes," she said, looking concerned in an annoyingly kind way, "but we don't do them here at this clinic."

"Well, why did I even come here, then? Why didn't they tell me on the phone that this appointment was pointless?"

"You want reception to tell everyone who calls in that we don't do abortions here, no matter what they're calling about?"

"YES," I yelled.

She didn't say anything. I heaved and cried a little bit more, then a little bit less, in the silence.

"Is there anything else I can do for you right now?" she asked, gently.

"No, I'm fine." I accepted a tissue. "I'm sorry I got upset."

"It's okay. This is a stressful situation. I know." She squeezed my shoulder.

I went home, curled up in bed, and called the clinic (which had some vague, mauve, nighttime soap name like "Avalon" or "Dynasty" or "Falcon Crest"), still wobbling on the edge of hysteria. Not for all the reasons the forced-birth fanatics would like you to think: not because my choice was morally torturous, or because I was ashamed, or because I couldn't stop thinking about the tiny fingernails of our "baby," but because life is fucking hard, man. I wanted someone to love me so much. I did want a baby, eventually. But what I really wanted was a family. Mike wasn't my family. Everything was wrong. I was alone and I was sad and it was just hard.

The woman on the phone told me they could fit me in the following week, and it would be $400 after insurance. It was the beginning of the month, so I had just paid rent. I had about $100 left in my bank account. Payday was in two weeks.

"Can you bill me?" I asked.

"No, we require full payment the day of procedure," she said, brusque from routine but not unkind.

I felt like a stripped wire. My head buzzed and my eyes welled.

"But...I don't have that."

"We can push back the appointment if you need more time to get your funds together," she offered.

"But," I said, finally breaking, "'I can't be pregnant anymore. I need to not be pregnant. I'm not supposed to be pregnant.'"

I didn't want to wait two more weeks. I didn't want to think about this every day. I didn't want to feel my body change. I didn't want to carry and feed this artifact of my inherent unlovability—this physical proof that any permanent connection to me must be an accident. Men made wanted babies with beautiful women. Men made mistakes with fat chicks. I sobbed so hard I think she was terrified. I sobbed so hard she went to get her boss.

The head of the clinic picked up the phone. She talked to me in a calm, competent voice—like an important businesswoman who is also your mom, which is probably fairly accurate. She talked to me until I started breathing again. She didn't have to. She must have been so busy, and I was wasting her time with my tantrum. Babies having babies.

"We never do this," she sighed, "because typically, once the procedure is done, people don't come back. But if you promise me you'll pay your bill—if you really promise—you can come in next week and we can bill you after the procedure."

I promised, I promised, I promised so hard. Yes, oh my god, yes. Thank you so much. Thank you. Thank you! (And I did pay—as soon as my next paycheck came in. They were so surprised, they sent me a thank-you card.)

I like to think the woman who ran the clinic would have done that for anyone—that there's a quiet web of women like her (like us, I flatter myself), stretching from pole to pole, ready to give other women a hand. She helped me even though she didn't have to, and I am forever grateful. But I also wonder what made me sound, to her ears, like someone worth trusting, someone it was safe to take a chance on. I certainly wasn't the neediest person calling her clinic. The fact is, I was getting that abortion no matter what. All I had to do was wait two weeks, or have an awkward conversation I did not want to have with my supportive, liberal, well-to-do mother. Privilege means that it's easy for white women to do each other favors. Privilege means that those of us who need it the least often get the most help.

I don't remember much about the appointment itself. I went in, filled out some stuff on a clipboard, and waited to be called. I remember the waiting room was crowded. Everyone else had somebody with them; none of us made eye contact. I recognized the woman working the front desk—we went to high school together (which should be illegal)*—but she didn't say anything. Maybe that's protocol at the vagina clinic, I thought. Or maybe I just wasn't that memorable as a teenager. Goddammit.

Before we got down to business, I had to talk to a counselor, I guess to make sure I wasn't just looking for one of those cavalier partybortions that the religious right is always getting its sackcloth in a bunch over. (Even though, by the way, those are legal too.) She was younger than me, and sweet. She asked me why I hadn't told my "partner," and I cried because he wasn't a partner at all and I still didn't know why I hadn't told him. Everything after that is vague. I think there was a blood test and maybe an ultrasound. The doctor, a brisk, reassuring woman with

---

* Same goes for you, dildo store cashier. (But thank you for the discount.)

gray hair in an almost military buzz cut, told me my embryo was about three weeks old, like a tadpole. Then she gave me two pills in a little cardboard billfold and told me to come back in two weeks. The accompanying pamphlet warned that, after I took the second pill, chunks "the size of lemons" might come out. LEMONS. Imagine if we, as a culture, actually talked frankly and openly about abortion. Imagine if people seeking abortions didn't have to be blindsided by the possibility of blood lemons falling out of their vaginas via a pink photocopied flyer. Imagine.

That night, after taking my first pill, as my tadpole detached from the uterine wall, I had to go give a filmmaking prize to my friend and colleague Charles Mudede— make a speech on a stage in front of everyone I knew, at the Genius Awards, the *Stranger*'s annual arts grant. It was surreal. Mike and I went together. We had fun—one of our best nights. There are pictures. I'm glassy-eyed, smiling too big, running on fumes and gallows humor. I remember pulling a friend into a dark corner and confessing that I had an abortion that day. "Did they tell you the thing about the lemons?" she asked. I nodded. "Don't worry," she whispered, hugging me tight. "There aren't going to be lemons."

She paused.

"Probably no lemons."

Afterwards, Mike didn't want to stay over at my place because he had to get up early to go to his high school reunion. That was fine. (It wasn't.) I've got some uterine lining to shed, bozo. I tried to drop him off Fonz-style, but he could tell I was being weird. It's hard to keep secrets from people you love, even when your love isn't that great.

"What's going on?" he said, as we sat in my quietly humming Volvo in the alley behind his house.

"I can't tell you," I said, starting to cry.

There was silence, for a minute.

"Did you have an abortion?" he said.

"Today," I said.

He cried too—not out of regret or some moral crisis, but because I'd felt like I had to keep this a secret from him. We were just so bad at being together. He felt as guilty as I felt pathetic, and it made us closer, for a while.

He still went to his reunion the next day, and he didn't text enough, and I cried a little. I lay in bed all day and ached. No lemons came out. It was like a bad period. The day after that, I felt a little better, and the day after that was almost normal. I wasn't pregnant anymore. But instead of going back to our old routine—him running, me chasing—something had shifted inside me. Within six months, we were broken up for good. Within seven months, I wasn't mad at him anymore. Within a year, he moved back east. He was a good guy.

I hesitate to tell this story, not because I regret my abortion or I buy into the right-wing narrative that pregnancy is god's punishment for disobedient women, but because it's so easy for an explanation to sound like a justification. The truth is that I don't give a damn why anyone has an abortion. I believe unconditionally in the right of people with uteruses to decide what grows inside of their body and feeds on their blood and endangers their life and reroutes their future. There are no "good" abortions and "bad" abortions, there are only pregnant people who want them and pregnant people who don't, pregnant people who have access and support and pregnant people who face institutional roadblocks and lies.

For that reason, we simply must talk about it. The fact that abortion is still a taboo subject means that opponents of abortion get to define it however suits them best. They can cast those of us who have had abortions as callous monstrosities, and seed fear in anyone who might need one by insisting that the procedure is always traumatic, always painful, always an impossible decision. Well, we're not, and it's not. The truth is that life is unfathomably complex, and every abortion story is as unique as the person who lives it. Some are traumatic, some are even regretted, but plenty are like mine.

Paradoxically, one of the primary reasons I am so determined to tell my abortion story is that my abortion simply wasn't that interesting. If it weren't for the zealous high school youth-groupers and repulsive, birth-obsessed pastors flooding the public discourse with mangled fetus photos and crocodile tears—and, more significantly, trying to strip reproductive rights away from our country's most vulnerable communities—I would never think about my abortion at all. It was, more than anything else, mundane: a medical procedure that made my life better, like the time I had oral surgery because my wisdom tooth went evil-dead and murdered the tooth next to it. Or when a sinus infection left me with a buildup of earwax so I had to pour stool softener into my ear and have an otolaryngologist suck it out with a tiny vacuum, during which he told me that I had "slender ear canals," which I found flattering. (Call me, Dr. Yang!)

It was like those, but also not like those. It was a big deal, and it wasn't. My abortion was a normal medical procedure that got tangled up in my bad relationship, my internalized fatphobia, my fear of adulthood, my discomfort with talking about sex; and one that, because of our culture's obsession with punishing female sexuality and shackling women to the nursery and the kitchen, I was socialized to approach with shame and describe only in whispers. But the procedure itself was the easiest part. Not being able to have one would have been the real trauma.

You're So Brave for Wearing Clothes and Not Hating Yourself!

Probably the question I get most often (aside from "Why won't you go on Joe Rogan's podcast to debate why rape is bad with five amateur MMA fighters in a small closet?") is "Where do you get your confidence?"

"Where do you get your confidence?" is a complex, dangerous question. First of all, if you are a thin person, please do not go around asking fat people where they got their confidence in the same tone you'd ask a shark how it learned to breathe air and manage an Orange Julius.

As a woman, my body is scrutinized, policed, and treated as a public commodity. As a fat woman, my body is also lampooned, openly reviled, and associated with moral and intellectual failure. My body limits my job prospects, access to medical care and fair trials, and—the one thing Hollywood movies and Internet trolls most agree on—my ability to be loved. So the subtext, when a thin person asks a fat person, "Where do you get your confidence?" is, "You must be some sort of alien because if I looked like you, I would definitely throw myself into the sea." I'm not saying there's no graceful way to commiserate about self-image and body hate across size-privilege lines—solidarity with other women is one of my drugs of choice—but please tread lightly.

Second of all, to actually answer the question, my relationship with my own confidence has always been strange. I am profoundly grateful to say that I have never felt inherently worthless. Any self-esteem issues I've had were externally applied—people *told me* I was ugly, revolting, shameful, unacceptably large. The world around me simply insisted on it, no matter what my gut said. I used to describe it as "reverse body dysmorphia": When I looked in the mirror, I could never understand what was supposedly so disgusting. I knew I was smart, funny, talented, social, kind—why wasn't that enough? By all the metrics I cared about, I was a home run.

So my reaction to my own fatness manifested outwardly instead of inwardly—as resentment, anger, a feeling of deep injustice, of being cheated. I wasn't intrinsically without value, I was just doomed to live in a culture that hated me. For me, the process of embodying confidence was less about convincing myself of my own worth and more about rejecting and unlearning what society had hammered into me.

Honestly, this "Where do you get your confidence?" chapter could be sixteen words long. Because there was really only one step to my body acceptance: Look at pictures of fat women on the Internet until they don't make you uncomfortable anymore. That was the entire process. (Optional step two: Wear a crop top until you forget you're wearing a crop top. Suddenly, a crop top is just a top. Repeat.)

It took me a while to put my foot on that step, though. So let me back up.

The first time I ever called myself fat, in conversation with another person, was in my sophomore year of college. My roommate, Beth—with whom I had that kind of platonically infatuated, resplendent, despairing, borderline codependent friendship unique to young women— had finally convinced me to tell her who I had a crush on, and didn't understand why the admission came with a Nile of tears. I couldn't bear to answer her out loud, so we IMed in silence from opposite corners of our dorm room. "You don't understand," I wrote, gulping. "You count."

Beth is one of those bright, brilliant lodestones who pulls people into her orbit with a seemingly supernatural inevitability. She wore high heels to class, she was a salsa dancer and a soprano, she could change the oil in a truck and field dress a deer, she got Distinction on our English comps even though she and I only started studying two days before (I merely passed), and she could take your hands and stare into your face and make you feel like you were the only person in the world. It seems like I spent half my college life wrangling the queue of desperate, weeping suitors who'd "never felt like this before," who were convinced (with zero input from her) that Beth was *the one.*

She regularly received anonymous flower deliveries: tumbling bouquets of yellow roses and trailing greens, with rhapsodic love letters attached. She once mentioned, offhand on the quad, that she wanted one of those Leatherman multi-tools, and a few days later one appeared, sans note, in her campus mailbox. In retrospect, these years were a nonstop, fucked-up carnivale of male entitlement (the anonymous Leatherman was particularly creepy, the subtext being "I'm watching you"), one young man after another endowing Beth with whatever cocktail of magic dream-girl qualities he was sure would "complete" him, and laboring under the old lie that wearing a girl down is "seduction." At the time, though, we laughed it off. Meanwhile, alone in my bed at night, the certainty that I was failing as a woman pressed down on me like a quilt.

I was the girl kids would point to on the playground and say, "She's your girlfriend," to gross out the boys. No one had ever sent me flowers, or asked me on a date, or written me a love letter (Beth literally had "a box" where she "kept them"), or professed their shallow, impetuous love for me, or flirted with me, or held my hand, or bought me a drink, or kissed me (except for that dude at that party freshman year who was basically an indiscriminate roving tongue), or invited me to participate in any of the myriad romantic rites of passage that I'd always been told were part of normal teenage development. No one had *ever picked me*. Literally no one. The cumulative result was worse than loneliness: I felt unnatural. Broken. It wasn't fair.

"You will always be worth more than me, no matter what I do," I told Beth, furious tears splashing on my Formica desk. "I will always be alone. I'm fat. I'm not stupid. I know how the world works."

"Oh, no," she said. "I wish you could see yourself the way I see you."

I resented her certainty; I thought she didn't understand. But she was just ahead of me.

The first time I ever wrote a fat-positive sentence in the newspaper (or said a fat-positive sentence out loud, really) was four years later, in December 2006 in my review of the movie *Dreamgirls* for the *Stranger*:

"I realize that Jennifer Hudson is kind of a superchunk, but you kind of don't mind looking at her, and that kind of makes you feel good about yourself. But... fat people don't need your pity."

It was early enough in my career (and before the Internet was just a 24/7 intrusion machine) that my readers hadn't yet sniffed out what I looked like, and coming this close to self-identifying as fat left me chattering with anxiety all day. My editor knew what I looked like. Would she notice I was fat now? Would we have to have a talk where she gave me sad eyes and squeezed my arm and smiled sympathetically about my "problem"? Because I *just said* fat people don't need your pity.

Of course she never mentioned it. I don't know if she even picked up on it—if she turned my body over in her head as she read that sentence. She probably didn't. I didn't know it at the time, but the idea of "coming out" as fat comes up a lot in fat-acceptance circles. I always thought that if I just never, ever acknowledged it—never wore a bathing suit, never objected to a fat joke on TV, stuck to "flattering" clothes, never said the word "fat" out loud—then maybe people wouldn't notice. Maybe I could pass as thin, or at least obedient. But, I was slowly learning, you can't advocate for yourself if you won't admit what you are.

At the same time, I was blazingly proud that I'd stuck that sentiment in my *Dreamgirls* review—right there in the opening paragraph, where it couldn't be missed. It was exhilarating to finally express something (even in the most oblique way possible) that I'd been desperately hiding for so long. From a rhetorical standpoint, it tidily expressed a few complex concepts at once: Fat people are not here as a foil to boost your own self-esteem. Fat people are not your inspiration porn. Fat people can be competent, beautiful, talented, and proud without your approval.

Not a ton had changed in my self-conception since that conversation with Beth. I had finally found someone to flirt and have sex with, but he wouldn't be seen on the street with me or call me his girlfriend. He also believed in Sasquatch, wore a T-shirt that said, "I'm the drunken Irishman your mother warned you about," and eventually dumped me for someone irritatingly named Mindy. We then had a screaming fight, which culminated in him attempting to "slam" the door in my face with a flourish, except he lived in a dank basement accessed via a garage and could only emphatically push the garage door button and stand there glaring as it *"whirrrrrrrrrrrrrrrrrrrrrr"*ed to the ground in slow motion. My cabdriver hit on me while I sobbed, and a small voice inside reminded me I should be flattered.

Lots of men wanted to have sex with me—I dated casually, I got texts in the night—they just didn't want to go to a restaurant with me, or bring me to their office party, or open Christmas presents with me. It would have been relatively simple to swallow the idea that I was objectively sexually undesirable, but the truth was more painful: There was something about me that was *symbolically shameful*. It's not that men didn't like me; it's that they hated themselves for doing so. But why?

The question, "Why am I like this?" gnawed at me.

The media tells me that I'm fat because a weird sandwich exists somewhere with Krispy Kreme donuts instead of buns. But I'm sure that's not it. I would definitely remember eating that sandwich. Internet trolls tell me I'm fat because I eat lard out of a bucket for dinner, which would be a weird thing to do, and use a Toblerone for a dildo, which really isn't an efficient way to ingest calories at all. The fact is that I'm fat because life is a snarl of physical, emotional, and cultural forces both in and out of my control. I'm fat because life is life.

Like most fat people who've been lectured about diet and exercise since childhood, I actually know an inordinate amount about nutrition and fitness. The number of nutrition classes and hospital-sponsored weight loss programs and individual dietician consultations and tear-filled therapy sessions I've poured money into over the years makes me grind my teeth. (Do you know how many Jet Skis I could have bought with that money? *One Jet Skis!!!*) I can rattle off how many calories are in a banana or an egg or six almonds or a Lean Cuisine Santa Fe–Style Rice and Beans. I know the difference between spelt bread and Ezekiel bread, and I know that lemon juice makes a great "sauce"! I could teach you the proper form for squats and lunges and kettle bell swings, if you want. I can diagnose your shin splints. I can correct your jump shot.

I never did manage to lose weight, though—not significantly—and my minor "successes" weren't through any eating patterns that could be considered "normal." The level of restriction that I was told, by professionals, was necessary for me to "fix" my body essentially precluded any semblance of joyous, fulfilling human life.

It was about learning to live with hunger—with feeling "light," I remember my nutritionist calling it—or filling your body with chia seeds and this miracle supplement that expanded into a bulky viscous gel in your stomach. If you absolutely had to have food in between breakfast at seven a.m. and lunch at one p.m., try six almonds* and if you've already had your daily almond allotment, try an apple. So crisp. So filling. Then everyone in nutrition class would nod about how fresh and satisfying it is to just eat an apple.

One day, during the Apple Appreciation Circle-Jerk Jamboree, the only other fat person in the class (literally everyone else was an affluent suburban mom trying to lose her last four pounds of baby weight) raised his hand and mentioned, sheepishly, that he sometimes felt nauseated after eating an apple, a weird phenomenon I was struggling with as well. What was that all about? Was there any way to fix it? The nutritionist told us she'd recently read a study about how some enzyme in apples caused nausea in people with some *other* elevated enzyme that became elevated when a person was fat for a long time. So, basically, if we fatties wanted to be able to eat

---

* "Six almonds."—All diet advice.

apples again, nausea-free, then we'd really need to double down on the only-eating-apples diet. The only real cure for fatness was to go back in time and not get fat in the first place. I started to cry and then I started to laugh. What the fuck kind of a life was this?

Around that time, just when I needed it, Leonard Nimoy's *Full Body Project* came to me like a gift. The photographs are in black and white, and they feature a group of fat, naked women laughing, smiling, embracing, gazing fearlessly into the camera. In one, they sway indolently like the Three Graces; in another they re-create Herb Ritts's iconic pile of supermodels. It was the first time I'd ever seen fat women presented without scorn.

I clicked, I skimmed, I shrugged, I clicked away.

I clicked back.

I was ragingly uncomfortable. *Don't they know those things are supposed to stay hidden?* I haven't been having basement sex with the lights off all these years so you could go show what our belly buttons look like!

At the same time, I felt something start to unclench deep inside me. What if my body didn't have to be a secret? What if I was wrong all along—what if this was all a magic trick, and I could just *decide I was valuable* and it would be true? Why, instead, had I left that decision in the hands of strangers who hated me? Denying people access to value is an incredibly insidious form of emotional violence, one that our culture wields aggressively and liberally to keep marginalized groups small and quiet. What if you could opt out of the game altogether? I paused and considered. When the nutrition teacher e-mailed, I didn't sign up for the next session of Almond Gulag.

I couldn't stop looking. It was literally the first time in my life that I'd seen bodies like mine honored instead of lampooned, presented with dignity instead of scorn, displayed as objects of beauty instead of as punch lines. It was such a simple maneuver, but so profound. Nimoy said, of his models, "I asked them to be proud." For the first time it struck me that it was possible to be proud of my body, not just in spite of it. Not only that, but my bigness is powerful.

I hate being fat. I hate the way people look at me, or don't. I hate being a joke; I hate the disorienting limbo between too visible and invisible; I hate the way that complete strangers waste my life out of supposed concern for my death. I hate knowing that if I did die of a condition that correlates with weight, a certain subset of people would feel their prejudices validated, and some would outright celebrate.

I also love being fat. The breadth of my shoulders makes me feel safe. I am unassailable. I intimidate. I am a polar icebreaker. I walk and climb and lift things, I can open your jar, I can absorb blows—literal and metaphorical—meant for other women, smaller women, breakable women, women who need me. My bones feel like iron—heavy, but strong. I used to say that being fat in our culture was like drowning (in hate, in blame, in your own tissue), but lately I think it's more like burning. After three decades in the fire, my iron bones are steel.

Maybe you are thin. You hiked that trail and you are fit and beautiful and wanted and I am so proud of you, I am so in awe of your wiry brightness; and I'm miles behind you, my breathing ragged. But you didn't carry this up the mountain. You only carried yourself. How hard would you breathe if you had to carry me? You couldn't. But I can.

I was hooked. Late at night, I started furtively clicking through fat-positive tags on Tumblr like a Mormon teen looking at Internet porn. Studies have shown that visual exposure to certain body types actually changes people's perception of those bodies—in other words, looking at pictures of fat people makes you like fat people more. (Eternal reminder: Representation matters.)

I discovered a photo blog called *"Hey, Fat Chick"* (now, crushingly, defunct) run by an effervescent Australian angel named Frances Lockie, and pored over it nightly like a jeweler or a surgeon or a codebreaker. It was pure, unburdened joy, and so simple: Just fat women—some bigger than me, some smaller—wearing outfits and doing things and smiling. Having lives. That's it. They were like medicine. One by one they loosened my knots.

First, I stopped reacting with knee-jerk embarrassment at the brazenness of their bodies, the way I'd been trained. I stopped feeling obscene, exposed, like someone had ripped the veil off my worst secrets.

Next, they became ordinary. Mundane. Neutral. Their thick thighs and sagging bellies were just bodies, like any other. Their lives were just lives, like any other. Like mine.

Then, one day, they were beautiful. I wanted to look and be like them—I wanted to spill out of a crop top; plant a flag in a mountain of lingerie; alienate small, bitter men who dared to presume that women exist for their consumption; lay bare the cowardice in recoiling at something as *literally fundamental* as a woman's real body. I wasn't unnatural after all; the cultural attitude that taught me so was the real abomination. My body, I realized, was an opportunity. It was political. It moved the world just by existing. What a gift.

The Red Tent

In August of 2010, the *Stranger* got an e-mail from an organization called "Vashon Red Tent," advertising that "A Red Tent Temple Sisterhood Is Coming to Vashon." Vashon is an island, accessible by ferry from Seattle, mainly populated by NIMBY-ish hippies, NIMBY-ish yuppies, boutique farmers, and wizards riding recumbent bicycles. A full quarter of the children in Vashon schools are unvaccinated. The "Red Tent Temple Movement," the press release read, "envisions a gathering honoring our stories and promoting healing in every town across the country where women of all ages meet regularly to support one another and monthly menstrual cycles."

The only thing I knew about Anita Diamant's novel *The Red Tent*, which inspired the movement, was that one time my college roommate read it and then announced to the rest of us that she wanted to go "bleed into the forest." It didn't feel like a good sign. This event, clearly, was my worst nightmare. The paper, clearly, RSVPed for me immediately.

I dragged my friend Jenny along with me, and we barely made the ferry. On the bench next to us there was a woman with long frizzy hair and high-waisted jeans. She was wearing a T-shirt with a picture of cats in sunglasses playing saxophones, and above the picture it said, "JAZZ CATS." "There are a lot of different ways to be a woman," I wrote in my notebook. Jenny and I were running late for menses tent, but we stopped by the grocery store anyway to buy some boxed wine and anxiety jelly beans. We sat in the parking lot and wolfed beans and got as tipsy as we could in the time allotted.

My sister is into this sort of thing. She loves ritual. She's forever collecting shells for her Venus altar, or tying a piece of ribbon to a twig in a secret grove, or scooping magic waters up into very small vials to make potions. Being around my sister feels magical. When we traveled through Europe together (following the path of Mary Magdalene, doyeeeee), we didn't miss a stone circle or a magic well—tromping over stiles and up tors and always leaving little offerings for the fairies. Once, in Cornwall, we looked down into an aquamarine cove and she said, "Do you see the mermaids? They're sitting on that rock." I said no, and she looked at me with pity. On the way to the Vashon Red Tent Temple, I texted my sister for advice. "I'm on my way to a new moon celebration at a menses temple," I said. "Liar," she said. "It's true! Any tips?" "Stay open to a new flow and wave good-bye to the blood of old that nurtured you well." I knew she'd know what to do.

I almost didn't go in. It was too intimate and foreign, and I am clinical like my mom. I like magic *as escapism*—I barely tolerate fantasy books set in our universe (the first time I cracked a Harry Potter novel I was like, "Yo, is this a documentary?")—pretending that the supernatural is real just drives home how much it's not. But we did, we walked in, removed our shoes, and joined the circle of women seated on pillows beneath the homemade canopy of red scarves. It wasn't really a "tent" so much as a pillow fort inside a community center, but it did the job.

The women were talking about chocolate, which was such an adorable cliché that I fell in love with them instantly. "There is *definitely* a goddess of chocolate." "I read somewhere that the molecular makeup of chocolate is so unique that it was probably brought here from another planet." One woman passed a Hershey's bar around the circle. "This chocolate is even better now that it's passed through the hands of so many goddesses," said the woman next to me, appreciatively.

There was chanting.

Isla, the leader of the circle, said that right now there is an astrological configuration—the Cardinal Cross—that has not occurred since Jesus was alive, and that she and the other local angel healers are very busy "holding that energy." She explained that the media tells us that things are terrible and violent, but that this is actually one of the most peaceful times in history. We should not focus on the negative. Later, I asked my sister what an "angel healer" is, and she said, "Well, you know, angels are just the same thing as aliens. They're probably the ones who brought the chocolate." I asked about the Cardinal Cross, and she told me, "If you're going to have a baby, have it like tomorrow. It'll be a superbaby. Dude, remind me to send you a picture of the cosmos right now. It's fucking out of control."

We went around the circle and stated our "intentions" for the coming moon cycle. Most of the women had intentions that I didn't understand, that involved "manifesting" and "balance" and "rhythm." One woman said that her intention was to "end rape." I said I intended to organize my apartment, and felt mundane. The women totally approved. Total approval is the point of menses tent. The press release had promised "a place where young women can ask questions and find mentors in absolute acceptance," and menses tent delivered.

"You look different today," said one woman to another. "Oh, I know," she replied. "It's because I did the twenty-four-strand DNA activation yesterday. I feel like a completely new person." The women around me tittered with excitement. I asked what that meant. She explained that in addition to our two physical DNA strands, we have twenty-two spiritual DNA strands, which can be "activated" by a specially trained lady with a crystal wand.

The process took ten hours. "There's also a golden gate that you can walk through," she said, "but that's more for larger groups." Then another woman explained that DNA activation has something to do with the Mayan calendar. I still didn't understand. My sister didn't know anything about DNA activation, but she did tell me a story about the time she went to see a shaman and the shaman had a spirit jaguar eat a ghost off her back. That sounded cooler than the DNA thing.

Jenny and I thanked our hostesses and hobbled out to the car, thighs asleep and buzzing with pain after hours of sitting cross-legged on pillows. We ate some more jelly beans and talked about our feelings.

It's true that I don't believe in most of this stuff—and I suspect that believing is the secret ingredient that makes this stuff work. But it *does* work for the gracious ladies on the pillows under the red tent, and it was surprisingly nurturing to sit cross-legged in their world for a few hours. And even though I would never phrase it like this, I agree that women don't always get a chance to "fill our own vessels." My dad worked all day. My mom worked all day, then came home and made dinner. Women do a lot. Women are neat.

Back at the office, I knew my job was to make fun of menses tent, but I just didn't want to. They were so nice and so earnest. What was the point of hurting them? Sincerity is an easy target, but I don't want to excise sincerity from my life—that's a lonely way to live.

I used to try to be cool. I said things that I didn't believe about other people, and celebrities, and myself; I wrote mean jokes for cheap, "edgy" laughs; I neglected good friendships for shallow ones; I insisted I wasn't a feminist; I nodded along with casual misogyny in hopes that shitty dudes would like me.

I thought I was immune to its woo-woo power, but if it hadn't been for menses tent, how long would it have taken me to understand that I get to choose what kind of person to be? Open or closed? Generous or cruel? Spirit jaguar or clinging ghost? A lazy writer (it's easy to hate things) or a versatile one? I don't believe in an afterlife. We live and then we stop living. We exist and then we stop existing. That means I only get one chance to do a good job. I want to do a good job.

Hello, I Am Fat

In 2009, I'd been at the *Stranger* about five years (four as a freelancer, one on staff), and was casually dating a dude who refused to kiss me on the mouth. He's a good person; he was good to me in other ways. They all were, really—even Sasquatch garage door guy—but, you know, we were all raised in the same fucking septic tank. No one teaches young men how to take care of fat girls.

The *Stranger* is the best thing that's ever happened to me. I got to learn how to write and run a newspaper from geniuses (David Schmader, Charles Mudede, Eli Sanders) I'd been obsessed with since I was a teen—we took chances, changed elections, ran our sections with nearly unfettered editorial freedom, and struck a balance between ethics and irreverence that I was always proud of. By the time I got on staff full-time, Dan Savage was already medium-famous and had orchestrated a more-power/less-responsibility promotion from editor in chief to editorial director, so he wasn't in the office so much. Nonetheless, the culture of the place was all Dan, and even mostly in absentia he did the hell out of that job.

Dan would run a meeting every few weeks, always our most productive and most boisterous; be gone traveling for months and then show up at a candidate interview to grill local politicians with the acuity of a day-to-day city hall reporter; emerge from his office like a groundhog to drop an infuriatingly brilliant mandate about precisely how to tweak whatever delicate story was stumping us; and send insistent e-mails the morning after every office party to ensure surplus sheet cake was placed, uncovered, on his desk. (Dan has a thing about stale cake.) I was taught a mantra, my first week, to manage my expectations about Dan as an editor: "Silence is praise." As long as you don't know he exists, you're killing it. I remember two editors improvising an extensive, Dan-themed Gilbert and Sullivan musical number over their cubicle walls: "I will laugh at you when you cry!" Dan, the great and terrible.

If his management approach is unique, Dan's editorial sense—for clear-headed satire and gleeful, pointed disobedience, for where to aim and from what angle to drop the hammer—is unparalleled in my decade of writing experience. Dan knows how to land a point better than anyone I've ever worked with. That preternatural ability is what has made him famous (he is a magnificent pundit), and it's also what gets him into trouble.

Like all of us, Dan fucks up. Like all of us, he is some-times slow to find the right side of an issue. And when he has an opinion on something, he expresses it in vivid, uncompromising prose to a rapt audience of millions—over and over and over again, because he is as prolific as he is stubborn. He also, like all of us, can be intracta-ble and defensive when criticized, and because he is very funny and very smart, he can also be very snide, and when such a person does actually happen to be wrong, but mistakes totally warranted criticism for petty sniping, and responds not with openness but with sneering acidity to a critic who is just trying to advocate for their own humanity, it can be a very bad look.

This is the great curse of popularity and the great luxury of obscurity: People only care about your mistakes when they can hear you. Only failures can afford to be cavalier and careless.

Unfortunately for my personal emotional cankers, in the mid-to-late aughts Dan was on something of an "obe-sity epidemic" kick. He wasn't alone. At the same time that I was tentatively opening to the idea that my human-ity was not hostage to my BMI, the rest of the nation had declared a "war on obesity." They'd whipped up a host of reasons why it was right and good to hate fat people: our repulsive, unsexy bodies, of course (the classic!), but also our drain on the healthcare system, our hogging of plane armrests, our impact on "the children," our pathetic inability and/or monstrous refusal to swap austerity for gluttony (like thin people, who, as you know, are moderate and virtuous in all ways). Oh, and our "health." Because they care. They abuse us for our own good. (Do you know what is actually not a good way to help a group of people, it turns out? Advocating for their eradication.)

Dan was on that train, and I don't blame him—it was a very popular (and, I imagine, gratifying) ticket at the time, and, even more so than today, it was considered very roguish to "tell it like it is" about fat people (as though that wasn't the status quo, as though we hadn't gotten the message). I understand; I had only recently snapped out of some of the same thought patterns myself. I had to learn how to look at pictures of fat people, and I am one.

The problem is, fat people are an extremely suboptimal bogeyman, the roots of America's "obesity epidemic" lying largely in systemic poverty and agribusiness, not in those exploited thereby; the problems with America's fucked-up healthcare system stemming entirely from America's preposterous healthcare system, not from the people attempting to survive within it (and use a service they pay tremendous amounts of money for); new research finding that it's a sedentary lifestyle, not size, that correlates with increased health risks; and fat people turning out to *be people* whose lives are impossibly complex snarls of external and internal forces and who do not, in fact, owe you shit. As Kate Harding and Marianne Kirby wrote in their book *Lessons from the Fat-O-Sphere*, health is not a moral imperative.

However, it is easier to mock and deride individual fat people than to fix food deserts, school lunches, corn subsidies, inadequate or nonexistent public transportation, unsafe sidewalks and parks, healthcare, mental healthcare, the minimum wage, and your own insecurities. So, "personal responsibility" was de rigueur, and my boss was on board.

It was the same bunk you were hearing everywhere around that time—imperious declarations about fat people's delusions and gluttony, soaked in plausible deniability about "health." Dan's main sticking point seemed to be fat people (like me) who insisted we weren't imminently dying—he fiercely and persistently defended his "refusal to take the self-esteem-boosting/public-health-shredding position that you can be obese and healthy."

In one 2004 column, the root of a whole pantload of his fatphobia accusations, Dan got grumpy about women, "particularly obese people," wearing low-rise jeans, and dismissed the impact that stigmatizing language has on young women:

"It's an article of faith that we can't talk about how much crap we're eating—or how awful we look in low-rise jeans—without inducing eating disorders in millions of silly and suggestible young women . . . Our obsession with anorexia . . . not only covers up America's true eating disorder (we eat too much and we're too fat!), but it also hamstrings efforts to combat obesity, a condition that kills almost as many people every year as smoking does. Eating disorders, by way of comparison, lead to only a hand-ful of deaths every year. If you're truly concerned about the health and well-being of young women ... worry more about the skyrocketing rates of obesity-related diseases in young people—like type 2 diabetes—and less about the imaginary link between anorexia and my low opinion of low-rise jeans."

Okay, man. We get it. You are not into those pants.

More than anything, though, this passage from his 2005 book *The Commitment* sums up the overall tone of his stance, at the time, on fatties:

> *Two days later, in a water park in Sioux Falls, South Dakota, I came to a couple of realizations: First, any-one who denies the existence of the obesity epidemic in the United States hasn't been to a water park in Sioux Falls, South Dakota. (The owners of water parks in the U.S. must be saving a fortune on water and chlorine bills; floating in the deep end of the wave pool with D.J., Terry observed that there was an awful lot of water being displaced. If the South Dakotans floating around us all got out of the pool at the same time, the water level would most likely have dropped six feet.)*

We are horrible to look at, we are in the way, we are a joke.

I could probably have dealt with that—after all, it really was coming from all sides—but in an unanticipated side effect, a few perspicacious trolls made the connection between my fat body and Dan's fatphobia. (Comments sections on any post about fatness were their own kind of horror—having my workplace host sentiments such as "I wouldn't fuck with these people. They might sit on you and crush you to death. If they can catch you, of course. Best bet: run uphill, you'll induce a heart attack, and the pursuer might even roll back downhill, taking out the other members of the fat mob" didn't exactly make me feel supported.)

I started to get comments here and there, asking how it felt to know that my boss hated me because of my body. I knew Dan didn't hate me—we had always gotten along, he made me a writer, and sometimes I even earned the vocal kind of praise!—but if that was true, why didn't he give this thing a rest? Why didn't he see that when he wrote about fat people, he was writing about me, Lindy West, his colleague and friend? Why should I, as an employee, have to swallow that kind of treatment at my job—in the same newspaper I was sweating blood into for $36k a year? What's more, what about our fat readers? I knew there were people reading the blog, clocking the fact that I wasn't sticking up for them—as though I was tacitly okay with what Dan was arguing. It implied complicity and self-hatred. Did I want to be the kind of person who didn't fight?

Crop tops, short shorts, no kissing on the mouth, the *whirrrrrrrrrrrrr* of the garage door, Beth's flowers, my perfect bloodwork, the trolls, a year in a basement talking about fucking Sasquatch ("I don't know why they don't just find out what it eats and then go to where that is!"), all of it, a lifetime of it, finally foamed up and spilled over. Something lurched awake inside of me. They talk to you this way until you "come out" as fat. They talk to you this way until you make them stop.

I e-mailed Dan, privately, in November of 2009. In my memory, I asked him to please, please consider his words more carefully before writing about fat people—to remember that we are human beings with complex lives, not disease vectors or animals. I begged him to extend some compassion to the fat people on his staff, and to imagine what it might feel like to read your boss parroting the same cruel words and snide insinuations that have been used to hurt you and hold you back your whole life. I was timid, pleading.

Or, at least, that's how I remember it.

While writing this chapter, I looked up the original exchange, and it turns out that my memory sucks. Here's the actual e-mail that I sent to my actual boss:

To: Dan Savage
Subject: "Hello! Could you lay off the fat people shit?"

Just curious: Who are these hordes of fat people chasing you around insisting that eating pot pies all day is awesome and good for your health? Because, um, I don't believe you. That sounds like a straw man, and

I know "some of your best friends are fat" or whatever, but you sound like a bigot. Also, your (super fucking obvious and regressive) point has been made—everyone in the world already thinks fat people are lazy and gross! WE GET IT. YOU ARE NOT BREAKING NEW GROUND HERE.

And just so you know, on top of the trolls who call me a fat cunty virgin every day of my life, now I also get trolls asking me, "How does it feel to know your boss thinks you're a disgusting cow?" Being fat is its own punishment. I don't give a shit if you think I lie on the couch all day under the Dorito funnel—I'd just rather not be abused on the Internet from inside my own workplace. Just a thought.

Love,

Lindy

Ohhhhh, past self. You are completely nanners. (I mean, let's be honest. I was really popular. I knew they wouldn't fire me.)

Dan's reply was nine words long. He asked, simply, if I'd ever detected any animus from him personally.

"Nope, not at all," I wrote. "Not my point at all, either."

He said he heard me, but I was accusing him of being a bigot—a serious charge against someone exhibiting, by my admission, no animus.

It was a dodge. He was deliberately missing the point.

SO THEN I REALLY WENT FOR IT:

> *Sorry I hurt your feelings?*
>
> *My points again: Being fat is its own punishment. Every day. Fat people know they're fat and that the rest of the world thinks they're disgusting. Have you experienced pop culture recently? You are crusading for a stereotype that is already the majority opinion. Why bother? Why is that interesting? There is no army of fat acceptance warriors poised to overthrow the earth and force-feed you gravy. Don't worry—all the stereotypes about fat people are solidly intact.*
>
> *I'm being sincere here. I don't really think you're a bigot—I just think you're acting like one. This is a really painful thing that I wake up with every morning and go to sleep with every night, AND I'M NOT EVEN THAT FAT.*

Dan never wrote back. We never talked about it in the office.

He couldn't really be mad, could he? The whole ethos of the *Stranger*—an ethos that Dan built—was editorial freedom, thoughtful provocation, and fearless transparency. Dan taught me to be bold and uncompromising, to confront bullshit head-on, to cultivate a powerful voice and use it to effect meaningful change. I learned it from watching you, Dan. *I learned it from watching you.*

For the next year, he went back to posting semi-regularly about the horrors of the obesity epidemic with no discernible interruption, and I went back to ignoring him. Then, a whole lot happened in the same week. I dumped no-kissing-on-the-mouth guy. I kissed (on the mouth!) the man who, four years later, would become my husband. Then, Dan wrote a *Slog* post entitled, "Ban Fat Marriage," using the supposed health risks of fatness as leverage to skewer some GOP dodo's argument that gay marriage should be illegal because gay people supposedly die younger:

"Even if it were true—even if gay people had lower life expectancies (which we do not)—and if that 'fact' all by itself was a justification for banning same-sex marriage, why stop with gay people? Iowa should ban fat marriage. There are, according to the state of Iowa, more than 1.4 million obese people living in Iowa. That's nearly 30% of the state's population, and those numbers just keep rising. The social costs of Iowa's obesity epidemic are pretty staggering—and those costs include premature death and lower average life expectancies for Iowans."

I get the point. I understand that, in context, Dan presents "ban fat marriage" as an instructive absurdity. This post is still dehumanizing. It still oversimplifies the connections between size and health, and, unfortunately, some anti-fat bigots actually have suggested that fat people shouldn't be allowed to have families (because of "the children"). Mainly, though, if you have a track record of treating my struggle with persistent disrespect and dismissal, then my struggle is not yours to use as a flippant thought experiment.

I threw up a quick *Slog* post:

Re: Ban Fat Marriage

Hey, Dan—so now that you're equating the stigmatization of fat people with the stigmatization of gay people, does that mean you're going to stop stigmatizing fat people on this blog?

Nothing. I waited a few days. Nothing.

I looked back over our old e-mail exchange—remembering how scary it had been to send, how roundly he'd dismissed me, and how quickly he'd gone back to posting fatphobic rhetoric. Passively attempting to earn my humanity by being smart, nice, friendly, and good at my job had gotten me nowhere; my private confrontation with Dan had gotten me nowhere; literally telling him "this harms me" had gotten me nowhere; taking a quick, vague swipe at him on the blog had gotten me nowhere. So I did what—honestly—I thought Dan would do: On Feb 11, 2011, I wrote a scorched-earth essay and, vibrating with adrenaline, posted it publicly at the tail end of a sunny Friday afternoon.

The post was called, "Hello, I Am Fat." It included a full-body photo of me, taken that day by Kelly O, our staff photographer, with the caption: "28 years old, female, 5'9", 263 lbs." Remember that, at this point in my life, I had never self-identified as "fat" except in that single e-mail exchange with Dan, and in private conversations with trusted friends. Even then, I spoke the word only with shame, not power. Never in public. Never defiantly. Something had snapped in me the week of this post. This was a big deal, a spasm of self-determination rendered in real time. This was the moment.

It read as follows (now with a few annotations and cuts for brevity):

This is my body (over there—see it?). I have lived in this body my whole life. I have wanted to change this body my whole life. I have never wanted anything as much as I have wanted a new body. I am aware every day that other people find my body disgusting. I always thought that some day—when I finally stop failing—I will become smaller, and when I become smaller literally everything will get better (I've heard It Gets Better)! My life can begin! I will get the clothes that I want, the job that I want, the love that I want. It will be great! Think how great it will be to buy some pants or whatever at J.Crew. Oh, man. Pants. Instead, my body stays the same.

There is not a fat person on earth who hasn't lived this way. Clearly this is a TERRIBLE WAY TO EXIST. Also, strangely enough, it did not cause me to become thin. So I do not believe any of it anymore, because fuck it very much.

This is my body. It is MINE. I am not ashamed of it in any way. In fact, I love everything about it. Men find it attractive. Clothes look awesome on it. My brain rides around in it all day and comes up with funny jokes. Also, I don't have to justify its awesomeness/attractiveness/healthiness/usefulness to anyone, because it is MINE. Not yours.*

I'm not going to spend a bunch of time blogging about fat acceptance here, because other writers have already done it much more eloquently, thoroughly, and radically than I ever could. But I do feel obligated to try to explain what this all means.

I get that you think you're actually helping people and society by contributing to the fucking Alp of shame that crushes every fat person every day of their lives— the same shame that makes it a radical act for me to post

---

* I've noticed that a lot of people have trouble with the basic definition of fat acceptance—they want to argue and nitpick about calories and cardio and insurance and health and on and on and on—and if you're one of those people, wallowing in confusion, fret no more. I can sum it up for you in one easy-to-remember phrase: GET THE FUCK OFF ME, YOU FUCKING WEIRDO. Print it, laminate it, be it.

a picture of my body and tell you how much it weighs.
But you're not helping. Shame doesn't work. Diets don't
work.* Shame is a tool of oppression, not change.

Fat people already are ashamed. It's taken care of.
No further manpower needed on the shame front, thx.
I am not concerned with whether or not fat people can
change their bodies through self-discipline and "choices."
Pretty much all of them have tried already. A couple of
them have succeeded. Whatever. My question is, what if
they try and try and try and still fail? What if they are
still fat? What if they are fat forever? What do you do
with them then? Do you really want millions of teenage
girls to feel like they're trapped in unsightly lard prisons
that are ruining their lives, and on top of that it's because
of their own moral failure, and on top of that they are

---

* Fatphobes love to hold this assertion up as evidence of how delusional and intractable fat activists are. "Calories in/calories out," they say. "Ever heard of thermodynamics?" "Uhhh, I've never seen a fat person in a concentration camp. High-five, Trevor." Leaving aside the barbarism of suggesting, however obliquely, that, well, at least concentration camp victims weren't fat, no fat activist who says "Diets don't work" is suggesting that you cannot starve a fat person to a thin death. Rather, we are referencing the rigorously vetted academic conclusion that traditional diets—the kind that are foisted upon fat people as penance and cure-alls and our entry exam for humanity—fail 95 percent of the time. Whether fat people fail to lose weight due to simple laziness and moral torpor or because of a more complex web of personal, cultural, and medical factors, those numbers are still real. Those fat people still exist. Pushing diet culture as a "cure" for fatness does nothing but perpetuate the emotional and economic exploitation of fat people.

ruining America with the terribly expensive diabetes that they don't even have yet? You know what's shameful? A complete lack of empathy.

And if you really claim to still be confused—"Nu uh! I never said anything u guyz srsly!"—there can be no misunderstanding shit like this:

"I am thoroughly annoyed at having my tame statements of fact—being heavy is a health risk; rolls of exposed flesh are unsightly—characterized as 'hate speech.'"

Ha!

1. "Rolls of exposed flesh are unsightly" is in no way a "tame statement of fact." It is not a fact at all—it is an incredibly cruel, subjective opinion that reinforces destructive, paternalistic, oppressive beauty ideals.* I am not unsightly. No one deserves to be told that they're unsightly. But this is what's behind this entire thing— it's not about "health," it's about "eeeewwwww." You think fat people are icky. Eeeewww, a fat person might touch you on a plane. With their fat! Eeeeewww! Coin- cidentally, that's the same feeling that drives anti-gay bigots, no matter what excuses they drum up about

---

* In his response to this post, Dan took me to task for cherry-picking that quote, explaining that he wasn't mocking the flesh rolls of fat people specifically, he was mocking the flesh rolls of all women who wear low-rise jeans without having the correct bodies for it. Oh, okay. FYI, feminism isn't super jazzed about men policing women's clothing choices either. (Also, it was totally about fat people, you liar.)

"family values" and, yes, "health." It's all "eeeewwwww."
And sorry, I reject your eeeeeewwww.

2. You are not concerned about my health. Because
if you were concerned about my health, you would also
be concerned about my mental health, which has spent
the past twenty-eight years being slowly eroded by
statements like the above. Also, you don't know any-
thing about my health. You do happen to be the boss
of me, but you are not the doctor of me. You have no
idea what I eat, how much I exercise, what my blood
pressure is, or whether or not I'm going to get diabetes.
Not that any of that matters, because it is entirely none
of your business.

3. "But but but my insurance premiums!!!" Bullshit.
You live in a society with other people. I don't have
kids, but I pay taxes that fund schools. The idea that
we can somehow escape affecting each other is deeply
conservative. Barbarous, even. Is that really what you're
going for? Good old-fashioned American individualism?
Please.

4. But most importantly: I reject this entire frame-
work. I don't give a shit what causes anyone's fatness.
It's irrelevant and it's none of my business. I am not
making excuses, because I have nothing to excuse. I
reject the notion that thinness is the goal, that thin =
better—that I am an unfinished thing and that my life
can really start when I lose weight. That then I will be

a real person and have finally succeeded as a woman. I am not going to waste another second of my life thinking about this. I don't want to have another fucking conversation with another fucking woman about what she's eating or not eating or regrets eating or pretends to not regret eating to mask the regret. OOPS I JUST YAWNED TO DEATH.

If you really want change to happen, if you really want to "help" fat people, you need to understand that shaming an already-shamed population is, well, shameful. Do you know what happened as soon as I rejected all this shit and fell in unconditional luuuuurve with my entire body? I started losing weight. Immediately. WELL LA DEE FUCKING DA.*

The post went up. I left the office early and went across the street to get a head start on our Friday afternoon ritual, "Ham Grab," so named because it consisted of getting drunk as fast as possible and then descending upon a meat and cheese platter like a plague of locusts with journalism

---

* If I had it to do over again, I would write this last part more clearly, because I think the way it stands undermines my point a bit. What I was trying to convey was that if anti-fat crusaders really want what they claim to want—for fat people to be "healthy"—they should be on the front lines of size acceptance and fat empowerment. There's hard science to back this up: Shame contributes measurably to weight gain, not weight loss. Loving yourself is not antithetical to health, it is intrinsic to health. You can't take good care of a thing you hate.

degrees. As the comment section churned away—two hundred, three hundred, four hundred comments—I heard nothing from Dan all weekend; unbeknownst to me, he was off the grid in a cabin somewhere with no cell or Internet service. It would be a jarring welcome back to civilization. Oops.

The following Monday, Dan posted his response. It was three times longer than my piece—2,931 words, to be exact—accused me of "ad hominem attacks" and being blinded by my own emotional problems, and featured, as its centerpiece, this condescending bit of armchair psychology:

> It sounds like you're externalizing an internal conflict about being fat—you're projecting your anger and self-loathing onto me, and seeing malice and bigotry where none exists, and perhaps that's useful because that anger seems to be liberating and motivating. If having your own personal boogeyman on Slog helps you conquer your shame and love your body and this helps you break out of old, self-destructive patterns and habits (you can't be losing weight now just because your attitude changed), then I'm happy to be your own personal boogeyman. But honestly, Lindy, you don't need one. You're stronger than that.

He said a lot of other things too, like "the bigotry in my posts exists only in Lindy's imagination," and "there are crazy fat people out there, Lindy…be careful who you crawl into bed [with] now that you're a 'brave' hero to the FA movement," and approvingly quoted a com-menter who suggested that "apparently, Lindy isn't very good with reading comprehension."

It was exhausting—it just felt so static and pointless. We hadn't moved an inch. The next day, there was a staff meeting about how I'd hurt Dan's feelings, with no men-tion at all of the climate that had led me to write the post in the first place. I was livid. I thought about quitting, but the *Stranger* meant everything to me—it was the place where I found my voice, and the family that emboldened me to use it. At the time, I couldn't imagine anything beyond that office, and besides, I loved working for Dan.

So, I dropped the argument (I'd said my piece, stood by it, and a lot of people agreed) and we fell back into a normal routine. Gotta get the paper out. Meanwhile, I started getting e-mails from friends and strangers, telling me that it had made their lives better in small ways—emboldened them to set a bound-ary of their own, or take in their reflection with care rather than disgust. To this day, those e-mails make my job worth it.

A few weeks later, Dan and I went out for beer and soft pretzels to make sure we were cool.

"It's like," I said, "here we are at this restaurant. Say both of our chairs are broken."

"Okay," said Dan.

"If my chair collapses under me right now, people will assume it's because I'm fat. But if your chair collapses under you, it's because you sat on a broken chair."

"Okay."

"Do you get it?"

"I get it."

I never wanted an apology, I just wanted it to be different. And, after all that, it was. While writing this chapter, when I went back and read Dan's response for the first time in years, I was shocked at how dated it feels. The Dan I know in 2016—I don't see much of him there. Whether I had anything to do with it or not, he writes about fat people differently now. When someone asks him for advice about body image, he reaches out to a fat person (sometimes me) for input. When fat people would make an easy punch line, he doesn't take it.

We, as a culture, discuss fat people differently now too. If you go back to just 2011, 2010, 2009—let alone 2004 or 2005, when Dan was writing about the Sioux Falls water park and low-rise jeans—the rhetoric, even on mainstream news sites, was vicious. Vicious was normal. It was perfectly acceptable to mock fat bodies, flatten fat humanity, scold fat people for their own deaths. You only have to look back five years to see a different world, and, by extension, tangible proof that culture is ours to shape, if we try.

Obviously there's no shortage of fat-haters roaming the Internet, the beach, and America's airports in 2016, but an idea has taken root in the hive mind: We do not speak about human beings this way.

I tell this story not to criticize Dan, but to praise him. Change is hard, and slow, but he bothered to do it. Sometimes people on the defensive rebound into compassion. Sometimes smart, good people are just a little behind.

Why Fat Lady So Mean to Baby Men?

I'm on hold with the FBI. I clack out an e-mail to a customer service rep at MailChimp, simultaneously filling out boilerplate help desk forms for Twitter, Google, and Yahoo. Intermittently, I refresh my e-mail and skim through hundreds and hundreds of spam letters ("Confirm your subscription for Subscribe2 HTML Plugin," "European Ombudsman Newsletter," "Potwierdzenie prenumeraty newsletter tvp.pl"), tweezing out legitimate messages from my agent, my editors, my family. I know I'm missing things. I'm probably losing money.

When the e-mails started trickling into my inbox that morning, I'd thought little of it. Some days are spammier than others. Around ten a.m., the trickle swelled to a flood, and then a creepy tweet popped up too: "Email me at [toiletperson@thetoilet.net] if you want the spam to stop. I simply want you to delete an old tweet."

I sigh, scrubbing my face hard with a dry palm. Does this have to be today? I was going to write about my abortion today!

The receptionist from the Seattle FBI office picks up.

"Hi," I say. "I have…a problem?" I'm already grasping for words. How do you explain to someone who might not even know what Twitter is that you're being anonymously extorted via e-mail newsletters into deleting an unspecified past tweet? Beyond that, how do you convince them that it actually matters? My understanding of the FBI is 90 percent *X-Files*. As far as I know, they're off trying to solve Sasquatch crime, and here I am begging them for tech support.

It does matter, though. It's costing me time, potential income, and mental health. If you consider Twitter part of my work, which I do, it is tampering with a journalist's e-mail to coerce them into pulling a story. It is, I think, illegal. More significantly, though, it's part of a massive, multifarious online harassment campaign that has saturated my life for the past half decade—and, on a broader scale, is actively driving women off the Internet. Disruption, abuse, the violent theft of time, then writing about it to illuminate what we go through online—this is my whole deal now. Unsurprisingly, the tweet that [the toilet] wanted deleted turned out to be a screenshot of a rape threat I'd received from a popular troll. He was harassing me to scrub Twitter of evidence of my harassment.

The FBI receptionist, sounding bored (I know the feeling), says she can't help me. She tells me to call the Washington State Patrol, which seems weird. It is unmistakably a brush-off. I call the number she gives me and nobody picks up. I drop it and try to get back to work. There is no recourse.

I didn't set out to make a living writing about being abused on the Internet.

As a child, I was really more looking for an open position as, say, the burly and truculent woman-at-arms protecting an exiled queen who's disguised herself as a rag-and-bone man using cinder paste and some light sorcery. Or a flea-bitten yet perspicacious motley urchin who hides in plain sight as a harmless one-man band jackanapes in order to infiltrate the duke's winter festival and assassinate his scheming nephew with the help of my rat army. Is that hiring? Any overweening palace stewards (who are secretly a pumpkin-headed scarecrow transfigured by a witch) want to join my professional network on LinkedIn?

I was an avoider, an escaper, a fantasist. Even as an adult, all I ever wanted was to write jokes, puns, and *Game of Thrones* recaps.

Instead, here I am, sitting at my computer dealing with some fuckface's insatiable boner for harassing women. Earlier, when I said the "violent theft of time," I meant it. Online harassment is not virtual—it is physical. Flooding in through every possible channel, it moves and changes my body: It puts me on the phone with the FBI, it gives me tension headaches and anxiety attacks; it alters my day-to-day behavior (Am I safe? Is that guy staring at me? Is he a troll?); it alienates my friends; it steals time from my family. The goal is to traumatize me, erode my mental health, force me to quit my job.

Anytime I complain about Kevins* harassing me online, no matter how violently, sexually, or persistently, someone always pipes up with this genius theory: Rape and death threats are part and parcel of the Internet; you just can't handle it because you're oversensitive. Never mind the fact that coding sensitivity as a weakness is bizarre (what do you think this is—the Ministry of Magic under Voldemort's shadow government?), it's also simply out of step with reality. You can't do this job if you have an emotional hair trigger. Undersensitivity is practically a prerequisite.

I was at the *Stranger* for the advent of comments but prior to the ubiquity of social media, so I sat through several years of relatively innocuous variations on "hipster douche bag" before my readers ever discovered what I look like, where I was vulnerable. In retrospect, it was bliss. I

---

* I call all anonymous Internet dill-holes "Kevin," not because I think "Kevin" is a bad name (you know I love you, my Kevins), but because—being from the *Home Alone* generation—it's so easy to hear a fed-up mom screaming it up a staircase. "KEVIN, WHAT IS A 'BRAZZERS' AND WHY IS IT ON MY BANK STATEMENT?"

never took those comments home with me. They were cumulatively tiresome, but they didn't sting. I think of my first real troll as the first person who crossed that line from the impersonal into the personal, the first one who made me feel unsafe, the first to worm their fingers into my meat-life and attack who I was rather than what I wrote.

At the time, I covered movies and theater. I didn't write anything political; I didn't write about being fat or being a woman. My name is gender-ambiguous, and for the first few years of my career, many readers thought I was a man. People's assumptions tend to default to white and male, especially when the writer is loud and unapologetically critical and sharp around the edges, which was kind of my brand. (Not that women aren't naturally those things, any more or less than men are, of course, but we are aggressively socialized to be "nice," and to apologize for having opinions.) So, while the tenor of my commenters was often snide, disdainful of the *Stranger*'s snotty teenage brand of progressivism, they stuck to hating the message, not the messenger.

Those years were liberating in a way I can barely imagine now—to be judged purely on ideas and their execution, not written off by people with preconceived notions about fat female bodies and the brains attached to them. Now I spend as much time doing damage control—playing whack-a-mole with my readership's biases against my identities (fat, female, feminist)—as I do writing new material, generating new ideas, pitching new stories, and promoting myself to new audiences. I received more benefit of the doubt as an unknown regional theater critic than I do as an internationally published political columnist. What could I have accomplished by now if I had just been allowed to write? Who could I have been?

I sometimes think of people's personalities as the negative space around their insecurities. Afraid of intimacy? Cultivate aloofness. Feel invisible? Laugh loud and often. Drink too much? Play the gregarious basket case. Hate your body? Slash and burn others so you can climb up the pile. We construct elaborate palaces to hide our vulnerabilities, often growing into caricatures of what we fear. The goal is to move through the world without anyone knowing quite where to dig a thumb. It's a survival instinct. When people know how to hurt you, they know how to control you.

But when you're a fat person, you can't hide your vulnerability, because you are it and it is you. Being fat is like walking around with a sandwich board that says, "HERE'S WHERE TO HURT ME!" That's why reclaiming fatness—living visibly, declaring, "I'm fat and I am not ashamed"—is a social tool so revolutionary, so liberating, it saves lives.

Unfortunately, my first troll, the first time an anonymous stranger called me "fat" online, was years before I discovered fat liberation. It was posted in the comments of some innocuous blog entry on June 9, 2009, at 11:54 p.m., what would become a major turning point in my life:

"I'm guessing Lindy's sexual fantasies involve aliens

that love big girls and release a hallucinogenic gas while making sweet love to a fat girl that instantly causes her to imagine herself as height/weight proportionate. With long sexy legs."

The comment was so jarring because it was so specific. It wasn't simply dashed off in a rage—it took some thought, some creativity, some calibration. Calories were burned. The subtext that got its hooks in me the most was "I know what you look like," implying that the author was either someone I knew who secretly despised me, or a stranger fixated enough to take the time to do research on my body. Only slightly less unsettling, the comment simultaneously sexualized me and reminded me that fat women's sexuality can only ever be a ghoulish parody. I cried. I went home early, feeling violated, and climbed into bed to marathon some *SVU*. I'd always known that my body was catnip for dicks, but up until that moment, writing had been a refuge. On paper, my butt size couldn't distract from my ideas. It hadn't even occurred to me that my legs weren't long enough. I added it to the list.

That night, I forwarded that comment to my editors and the tech team, begging for some sort of change in the comment moderation policy. How was this not a hostile work environment? How was it not gendered harassment? These people were my friends (they still are), but the best they could give me was a sympathetic brow-knit and a shrug. The Internet's a cesspool. That's just the Internet.

We all get rude comments. Can't make an Internet without getting a little Internet on your Internet!

Why, though? Why is invasive, relentless abuse—that disproportionately affects marginalized people who have already faced additional obstacles just to establish themselves in this field—something we should all have to live with just to do our jobs? Six years later, this is still a question I've yet to have answered.

At pretty much every blogging job I've ever had, I've been told (by male managers) that the reason is money. It would be a death sentence to moderate comments and block the IP addresses of chronic abusers, because it "shuts down discourse" and guts traffic. I've heard a lot of lectures about the importance of neutrality. Neutrality is inherently positive, I'm told—if we start banning trolls and shutting down harassment, we'll all lose our jobs. But no one's ever shown me any numbers that support that claim, that harassment equals jobs. Not that I think traffic should trump employee safety anyway, but I'd love for someone to prove to me that it's more than just a cop-out.

Years later, when I moved on to a staff writer position at *Jezebel* (and trolls like sex-alien guy had become a ubiquitous potpourri), Gawker Media publisher Nick Denton unrolled a new platform called Kinja, with the express mission of "investing in commenters." On Kinja, any commenter could start their own blog, hosted by Gawker, which could then be mined for re-posting on the main sites. Your commenter handle became the URL of your blog—so, for example, mine was lindywest.kinja. com. This was an alarming precedent from an editorial standpoint: Our employer was intentionally blurring the lines between our work as professional, experienced, vetted, paid journalists and the anonymous ramblings of the unpaid commentariat, which seemed to exist, most days, simply to antagonize us. It did not go over particularly well at the all-hands meeting. In Kinja, as the trolls quickly learned, comments are moderated by the writers, so to keep our work readable we had to dismiss and ban each one by hand. At *Jezebel*, that meant fielding a constant stream of gifs depicting graphic violence and rape. It was emotionally gruesome. But it was "part of the job."

The problem with handing anonymous commenters the tools of their own legitimization soon became even clearer for me. One user registered the handle Lindy-WestLicksMyAsshole" and began merrily commenting all over Gawker. Under Kinja, that meant there was now a permanent blog, hosted by my employer, side by side with my work, called lindywestlicksmyasshole.kinja.com. Can you imagine? At your job? That's like if your name was Dave Jorgensen and you worked at Walgreens, and one day you got to work and right in between the fiber supplements and the seasonal candy there was a new aisle called Dave Jorgensen Is a Sex Predator. And when you complained to your manager she was like, "Oh, you're so sensitive. It's a store! We can't change what goes in a store—we'd go out of business! We all have stuff we don't like, Dave. I don't like Salt and Vinegar Pringles, but you don't see me whining about aisle 2."

I e-mailed my boss and insisted the page be taken down. She told me she'd see what she could do, but not to get my hopes up. Sure enough, Gawker higher-ups claimed it didn't violate the harassment policy. It isn't explicitly gendered or racist or homophobic. Anyway, that's just how the Internet is! If we start deleting comments because people's feelings are hurt, it'll stifle the lively comment culture that keeps the site profitable. What if LindyWestLicksMy Asshole has some really tasty anonymous tip about a congressman who did something weird with his penis? Don't you care about free speech and penis news?

It is gendered, though. Of course it's gendered. It's sexualizing me for the purpose of making me uncomfortable, of reminding my audience and colleagues and detractors that I'm a sex thing first and a human being second. That my ideas are secondary to my body. Sure, if you strip away cultural context entirely, you could construe "Lindy WestLicksMyAsshole" as having nothing to do with gender, but that's willful dishonesty.* I didn't have a choice, however, so I put LindyWestLicksMyAsshole out of my

---

* I did once receive an angry e-mail from a man informing me that "asshole" is an anti-male slur, which is about the level of understanding of female anatomy that I'd expected from someone who believes in "reverse sexism." (Just kidding—women poop out of our vaginas like a parrot.)

mind and tried to stay out of the comments as much as possible.

It's just the Internet. There's nothing we can do.

When I was right in that sweet spot—late *Stranger*/ early *Jezebel*—when the trolls were at full volume about my Michelin Man thorax and Dalek thighs, but my only line of defense was the fetal position, I was effectively incapacitated. I had no coping mechanisms. I felt helpless and isolated. I stayed in bed as much as possible, and kept the TV on 24/7; I couldn't fall asleep in silence. I don't know if trolls say to themselves, explicitly, "I don't like what this lady wrote—I'm going to make sure she never leaves her apartment!" but that's what it does to the unprepared.

I know those early maelstroms pushed some of my friends away. To someone who's never experienced it, large-scale online hate is unrelatable, and complaints about it can read like narcissism. "Ugh, what do I do with all this attention?" The times I did manage to get out and socialize, it was hard not to be a broken record, to recount tweets I'd gotten that day like a regurgitating toilet. Eventually, people got bored. Who wants to sit around in person and talk about the Internet?

Gradually, though (it took years), I got better. I learned how to weather the mob without falling out of my skin, becoming my own tedious shadow.

PLAN A: Don't click on anything. Don't read anything. Don't look at any words below any article, or any forum to which the public has any access, or any e-mail with a vaguely suspicious subject line like "feedback on ur work" or "a questions about womyn" or "feminism= female supremacy?" EVER. Because why on earth would you do that? I can understand if the Internet had just been invented Tuesday, and you sincerely thought, "Oh, perhaps sniffmychode89 has some constructive perspective on the politics of female body hair." However, I, Lindy West, have now been using this virtual garbage dispenser for literally twenty years, and maybe one comment in fifty contains anything other than condescending, contrarian, and/or abusive trash. I have no excuse. When I click, it is because I am a fool.

It's as if there were an international chain of delis that—no matter what franchise you went to and what you ordered and how clearly you articulated "PAHH-STRAWWW-MEEE"—forty-nine out of fifty times they just served you a doo-doo sandwich. A big, fat, steaming scoop of doo-doo on a sesame seed bun (special sauce: doo-doo). Then you went ahead and ate the sandwich. And you didn't just eat the sandwich one time, or fifty times, or even one hundred, but you went back and ate there—with hope in your heart, paying for the privilege—every single day of your life. Thousands and thousands of days in a row. Plus, pretty much everyone you ever met had been to that deli too, and they all ate mouthfuls of straight stank doo-doo over and over again, and they told you about it. They warned you! Yet you still went back and ate the sandwich.

Because maybe this time it'd be different! Maybe—just maybe—this time you'd get the most delicious and fulfilling sandwich the world had e'er known, and the sandwich guy would finally recognize the trenchant, incisive brilliance of your sandwich-ordering skills, and doo-doo would be abolished, and Joss Whedon would pop out of the meat freezer and hand you a trophy that said "BEST GUY" on it and option your sandwich story for the plot of the next Avengers movie, *Captain Whatever: The Sandwich Soldier.* (Full disclosure: I do not know what an Avenger is.)

That's not what happens, though. That's never what happens. Instead, I keep slogging through forty-nine iterations of "kill yourself, pig lady" per day in my Twitter mentions, because one time in 2013 Holly Robinson Peete replied to my joke about Carnation instant breakfast.* Cool cost/benefit analysis, brain.

Still, I TRY not to click. I try.

PLAN B: When the temptation is too strong, when Plan A falls in the commode, I turn to the second line of defense—the mock and block. I take screen grabs of the worst ones—the ones that wish for my death, the ones that invoke my family, the ones with a telling whiff of pathos—and then re-post them with a caption like "way to go, Einstein" or "goo goo ga ga baby man" or some-

---

* THIS ACTUALLY DID HAPPEN. I WOULD NOT JOKE ABOUT HOLLY ROBINSON PEETE.

times just a picture of some diaper rash cream. (As Dorothy Parker or someone like that probably once said, "Goo goo ga ga baby man is the soul of wit.") My friends and I will toss the troll around for a while like a pod of orcas with a baby seal, and once I've wrung enough validation out of it, I block the troll and let it die alone. Maybe it's cruel. I know that trolls are fundamentally sad people; I know that I've already defeated them in every substantive arena—by being smart, by being happy, by being successful, by being listened to, by being loved. Whatever. Maybe if Mr. "Kill Yourself You Fat Piece of Shit" didn't want to get mocked, shredded, and discarded, he should be more careful about how he talks to whales.

PLAN C: Wine.

Overall, my three-pronged defense holds up...pretty well. I am...okay. I cope, day to day, and honestly, there is something seductive about being the kind of person who can just take it. Challenging myself to absorb more and more hate is a masochistic form of vanity—the vestigial allure of a rugged individualism that I don't even believe in.

No one wants to need defenses that strong. It always hurts, somewhere.

Besides, armor is heavy. My ability to weather online abuse is one of the great tragedies of my life.

You never get used to trolls. Of course, you are an adaptable thing—your skin thickens, your stomach settles, you learn to tune out the chatter, you cease self-Googling (mostly), but it's always just a patch. A screen. A coat of paint. It's plopping a houseplant over the dry rot. It's emotional hypothermia: Your brain can trick itself into feeling warm, but the flesh is still freezing. Medically speaking, your foot's still falling off. There's a phenomenon called "paradoxical undressing," common when a person dies of hypothermia, wherein they become so convinced they're overheating that they peel off all their clothes and scatter them in the snow. They get colder, die faster. There's something uncanny about a cold death; a still, indifferent warping of humanity.

I struggle to conceive of the "resilience" I've developed in my job as a good thing—this hardening inside me, this distance I've put between myself and the world, my determination to delude myself into normalcy. From the cockpit, it feels like much more of a loss than a triumph. It's like the world's most not-worth-it game show: Well, you've destroyed your capacity for unbridled happiness and human connection, but don't worry—we've replaced it with this prison of anxiety and pathological inability to relax!

Yet, it seems like the more abuse I get, the more abuse I court—baring myself more extravagantly, professing opinions that I know will draw an onslaught—because, after all, if I've already adjusted my body temperature, why not face the blizzard so that other women don't have to freeze?

Paradoxical undressing, I guess.

But it's just the Internet. There's nothing we can do.

This is my reality now. Pretty much every day, at least one stranger seeks me out to call me a fat bitch (or some pithy variation thereof). Being harassed on the Internet is such a normal, common part of my life that I'm always surprised when other people find it surprising. You're telling me you don't have hundreds of men popping into your cubicle in the accounting department of your midsized, regional dry-goods distributor to inform you that—hmm—you're too fat to rape, but perhaps they'll saw you up with an electric knife? No? Just me, then. This is the barbarism—the eager abandonment of the social contract—that so many of us face simply for doing our jobs.

I'm aware of the pull all the time: I should change careers; I should shut down my social media; maybe I can get a job in print somewhere; it's just too exhausting. I hear the same refrains from my colleagues. Not only that, but those of us who are hardest hit often wind up writing about harassment itself. I never wanted Internet trolls to be my beat—I want to write feminist polemics, jokes about wizards, and love letters to John Goodman's meaty, sexual forearms. I still want that.

I wonder if I'll ever be able to get back to work.

Strong People Fighting Against the Elements

I never wanted to fight virtual trolls; I wanted to fight real ones. With a sword.

My fixation on the fantastical is not difficult to trace. When I was very small, my dad read out loud to me every night before bed. It was always fantasy: Tolkien, Lewis, Baum, Tolkien again. I remember him nodding off in the chair, his pace and pitch winding down like he was running out of batteries—Bifur, Bofur, Bommmmbuuurrrrrrrrrrrr. To this day, if someone even mentions riding a barrel down the Celduin to Lake-town at the gates of Erebor, the Lonely Mountain (even if they're just talking about spring break), I am incapacitated by nostalgia. I made him read *The Lion, the Witch and the Wardrobe* so many times that I could recite much of it from memory—

I didn't know what "air raids" were, but I knew that when they happened, you went on a permanent vacation to a country manse where a wizard let you use his inter-dimensional closet. I wonder if we can get "air raids" in Seattle, I thought.

Dad was a jazz pianist and an ad copywriter—an expressive baritone who was often employed as a kind of one-man, full-service jingle factory. By night, he worked in bars, sometimes seven nights a week, a lost breed of lounge entertainer who skipped dizzyingly from standards to Flanders and Swann to Lord Buckley and back again. Once in a while, I still meet Seattle old-timers who blush like teenagers. "I loved your dad. Used to go see him every night."

My grandfather was a radio producer (*The Burns and Allen Show, Lucky Strike Hit Parade*), and in the 1940s, when he took a job at CBS, it was suggested that he change his name from the unwieldy and, perhaps, at the time, uncomfortably Austrian, "Rechenmacher" to the more radio-friendly "West." So my dad became Paul West Jr., and now I am Lindy West. Sometimes people think "Lindy West" is a pseudonym. I guess they're right.

Eighty years removed, my grandparents' Old Hollywood existence seems impossibly glamorous. I imagine shimmering laughter and natty suits. Hats on heads, hats in hat boxes. Scotch in the winter, gin in the summer.

Grandma Winnie sang with Meredith Willson's orchestra, and when my dad was a little boy in the '30s, she worked in movies (under her maiden name, Winnie Parker, and her stage name, Mona Lowe), dubbing the vocal parts for Carole Lombard, Dolores del Rio, and other leading ladies who, apparently, couldn't sing. Dad had stories of going to Shirley Temple's birthday party, of nearly fainting when his dad nonchalantly introduced him to his friend Lou Costello, of Gene Autry trying to give little Paul a pony to keep in their Glendale backyard.

They drank hard—"eating and drinking and carrying on," as my dad would say. He once e-mailed me a little vignette he wrote in his creative writing night class:

"The living room is the part of the house I remember least, from the inside anyway. I remember it a little better from the sidewalk in front, along Kenneth Road. I remember standing there looking at the bright gold harp that stood framed by the green brocade draperies— draperies I once hid behind when my mother and father were screaming drunk.

"I heard a dull 'thunk,' followed by a big crash, and when I peeked out from behind the drape, my father was lying on the living room floor, blood spurting from his big, already knobby nose. Mother and the other couple in the room, my uncle and his wife, were laughing hysterically when my grandmother came down the wide staircase. 'Vas ist?' she said—with stern, Viennese dignity. 'An orange,' my uncle giggled, 'Winnie hit him in the nose with an orange!' They were all helpless with laughter. 'Be ashamed,' Gramma said."*

I never met any of those people. In fact, I've never met any family from my dad's side at all. My grandfather had a heart attack and died unexpectedly in 1953 when he was just forty-four, two days before my dad's high school graduation. There was some dispute about the burial, between the deeply Catholic Rechenmachers in southern Illinois, who wanted a Catholic funeral, and my dad's lapsed Hollywood branch, who didn't. Paul West Sr. ended up in a Catholic cemetery in Culver City, where lingering animus led to nobody visiting him for the next fifty-five years, until, on a whim, my sister and I tracked down the grave. We called Dad and told him where we were. "Golly," he said, his voice rough.

You could tell that my dad never fully recovered from that loss (and it wasn't his last). My sister and I called him "sad dad"—underneath the exuberance there was a towering melancholy. I sometimes told people my dad reminded me of Robin Williams, and they would assume I meant the drive to entertain, the old showbiz patter. But

---

* There's more: "I called my blanket Hi Ho. It didn't follow me everywhere, but it was the comfort I sought when fear and injury came. On the day of the car accident on the way to the pre-school, I had Hi Ho with me. It was forever stained with my blood, and while it remained beside me in my crib at night after it had been washed, the brown stains remained and tarnished the magic. The warmth was still there but the reassurance was gone. A year or so later we named our new Cocker Spaniel Hi Ho."

it was really that ever-present Pig-Pen cloud of kind-eyed sadness.

My dad had four wives; my mom was the last. I think about how much faith it must have taken to keep going—to insist, over and over again, "No! I really think it's going to work this time!" Plenty of people are irretrievably jaded after one divorce, let alone three. My dad went for it four times, and the last one stuck. You could frame that as irresponsibility or womanizing or a fear of being alone, but to me it was a distillation of his unsinkable optimism. He always saw the best in everyone—I imagine, likewise, he stood at the beginning of every romance and saw it unspooling in front of him like a grand adventure, all fun and no pain. "Oh boy!" I can hear him saying each time. "Isn't she just terrific?" The idea that a relationship is a "failure" simply because it ends is a pessimist's construct anyway. Dad loved lots of people, and then found the one he loved the best.

It made sense that he was so drawn to magic and escapism, just like me. His life was beautiful and marked with loss; maybe not more than anyone else's, but when you only expect the best, heartbreak is a constant.

My mom, by contrast, never liked fantasy. When I was little, this made as much sense to me as not liking gravity, or Gordon from *Sesame Street*. "I just like things that are true," she'd say. "Strong people fighting against the elements." I grilled her so often on why she wasn't obsessed with dragons LIKE A NORMAL PERSON that it became kind of a catchphrase in our house—strong people fighting against the elements.

That made sense too. My mom's parents came from Norway: Grandma Clara first, the eldest of ten, when she was a little girl and the family homesteaded in North Dakota. We visited the old dirt farm once during a family reunion: just a hole and the remnants of the foundation and some dead grass and the big, red sun. In summer the North Dakotan prairie is flat and brown. In winter, flat and white. "The elements," I imagine, had a seat at the table like family.

When the Depression hit and my great-grandparents just couldn't feed so many mouths, they shipped eighteen-year-old Clara back to Norway to raise two of her little sisters on her own. While Grandpa Rechenmacher's early death shaped my dad's life like a tide, absent mothers tugged on my mom's side. My great-aunt Eleanor, one of the little girls sent off to the old country, requested that "Sometimes I Feel Like a Motherless Child" be played at her funeral, and it was.

Clara met and married my grandfather, Ole, who grew up on a farm called Gunnersveen, just down the lake. His father died in the flu pandemic of 1918, when Ole was nine. "The boys didn't have much of a childhood," my mom told me once, when she e-mailed to scold me about washing my hands during the 2009 swine flu scare (subject line: "GERMS!"*). In 1945, during the Nazi occupation, Grandpa Ole and his brother were among twelve resistance fighters who skied out into the dark hills to retrieve packages parachuted by an Allied spy plane—bundles of weapons, radio equipment, provisions. Strong people, elements, blah blah blah, the whole thing.

Ole and Clara married and moved to Seattle and raised seven children; my mom, Ingrid, was number six. Clara kept house—canning fruit, sewing the family's clothes, a pot of coffee perpetually perking for anyone who dropped by—and Grandpa Ole was a carpenter, never quite mastering English because, privately, he always just wanted to go home. They took in strays; sometimes as many as thirteen people lived in that three-bedroom, one-bath house; the kids shared beds and bathwater. "My trick was to help my mother in the kitchen," my mom always says when someone compliments her cooking. "It was hard to get one-on-one time otherwise, she was so busy." (Maybe that's why my mom stopped at one child herself.) She speaks of the cramped chaos with pride. Her ability to get by is part of her identity.

---

* Body of e-mail: "My rules are: Wash your hands as soon as you get home. Then go around with a Clorox wipe and clean the doorknobs, light switches, and faucets. Of course, wash before you eat and keep your hands away from your mucous membranes, including eyes. I wish I could quarantine you until this thing settles down, but I will trust you to keep yourself safe. If everybody in your house does the same, then you can feel safe at home . . . unless you accidentally let a sick person inside. Love you. Mom."

My mother is aggressively competent. She was an RN for forty years—yes, she will look at your infected toe—and her rigid expectations about the Correct Way to Do Things border on disordered (motto: "If you clean your bathroom every day, you never have to clean your bathroom"). When she and my dad fell in love, he was playing the piano in bars every night, living off credit cards, occasionally accepting gin and tonics as currency, and had decorated his apartment entirely in zebra-themed bric-a-brac—due, no doubt, to some passing, impetuous whim. ("Hey, zebras are trick!") By the time I was born, a few years later, they were financially stable, he had a day job at an ad agency, and the zebra merch was limited to one vase, two paintings, a set of directors' chairs, and a life-sized F. A. O. Schwarz stuffed zebra named Simon. You know, a reasonable amount.

He wrote a song for my mom called "I Like You So Much Better (Than Anyone I've Ever Loved Before)"—"Time was I took a lot of chances/on passions and romances/but you're the one who helped me get my feet back on the floor/That's why I like you so much better/than anyone I've ever loved before."

Dad was the entertainer, but I'm funny because of my mom. She has a nurse's ease with gallows humor, sarcastic and dry; she taught me to cope with pain by chopping it up into bits small enough to laugh at. (My dad would go full Swamps of Sadness when anything went wrong. If the printer ran out of toner, he couldn't speak above a whisper for days.) When I was little, a neighbor opened a small temping agency called Multitask and, in an early stab at guerrilla marketing, purchased a vanity plate that read, "MLTITSK." Around the house, my mom called him "M. L. Titsky." Later, just "Mr. Titsky." Empirically, that's a great riff.

Once, at a block party, she forgot that Mr. Titsky wasn't actually his name, and introduced him as such to a new neighbor. Mr. Titsky, it turned out, was not a comedy connoisseur.

My dad took care of unbridled enthusiasm and unconditional encouragement—everything was "Killer!" "WowEE!" "You can be anything you want to be!"—while my mom's role was, "Not today," "Hmmm," and "Not if you don't learn how to balance a checkbook."* In fact, she recently told me that part of her parenting philosophy was to make sure I knew I couldn't be anything.

"Well, you can't," she said. "I didn't want you to be disappointed."

If my dad supported us with words, head in the clouds, my mom supported us with structure, roots in the ground. That degree of harmonious opposition has to fulfill some cosmic archetype. (Not that my mom would allow such arcane silliness to be discussed in her house.)

Between those far-flung poles—escapism vs. realism,

---

* Still haven't. Only 20 percent clear on the definition, to be honest.

glamour vs. austerity, wild hope vs. Nordic practicality—I
grew.

People say to me all the time, "I couldn't do what you
do; I couldn't cope with trolls," but it's just part of my job.
I bet they could if they had to.

Once in a while, though, I wonder: Is it more than that?
Did I somehow stumble into a job—one that didn't even
exist when I was born in 1982—for which I am supremely,
preternaturally suited? I do fight monsters, just like I always
dreamed, even if they are creeps in basements who hate
women instead of necromancers in skull towers who hate
lady knights. Without my mom, would I have the grit to
keep going? Without my dad, would I have the idealism
to bother?

The Day I Didn't Fit

One time, I flew first class on an airplane, because when I checked in they offered me a fifty-dollar upgrade, and when you are a fat person with fifty dollars and somebody offers you a 21-inch recliner instead of a 17-inch trash compacter, you say YES. It was a new world up there, in front of that little magic curtain, among the lordlings. I was seated next to a businessman in leather shoes that cost more than my car, and behind a man who kept angrily attempting to sell a boat over the phone even after they told us to stop making phone calls.

The first rule of first class, apparently, is that there are no rules. (The second rule is don't let the poor people use the rich people bathroom.)

I wondered if my fellow first-classers—all virility and spreadsheets—could discern that I was a fraud, that I could only afford the upgrade because my job covered the rest of my ticket. I may have betrayed myself when the flight attendant asked if I'd like a "special drink" before takeoff and I yelled, "A SPECIAL DRINK?" and then ordered three. Why just have coffee like some row-26 peasant when you could have coffee, ginger ale, and a mimosa!? This, as I'd been assured by the airline industry, was the life.

As the flight progressed, first class got less exciting. At some point, once the initial thrill of being adjacent to a four-figure boat sale had worn off, I realized: These special drinks weren't remotely special. This roast beef sandwich, though presented with a *cloth napkin*, was in no way luxurious. (Also, "sandwich" is a rather generous term for a microwaved wad of airborne gray beef.) My first-class chair wasn't a plush throne stuffed with Richard Branson's hair, as air travel's mythology would have you believe—it was simply an average-sized chair with a human amount of leg room (as opposed to coach seats, which are novelty-sized file drawers with a elfin amount of leg room). It wasn't unbearable. The highest praise I can give it is that it was adequate. It had succeeded at being a chair instead of a flying social experiment about the limits of human endurance. The rich aren't paying for luxury—they're paying for basic humanity.

For me, the primary advantage of flying first class was that it precluded the dread. I didn't know about the dread until the fall of 2013—the first time I got on a plane and discovered that I didn't quite fit in the seat. I've always been fat, but I was the fat person that still mostly fit. While I couldn't fit into regular-lady clothes (more bejeweled tunics covered with skulls, cherries, and antique postage stamps, please!), and I had to be careful with butt safety (I once Godzilla'd an entire lunch setting while trying to sidle through a Parisian cafe), I was still the kind of fat person who could move through the straight-sized world without causing too many ripples. Until I couldn't.

It had been an incredibly busy year for me professionally—I'd probably flown twenty times in the preceding eight months, and there's nothing like a steady diet of stress and Chili's Too to keep the waistline trim— and one day I sat down and it just didn't work. I was on a flight home from Texas, and the flight out there had been fine. Suddenly, on the return flight, I had to cram myself in. I mean, I know I ate that brisket, but I was only gone for two days! I'm no butt scientist (just two credits away, though!), but how fast could a person's butt possibly grow?

If you've never tried cramming your hips into an angular metal box that's an inch or two narrower than your flesh (under the watchful eye of resentful tourists), then sitting motionless in there for five hours while you fold your arms and shoulders up like a dying orchid in order to be as unobtrusive as possible, run, don't walk. It's like squeezing your bones in a vise. The pain makes your teeth ache. I once spent a tearful eight-hour flight from Oslo to Seattle convinced I could feel my femurs splintering like candy canes. It hurts.

Much worse than any physical pain is the anxiety—the dread—of walking up the aisle and not knowing what type of plane you're on. Every model has different seat widths and belt lengths, which also vary from airline to airline. Am I going to fit this time? Will I have to ask for a seat-belt extender? Is this a 17-incher or an 18-incher? Is the person next to me going to hate me? Does everyone on this plane hate me? I paid money for this?

I have, in my life, been a considerably thinner person and had a fat person sit next to me on a plane. I have also, more recently, been the fat person that makes other travelers' faces fall. Being the fat person is worse.

Here's how I board a plane. I do not book a ticket unless I can be assured a window seat—I will happily sit in the very back row, or change my flight to the buttcrack of dawn—because the window well affords me an extra couple of inches in which to compress my body to give my neighbor as much space as possible. It's awkward and embarrassing to haul and cram myself in and out of the seat, so I also prefer the window because I'm not blocking anyone's bathroom access. I've learned from experience that emergency exit rows and bulkhead rows are often narrower, so those are out. My preflight anxiety begins the day before, when I remember that I have a trip coming up. I arrive at least two hours early, even for domestic flights, to preclude any risk of having to run, because the only thing worse than being fat on a plane is being fat, red, sweaty, and huffing on a plane. I go to the bathroom multiple times before boarding because, again, I avoid getting out of my seat at all cost, even on international flights. (The path from fat-shaming to deep vein thrombosis is short and slick.) I linger by the gate so I can board as early as possible and be the first one in my row; that way I don't have to make anyone wait in the aisle while I get my body folded up and squared away. As I pass the flight attendants at the front of the plane I ask, discreetly, if I can have a seat-belt extender, to minimize the embarrassment of having to ring the call button once I'm seated and let my seatmates know they're next to the too-big kind of fat person. Finally, I press myself up against the wall like a limpet and try to go to sleep, avoiding any position in which I might snore and remind everyone about my fat, lumpy windpipe.

That's the amount of forethought, anxiety, and emotional energy that goes into every single flight. Fat people are not having fun on planes. There is no need to make it worse.

Just a month or two after the first time I didn't fit, on a crack-of-dawn flight from New York City to Seattle, I had my first ever, um, disagreement with a seatmate. Despite my online irascibility, I'm pathologically polite in person, so face-to-face hostility is foreign to me. I'd almost missed the plane—I was that person staggering on board just before the doors closed—and I'm sure this dude thought he was going to have the three-seat row all to himself. He was about my age, maybe midthirties, an average kind of Jon Gosselin–looking guy. Probably works in an office; hangs out at, like, an Irish pub because he's too old for clubs but still wants to hit on chicks; has always wanted to learn to surf but will never get around to it. I don't know, just a guy. I flashed him an apologetic smile and pointed to the middle seat. "Hey, sorry, I'm over there." He didn't respond or make eye contact, just glared blankly at my hips. Then, as I went to put my bag in the overhead bin, I heard him mutter something sour.

"[Something something], say excuse me."

I froze. Was someone being a dick to me? In person? At seven a.m.? In an enclosed space? For no reason? When I have a hangover? And we're about to be stuck next to each other for the next five hours? I'm used to men treating me like garbage virtually, or from fast-moving cars, but this close-quarters face-to-face shit-talking was a jarring novelty.

"What?" I asked.

"Nothing," he muttered, still refusing to look at me.

"No," I said. If I'm going to make a living telling women to stick up for themselves, I need to do it too. "You said something. What did you say?"

"Nothing," he repeated.

"No," I repeated. "What did you say? Tell me."

"I said," he snapped, "that if you want someone to move, it helps to say 'excuse me' and then get out of the way. You told me to move and then you just—" He gestured with a large circular motion at my body.

"I'm putting my bag in the overhead bin," I said, anxiety thundering in my ears. "You know, because that's how planes work?"

"Yeah," he said, dripping with disdain. "Okay."

He stood up so I could slide into the middle seat, keeping his gaze fixed on the far bank of windows, avoiding my eye contact. I sat, trying not to touch him. My head felt like a hot-air balloon. I hadn't said "excuse me" yet because I was still in the process of putting my bag in the overhead bin. The "excuse me" part of the transaction comes when you ask the other person to get up. I hadn't leaned over him or touched him or dropped anything on him. No éclairs had tumbled out of my cleavage and into his hair. Was a preemptive "sorry" really not enough? Had I violated some custom I was unaware of? Had I fallen through a tesseract and into a dimension where "sorry" means "No offense, but you have a Jon Gosselinesque face and a Kate Gosselinesque personality"? If not, I could not fathom where I'd gone wrong.

The last few passengers boarded and they closed the doors. No one came to claim our window seat, so I slid over, saying, "Looks like there's no one in the middle seat, so you won't actually have to sit next to me. Since I apparently bother you so much."

"Sounds great to me," he droned, eyes front.

As soon as he fell asleep (with his mouth open like a nerd), I passive-aggressively jarred his foot with my backpack and then said, "Oh, excuse me," because I am an adult (and he loves to hear "excuse me"!). We ignored each other for the rest of the flight.

It felt alien to be confronted so vocally and so publicly (and for such an arbitrary reason), but it also felt familiar. People say the same kind of thing to me with their eyes on nearly every flight—this guy just chose to say it with his mouth.

This is the subtext of my life: "You're bigger than I'd like you to be." "I dread being near you." "Your body itself is a breach of etiquette." "You are clearly a fucking fool who thinks that cheesecake is a vegetable." "I know that you will fart on me."

Nobody wants to sit next to a fat person on a plane. Don't think we don't know.

That's why—to return to my first-class flight—my foray into "luxury" was so disheartening. It wasn't a taste of the high life so much as an infuriating illumination of how dismal it is to fly any other way. I realized: Oh. Flying first class wasn't intrinsically special, but it was the first time in recent memory that I've felt like a human being on a plane.

We put up with economy class because most of us have no choice—we need to get from here to there and we want cheaper and cheaper tickets. I can't blame airlines for trying to stay in business by compressing as many travelers as possible into coach like a Pringles can lined with meat glue. It seems like a straightforward business decision, which is why it's confusing, as a fat person, to hear so much about how I, personally, have ruined air travel. There are entire blogs devoted to hating fat people on planes—describing their supposed transgressions and physical particulars in grotesque, gleeful detail, posting clandestine photos, and crowing about the verbal abuse that posters claim to have heaped on their bigger neighbors. As though there were a time when 1) there were no fat people, and 2) everyone passionately loved flying.

As a counterpoint, I would like to lodge a gentle reminder that air travel has been terrible for a long time. It's terrible because a plane is just a flying bus, trapped in an eternal rush hour, with recycled farts and vaporized child sputum instead of air, seats barely wider than the average human pelvis, and a bonus built-in class hierarchy. Barring a brief period in the '50s and '60s, when airplanes were reportedly flying, smoke-choked bacchanals staffed by Bond girls wearing baby onesies, air travel has been a study in discomfort giving way to ever more profitable methods of making people uncomfortable. That has nothing to do with fat people's bodies.

I'm sure some fat people are fat by their own hand, without any underlying medical conditions, but a lot of other fat people are fat because they're sick or disabled. Unless you're checking every human being's bloodwork before they pull up Kayak.com, you do not know which fat people are which. Which means, inevitably, if you think fat people are "the problem" (and not, say, airlines hoping to squeeze out extra revenue, or consumers who want cheap airline tickets without sacrificing amenities), you are penalizing a significant number of human beings emotionally and financially for a disease or disability that already complicates their lives. Ethically, that's fucked up.

That dude next to me didn't call me fat to my face. I don't even know if that's what was bothering him, although I recognized the way he looked at my body (my body, not my face, not once, not ever). I can't be sure why that guy was mad at me, but I know why people are usually mad at me on planes. I know that he disliked me instantly, he invented a reason to be a jerk to me, and then he executed it. More importantly, I see other people staring those same daggers at other fat people's bodies every day, in the sky and on the ground, and congratulating themselves for it, as though they're doing a righteous public service.

Even less popular than being fat on a plane, I soon discovered, was talking about being fat on a plane with anything but groveling, poo-eating penitence.

Not long after it happened, I wrote about "say excuse me" guy in a little essay for *Jezebel*, about holiday air travel, not expecting anything beyond the usual "eat less/exercise more" anti-fat backlash. It was a vulnerable story, and a sympathetic one, I thought, about the low-grade hostility that fat people face every day (and about the debilitating self-doubt bred by micro-aggressions—does this person really hate me or am I being oversensitive?), and I told it plainly, as it happened. I assumed that people could connect with me, the person, and potentially break down some of the prejudice that makes fat people such popular pariahs. The actual response caught me off guard, though it shouldn't have.

Without considering for a moment that I might have interpreted my own experiences accurately—that this very simple and famously common interaction, an airplane passenger feeling resentful about sitting next to a fat person, might be true—readers bent over backwards to construct elaborate alternate narratives in which I was the villain. I was the one being rude, by saying "sorry" instead of "excuse me." (What rule is that?) I had smothered him with my gut when I reached up to stow my bag. (Ew, as if I like touching people.) I had delayed the flight with my entitled, irresponsible failure to show up on time. (I was there within the boarding window, I just wasn't early, the way I like to be.) I was the last person on the plane (nope). I was still drunk, looking for a fight, ranting and raving and reeking of booze. (What do I look like—a freshman?)

In the same breath that commenters were telling me I was overreacting, I was delusional, I was lying—a man couldn't possibly have been hostile to me on an airplane— they were also chiming in with and commiserating over their own anecdotes about the horrors of flying near disgusting, smelly, presumptuous fat people. So which is it? Are fat people treated just fine on planes or is flying with fat people such a torment that it warrants a public crusade?

Part of writing is choosing which details to include and which to discard. Part of reading is deciding whether or not you can trust your narrator. The Internet made it very clear, very quickly, once my post went up, that trusting me was not on the table. I didn't bother to mention, for instance, that the dude was sitting with his legs splayed wide in classic "MAN'S STEAMING BALLS COMING THROUGH" fashion, with his foot in the middle footwell (my footwell) where I'd stowed my backpack. (If I had, I would have been accused of feminist hysteria, the way women who call out subway "manspreading" have been.) I didn't waste words on the fact that when they closed the cabin doors and it became clear that our window seat was going to be unoccupied, I moved my backpack to the window seat, where I'd already been sitting. So, yeah, I jostled the guy's foot when I moved my bag, because the guy's foot was blocking my bag. The guy didn't even wake up. I thought it was tedious and unnecessary exposition (and, if you're still awake at this point in this boring-ass paragraph, you'll see that I was right). I assumed that *Jezebel* readers would trust that I am as I have always presented myself—a kind, pragmatic, nonviolent, reasonable human being—and read my story with a modicum of empathy, or at least the benefit of the doubt.

Within hours of my post cycling through the Internet sausage factory, I was barraged with bizarre fictions on Twitter: I had stumbled onto the plane drunk, delayed takeoff as I screamed at the guy to move, sat on him, viciously kicked him with my wide-calf boot, brutally beaten him with my backpack, continued to harass and mock him for the duration of the flight as he quivered in terror and pretended to sleep, then eagerly libeled him on the Internet. One particularly putrid community of misogynists threatened to "report me to the FBI" for "assault and battery in a federal airspace." (LOL, go for it, sluggers.) They also coordinated a (temporarily successful) effort to Google bomb my name so that their "article"—"Fat Feminist Lindy West Goes Berserk Because She No Longer Fits in Airplane Seats"—came up on the first page of search results.

Here's an excerpt from that totally reasonable and not-at-all-bigoted-because-fatphobia-isn't-a-real-thing reaction to my article ([sic] throughout):

> *Is this who we want having influence in our country? Society must realize there are consequences to fat feminist beliefs. They range from the concrete (not fitting on airplanes) to creating a class of perennial female victims-seekers who have no notion of personality responsibility. Instead of focusing on self-improvement, they seek to blame everyone else for their problems, even innocent men on airplanes who have their property damaged from the canckled legs of deranged women.*

On a different site, a commenter wrote: "Man FUCK HER. I wouldn't want to stoop to feminist levels and wish bodily harm—castration/acid burning her face, etc.—on her, but if I did, then I'd say I wish that Buffalo Bill taught her a lesson or two."

And another: "My god, what a putrid and deluded fucking cunt. I'm so glad that her health decisions that are none of my business will see her in an early grave. I'm sure when she loses her legs from diabetes or has a heart attack at forty due to lard clogged arteries that will be the patriarchy's fault too. Bitch."

Very astute, boys. I was probably just imagining the whole thing. I'm certainly not an adult human being who's been successfully reading social cues for thirty years. And we certainly don't have any evidence of general animosity toward fat people, particularly fat people on planes.

Before the day I didn't fit, this conversation was largely an abstraction for me. My stance was the same as it is now (if people pay for a service, it's the seller's obligation to accommodate those people and provide the service they paid for), but I didn't understand what that panicky, uncertain walk down the aisle actually felt like. How inhumane it is.

I'm telling you this not to garner sympathy or pity, or even to change your opinion about how airplanes should accommodate larger passengers. I'm just telling you, human to human, that life is complicated and fat people are trying to live. Same as you. Reasons I have had to fly within the past five years: For work (often). To see beloved friends get married. To speak to college students about rape culture and body image. To hold my father's hand while he died. I'm sorry, but I'm not constraining and rearranging my life just because no one cares enough to make flying accessible to all bodies.

Airlines have no incentive to fix this problem until we, collectively, as a society, demand it. We don't insist on a solution because it's still culturally acceptable to be cruel to fat people. When even pointing out the problem— saying, "my body does not fit in these seats that I pay for"—returns nothing but abuse and scorn, how can we ever expect that problem to be addressed? The real issue here isn't money, it's bigotry. We don't care about fat people because it is okay not to care about them, and we don't take care of them because we think they don't deserve care.

It's the same lack of care that sees fat people dying from substandard medical attention, being hired at lower rates and convicted at higher ones, and being accused of child abuse for feeding their children as best they can.

You can't fix a problem by targeting its victims. Even if you hate fat people with all your heart, if you actually want to get us out of "your" armrest space, defending our humanity is the only pragmatic solution. Because no matter how magnificently you resent them, you cannot turn a fat person into a thin person in time for the final boarding call (nor a full bladder into an empty one, nor a crying baby into a baked potato). The only answer is to decide we're worth helping.

Chuckletown, USA, Population: Jokes

For my junior year English requirement in high school, I took a class called "Autobiography," because it was taught by my favorite teacher. I didn't have anything remotely noteworthy to say about myself (*Today after Basketball I Tried Red Powerade Instead of Blue Powerade but I Think I'll Switch Back Tomorrow, I Don't Know, I Am Also Considering Mandarin Blast: A Life*, by Lindy West), nor was I particularly interested, at the time, in reading the memoirs of others (*I Read This Entire Book about Florence Griffith Joyner and It Did Not Contain a Single Gryphon, Chimera, or Riddling Sphinx, BOOOOOOOO: A Life*, by Lindy West). My friends and I signed up for all of Ms. Harper's classes religiously, though, so "Autobiography" it was.

Ms. Harper was one of those young, cool teachers who

understood jokes and wore normal clothes, and you could tell she still had a social life and probably went to bar trivia and maybe even a Tori Amos concert once in a while for a fun gals' night. We were mildly infatuated with her because she was a relatable human being in the alienating, chaotic landscape of public high school—unlike, say, the primordial Spanish teacher who seemed to be carved out of desk, whose favorite lesson plan was to turn on *Lambada: The Forbidden Dance*** and doze off. Ms. Harper was the kind of baby-showers-and-brunch friend I imagined myself having mimosas with when I was, like, thirty-two. (Coincidentally, I ran into Ms. Harper at a movie theater when I was thirty-two, moved to giddily embrace her, and she did not remember me. FINE. IT'S FINE.)

For the final exam, we were supposed to make a presentation, ten or fifteen minutes long, about anything we wanted. Any hobby or interest that we felt made us unique—whatever our thing was. One guy showed us his scuba gear and talked about why he liked scuba diving. (I don't remember, but "fish," probably?) A quiet, unassuming dude brought in a massive easel, on which he displayed his painstakingly detailed step-by-step guide to "Gettin' Dipped," which was a kind of proto–Tom Haverford swagger manual ("Step One: Get Money"). The band

---

* Once we got bored of *Lambada*, a few months into the school year, he'd switch to a Spanish dub of the 1996 Michael Keaton human cloning comedy *Multiplicity*, or *Mis Otros Yo*.

kids showed off their spit valves, and the outdoor ed kids bragged about their search and rescue pagers and someone served pupusas that she made with her mom.

As the date of my presentation loomed, so did my despair. Anything that could remotely be considered "my thing" was either too childish, too insignificant, or too dorky to say out loud in front of a room full of teenagers. What—collecting miniature ceramic cat families? Choir? Feminist young adult high fantasy? I might as well do my presentation on "my binky" or "calling the cops on Jeremy's house party" or "[whatever style of jeans is most unfashionable during your era, deep in the future, in which scholars and kings are no doubt still reading this classic book]."

How are you supposed to choose what represents you as a human being when you have no idea who you are yet? When I asked myself the question honestly—what is my thing?—the only answer I could come up with was that I liked watching TV, eating hot sandwiches, and hanging out with my friends. Tragically, I was not enough of a visionary at the time to turn "Leah, Hester, Emily, Aditi, Tyler, Claire, and a panini" into an oral report, so I was like, shrug, guess I'll go with "watching TV."

I really did. I stayed up all night the night before my presentation, two VCRs whirring hot on the floor of our basement, editing together a montage of all of my top clips. I arranged them chronologically—not by release date, but in the order in which I'd loved them—from my favorite when I was a toddler (John Cleese guesting on *The Muppet Show*) all the way up to what my friends and I were having giggle fits over at the time (*Mr. Show*). Even though this was pre-YouTube, pre-torrenting, pre-home-editing-software, I had everything I needed on hand: Since sixth grade, I'd been obsessively recording off the TV, and had amassed a mountain of painstakingly labeled VHS tapes. I taped Letterman and Conan every night. I taped *Talk Soup*, *SNL*, *Politically Incorrect*, every stand-up special on Comedy Central, *Fawlty Towers*, *Garfield's Halloween Adventure*, the earliest episodes of *The Daily Show*. Anything I thought was funny, I taped it, and watched it over and over, hoping to absorb its powers.

I don't remember everything that ended up in my montage, but I know I used the part in *Bill & Ted's Excellent Adventure* (favorite movie, 1989 to present), when Bill's trying to keep his stepmom from noticing that he and Keanu Reeves are forcing six kidnapped historical figures to do his chores: "These are my friends...Herman the Kid, Socrates Johnson, Bob Genghis Khan..." There was this Conan clip I thought was so fucking funny—a character called the "Narcoleptic Craftsman," where the entire bit was that the Narcoleptic Craftsman would fall asleep during a woodworking segment and cut all his fingers off. "See," Andy Richter deadpanned, "have a craftsman on, OR have a narcoleptic on. It's when you combine the two that you get something like this."

I cut all my treasures together on one tape, wrote

up some hasty trash about how my "favorite pastime is laughing,"* claimed that this was a highly academic audit of "the evolution of my sense of humor," and sped to class. As I floundered through my speech and the tape rolled, I could see disappointment solidifying on Ms. Harper's face. She liked me—she said I was smart, and a good writer—and this was such an obvious cop-out. My tape was too long, and the bell rang before it was over. People wandered out without finishing it, bored. For years afterwards, thinking of that presentation made me a little sick.

The following year, just months before graduation, I met a girl named Meagan in Shakespeare class. We ran in overlapping circles, but somehow had never connected. From afar, I found her intimidating, and she never noticed me at all. I had that effect on people. In close quarters, though, assigned to the same group project, we were platonically, electrically smitten—both of us, I think, relieved to finally meet someone else who was "a bit much" for people in all the same ways. Too loud, too awkward, too boisterous, too intense. Meagan is aggressively exuberant. She doesn't say anything that isn't funny, which sounds like an exaggeration, but isn't. She was bold in ways that I had never imagined, even though I'd shrugged off most of my shyness years before: Meagan was honest. She wasn't

---

* [Fire hose of vomit]

nice to people she didn't like. She talked back to authority figures if she thought they were feeding her bullshit. She delivered hard *"no"*s and didn't waver.

I discovered that Meagan was an obsessive comedy archivist, just like me. It was uncanny: Her bedroom was stacked with fat loaves of VHS tapes, also painstakingly labeled (in her handwriting weirdly like mine), that she'd been recording off the TV for years, just like me. We'd drive around for hours in my Volvo, listening to Mitch Hedberg and David Cross; with the advent of Napster, we could make each other entire mix-CDs that were just audio clips from *The Simpsons*. Meagan spent fifty dollars on eBay—an exorbitant amount of money at the time—to get a bootleg VHS copy of every *Tenacious D* episode. We wore the tape out. Within months, our vocal cadence merged, until even we couldn't tell our voices apart, and sometimes we went so long without saying anything that wasn't a reference or an inside joke that we might as well have been speaking some feral bog twin language. We won "funniest" in the senior class poll.

We were fucking unbearable.

Comedy has always been a safe harbor for the *"a bit much"*es of the world. The things that made Meagan and me horrible to be around—the caterwauling, the irreverence, the sometimes inappropriate honesty, the incessant riffing—aren't just welcome in comedy, they're fundamental. For me, as a kid who felt lonely, ugly, simultaneously invisible and too visible, comedy felt like a friend. That's its greatest magic—more than any other art form, it forces you to interact with it; it forces you to feel not alone. Because you can't be alone when someone's making you laugh, physically reaching into your body and eliciting a response. Comedy is also smart. It speaks the truth. It was everything I wanted to be. Plus, if you're funny, it doesn't matter what you look like.

During college, in Los Angeles, I went to comedy shows as often as I could (usually alone; my roommates didn't much care): Patton Oswalt working out new material at M Bar, Paul F. Tompkins singing "Danny Boy" at Largo, Mitch Hedberg at the Improv soon before he died. It was rapturous. We were between comedy booms at the time, and I didn't understand that normal people weren't starstruck by Marc Maron and Greg Proops and Maria Bamford. Why were they so accessible? Don't they keep the celebrities in a bunker somewhere? Why was Bob Odenkirk, the most important man in the world, sitting next to me at the bar, where anyone could talk to him? How was it possible that I just accidentally body-slammed Bobcat Goldthwait outside the bathroom? Also, was he okay? (He is very small!)

Once, at the Paul F. Tompkins Show (which I never missed), I was seated at a cocktail table next to Andy Richter and his wife, Sarah Thyre. "Have a craftsman on," I thought, "OR have a narcoleptic on. Have a craftsman on, OR have a narcoleptic on!" I ran to the bathroom and called Meagan. "Fuck you," she said.

I wanted to be immersed in comedy—the creation of it and the consumption of it—all the time. I couldn't sleep without Ricky Gervais and Stephen Merchant's XFM radio show playing; I've probably fallen asleep to Gervais's voice more than my own mother's. I never wanted to do stand-up, particularly, though I certainly nursed an idealized notion of how "fun" it would be to hang out in comedy club greenrooms ("HAHAHAHAHAH" — Me now). My real Xanadu was the TV writers' room. I couldn't believe that people got paid to sit around a table and riff with their friends—building from scratch the kind of rich, brilliant TV universes that had felt like family to me growing up.

I graduated in 2004 with an English degree and a case of impostor syndrome so intense that I convinced myself I "didn't have enough ideas" to become a writer of any kind.

Instead, when people asked me what I wanted to do with my life, I'd say this: "Well, I only have one skill, which is that I know how to make sentences, kind of, but I don't know, I'm not, like, a writer." A COMPELLING PITCH, YOUNG WEST. With no other options, or ideas, or interests, I took an unpaid internship at a free "parenting magazine" in the Valley. It was essentially a packet of coupons and ads for backyard clowns, padded with a handful of "articles" written by interns (me) and a calendar highlighting what time Three Dog Night would be appearing at the Antelope Valley Fair (four p.m.). There were three people in editorial (including me), and what seemed like hundreds in sales.

Despite still being a child myself in, like, nine out of ten ways (exception: boobs), I threw myself gamely into the "job." If I'm going to sit in a windowless office in Encino for twenty hours a week for zero dollars, I might as well try to get some clips out of it. The slimy Young Businessman who owned the place didn't care that I was alarmingly, dangerously unqualified to dispense parenting advice, so I was assigned pieces on anything from "what to do if your child is a bully" to "should you bank your baby's umbilical cord blood?" (I believe my answers were, "IDK, talk to it?" and "uuuuuuhhhhhhhhhhhhhhhhhhhhhhhhhhhhhhhhhhhhh hhhhhhhhhhhhhhhhhhhhhhhhhhhhhhhhhhhhhhhhhhhh hhhhhhhhhhhhhhhhhhhhhhhhhhhhhhhhhhhhhhhhhhhh hhhhhhhhhhhhhhhhhhhhhhhhhhhhhhhhhhhhhhhhhhhh hhhhhhhhhhhhhhhhhhhhhhhhhhhhhhhhhhhhhhhhhhhh hhhhhhhhhhhhhhhhhhhhh............yes?" respectively.) I can only hope that no families were destroyed during my tenure. To be fair, though, DON'T GET YOUR BABY BLOOD TIPS FROM A CLOWN PAMPHLET.

I finally quit the day one of the slimers made me drive to a lumberyard in South Pasadena to pick up a cord of firewood for his motivational corporate firewalking side business. This was *not* in the terms of my internship. He instructed me to drop the wood off—and unload it myself, alone, log by log—at this creepy, barren porn-condo that apparently was Slimer Firewalking Inc.'s HQ. He touched my arm, slipped me twenty dollars, and asked, huskily, if I'd ever walked on hot coals. "Yeah, no," I said, moving toward the door.

"Do you want to?" he called after me. "It'll change you."

"I'm good!"

In retrospect, I should have sued that place for all of its dirty, on-fire clown money. Instead, I gave up on L.A. and moved back home.

Seattle, in 2005, had our own little comedy boom. I started hanging around open mics because Hari Kondabolu—college roommate of a friend—had moved to town and joined our social circle. (Coincidentally, he lived in a house with the guy who brought the scuba gear into Autobiography class, because Seattle is only four people big.) When I looked at Hari's Friendster profile, before we'd even met, and discovered that he was a comic, I thought, "Holy shit. I'm about to have a comedy friend."

People who were around at the time still talk about that scene with reverence. It did feel special—some lucky confluence of the right people, the right rooms, the right mentorship, the right crowds, the right branding. Comics did weird, experimental stuff and filled seats at each other's shows. You could feel something happening. Meanwhile, the national comedy boom was percolating—Louis

CK was becoming a household name, people were starting to realize the potential of podcasting.

At those early Seattle shows, a few faces were ubiquitous: Hari, Emmett Montgomery, Dan Carroll, Derek
Sheen, Andy Peters, Scott Moran, Andy Haynes (WHO
WAS ALSO IN AUTOBIOGRAPHY CLASS OH MY
GOD), and Ahamefule J. Oluo, a tall, gloomy single dad
who quickly formed a writing partnership with Hari and
was folded into our social circle as well.

I did stand-up once in a while too, usually at Hari's
urging, but knew pretty quickly that it wasn't my thing. I
hated telling the same jokes over and over, and I hated the
grind, which means I never tried hard enough to actually
get good. (If you've never done stand-up in a brightly lit
pizzeria at six p.m. in front of four people who were not
informed that there would be comedy, try it, it's great.) I
liked performing, though, and eventually I started hosting
the Seattle outpost of The Moth, a live storytelling show—
three hours of crowd work twice a month. I was good at it.

Through some dark sorcery, I managed to parlay my parenting magazine clips into an internship in the theater
department of the *Stranger*, which turned into freelance
writing work, which turned into a staff position as a film
critic, where I wrote goofy movie reviews and a column
covering Seattle comedy called "Chuckletown, USA, Population: Jokes." A representative excerpt:

WEDNESDAY 6/1
ROB DELANEY
Rob Delaney is the best person on Twitter. He loves
pussy. Rendezvous, 10 pm, $15, 21+.

I was going to comedy shows at night, interviewing comics, watching movies and TV for a living, and writing jokes in the newspaper all day. Then, one day, it struck me: I did it. I got paid to watch comedy and make people laugh. In just seven years, I'd actually lived up to that stupid Autobiography presentation.

Like, Toby isn't a professional scuba diver and Jessica C. isn't an itinerant bassoonist and Jessica R. doesn't run a pupusa stand, although maybe she should get on that already because those things were hella good. I did hear a rumor that "Gettin' Dipped" guy is a male model now, so technically he is professionally "dipped" (touché), but other than that, I couldn't think of anyone else from class whose presentation actually foreshadowed the course of their life. Not that they were supposed to, of course— it was just a throwaway assignment. But for me, who'd struggled to define myself for so many years, it was an unexpected wonder to realize that my presentation wasn't an embarrassment—it was a goddamn prophecy.

At the Bridgetown Comedy Festival in Portland (in 2010, its third year), I found myself standing next to Ahamefule in the back of a club, watching an old friend's set. The guy was doing a bit about sex, or maybe online dating—I don't remember the premise, but I remember that the punch line was "herpes," and it was killing. It wasn't a self-deprecating joke about the comic's own herpes. It was about other people. People with herpes are gross, ha ha ha. Girls with herpes are sluts. I hope I never accidentally have sex with a gross slut with herpes! Let's all laugh at people with herpes and pretend like none of the people in the room has herpes, even though, depending on which statistics you believe, anywhere from 15 per cent to 75 percent of the people in the room have herpes. Let's force all of those people to laugh along too, ha ha ha.

It's a lazy joke, but a common one, and a year earlier I might not have thought anything of it. Just then, though, a friend was going through some shit—a partner had lied about his STI status, then slipped the condom off without her consent, and a few weeks later she erupted in sores so painful she couldn't walk or sit, move or not move. She was devastated, not just because of the violation, the deception, and the pain, but because the disease is so stigmatized. She was sure she'd never be able to date again. It seemed entirely possible to her that she might be alone forever, and, she thought, maybe she deserved it. "You know," I remember telling her, "it's just a skin condition. A rash, like acne or hives or eczema. Are those shameful?" I rubbed her back while she sobbed in my car.

That interaction was fresh in my mind as I watched this

dude—who is a funny, good person—tell his joke, and I thought about all the people in the audience who were plastering smiles over their feelings of shame, of being tainted and ruined forever, in that moment. I thought about my friend, who—unless you believe recreational sex is an abomination and STIs are god's dunce caps—didn't "deserve" this virus. Neither did anyone else in that room. So, did she deserve to have her trauma be the butt of a joke? Even if you could milk a cheap laugh out of the word "herpes," was it worth it to shore up the stigma that made real people's lives smaller and harder? Was the joke even that funny anyway?

Stigma works like this: Comic makes people with herpes the butt of his joke. Audience laughs. People with herpes see their worst fears affirmed—they are disgusting, broken, unlovable. People without herpes see their worst instincts validated—they are clean, virtuous, better. Everyone agrees that no one wants to fuck someone with herpes. If people with herpes want to object, they have to 1) publicize the fact that they have herpes, and 2) be accused of oversensitivity, of ruining the fun. Instead, they stay quiet and laugh along. The joke does well. So well that maybe the comedian writes another one.

I cycled through that system over and over in my head. It was maddeningly efficient—what were people supposed to do? More broadly, in a nation where puritanical gasbags have a death grip on our public education system, can we really expect ironclad safe sex practices in people from whom comprehensive sex ed has been withheld? Blaming and shaming people for their own illnesses has always been the realm of moralists and hypocrites, of the anti-sex status quo. Isn't comedy supposed to be the vanguard of counterculture? Of speaking truth to power? The longer I turned it over the more furious I became. Why do we all just laugh along with this?

I moved close to Aham's ear and said, over the boisterous crowd, "You know, I could have herpes."

He looked at me, clearly startled. A little thought throbbed in the back of my head—how handsome Aham was, with his broad shoulders and mole-brown eyes, towering over me at six foot five. He was an incredible comedian—insightful and fearless, always one of my favorites—and I'd recently found out he was a jazz musician too, like my dad. (He'd also been divorced multiple times, like my dad, and had two kids and a vasectomy, like my dad when he met my mom.) A mutual friend had mentioned the other day that Aham was a great cook. Was this really a dude I wanted to say "I might have herpes" to? I shoved the thoughts aside. It's just a skin condition.

"A ton of people in this audience probably have herpes," I went on, "but they have to pretend to laugh anyway. That has to be the worst feeling. Why do that to people when you could just write a different joke?"

"I don't know," he said. "But you're right. I could have herpes too."

Aham and I had been chatting at house parties and open mics for five years, but we didn't really know each other well. Years later, he told me that he'd always been a fan of my writing, but that moment shifted his perception of me forever. "I was just blown away to hear a woman talk like that," he said. "I started to realize that you weren't just funny—I'd always thought you were funny—but that you might be a really, really, radically good person." Sometimes it pays to tell hot guys you might have herpes, kids!

We were inseparable for the rest of the weekend—we went to an arcade, played hours of Plinko, drank beer, helped Hari come up with burns in a text fight he was having with Marc Maron. Within a year, Aham and I were a couple and he and my dad were playing gigs together.

This was the life I'd dreamed of at twenty-two: hanging out with comics, falling in love, riffing all day. But, in the same moment, I felt my relationship with comedy changing.

Death Wish

Comedy doesn't just reflect the world, it shapes it. Not in the way that church ladies think heavy metal hypnotizes nerds into doing school shootings, but in the way it's accepted fact that *The Cosby Show* changed America's perception of black families. We don't question the notion that *The Daily Show* had a profound effect on American politics, or that *Ellen* opened Middle America's hearts to dancing lesbians, or that propaganda works and satire is potent and Shakespeare's fools spoke truth to power. So why would we pretend, out of sheer convenience, that stand-up exists in a vacuum? If we acknowledge that it doesn't, then isn't it our responsibility, as artists, to keep an eye on which ideas we choose to dump into the water supply? Art isn't indiscriminate shit-flinging. It's pure communication, crafted with intention and care. Every comedian on every stage is saying what he's saying on purpose. So shouldn't we be welcome to examine that purpose, contextualize it within our culture at large, and critique what we find?

The short answer, I'd discover, is "nah shut up bitch lol get raped."

For years, I assumed it was a given that, at any comedy show I attended, I had to grin through a number of brutal jokes about my gender: about beating us, about raping us, about why we deserve it, about ranking us, about fucking us, about not fucking us, about reducing our already dehumanized existence to a handful of insulting stereotypes. This happened all the time, even at supposedly liberal alt shows, even at shows booked by my friends. Misogyny in comedy was banal. Take my wife, please. Here's one I heard at an open mic: "Last night I brought this girl home, but she was being really loud during sex, so I told her, 'Sssshhh, you don't want to turn this rape into a murder!'" Every time, I'd bite back my discomfort and grin—because, I thought, that's just how we joke. It's "just comedy." All my heroes tell me so. This is the price if I want to be in the club. Hey, men pay a price too, don't they? People probably make fun of Eddie Pepitone for being bald.

When a comedian I loved said something that set off alarm bells for me—something racist, sexist, transphobic, or otherwise—I thought: It must be okay, because he says it's okay, and I trust him. I told myself: There must be a secret contract I don't know about, where women, or gay people, or disabled people, or black people agreed that it's cool, that this is how we joke.

But in that moment at Bridgetown, it dawned on me: Who made that rule? Who drew up that contract? I don't remember signing anything, and anyway, it seems less like a universal accord and more like a booby trap that powerful men set up to protect their "right" to squeeze cheap laughs out of life-ruining horrors—sometimes including literal torture—that they will never experience. Why should I have to sit and cheer through hours of "edgy" misogyny, "edgy" racism, "edgy" rape jokes, just to be included in an industry that belongs to me as much as anyone else?

When I looked at the pantheon of comedy gods (Bill Hicks, Eddie Murphy, George Carlin, Lenny Bruce, Louis CK, Jon Stewart, Richard Pryor, Chris Rock, Jerry Seinfeld), the alt-comedy demigods (Patton Oswalt, Zach Galifianakis, David Cross, Marc Maron, Dave Attell, Bill Burr), and even that little roster of 2005 Seattle comics I rattled off in the previous chapter, I couldn't escape the question: If that's who drafted our comedy constitution, why should I assume that my best interests are represented? That is a bunch of dudes. Of course there are exceptions—maybe Joan Rivers got to propose a bylaw or two—but you can't tell me there's no gender bias in an industry where "women aren't funny" is widely accepted as conventional wisdom. I can name hundreds of white male comedians. But how about this: Name twenty female comics. Name twenty black comics. Name twenty gay comics. If you're a comedy nerd, you probably can. That's cool. Now ask your mom to do it.

In the summer of 2012, a comedian named Daniel Tosh was onstage at the Laugh Factory in Hollywood. Tosh is a bro-comedy hero, specializing in "ironic" bigotry—AIDS, retards, the Holocaust, all with a cherubic, frat-boy smile—the kind of jokes worshiped by teenagers and lazy comics who still think it's cool to fetishize "offensiveness." Here's one of Tosh's signature I'm-just-a-bad-baby wape jokes, about playing a prank on his sister: "I got her so good a few weeks ago—I replaced her pepper spray with silly string. Anyway, that night she got raped, and she called me the next day going, 'You son of a bitch! You got me so good! As soon as I started spraying him in the face, I'm like, "Daniel! This is going to really hurt!"'" See, it's a good one, because being raped really hurts.

This particular night at the Laugh Factory, Tosh was working a bit more meta: according to an audience member who later posted her account anonymously online, he was "making some very generalizing, declarative statements about rape jokes always being funny, how can a rape joke not be funny, rape is hilarious, etc." Uncomfortable, the woman heckled: "Actually, rape jokes are never funny!"

Tosh paused, then addressed the packed house. "Wouldn't it be funny if that girl got raped by, like, five guys right now? Like right now? What if a bunch of guys just raped her?"

Horrified and frightened, the woman gathered her things and rushed out. She wrote later: "Having to basically flee while Tosh was enthusing about how hilarious it would be if I was gang-raped in that small, claustrophobic room was pretty viscerally terrifying and threatening all the same, even if the actual scenario was unlikely to take place. The suggestion of it is violent enough and was meant to put me in my place."

After the predictable viral backlash, Tosh offered a predictably tepid non-apology, and comedians lined up to support him: Patton Oswalt, Jim Norton, Anthony Jeselnik, Doug Stanhope. Oswalt wrote, "Wow, @danieltosh had to apologize to a self-aggrandizing, idiotic blogger. Hope I never have to do that (again)." Stanhope tweeted, "#FuckThatPig." They were standing up for free speech, for their art. These crazy bitches just didn't get it.

It was a few months into my time at *Jezebel*, and I was tapped to write a response. I felt confident, like I was a good fit for the assignment. I knew I had a more comprehensive understanding of the mechanics and history of comedy than your average feminist blogger. I'd been writing straight-ahead humor since the beginning of my career—you couldn't say I didn't get jokes. I had enough cred on both sides to bridge the gap between the club and the coven, to produce something constructive. The piece was called "How to Make a Rape Joke."

"I actually agree with Daniel Tosh's sentiment in his shitty backpedaling tweet ('The point I was making before I was heckled is there are awful things in the world but you can still make jokes about them #deadbabies')," I wrote. "The world is full of terrible things, including rape, and it is okay to joke about them. But the best comics use their art to call bullshit on those terrible parts of life and make them better, not worse."

Then: "This fetishization of not censoring yourself, of being an 'equal-opportunity offender,' is bizarre and bad for comedy. When did 'not censoring yourself' become a good thing? We censor ourselves all the time, because we are not entitled, sociopathic fucks...In a way, comedy is censoring yourself—comedy is picking the right words to say to make people laugh. A comic who doesn't censor himself is just a dude yelling. And being an 'equal-opportunity offender'—as in, 'It's okay, because Daniel Tosh makes fun of ALL people: women, men, AIDS victims, dead babies, gay guys, blah blah blah'—falls apart when you remember (as so many of us are forced to all the time) that all people are not in equal positions of power. 'Oh, don't worry—I punch everyone in the face! People, baby ducks, a lion, this Easter Island statue, the ocean...' Okay, well, that baby duck is dead now."

I analyzed four rape jokes that I thought "worked"—
that targeted rape culture instead of rape victims (in retrospect, I should have been harder on Louis CK, whom I
basically let off on a technicality)—and then I explained,
"I'm not saying all of this because I hate comedy—I'm
saying it because I love comedy and I want comedy to be
accessible to everyone. And right now, comedy as a whole
is overtly hostile toward women."

My point was that what we say affects the world we
live in, that words are both a reflection of and a catalyst
for the way our society operates. Comedy, in particular,
is a tremendously powerful lever of social change. Tina
Fey's Sarah Palin impression may have tipped the 2008
election for Obama. Plenty of my peers cite *The Daily Show*
as their primary news source. When you talk about rape,
I said, you get to decide where you aim: Are you making fun of rapists? Or their victims? Are you making the
world better? Or worse? It's not about censorship, it's not
about obligation, it's not about forcibly limiting anyone's
speech—it's about choice. Who are you? Choose.

I do get it. Tosh plays a character in his act—the
charming psychopath. He can say things like "rape is
hilarious" because, according to his defenders, it's obviously not. Because "everyone hates rape." It's not an
uncommon strain in comedy: Anthony Jeselnik, Jeff Ross,
Lisa Lampanelli, Cartman. The problem is, for those of
us who actually work in anti-rape activism, who move

through the world in vulnerable bodies, who spend time online with female avatars, the idea that "everyone hates rape" is anything but a given. The reason "ironically" brutal, victim-targeting rape jokes don't work the way Tosh defenders claim they do is because, in the real world, most sexual assault isn't even reported, let alone taken seriously.

Feminists don't single out rape jokes because rape is "worse" than other crimes—we single them out because we live in a culture that actively strives to shrink the definition of sexual assault; that casts stalking behaviors as romance; blames victims for wearing the wrong clothes, walking through the wrong neighborhood, or flirting with the wrong person; bends over backwards to excuse boys-will-be-boys misogyny; makes the emotional and social costs of reporting a rape prohibitively high; pretends that false accusations are a more dire problem than actual assaults; elects officials who tell rape victims that their sexual violation was "god's plan"; and convicts in less than 5 percent of rape cases that go to trial. Comedians regularly retort that no one complains when they joke about murder or other crimes in their acts, citing that as a double standard. Well, fortunately, there is no cultural narrative casting doubt on the existence and prevalence of murder and pressuring people not to report it.

Maybe we'll start treating rape like other crimes when the justice system does.

No, no one thought that a spontaneous gang rape was

going to take place just then on the stage of the Laugh Factory. But the threat of sexual violence never fully leaves women's peripheral vision. The point of Tosh's "joke" was to remind that woman that she is vulnerable. More importantly, it reinforces the idea that comedy belongs to men. Therefore, men must be correct when they tell us what comedy is.

There are two competing narratives here. One is the "Women Aren't Funny" narrative, which posits that women are leading the charge against rape jokes because we are uptight and humorless, we don't understand the mechanics of comedy, and we can't handle being the butt of a joke. Then there's the narrative that I subscribe to, which is "Holy Shit Women Are Getting Fucking Raped All the Fucking Time, Help Us, Please Help Us, Why Are You All Laughing, for God's Sake, Do Something." As a woman, I sincerely wish it were the first one.

"How to Make a Rape Joke" wasn't perfect, but it accomplished what I'd hoped: It bridged the gap between feminists and shock comics in a definitive, reasoned way. It went viral like nothing I'd ever written before, the response overwhelmingly supportive from both sides. Many female comedy fans, who'd long been told their voice wasn't welcome in this "debate," expressed relief. A lot of people said I'd finally shut the lid on the conversation. Even Patton Oswalt retweeted it. The reception was positive enough that I was able to shrug off the relatively small amount of snide abuse from the Tosh faithful:

"Shut the fuck up Lindy West (who?)"

"Just read @thelindywest's article about Tosh on Jezebel. Two things: 1) Rape is hilarious. 2) I have no idea who she is. Shut the fuck up."

"I hope Lindy and all the people who commented on this article are raped"

A few characterized my critiques of Tosh as a "witch hunt," calling me a "fascist" who was trying to destroy his career and the career of any man who challenged the feminazi orthodoxy. Contrary to their dire warnings, Tosh's popularity soared. As of the writing of this book, he's still on the air.

Overall, I was pleased. It felt like we'd made progress.

A year passed. The following summer, 2013, a feminist writer named Sady Doyle published an open letter to a young comic named Sam Morril. She recently saw him in a show and found his jokes about raping and brutalizing women questionable. Like me the previous year, she hoped to engage him in a constructive dialogue rather than just throwing the same old talking points back and forth.

"One in five women reports being sexually assaulted," Doyle wrote. "For women of color, that number is much higher; one study says that over 50% of young black women are sexually assaulted. (One of your jokes: 'I'm attracted to black women. I had sex with one once. The whole time

I was fucking her, she kept using the n-word. Yeah, the whole time, she was yelling NO!') On your Twitter, you warned people that they shouldn't attend one particular set of yours if they'd recently had a miscarriage or been raped. So, like: Are you comfortable excluding that big a chunk of the population from your set?"

Reasonable questions, in my opinion. If you're leveraging people's trauma for laughs, the least you can do is look them in the face. Why make art if you don't have a point of view?

The same week, feminist writer and comedian Molly Knefel published an impassioned essay about the contrast between Patton Oswalt's brutal dismissal of rape joke critiques and his "too soon" reverence for the victims of the Boston Marathon bombing and the Aurora theater shooting: "The suffering in Boston, as horrifying as it is, is largely abstract to a nation that has, for the most part, never experienced such a thing. On the other hand, in every room Oswalt performs comedy in, there will be a rape survivor. Statistically speaking, there will be many. There will be even more if he is performing at a university. If exceptional violence illuminates our human capacity for empathy, then structural violence shows the darkness of indifference."

Both pieces are eminently reasonable and fair—they read beautifully, even years later. The response from comedy fans, however, was horrific. Doyle and Knefel were interlopers, frauds, unfunny cunts, Nazis. Oswalt fans harangued Knefel for days until she took a break from the Internet. Sam Morril eventually replied to Doyle's letter with a lengthy blog post. The key quote? "Stand-up comedy is a performance, not a discourse." A dead end. A wall. You are not welcome. Women, it seemed, were obliged to be thick-skinned about their own rapes, while comics remained too thin-skinned to handle even mild criticism.

I was done. I wrote an essay in defense of Knefel and Doyle. It was plainer than "How to Make a Rape Joke," less affectionately fraternal, less pliant. "Comedy clubs are an overtly hostile space for women," I said. "Even just presuming we can talk about comedy gets women ripped to shreds by territorial dudes desperate to defend their authority over what's funny. 'Jokes' about rape and gendered violence are treated like an inevitability instead of a choice; like they're beyond questioning; like they're somehow equally sacred alongside women's actual humanity and physical sanctity. When women complain, however civilly, they're met with condescension, dismissal, and the tacit (or, often, explicit) message that this is not yours, you are not welcome here."

To my surprise, Oswalt tweeted a link to my post, saying that THIS was feminist discourse he could respect—not like Molly's hit piece. It was a savvy move, to use me for some feminist cred while discrediting the piece that called him out most damningly by name. I replied that if he agreed with me, he agreed with Knefel; our views were not at odds. As we volleyed back and forth, I thought about a night at M Bar in 2003 or 2004, when I'd shyly approached him after a show and told him he was my favorite comic. He was kind and generous with his time. We talked about Seattle; neither of us could remember the name of the movie theater on the Ave that wasn't the Neptune. Later, when I remembered, I e-mailed him: the Varsity. He thanked me, warm and sincere.

Fighting about rape on the Internet was not how I envisioned our next encounter.

I was in a cab to JFK, heading home from a New York business trip, when my friend W. Kamau Bell called my cell. Kamau, at the time, had a weekly show on FX, produced by Chris Rock, called *Totally Biased*—a sort of news-of-the-day talk show structured vaguely like *The Daily Show*, but with a social justice bent. Hari wrote for the show; so did Guy Branum. It was a rare writers' room—straight white men were a minority. It was a rare show.

"I want to talk to you about a crazy idea," Kamau said. "We want to do a debate about rape jokes, on the show. You versus a comic—it looks like it'll be Jim Norton."

"Oh, god," I laughed. "Do I have to?" Norton is a darling of dark comedy, a prince of the *Opie & Anthony* set—a scene that makes Howard Stern look like Terry Gross.

"Jim's not like a lot of those guys, I promise," Kamau assured me. "He's not just like, 'Ugh, feminists.' You can actually have a conversation with him. We tried to get

Colin Quinn, but honestly I think you'll be better off with Jim."

"Is this a trap?" I said.

"I promise it's not a trap."

I made arrangements to fly back to New York the following week. Now, the thing about *Totally Biased* was that it was a national television show, and the thing about me was that I was just some fucking lady. Aside from one bizarre time when the Canadian prime-time news had me on to make fun of James Cameron, I think because the anchor had a vendetta, I had never in my life been on television. I didn't have, like, a reel. I wasn't trying to be an actor or a pundit. Me being asked to be on TV was exactly the same as, say, you being asked to be on TV. Or your math teacher, or your dog, or your mommy. It was bizarre and terrifying, but I agreed, because, hey, maybe I could make a difference. Maybe I could win and comedy would open up just a crack more to female comics and audiences.

My segment was going to be framed as either comedian vs. feminist, or feminism vs. free speech—neither of which, Kamau told me, was his preference, but you had to package things a certain way on television. Fine by me, I said, tamping down my anxiety about debating whether or not it's a good idea to glorify the victimization of women onstage within a framework that explicitly excludes women from even being capable of comedy. What does just some fucking lady know of television?

Totally Biased taped in a haunted hotel in Midtown—the set a penny-bright, Technicolor diorama, while behind the scenes was this sort of moldering, dripping, Soviet gray dungeon tower. I gave it fifty-fifty odds that I'd be kidnapped by a masked, erotic ghost on my way to the bathroom. I had a quick sit-down with Kamau and Guy to go over my general talking points. "The time is going to go faster than you think," Guy warned me. "Don't save all your best shit for the end—you won't get to say it."

Producer Chuck Sklar took me aside and told me that Chris Rock was coming to my taping. "He doesn't usually come," he said, "but he kind of hates this whole rape joke thing. Thinks it's whiny. So he's curious to see how you're going to do." First of all, solid pep talk, boss. Thanks. Second of all, what the fuck?

One flawed but instructive plank in the debate over rape jokes is the concept of "punching up" versus "punching down." The idea is that people in positions of power should avoid making jokes at the expense of the powerless. That's why, at a company party, the CEO doesn't roast the janitor ("Isn't it funny how Steve can barely feed his family? This guy knows what I'm talking about!" [points to other janitor]). Because that would be disgusting, and both janitors would have to work late to clean up everyone's barf. The issue isn't that it's tasteless and cruel (though it is), but that it mocks the janitors for getting the short end of an oppressive system that the CEO actively works to keep in place—a system that enables him to be a rich dick.

In a 1991 interview with *People* magazine, Molly Ivins put it perfectly: "There are two kinds of humor. One kind that makes us chuckle about our foibles and our shared humanity—like what Garrison Keillor does. The other kind holds people up to public contempt and ridicule—that's what I do. Satire is traditionally the weapon of the powerless against the powerful. I only aim at the powerful. When satire is aimed at the powerless, it is not only cruel—it's vulgar."

Punching up versus punching down isn't a mandate or a hard-and-fast rule or a universal taxonomy—I'm sure any contrarian worth his salt could list exceptions all day—it's simply a reminder that systems of power are always relevant, a helpful thought exercise for people who have trouble grasping why "bitch" is worse than "asshole." It doesn't mean that white people are better than black people, it means that we live in a society that treats white people better than black people, and to pretend that we don't is an act of violence.

Here's the reason I bring this up: I've always been told that "punching up" was a concept coined by Chris Rock. That attribution might be apocryphal—I can't find a direct quote from Rock himself—but my enduring comedy hero Stewart Lee said it with some authority in a *New Statesman* column about why right-wingers make terrible comedians:

"The African-American stand-up Chris Rock maintained that stand-up comedy should always be punching upwards. It's a heroic little struggle. You can't be a right-wing clown without some character caveat, some vulnerability, some obvious flaw. You're on the right. You've already won. You have no tragedy. You're punching down . . . Who could be on a stage, crowing about their victory and ridiculing those less fortunate than them without any sense of irony, shame or self-knowledge? That's not a stand-up comedian. That's just a cunt."

Are rape jokes so sacred—and misogyny so invisible— that the dude who literally invented the model for social responsibility in comedy can't imagine a world without them? I never got an answer. Rock didn't come to the taping after all.

Backstage, before we got started, I met Jim for the first time—he told me he loved my "How to Make a Rape Joke" piece, said we agreed more than we disagreed. "Duh," I joked. "I'm right." We had a good rapport. I felt jumpy but righteous.

When we got onstage, my heart sank quickly. In my intro, to an audience that largely had never heard of me, Kamau explained, "She's a staff writer for *Jezebel* [who's] called out everyone from Louis CK to Daniel Tosh, and now she's ready to put Jim on blast." The majority of *Totally Biased* viewers would have no idea who I was, and they heard no mention of my lifelong comedy obsession, the fact that I've done comedy, that I write about comedy, that (at least at the time) I was most widely known in my career for writing humor. They had no reason to assume I had any standing to critique comedy at all.

Before the debate had even started, I was framed as combative, bitchy, shrill. I wasn't there to have a constructive discussion, I was there to put Jim "on blast." "Call-out culture" and putting people "on blast" are both loaded terms that the anti-social-justice right loves to throw scornfully back at activists. To unfriendly ears—of which, I'd soon learn, there were many pairs listening—the terms connote overreaction, hysteria, stridence. "Comedian vs. feminist." I felt uneasy.

Kamau addressed his first question to Jim. "Jim, do you think comedians should be able to say anything they want to say without any repercussions?"

Silently, I thanked Kamau. Whether intentional or not, the question was framed in a way that forced Jim to concede a few points right off the bat. Everything has repercussions, obviously. The audience laughs, or they don't. They come see you again, or they don't. They buy your album, or they don't. You get booked again, or you don't. He couldn't possibly deny that with a straight face.

Jim nodded enthusiastically, eyes wide. "If you're trying to be funny, I think! Everybody knows the difference—Michael Richards said something in anger. Reasonable people can sense when you're trying to be funny and when you're trying to be angry. I think, like Matt and Trey said on *South Park*, it's either all okay or none of it's okay."

He referenced a joke about Hitler that Kamau had made in an earlier segment, then added: "If we go down the road of 'Hey, don't make fun of this, don't make fun of that,' well, then people have a very legitimate argument to go, 'Well, don't mention Hitler in any context, because it's never humorous!' So I'm just not comfortable going down that road. I just think as long as you're trying to be funny, you're okay."

"Everybody knows the difference," he said. "Reasonable people can sense when you're trying to be funny." There's a nasty implication there. The entire rape joke debate can be boiled down to women saying, "These are not just jokes. These bleed into the world and validate our abusers and reinforce our silence. These are rooted in misogyny, not humor. These are not funny." Therefore, Jim implied, women are not "reasonable people." "Everybody knows the difference" except feminists, apparently.

Kamau threw the question to me. I breathed sharply through my nose, trying to slow my heart. I wanted to establish myself as someone who wasn't there to equivocate, to bow and scrape, to cede ground to an older, more famous man who talks for a living. I know what I'm talking about, and I mean it. Don't fuck with me. I also wanted to open with a laugh. "I think that question is dumb," I said.

"Everything has repercussions. If you're talking about legal repercussions, yeah, I do not think that comedy should be censored, and we're not here to talk about censorship, and"—I gestured to Jim—"I'm pretty sure we agree." The censorship argument is a boring red herring—I wanted to knock it down early. Rape joke apologists are quick to cry "free speech," to use the word "allowed," as though there are certain things comedians are and aren't "allowed" to say "anymore." Barring the most extreme forms of hate speech and credible, specific threats of violence, there is no legislative body governing comedy club stages. The "thought police" is not a real law enforcement agency.

"What I'm talking about is the kind of repercussion where you choose to say something that traumatizes a person who's already been victimized, and then I choose to call you a dick."

Jim cut in. "I totally agree with you..."

(Great. Are we done?)

"...and if you think somebody sucks for what they said onstage, you should blog about it! You should write about it! As long as a person isn't calling for somebody to get in trouble for an opinion or a joke."

The vagueness of "trouble" felt like a misdirection. "But what do you mean by trouble?" I asked, trying to pin him down. "Is the trouble 'people are mad at you'?"

"The trouble is, I do *Opie & Anthony*, the radio show. So a lot of time, the trouble people will do is if you're doing jokes they don't like, they begin to target your advertisers. Because the market should dictate whether or not people enjoy you. But they'll go to the advertisers and say, 'They're making jokes that we don't like, so remove your advertising support,' which is a way to punish them. That's the type of trouble I'm talking about."

So Jim was fine with people complaining about comedians, as long as we do it where no one can hear us—as long as we don't complain in any of the ways that actually produce change. No petitions, no letter-writing campaigns, no boycotts. It's odd to invoke "the market" in such an anti-market sentiment. People boycott because boycotting works—and, more importantly, because it is the only leverage available to us. People target advertisers because they're tired of their hard-won consumer dollars going to pay sexists and racists and homophobes who got those jobs, at least partially, by coasting on the privileges and benefit of the doubt conferred by sexism and racism and homophobia. Also, you know, you're not entitled to a job. It is okay for a white dude to be fired.

It is also okay to draw hard-and-fast distinctions between different ideas—to say that some ideas are good and some ideas are bad. There's a difference between church groups boycotting JCPenney because JCPenney put a gay couple in their catalog and gay people boycotting Chick-fil-a because Chick-fil-a donated millions of dollars to groups working to strip gay people of rights and protections. Gay people wearing shawl-collar half-zip ecru sweaters does not oppress Christians. Christians turning their gay children out on to the streets, keeping gay spouses from sitting at each other's deathbeds, and casting gay people as diseased predators so that it's easier to justify beating and murdering them does oppress gay people.

That said, right-wing Christians should have the right to boycott and write letters to whomever they please. The goal is to change the culture to the point where those boycotts are unsuccessful. You do that by being vocal and uncompromising about which ideas are good and which are bad—which ones we will tolerate, as a society, and which ones we will not. I do not tolerate rape apologia. And, yes, I want to actively work to build a society in which rape apologists face social consequences.

The next few minutes of the debate were more of the same: Kamau asked me if I thought that comedy clubs are "inherently hostile environments for women," to which I joked, "Well, they're dark basements full of angry men." (I took a tremendous amount of abuse for that quip later on, from male comedians who were "offended" by my characterization of them. Weird—I thought "reasonable people can sense when you're trying to be funny.") Jim compared feminists complaining about sexism to religious people complaining about mockery of their religion. He hammered away, yet again, at the idea that "we all know the difference" between "a comedy club where you understand that we're trying to have an emotion pulled out of us, which is laughter, and standing up at the office party"—here he pantomimed raising a toast—"and going, 'to rape!'"

I was frustrated. What the fuck is the point of debating the cultural impact of jokes if your opponent's only argument is "They're jokes!" It's a cheap trick, forcing me into a position where I have to argue that jokes aren't jokes. So, he's the "Yay, jokes!" candidate, and I'm the twenty-minutes-of-nuanced-feminist-jargon-that-kind-of-makes-you-feel-guilty candidate.

"I'm sure it's super-comfortable and nice to believe that there aren't systemic forces that are affected by speech," I said, "but that's not true, and those of us who are affected by these forces know that's not true. I'm sure sixty years ago there were some 'hilarious' jokes about black people, and comedy was way more overtly racist sixty years ago, and it's not a coincidence that life was more hostile and dangerous for black people—not that it's great now, by the way!—and you literally think that's a coincidence? You don't get to say that comedy is this sacred, powerful, vital thing that we have to protect because it's speaking truth to power, blah blah blah, and also be like, 'Well, it's just a joke, I mean, language doesn't affect our lives at all, so shut up.'"

Jim turned to the audience with a kind, paternalistic smile, as though he felt sorry for me. "Comedy is not a cause of what happens in society. A lot of times it's a reaction to what's happening and a reflection of what's happening. And comics' speech has never inspired violence." He then segued into a weird rant against "the press," who, he said, is "the only group that I think owes an apology," because they sometimes report on the identities and manifestos of mass shooters, which "contributes to violence." Applause.

It was such a transparently irrelevant tangent that I was momentarily speechless. Rape jokes couldn't possibly contribute to the trivialization of rape, because Columbine? It was the rhetorical equivalent of distracting the audience with a squeaky toy. My speechlessness didn't matter, though, because Jim was forging ahead:

"I think the next time somebody walks through a museum and sees a painting that they find highlights or perpetuates a thought that they find objectionable—even a thought that they should find objectionable—then they should take a towel and throw it over the painting. Or I think the next time that person goes to a movie and there's a rape in a movie, they should stand up and hold a board in front of a screen so nobody else can see it. Now, if you did that, people would—what happened to Giuliani when he went after the Brooklyn Museum of Art! People were like, 'You fascist! You're going after art for something you don't like!' But if you get mad at a comedian for telling a joke you don't like, people are like, 'You go girl.' It's either all okay or none of it's okay. I understand why rape is an offensive, awful thing. No one is saying it's not. But sometimes comedy does trivialize what is truly horrible. The roughest set I ever saw a comedian do is Joan Rivers—I saw her at the Cutting Room a few years ago—and I think she's one of the most underrated comics ever [applause] and she did a brutal set. She talked about 9/11, she talked about AIDS, and I mean it was *rough*. And she had zero respect for the boundaries of society. And we all knew why we were there, and we all knew why she was taking everything that hurts us and everything that's sad, and everything that's miserable, and just turning it upside down and looking at it, and we all walked out of there the same as when we walked in. Nobody walked out thinking, 'Hey, AIDS is hilarious! AIDS isn't sad and terrible! 9/11 is irrelevant!' We all walked out feeling the same about those subjects, but the relief of comedy is it takes things that aren't funny and it allows us to laugh about them for an hour, and then we have the rest of the day to look at them like they're as horrible and sad as they really are."

At this point, I had genuinely lost the plot. I stammered and grasped for words. What does Giuliani have to do with rape jokes? How was criticizing comedians on Twitter the same as throwing towels over paintings? Isn't a towel kind of small? Wouldn't a bedsheet do the job better? Also, how many art museums traffic in explicit rape apologia and then brush off any criticism by scoffing, "Calm down, it's just art"? Again, context matters. Hanging a giant swastika flag in a Holocaust museum, as a historical artifact, is not the same as painting a giant swastika on the wall of the Brooklyn Museum and titling it, "Kill All Jews." Culturally, we've evolved to the point where that second piece would never make it into a museum, because we, as a society, have made a decision about which ideas are good and which ideas are bad. We don't have to convene a panel of Holocaust deniers to sign off on that fact in the name of "free speech." That's the difference between commenting on rape culture and perpetuating rape culture; choosing to be better, collectively, and caving to the howls of misogynists who insist that sexist abuse is a fair and equal counterpoint to women asking not to be abused.

As for Jim's Joan Rivers anecdote, I'm glad he saw Joan do a great, dark set once. But it's bafflingly presumptuous (and, I'd wager, deliberately disingenuous) to assume that he knew what everyone's opinion on AIDS was when they walked into and out of that theater. There are plenty of people who consider themselves compassionate, moral, and kind—who have a gay friend and support same-sex marriage—who still, on some level, think of AIDS as a deviant's disease that gay men deserve because of their promiscuity. No, a few off-color AIDS jokes aren't going to implant prejudice in anyone's brain, but they can damn sure validate and stoke any prejudices that are already lurking.

People like Jim desperately want to believe that the engines of injustice run on outsized hate—stranger rapes in dark alleys, burning crosses and white hoods—but the reality is that indifference, bureaucracy, and closed-door snickers are far more plentiful fuels.

At the time, the Steubenville rape case had a monopoly on the news—at a high school party in Ohio, two popular football players digitally penetrated an unconscious sixteen-year-old classmate; one also exposed her breasts and put his penis in her mouth. Multiple teenage partygoers took photos and videos of the rape, which they then shared gleefully on social media, accompanied by a proliferation of rape jokes. In another video, friends of the boys reflect on the rape, joking about how "dead" the victim was. "She is so raped right now," one kid says. "They raped her quicker than Mike Tyson raped that one girl." The boys' coaches and school administrators attempted to cover up the crime. Media coverage of the investigation and trial repeatedly lamented the loss of the rapists' "bright futures." The victim's identity was leaked and her character flayed on live TV.

I practically begged Jim to understand. "Maybe there's a woman [in the audience] who's wondering whether she should report her rape," I said, "and she's sitting there, and everyone's laughing at the idea of how funny rape is, not in a way that is releasing any tension, but in a way that is causing tension, tangibly. Tension that filters out into the world, where we now live in a country where teenage boys think it's totally cool and hilarious to just put their fingers in the vagina of a passed-out child and then videotape it and put it on the Internet."

Jim cut me off. "And people reacted appropriately."

"*Really?*"

"People who saw that were disgusted by that. I'm not

talking about the school that covered it up, but the fact that society looked at that and all of us were repulsed by it."

"All of us were not repulsed by it. No. A lot of people supported those boys."

Kamau backed me up. "Have you been on Twitter lately?"

There was the crux. It's easy for Jim and his fans and all the young comedy dudes to pretend like rape culture doesn't exist, because they have the luxury of actively ignoring it. Confronted with a case like Steubenville, he only bothers to look at the parts that reinforce his world-view. He brushed it off with a shrug, because he can, and barreled on:

"Your Twitter picture is Jeff Goldblum. Jeff Goldblum's first role was a brutal rapist in *Death Wish*. Now I'm not saying anything against Jeff Goldblum, but—"

At this point a producer brought up a screen grab of my Twitter profile—featuring a sweaty Jeff Goldblum in repose, erotically dying from dinosaur bites, in *Jurassic Park*—on the screen behind us. They knew this "point" was coming. Jim must have told them in his pre-interview. They were prepared.

"—he picked up a blackjack and he said, 'you rich C,' and he called her the c-word, and they beat her to death in *Death Wish*. Now, we all understand, 'Oh, that's an actor doing a role.' But why, as an artist, do we give an actor a pass for convincingly playing a brutal rapist, but go after a comedian for making fun of something and mocking something? Like, why do we allow an artist to do something convincingly—what's going to affect a rape victim more? Seeing that rape acted out properly? Or hearing some comedian make fun of it?"

Bad-faith bullshit. Fuck this, I thought. Are you supposed to like and sympathize with Jeff Goldblum's character in *Death Wish*? When people go to watch it, is Jeff Goldblum physically in the room with them pretending to rape people? Does he sometimes break the fourth wall, point into the camera, and say, "Hey, Karen Ferguson, wouldn't it be hilarious if everyone in this theater raped you right now?" Why is it a given that seeing a rape acted out is more traumatizing than hearing the concept of rape turned into a joke? Who appointed Jim Norton the arbiter of every rape victim's feelings? If moviegoers just had to deal with the fact that any movie, at any time, could have a random rape scene spliced into it, out of nowhere, that might be a parallel example. A parallel example is not a movie CALLED *DEATH WISH*, with a rating on it that literally warns you about what's in it, that you've presumably gone to see deliberately because you watched a trailer and decided, "Yes, this is up my alley."

For fucking fuck's sake.

"We don't have to choose between those two things," I said, cold. "If someone went and saw that movie and they were offended by it, they are more than welcome to complain about it, which is all that I'm doing right now. It's about accountability—if you want to make that product and stand by that, that's fine, but I get to call you a dick, I get to call you out. And if we all agree that it's just a crutch, a hacky premise that people use because you want to get a reaction, you want to shock people, like, why does my vagina have to be your crutch? Can't you use something that's yours? Why do you have to come into my oppression and use me for your closer?"

"I think the best way to end this is for Lindy and I to make out for a while," Jim joked over Kamau's outtro—deliberately sexualizing me for a laugh at the end of a debate about the dehumanization of women in comedy.

Then it was over. Guy had been right. The time did go too fast, and I didn't get to my best material. I felt pretty good, though. Mostly I just wanted to sleep.

My hotel room didn't have FX, so I couldn't watch myself. I was grateful.

It's About Free Speech, It's Not About Hating Women

The first day, it was just a few tweets here and there—regular *Totally Biased* viewers, plus the small number of my fans and Jim's who made it a point to tune in on cable. These broke down pretty uniformly along preexisting ideological lines: Jim's fans thought Jim "won"; mine sided with me. Everyone seemed to feel that their previously held opinion on rape jokes was validated, and, seemingly, no minds were changed. "Maybe this'll just be a blip," I thought as the chatter subsided, honestly a little disappointed. I agreed to do this debate because these ideas are important to me (and, in my opinion, to the development of a more civil, inclusive world)—I wanted to have an impact, maybe shift the conversation, just a hair. I felt good about my performance; I'd held my own against a TV veteran on his turf. You don't go through that much stress to let it just vaporize and blow away.

The second day, my phone buzzed me awake.

Bzzt.

no need for you to worry about rape uggo

Bzzt.

Jesus Christ this woman is about as fun as dry rape. Lighten up Lindy!

Bzzt.

you are really annoying. Don't worry no one would ever rape u. Worry about ur Health & the heart attack that's coming #uglycow

The debate had gone up on YouTube, and Jim had posted it to his social media accounts.

I love how the Bitch complaining about rape is the exact kind of Bitch that would never be raped. Bitch have you looked in the mirror?

There were hundreds and hundreds of them. Thousands, maybe. I had never encountered such an unyielding wall of vitriol. They flooded in, on Twitter, Facebook, YouTube, my e-mail, the comments on *Jezebel*.

Who the fuck, in their right mind, would want to rape you?

I had been trolled before—for confronting Dan, for mocking men's rights activists, for disliking *Sex and the City 2*—but nothing like this. Nothing could compare to the misogynist rage of male comedy fans at being challenged by an unfuckable woman.

I wanted to rebut every one, but didn't. There was no point. This thing was alive.

She wants to get screwed so badly I bet you all the rape she is shaking her finger at is exactly what she wants.

You cannot "want" rape.

That big bitch is bitter that no one wants to rape her do some laps lardy holly shit her stomachs were touching the floor

Rape is not a compliment.

No one would want to rape that fat, disgusting mess.

Rape is not a gift or a favor or a validation.

lets cut the bullshit that broad doesnt have to worry about rape

Fat women get raped too.

You're fat, ugly, and unfuckable. You don't have to worry about rape!

Are you sure?

There is a group of rapists with over 9000 penises coming for this fat bitch

There is nothing novel or comedic or righteous about men using the threat of sexual violence to control non-compliant women. This is how society has always functioned. Stay indoors, women. Stay safe. Stay quiet. Stay in the kitchen. Stay pregnant. Stay out of the world. If you want to talk about silencing, censorship, placing limits and consequences on speech, this is what it looks like.

She won't ever need to worry about rape, ever!

I don't know any woman who hasn't experienced some level of sexual predation, from catcalls, to unwanted advances at bars, to emotional manipulation, to violent rape. I certainly have—even "unrapeable" me. All women do need to worry about rape.

*Don't disrespect ppls way of calming themselves down.
Embracing the sick idea of rape keeps some from ever
actually doing it*

You are a rapist.

What a fucking cunt. Kill yourself, dumb bitch.

No.

*Why is it almost all women that hate men are the most
un-fuckable people ever.*

I stepped off the plane in Seattle, my phone vibrating
like a pocket full of bees. The local comedy scene had
started in on me at this point: I was a cunt, a fraud, a
failed comic, I knew nothing about comedy and had no
right to comment on it. (Strangely, they'd had boundless
confidence in my expertise back when they were kissing my ass for a mention in the paper.) Someone made a
"parody" Twitter account called "Lindy East" (wow, you
guys really are comedy experts), its avatar a stolen photo
of me, my neck and face grotesquely inflated into a massive gullet. One guy—someone I'd never met personally
but who was a regular at the same clubs I frequented—
wrote on Facebook that he wished I'd fall down a flight of
stairs. (Let's call him Dave.) People I knew "liked" Dave's
comment—one was a regular at The Moth, whom I had

to intro with a smile onstage a few weeks later. But it's just comedy. To worry about my safety was a form of hysteria. Insulting, if you think about it. Can't a nice guy just defend his art?

Jabba has nothing to worrie about, not even a prison escapee would rape her.

I was determined to show my face at the open mics that week—to make it clear that I wouldn't be cowed or chased away. "I'll be at the Underground tonight if anyone wants to talk," I wrote on Facebook and Twitter. I'd have Aham with me. Nothing would happen. We'd be safe. I hadn't done stand-up in at least a year, so I threw together a few new jokes: "When people want to insult me, it's always 'Jabba the Hutt.' Which is really insulting. To Jabba the Hutt. The dude is an intergalactic warlord. He *owns a monster.* I'm a feminist blogger, you guys."

Aham and I went to the open mic, did our sets, had fun, and went home.

There is no way a straight dude would fuck or even rape that ugly heifer. What an annoying cunt.

Nearly a year later, a mutual friend would show me his text exchange with Dave about that open mic night.

Unbeknownst to us, Dave was convinced that Aham was going to attack him over his "fall down the stairs" comment. "I'm a big boy," he wrote (sic throughout), "and I can fight my own battles and take any punches thrown at me but Ill be honest until we squared that away I thought for sure I was going to get in a street fight with that guy. I worked out for two hours just visualizing the fight before the Underground that night, I had a switchblade on me, a 9mm in my trunk and I was ready for anything."

Dave brought a knife and a gun to a comedy show. Because of a disagreement about whether or not comedy clubs are safe for women. Because the way people talk onstage has no bearing on how they behave in real life.

It's so pathetic, the tough-guy posturing, but so sinister, because, to put it plainly, that's how black men die. Insecure, pee-pants white men assume that any disagreement is a life-threatening situation. Dave assumed Aham was dangerous, and was prepared to shoot him with a gun, even though Dave was the only one in the equation who'd issued a threat of any kind. I've only had a handful of moments like that in my life—where I could see how thin the veil was between my happy, intact world and its complete destruction. How few steps there were between the mundane and the unthinkable. You can see why people stay quiet. Can you see, yet, why I speak up?

Wouldn't the best ending be that Jim Norton rapes the fat girl.

Everyone hates rape. Rape is illegal. There is no rape cul-ture. Everyone takes rape seriously. Everyone was horrified by Steubenville. Everyone knows when you're joking and when you're not. Famous men laughing about rape has no effect on the way their fans speak to women they don't like.

My detractors paint me as some out-of-touch idealist, but Jim's the one assuming that all comics approach their art with good intentions—that they're all just trying to make people laugh. That's simply untrue. It's also deeply naive. There's not a single comic working today who's not doing it to fill a personal void; that's why it means so much to them. The idea of someone else laughing is not remotely a good enough payoff to devote your life to something so difficult. Anyway, if Jim's assumptions were true—that comics always have virtuous intentions and people can always tell when someone is joking and when they're not—then we wouldn't be having this discussion.

Holes like this make me want to commit rape out of anger, I don't even find her attractive, at all, she's a fat idiot, I just want to rape her with a traffic cone

"Hole" has its own entry on OApedia, an *Opie & Anthony* fan wiki: "Hole is the Opie and Anthony term for the woman who sits in on and ruins most radio shows. The hole opens her mouth saying God-knows-what, adds nothing to the conversation, and chastises the guys for being politically incorrect." But no, I was told, these people weren't representative of comedians and comedy fans. They were anomalous Internet trolls, and the Internet isn't real life. Except for the guy from real life, the comedian, the one with the gun.

If you've never been on the receiving end of a viral Internet hate mob, it's hard to convey the confluence of galloping adrenaline and roaring dread. It is drowning and falling all at once. In my lowest moment, when it seemed like the onslaught would never stop, an idea unfurled in my mind like some night-blooming flower: They'd handed me a gift, I realized. A suffocating deluge of violent misog-yny was how Amomh in a comedy fans reacted to a woman suggesting that comedy might have a misogyny problem. They'd attempted to demonstrate that comedy, in general, doesn't have issues with women by threatening to rape and kill me, telling me I'm just bitter because I'm too fat to get raped, and suggesting that the debate would have been better if it were just Jim raping me.

Holy shit, I realized. I won.

Their attempts to silence me made my point more effectively than any think piece or flawless debate performance ever could—they were churning out evidence as fast as they could type, hundreds of them working for me, for free. In trying to take down feminism, they turned themselves into an all-volunteer feminist sweatshop. I compiled a sheaf of comments. (They were so uniformly vile I didn't need to dig for the "worst" ones.) I sat in a big gray easy chair in my living room. Aham filmed me as I read aloud, in one relentless, deadpan beam, staring into the camera for nearly five minutes. Stripping emotion out of such a horror lays the humanity bare: If my feelings are absent, you can't say I'm manipulating you or pushing an agenda. I am a person, and other people said these words to me. They sat down at their computers and chose to type this and send it to another human being. Here is my face. Here are these words. "It's just the Internet" doesn't seem so true anymore.

That video handily exploded myths about me—that I'm working for censorship. That I'm emotionally frail. That I'm against free speech. That I'm afraid of bad words. How could I be? "I'd like to take a stick and shove it through that mouth of yours and roast you, sexy thing" is hardly going to make it to Thursday nights on NBC. Show me any joke that's more raw than that video. Show me a comedy routine that takes more risks. If you're so raw. If you're so edgy. Show me.

It worked.

My phone started vibrating for a different reason. The tenor of my Twitter feed had changed. The toilet was swirling the other way, if you will. Every comedian I'd ever loved—even ones who'd dug their heels in on rape jokes the previous summer—threw their support behind me. Joss Whedon got involved. Lena Dunham. It quickly became surreal. The mayor of Seattle tweeted, "I stand with Lindy West!" Cool, thanks, the mayor.

There was still resistance, but it was sad. You could feel it shaking. Beyond a vocal minority of actual rapists and abusive nihilists, the bulk of my harassers were just bandwagoners trying to impress their comedy heroes. When famous comics realized it was a PR disaster (not to mention a moral one) to align themselves with people who thought "get raped, piggy" was a constructive avenue of discourse, their ass-kissers had no choice but to follow suit. The tide of public opinion has always turned, invariably, on coolness. People just want to be cool.

Jim, presumably disturbed at the litany of abuse being heaped on me in his name (though still unwilling to admit any connection between misogynist comedy and misogynist comedy fans) wrote an essay for *xoJane*, of all places—the much-derided bastion of teen girl feelings—asking his fans to lay off:

"I am very careful about telling people what they should write or how they should express themselves, but I truly hate a lot of the things that have been directed at Lindy. The anger she's facing is wrong and misguided. If you have a problem with her opinion that's one thing, but to tweet that you hope she gets raped, or that you'd want her to be raped is fucking ignorant."

What's more, he actually explained the concept of rape culture on *Opie & Anthony*.

"Her point is"—Jim felt around for words that would make sense to this audience—"uh, the term 'rape culture' gets thrown around a lot."

"Rape culture." You could hear the snarl of disgust on Opie's face.

Jim cut in, gently contradictory. It's expected of

him to pile on—piling on feminists might even be in his contract—but he wouldn't: "And maybe if someone explains exactly what [rape culture] is, maybe we are..."

After the smallest of pauses, Opie offered, "A little rapey?"

"Yeah. Possibly."

You can feel them figuring it out. They reject it immediately, of course, but the spark is there. Two famous white men sniffing imperiously at the existence of rape culture (as though it's theirs to validate or deny) might not seem revolutionary, but to me it was a miracle. Millions of men listen to *Opie & Anthony*—a scene where misogyny isn't just unchecked, it's incentivized—and Jim Norton had not only introduced them to the concept of rape culture, he acknowledged that it could be real. (The question of whether or not Opie and Jim give a shit that our culture might be "a little rapey" is another matter.) Jim Norton threw rape culture into the fires of Mount Doom. The fires of Mount Doom are still harassing me over rape jokes three years later, but some victories are incremental.

Then, the final nail, Patton Oswalt wrote an open letter about rape jokes on his blog, in which he acknowledged that men might not understand what it's like to be a woman. You can feel the same dawning recognition that Opie and Jim were groping for.

"Just because I find rape disgusting, and have never had that impulse, doesn't mean I can make a leap into the minds of women and dismiss how they feel day to day, moment to moment, in ways both blatant and subtle, from other men, and the way the media represents the world they live in, and from what they hear in songs, see in movies, and witness on stage in a comedy club."

Just because you haven't personally experienced something doesn't make it not true. What a concept.

And it was over. (Temporarily.) Only the darkest contrarians were willing to posit that Patton Oswalt wasn't a comedy expert. People scrambled to find new trajectories by which their lips could caress his bunghole—suddenly, many open-micers discovered they'd been passionately anti-rape joke all along. Patton was heaped with praise; finally, someone was telling it like it is; he was so, so brave.

I was grateful to him, though it wasn't lost on me and Sady and Molly and all the female comics who have been trying to carve out a place for themselves for generations, that he was being lauded for the same ideas that had brought us nothing but abuse. Well, what else is new. Nobody cared about Bill Cosby's accusers until Hannibal Buress repeated their stories onstage with his veneer of male authority. Regardless, some thirteen-year-old comedy superfan was on his way to becoming a shitty misogynist, but he read Patton's post, and it might not have changed anything in him right away, but it's going to stick in his head the way things do when you're thirteen. He's going to do what Patton's generation didn't have the guts for. I'll take that victory.

Jim made one throwaway, jokey remark during our debate that's stuck with me more than any other. Referring to comedians milking great material out of life's horrors, he said, "The worse things are, the better they are for us." He was being flippant, but it's hardly a rare sentiment among comedians, and it betrays the fundamental disconnect between Jim and me. To Jim, all of life's horrors belong to him, to grind up and burn for his profit and pleasure, whether he's personally experienced said horrors or not. A straight, cis, able-bodied white man is the only person on this planet who can travel almost anywhere (and, as the famous Louis CK bit goes, to almost any time in history), unless they're literally dropping into a war zone, and feel fairly comfortable and safe (and, often, in charge). To the rest of us, horrors aren't a thought experiment to be mined—they're horrors.

Bad presidents are a great business opportunity for comedians like Jim. For families trapped in cycles of grinding poverty, bad presidents might mean the difference between electricity and darkness, food or hollow stomachs. Rape means something to me because I've been trapped in a bathroom with a strange drunk man demanding a blow job. Racism means something to my husband because when we drive through Idaho he doesn't want to get out of the car. Misogyny in comedy means something to me because my inbox is full of messages from female comics and comedy writers—some fairly high-profile—who need someplace to pour out their fears and frustrations about their jobs. They can't complain at work; they'll be branded as "difficult." They can't complain in public; jobs and bookings are hard to come by as it is. So they talk to me.

If you're a man who works in comedy full-time and you aren't aware of what your female colleagues go through (if you have female colleagues at all), stop assuming that their experience is the same as yours, and start wondering why they aren't talking to you.

The most-viewed segment on *Totally Biased*'s You-Tube channel is a profile of a teenage metal band called Unlocking the Truth, which went viral. At the time of this writing, it has 840,949 views and 1,507 comments. The second-most-viewed clip is an interview with *Daily Show* host Trevor Noah—612,498 views and 355 comments. My debate with Jim Norton comes in third with 404,791 views.

And 6,745 comments.

Three years later, the thing still gets at least several new comments a week. Honestly, it could be a case study in online misogyny. It has scientific merit. Neither Jim nor I are particularly famous. The debate itself isn't particularly interesting—I mean, it's fine, but it's a niche topic. So what's the draw? The draw is that I'm a disobedient woman. The draw is that I'm fat and I'm speaking authoritatively to a man. The draw is that I've refused to back down even after years of punishment. Nearly every comment includes a derogatory term—cunt, fat, feminazi. Many specifically call out the moment when Jim suggests we make out and I roll my eyes. He was just trying to be funny, they say.

Recently, an *Opie & Anthony* listener started bombarding me with images of mangled bodies, gruesome auto accidents, brains split open like ripe fruit. Others cheered him on—high-fiving, escalating, then rehashing it all later in online forums. This cycle isn't some crackpot theory of mine: Misogyny is explicitly, visibly incentivized and rewarded. You can watch it self-perpetuate in front of your eyes. I forwarded the links to Jim and pleaded, "This is still happening to me. Do you see? How can you not see it?"

His response was terse and firm and invoked Bill Cosby, of all people. The comedy people consume has no bearing on how they behave any more than Bill Cosby's comedy reflected his behavior.

But . . . Bill Cosby literally joked about drugging and raping women. And, in "real life," he drugged and raped women.

Comedy is real life. The Internet is real life. Jim, I realized, doesn't care if his argument is sound—for him, this was never a real debate to begin with. Admitting that I'm right would mean admitting that he's complicit in some truly vile shit. He's planted his flag. He's a wall, not a door.

But comics are a little more careful when they talk

about rape now. Audiences are a little bolder with their groans. It's subtle, but you can feel it. That's where change comes from: these tiny incremental shifts. I'm proud of that. I won. But I also lost a lot.

I can't watch stand-up now—the thought of it floods me with a heavy, panicked dread. There's only so much hostility you can absorb before you internalize the rejection, the message that you are not wanted. My point about rape jokes may have gotten through, but my identity as a funny person—the most important thing in my life—didn't survive. Among a certain subset of comedians and their fans, "Lindy West" is still shorthand for "humorless bitch." I sometimes envy (and, on my bad days, resent) the funny female writers of my generation who never get explicitly political in their work. They're allowed to keep their funny cards; by engaging with comedy, by trying to make it better, I lost mine.

The anti-feminist drumbeat is always the same in these conversations: They're trying to take comedy away from us. Well, Tosh got a second TV show, while the art that used to be my catharsis and my unqualified joy makes me sick now.

The most frustrating thing is that my silly little Autobiography report dreams are finally coming true: I've been offered TV writing gigs, been asked to write pilots, had my work optioned, watched jokes I wrote for other comics get laughs on the air while wannabe open-micers were still calling me "the anti-comedy" on Twitter. Andy

Richter and Sarah Thyre are friends of mine now. (Coincidentally, he's one of the few big-name comedians who's been tirelessly supportive.) I finally clawed my way to the plateau where my seemingly impossible goals were within reach, and I don't even know if I want them anymore.

Video-game critic Leigh Alexander, who is perpetually besieged by male gamers for daring to critique a pastime that is hers as much as theirs, wrote a beautiful meditation on her weariness—on the toll of rocking the boat in an industry you love—for *Boing Boing*: "My partner is in games, and his friends, and my guy friends, and they run like founts of tireless enthusiasm and dry humor. I know sometimes my ready temper and my cynicism and the stupid social media rants I can't always manage to stuff down are tiring for them. I want to tell them: It will never be for me like it is for you. This will only ever be joy, for you."

Men, you will never understand. Women, I hope I helped. Comedy, you broke my heart.

The Tree

The tree fell on the house when I was sleeping, alone, in the bed that used to be ours, two weeks before my father died, four weeks after Aham told me he was leaving, eight weeks after we moved in together in a new state with grand plans. We shouldn't have gone.

Because even that—"grand plans"—that's just some nothing I tell myself, still, even now, four years later, when I shouldn't need it anymore. It was wrong before we left. It was wrong in the moving truck, it was wrong in my parents' driveway, waving good-bye, my dad wrapped in a plaid blanket and leaning on my mom, probably one of the last times he was out of bed (and I left; I left), it was wrong in Portland, Eugene, Grants Pass, Ashland, Yreka, Weed, Redding, Willows, Stockton, Buttonwillow/ McKittrick, and Castaic, and east on the 210 and south on the 2, and off on Colorado, left, right, right, and right.

It was right two months before we moved, at the end of a day with his kids, when we swam in Lake Washington and played his favorite game, "see who can throw everyone else on the ground first," which he always wins, which is the point, because he is a giant toddler, and we stopped by a garage sale because the sign read "RARE JAZZ VINYL" and the woman there thought I was the girls' mom—me!— and complimented us on our beautiful children. "Your mom," she called me, to them. They looked up at me and I panicked, and said, too loud, "Oh no, I'm not their mom, I'm just SOME LADY!" because I wanted so badly not to fuck this up, not to let him think I was getting any ideas. Don't worry, I'm just some lady. We've only been dating for four months. You just got divorced. I'm not trying to be your family. That would be weird. I know. I'm normal. But.

Then we picked blackberries and made a pie and we swung by my parents' house—it was still my parents' house then, not my mom's house, not truncated and half-empty— and after the kids went inside with the pie he held me back.

"I loved hanging out with you and the girls today," he said, staring at me with that face.

"I know!" I said.

"I like your parents' house," he said, looking up at their white Cape Cod blushing in the sunset.

"Me too!" I said.

"What do you think our house is going to be like?" he said.

Meaningful pause.

"In L.A."

"Really? Are you sure?" I jumped up and down, squeezing him.

We weren't moving to L.A. together, we both insisted. We were each independently, coincidentally, moving to L.A. at the same time. He was going to live with some female friend I didn't know; I was going to live with our mutual friend Solomon Georgio. It had to be that way. People didn't move in together after four months. But on that perfect day, heat-drunk and berry-stained and bruised from roughhousing, from playing family, the ruse didn't make sense anymore.

We should live together, obviously. We were best friends, and we were in love, even if we didn't say it, and that had to be enough, even though he'd been telling me he was broken since the first night we spent together—broken from abandonment, poverty, kids at nineteen, two divorces by twenty-seven ("that's as bad as being thirteen and a half and divorced once...*times two*," his bit goes), single fatherhood, depression, a hundred lifetimes of real-ass shit while I was rounding the corner toward thirty still on my mommy and daddy's phone plan. We were friends for eight years before we even kissed. "Didn't you ever have a crush on me? I'm so handsome," he asked me later, teasing. "No. It literally never occurred to me," I replied, honestly. He was a man. I was still a stupid little girl. Kids? Divorce? That was above my pay grade.

In the summer of 2011, Aham and Solomon were both in the semifinals of NBC's Stand Up for Diversity contest, an annual comedy competition that awards development deals to underrepresented minorities, particularly people of color. (Every year, some straight white shithead would insist on entering, nobly, in protest, because "Irish is a minority.") I'm not sure if the deals ever went anywhere, particularly, but it was a good way to "get seen" by L.A. industry folks, and it made NBC look progressive.

All three of us were feeling like big fish in those days; we were ready to flop into the L.A. River and see if it'd take us all the way to the sea. (If you know anything about the L.A. River, you know we were screwed from the start.*)

Not to mention the fact that Aham couldn't really move to L.A. anyway. You can't just move when you're an adult man with two kids—he was only going for a few months, six tops, to see if this NBC thing panned out, because you never know, and maybe he'd "get seen" and become the next David Schwimmer and be able to move out of his three-hundred-square-foot place and he and the girls could have a big new life and no one would have to sleep in the laundry room anymore. If not, no foul. Nothing to lose.

---

* Every time we drove across a certain bridge, near my sister's house in Silver Lake, my dad would bring up the great flood of 1938 when the river broke its concrete banks: "Your grandfather always told me the water came right up level with this bridge. Hoo-wee, boy, all the way up here! Can you imagine?" I couldn't. The L.A. River I knew was a brown, trickling ditch. A joke. Dad was three in 1938, fifteen years before his dad died. My widowed grandmother was so bereft at the loss of her still-young other half that she drank herself into early dementia. She was gone before I was born—it was love that killed her. I'd grind some portent out of that if it wasn't the commonest thing in the world.

Meanwhile, I was signing a year-long lease in Los Angeles. My love story had a six-month shelf life, at most, in all but the most unlikely circumstances. But I forged ahead. Fuck reality. This was going to be my person. I knew it.

Then, in the driveway, Aham said it out loud—we'd live together, be a real couple—and all of those warnings, overt and covert, that he'd been sending me for the past four months, that he wasn't ready for this, he couldn't do this, his divorce was too recent, their fights were too loud and too mean, his life had too many moving parts, were going to fall away. I had been right to ignore him all along. I knew it I would make him okay through sheer force of will. He said it. Binding oral contract. Breaking it now wouldn't be *fair*. That's how a little girl thinks. Love was perseverance.

Later, I'd ask him, heaving, "Why the FUCK would you say that? Why did you trick me? Why did you come here?"

"I just loved you," he'd say. "I just wanted to be around you. I told you I couldn't do it. Why didn't you believe me?"

I rented the three of us a little yellow house in Eagle Rock with a big eucalyptus tree in the backyard. The house was owned by a church, which was two doors down, and every so often some church people would come by and try to guilt trip us into coming to one of their "activities." The church owned another, identical house next door to ours, where a middle-aged couple lived with their teenage son. The wife, Kathy, had severe early-onset Alzheimer's—she couldn't have been over fifty—and every couple of days she'd wander through our front door, lost and crying. "Where am I? Where's Jeff? I can't find Jeff!" We'd try to soothe her, walk her home, back into the house that was a dim, dirty funhouse mirror of ours—towels tacked up over the windows, counters piled with fast-food takeout containers, empty of furniture except for a few mattresses on the floor. One particularly sweltering afternoon, trying to get her settled in the back bedroom to wait until her husband got home from work, I realized with a start that he was there, passed out drunk under a pile of blankets. "Jeff," I said, shaking him. "JEFF. JEFF." He just kept sleeping.

Jeff was a really nice guy. Once, when he came rushing over to collect Kathy from our house, his perpetual cheer slipped for a second and he said, so quietly, "She used to take care of everything."

A week before my life broke, I met my sister for coffee and told her that Aham never laughed at my jokes anymore.

"Dude," she said, like it was the most obvious thing in the world, "don't you know you have to love with an open hand?"

"What?"

Her eyes rolled.

"If you have a bird that you love, and you want the bird to stay and hang out with you and sing for you, you don't clutch it in your fist so it can't get away. You hold your hand out, open, and wait for it to perch there. If you're holding it there, it's not your friend—it's your prisoner. Love with an open hand. DUH."

"Oh," I said, stuffing the thought far away.

I didn't see it coming, because I was a child. I didn't understand what a relationship was—that the whole beauty of the thing is two people choosing, every day, to be together; not one person, drunk on love stories, strangling them both into a grotesquerie of what she thinks she wants. It didn't help that the little yellow house next door to Jeff and his there-but-not-there Kathy was just a few blocks from Occidental, the college campus where, a decade earlier, the certainty that I was worthless and unlovable had calcified into a heavy, dragging, extra limb. That was the limb I draped eagerly around Ahani's shoulders, without asking—the weight that broke his back and pulled us under. It had never occurred to me that what I needed wasn't to find someone to help me carry it; what I needed was to amputate.

The descent was swift and boring: I was too much and too little. He was depressed, distant, and mean. I pressed myself against him harder, more frantic. His eyes lost focus; he was always somewhere else. I pressed. He pulled. I cried every day. He was eliminated from the comedy competition. He was angry. On Halloween, he went to a party. I couldn't come, he said. Sorry. No plus-ones. He came back at five a.m. We had sex, and then I cried.

"We're going to be okay, right?"

His back was turned.

"No," he said, and everything changed. "I don't think we're going to be okay."

I had been sad before. I had been very sad. This was

something new. I felt liquefied. Even writing this, years later, I'm sobbing like he's dead.

I had waited so long for someone to pick me. And then he changed his mind.

I went across town to my friends Ella and Owen's house for a few weeks, and they let me sit on their couch all day and stare and cry; Ella made me a therapy appointment and tried to get me to eat; Owen made me laugh by narrating elaborate parlor dramas between their three enormous, idiot dogs; at night, the dogs would forget who I was and trap me in the bathroom, barking wildly, until someone got up and rescued me.

I wrote Aham a long, impassioned e-mail, like a teenager—the gist of which was, "I don't understand. We love each other. It's enough."

He wrote back, in short, "You're right. You *don't* understand. It's not."

I drove him to the airport and he chattered the whole way about a radio show that was going to produce one of his stories; he thought we were just going to be friends now. He thought I knew how to compartmentalize, like he did. "I've missed talking to you so much," he said, beaming. I watched him blankly. He was going back to Seattle for Thanksgiving; I was going too, the next day.

That afternoon, I noticed a weird charge on my bank statement. Someone had stolen one of my checkbooks—I must have dropped it—and written a $750 check to herself. I called the bank's fraud department; they said they would take care of it. I woke up the next morning with a balance of negative $900,000. Apparently, that's the policy when someone reports check fraud to Bank of America; the bank subtracts $900,000 from their balance to preclude any further fraudulent withdrawals.*

I was a negative-millionaire. I shrugged and flew home to Seattle.†

At Thanksgiving dinner, we ate mashed potatoes and bad stuffing from the grocery store deli counter down the street. My dad threw up at the table and then started to cry. Aham called me to tell me about something goofy his mom had done to the turkey. I approximated a laugh. Downstairs, I took off my clothes and shambled toward bed. A massive period clot fell, *right out of me*, like a crimson water balloon, onto my mom's white carpet. I looked at it and got in bed.

The plane shook and lurched in the Santa Ana winds, but we returned to Burbank without particular trouble. I took a cab home. Solomon was out of town. Aham was still in Seattle. The wind picked up. The power went out. The windows rattled. I took an Ambien and curled into a ball and tried to hide from the dark and the wind in the bed that had been

---

* Yo! Bank! Other policy suggestion! TELL PEOPLE ABOUT
THE NEGATIVE-A-MILLION-DOLLARS POLICY BEFORE YOU
NEGATIVE-A-MILLION-DOLLARS THEM RIGHT WHEN THEIR
DAD IS DYING AND THEIR PERSON JUST CHANGED HIS MIND.
† The bank eventually refunded my $750 and said I could decide
whether or not to file a police report. I didn't. I'm glad that lady got to
keep that money—I hope it helped her out of a jam.

ours, the first bed I'd ever shared with someone who loved me and picked me and then changed his mind. At a certain point, a groaning started, then a cracking, then a pounding. It sounded like enormous beasts were hurling themselves against the house. Nothing had ever been louder. Growing up, I'd had a recurring nightmare about a flood, where the water rose right up to the level of my bedroom window, and animals—monstrous hippos, rampaging elephants—would lunge out of the storm, smashing their bulk against the glass. It must be the Ambien, I thought. A nightmare bleeding into real life. It sounded like the walls were coming down around me, like something was prying away the roof. I took another Ambien and shook.

I woke up in the morning embarrassed at my hallucination. It was just a storm. Was I really so pathetic? I walked into the kitchen.

The world was gone. Everything was leaves. Leaves pressed up against every window, through the screens, over the sills. The glass back door was a wall of leaves, Solomon's room was leaves, leaves, leaves. Someone banged on the door. I jumped.

The Santa Anas had been too much for the old eucalyptus tree; it had keened and struggled as I half slept, eventually cracking right in half and crushing our little yellow house. The little house that was supposed to be our love story. It's a metaphor you couldn't use in fiction. Too on the nose. Any good editor would kill it, and probably fire you.

My mom called. She was crying. It was time. I went back to the airport.

The End

Until I watched a death up close, I always felt avoidant around grief and grieving people. It was one of the things I hated most about myself—my complete loss of social fluidity among the heartbroken—though I know it's common. I am a shy person at heart, and a grieving acquaintance is a shy person's nightmare: The pressure to know the "right" thing to say. Seeing a person without their shell. The sudden plunge, several layers deeper than you've ever been, into someone's self, feigning ease in there so you don't make them uneasy. Navigating, by instinct, how much space you should be taking up—or, even worse, bringing yourself to ask.

I spent a lot of time alone as a kid. I've never been an easy hugger. The social conventions that keep human beings separate and discrete—boundaries, etiquette, privacy, personal space—have always been a great well of safety to me. I am a rule follower. I like choosing whom I let in close. The emotional state of emergency following a death necessarily breaks those conventions down, and, unfortunately, I am bad at being human without them.

I never caved to the impulse, of course—it's repulsively selfish and I've chewed my cheek bloody just admitting it here. Other people's grief is not about you; letting self-consciousness supersede empathy is barbaric. I'm the first to drop off a casserole, send flowers and a card. "Anything I can do." "Thinking of you so much right now." But before death had ever touched me directly, those interactions felt like trying to dance, sober, in a brightly lit room.

Someone picked me up at the airport and drove me to my parents' house, where my dad either was or wasn't, I can't remember. He was in and out of the hospital so often at that time it was hard to keep track, elation swapping places with despair at flickering speeds like a zoetrope animating the last days of my childhood. Flick, flick, flick.

Even though my mother was a nurse and I grew up immersed in hospital culture—talking eyeball surgery over dinner, specimen cups full of mandarin oranges in my school lunch—I didn't understand shit about hospitals. I didn't know that even the best ones were miserable and lonely places where you couldn't sleep more than a couple of hours at a stretch; where, with each second you weren't discharged, you could see the outline of your death shiver into focus. Hospitals were full of medicines and machines and doctors and hyper-competent people like my mother. I thought they were a place you went to get better, not a place you went to die.

Cancer doesn't hand you an itinerary. It's not like, up to a certain point, you have an okay amount of cancer, and then one day the doctor's like, "Uh-oh! Too much cancer!" and then all your loved ones rush to your bedside for some stoic, wise good-byes. Cancer, at least in my dad's case, is a complex breaking down of multiple systems, both slow and sudden. You have six months and then you have six hours. Treatments are messy, painful, and often humiliating. The cost/benefit is anything but clear.

My dad didn't want to die. He turned seventy-six that year, but until his prostate fucked everything up, he radiated the same tireless exuberance as he always had. My mom said he didn't like hearing his own prognoses, so she met with the doctors herself, carried the future inside her all alone. She, the realist, and he, the fantasist, as ever.

In those final weeks, though, even Dad couldn't deny that his body was failing. That horrible Thanksgiving, when he vomited into the empty margarine tub at the dinner table, was when I first noticed it. He had begun grieving—for himself, for the life he wasn't ready to leave behind. I, true to form, was terrified of his grief.

Those days eat at me. Why didn't I spend more time sitting with him? Why did I sleep so much? Why didn't I read out loud to him, our favorite books, the ones he read to me when I was little? Why was I so fucking chirpy in all of our interactions, desperate to gloss over the truth, instead of letting myself be vulnerable with him? Why the fuck did I move to L.A. three months before he died? What was wrong with me? Who does that?

He wanted me to go, though. That was before he admitted he was dying—if I had stayed, it would have been confirmation that something was really wrong—and there was nothing he loved more than watching his children stride out into the world and flourish. "Knock 'em dead, kid," he said. And I did. It's so fucking unfair that he didn't get to see it.

Eventually, I ran out of chances to sit with him, to be vulnerable, to tell the truth. We went to the hospital for the last time.

As Dad drifted in and out of consciousness, my sister and I read to him from the book he was halfway through at the time: *A Jazz Odyssey: The Life of Oscar Peterson*. Aham once told me that Oscar Peterson, my dad's hero, was the lovable dork of the jazz pantheon. "He's incredibly well respected," Aham hedged. "He's amazing—just the least edgy player ever. He's kind of like Superman." Peterson never had a drug problem; he loved his wives; he was huge in Canada. Unsurprisingly, then, where my sister and I picked up in *A Jazz Odyssey*, Peterson was describing a hobby that I can confidently declare the exact opposite of being a philandering New York needle junkie: pottering around America's parks and monuments with his wife Kelly in their brand-new Winnebago.

My dad roused every once in a while and chuckled as Peterson detailed with reverence the Winnebago's gleaming chrome accents and spacious over-cab loft bed. The open road, the great plains, Kelly by his side—this was the life. Until it came time to empty the Winnebago's sewage tank. Oscar was pretty sure he could figure it out unassisted.

I looked up from the book, into my sister's expectant face and over at my dad's unconscious one. Was Oscar Peterson about to tell us a story about gallons and gallons of his and his wife's liquefied feces spraying out of a Winnebago? Was I about to read it out loud, in a soothing voice, at my father's deathbed? Yes. Yes, I was.

Dad's hospital room was small—only two guests could hang out in there comfortably—so my mom, my sister, and I took turns sleeping in the chair next to his bed, holding his hand, while one of us lounged on the cushioned bench under the window and the odd woman out decamped to the cafeteria or the "family lounge" down the hall. The family lounge was a small, windowless room with an old TV, a couch upholstered in what looked like leftover airport carpet, and a pile of battered, cast-off VHS tapes, because nothing takes the edge off your father's slow suffocation like *Speed 2: Cruise Control*.

Did you know that sometimes there just isn't anything else that doctors can do to save your dad? I knew it intellectually, before this experience, but I didn't understand it in practice. In practice, it means that, at a certain point, a fallible human being called a doctor has to make a subjective decision that it is no longer feasible to mitigate both the internal bleeding and concomitant dehydration of your father, so all you can do is give him enough morphine that it doesn't hurt so much when he drowns inside of his own body. And you have to go, "Okay," and then let them do that. And then wait.

My dad lost consciousness on Saturday night. My mom told me to go home and sleep, that she'd call me if it looked like he was going to go. I passed out on my parents' couch, making peace with the fact that I would probably miss the end. It was okay. I had said good-bye, told him I loved him. But the next morning, when I woke up, he was still holding on (he was always strong, he didn't want to go), so back I went. We picked up our routine again—chair, bench, family lounge—and we sat there. Waiting. All day Sunday, into Monday. Each breath got slower and rougher—I use a French press now because I can't bear the percolator—and we sat and listened to every one.

Sometimes a team of doctors would come in and loom over us with well-rehearsed but clinical concern. "How are you doing?" they would ask. Oh, you mean besides sitting here on this plastic hospital chair listening to the world's best dude struggle for breath for the past thirty-six hours? Um, fucking gangbusters, I guess. "Is there anything we can do?" Apparently not, considering this whole long-slow-death thing that's happening in this room right now. Also, you're the doctor. You tell me.

I have never wanted anything as much as I wanted that shitty purgatory to be over. Except for one thing— which was for that shitty purgatory to never be over. Because when it's over, it's over. And eventually it was. Monday afternoon, my dad stopped breathing, faded to black-and-white like an old movie, and—I don't know how else to describe it—flattened slightly, as though whatever force was keeping him in three dimensions had abruptly packed up and moved on. He was, and then he wasn't. One moment his body was the locus of his personhood, the next moment our memories had to pick up the slack.

A nurse brought in granola bars and juice boxes on a little rolling cart, like a "your dad died" door prize. A guy with a mop came in to start cleaning up the room for the next patient. There was someone with a clipboard, asking questions. "Could you give us a fucking minute?" my mom snapped. "My husband just died thirty seconds ago."

We sat with the body that used to be him. I didn't understand the point, honestly.

Back in November, before Thanksgiving, before the tree fell on the house, before the hospital, Aham and I met up at a bar on Capitol Hill. We hadn't spoken in a week or so, and my pain and anger had cooled to something more permeable. I'd spent that time with friends and family, eating and drinking and carrying on, coming back to myself—getting reacquainted with the person I'd been before Aham, even before Mike. I had an identity other than my relationship—I remembered it now—and this grimy fish tank I built around us hadn't been good for me either.

Grudgingly, I'd come to see Aham's point a little bit. He fell in love with *this* person, and in my desperation to hang on to him, I morphed myself into something else entirely. He wanted a partner but I gave him a parasitic twin. Except worse than that. A parasitic twin that cried all the time. Worst *X-Files* episode ever.

At the bar, Aham and I ate tater tots and got drunk. We didn't talk about our relationship and I didn't cry. I felt detached; my capacity for sadness was maxed out. I had given up on trying to force him to come back to me, and he apologized for trying to force me to be his friend. Somehow, we had fun. Relief poured back and forth between us, quietly electric. Aham had a gleam I hadn't seen in months. For a minute, we held hands, and something woke, tiny but palpable, in my chest. Outside, it snowed, big, fat, wet flakes. I dropped him at the bus stop and said I'd see him in L.A., feeling something that wasn't quite despair for the first time in a month. He said we'd talk. Of course, that never happened—he flew back down the day after the tree fell, and I was already gone.

I took my bereavement juice box to the family lounge and called Aham in L.A.

"Can you just come?" I sobbed.

"Of course," he said.

We weren't back together, but we weren't not together. We weren't sleeping together, but he slept in the bed with me and held on to me as much as I needed. He ran errands for my mom, made her laugh, cooked eggs Benedict, booked a piano player for the funeral, figured out how to get a banquet license while I cried in the liquor store. My aunt and uncle came up from Arizona and stayed with us; Aham's girls would come on the weekends; friends and family dropped by nearly every day. We sat around and drank beer and watched football, all piled together in that little white house. It was a beautiful chaos, the same kind my mom grew up in and loved so much, the kind that I never understood growing up alone. It's weird to look back at the saddest month of my life and see that little vein of joy.

Aham and I weren't getting back together—we swore we weren't, we couldn't—but when I wasn't looking, he had become my family anyway.

The Beginning

We went back to L.A. and lived in limbo for a few months. Aham went on tour; I started working at *Jezebel*. We weren't "together," but we were happy in a totally unfamiliar way.

I'm not saying that if your relationship is in trouble you should cross your fingers that your dad dies.* But after my dad's funeral, I was older. Aham wasn't the only thing in my world anymore. My pain (and, later, my career) had pushed him aside a little bit, and that space was exactly what he needed. "I am a narcissist," he jokes, "but I didn't actually want to date my own reflection."

---

* Unless you hate your dad, I guess, in which case you can cross your fingers for whatever you want, *as long as you are not crossing them around the trigger of a dad-murdering gun!!!* (Look. Don't murder your dad. It will not make your boyfriend get back together with you. I DON'T KNOW HOW MUCH MORE CLEARLY I CAN SAY THIS.)

Aham had come through for me, in that month of emotional triage, with a selflessness that I think surprised us
both—not out of some sense of obligation, but because he
really wanted to be there, in my mom's basement, mixing
gin and tonics for my auntie Astri.

It was a horrendous period, but somehow we had fun.
We worked so hard to make each other laugh. We were
just ourselves again. It was like a reset.

When Aham got back from tour, we sat down for a
two-day feelings marathon. Even for me, a professional
leaking sad-bag, it was a nightmare. There were sched-
uled breaks. We punched in and out like trudging coal
miners. We wrote up a contract specifying how much
crying was allowed. (My opening offer was "100 percent
of the time"; Aham low-balled with a blank stare.) The
details are boring, and some of them are just mine, but at
the end of it, we were a couple again. I don't even think
of it as "getting back together," because it didn't feel like
a reconvening of the old relationship—it was a new one.

"If we're going to do this," he told me, giving me his
most Intense Face, "we're really doing it. Don't change
your mind on me."

It's hard to talk about, because the realist in me (i.e.,
my mom) kind of doesn't believe that "couples getting back
together" is a real thing. It's something I believed in when
I was a child, when I understood a relationship as something that happened to you, not something you built, and
I thought *The Parent Trap* was the ultimate love story. But

we really did do it, and the only explanation I can offer is that we weren't the same people in Relationship: Part Deux as we were in Relationship: The Phantom Menace.

Aham still wasn't sure that he believed in marriage anymore. It was understandable—he'd been divorced twice in the previous six years. I used up some of my tear allotment on that, not because I have any particular attachment to the institution of marriage, but because I just wanted to prove to the world that I was worth marrying. I grew up assuming that I would never get married, because marriage was for thin women, the kind of women who deserved to be collected. How could I be a bride when I was already what men most feared their wives would become? I was the mise en place for a midlife crisis. I was the Ghost of Adultery Future. At least, that's what I'd been taught. Aham was my shot at vindication. Come on, man. Think of all the fat girls we can inspire with our lifelong legal commitment!

"Okay, what if we still like each other this much in five years?" I bargained, annoyingly persistent *but in a charming way, I'm sure.* "Can we talk about getting married then?"

"In five years, if we still like each other exactly this much, sure, we can *talk* about getting married," Aham said, rolling his eyes. "You are the most annoying person on earth." That was good enough for me. It was basically a proposal.

We moved back to Seattle a few weeks after that. We rented a house and settled into a routine, our pre-breakup life already distant and foreign, like it happened to someone else. Every day I take his face in my hands and squeeze, because I think he might be a mirage; he declares "Crab Fingers," his second-favorite game, and pinches me until I fall out of bed. I call him and say gross stuff like, "I want to hug you and kiss you!" and he goes, "Who is this? Jessynthia?" and pretends to have a secret family. We show our love in different ways. But being in love holds its own kind of challenges.

Once, Aham and I were sitting at a bar, holding hands, and a woman recognized me. She was a fan of my writing, so she came up to introduce herself, and we shambled through a few minutes of pleasant chitchat. Sensing the conversation was running out of steam, she asked me one of the questions that people always ask me in those awkward, floundering moments: "So, what's it like to work from home? Aren't you lonely?"

"Not really," I said. I gestured to Aham. "He works from home, too. It's hard to feel alone when there's a guy constantly playing the trumpet in your face."

She laughed and turned to him. "So, you two are roommates?"

Yes, lady. We are platonic adult roommates who hold hands at bars. This is, clearly, the only logical explanation. Actually, since you asked, I recently sustained a pulsing gash to the palm and he's just holding the wound closed until paramedics arrive. Also, every night before bed, a rattlesnake bites me on the mouth and he has to suck out the poison. It's the weirdest thing. We should probably move.

I wasn't surprised that this woman took so many willful leaps past "couple" and landed on "roommates" in her split-second sussing-out of our relationship—it happens all the time. But it was a disheartening reminder of an assumption that has circumscribed my life: Couples ought to "match." Aham and I do not. I am fat and he is not. He is conventionally desirable and I am a "before" picture in an ad for liquefied bee eggs that you spray on your food to "tell cravings to buzz off!" (COPYRIGHTED. SEND ME ALL THE MONEY.) It is considered highly unlikely— borderline inconceivable—that he would choose to be with me in a culture where men are urged to perpetually "upgrade" to the "hottest" woman within reach, not only for their own supposed gratification but also to impress and compete with other men. It is women's job to be decorative (within a very narrow set of parameters) and it is men's job to collect them. My relationship throws off both sides of that equation, and a lot of people find it bewildering at best, enraging at worst.

There are long, manic message board threads devoted to comparing photos of me with photos of Aham's thin, conventionally pretty second ex-wife (number one is blessedly absent from the old MySpace page he doesn't know how to take down; number two is not so lucky), and dissecting what personality disorder could possibly have caused him to downgrade so egregiously. Servers always assume we want separate checks. Women hit on him right in front of me—and the late-night Facebook messages are a constant—as though they could just "have" him and he would say, "Oh, thank god you finally showed up," and leave me, and some dire cosmic imbalance would be corrected. It's nothing personal, it's just that they "match." They can talk about hot-people problems together—like "too many clothing options" and "haters." I wouldn't understand.

It's not that I'm not attracted to fat men—I've dated men of all sizes—but the assumption that fat people should only be with fat people is dehumanizing. It assumes that we are nothing but bodies. Well, sorry. I am a human and I would like to be with the human I like the best. He happens to not be fat, but if he were, I would love him just the same. Isn't that the whole point? To be more than just bodies?

When I think back on my teenage self, what I really needed to hear wasn't that someone might love me one day if I lost enough weight to qualify as human—it was that I was worthy of love now, just as I was. Being fat and happy and in love is still a radical act. That's why a wedding mattered to me. Not because of a dress or a diamond or a cake or a blender. (Okay, maybe a cake.*)

Aham took me out for dinner on my thirty-second birthday, then suggested a "quick nightcap" at our

---

* We had like six.

neighborhood bar. Everyone was there—it was a surprise—
our friends, our families, the kids, a cake. I was so happy.
Aham took my hand and led me to the back; there was
a paper banner that said my name (the bartender made
it—we go there a lot); our friends Evan and Sam were
playing a duet on cello and bass. I was confused. Why
were there somber strings at my birthday party? Why
was Aham doing Intense Face? Wait, it's almost ten p.m.
on a school night and we're at a bar—why ARE the kids
here? Then it all happened at once: the knee, the ring,
the speech, the question, the tears. All the hits. It was a
full-blown grand gesture.

He tricked me! He said five years. I was ready to wait
five years. He only lasted two.

Later, I asked him why he did it that way—such a big
spectacle, such an event, not precisely our style—and I
expected something cliché but sweet, like, "I wanted to
make sure our community was a part of our marriage,"
or, "I wanted everyone to know how much I love you."
Instead, he said, "One time when you were drunk you
told me, 'If you ever propose to me, don't do it in the
bullshit way that dudes usually treat fat girls. Like it's
a secret, or you're just trying to keep me from leaving
you. Thin girls get public proposals, like those dudes are
winning a fucking prize. Fat chicks deserve that, too.'"

It's not that I'd ever particularly yearned for a grand
gesture—the relationship I cherish lives in our tiny private
moments—but the older I get and the longer I live in a

fat body, the harder it is to depoliticize even simple acts. A public proposal to a publicly valued body might be personally significant, but culturally it shifts nothing. A public proposal to a publicly reviled body is a political statement.

As soon as you start making wedding plans, you're bombarded with (among a million other beckoning money pits) a barrage of pre-wedding weight-loss programs. Because you're supposed to be as thin as possible on your special day. After all, there will be pictures! And what if someone remembers your butt as looking like what your butt looks like!? "I'm only eating grapefruit and steam until my wedding." "I enrolled my whole wedding party in bridal boot camp." "I bought my dress in a size 4 even though I'm a size 6." And that's totally fine, of course, if that's your priority. It wasn't mine.

I don't hide anymore in my everyday life, and I definitely wasn't going to hide at my wedding.

We got married a year and a half after the proposal, in July, at my parents' cabin a few hours outside of Seattle. Even though I believe that death is a hard return, I can always feel my dad at the cabin. It was his favorite place. I walked down the aisle to a recording of him playing "Someone to Watch Over Me" on the piano; Aham wore a blue plaid suit; a bald eagle flapped over the ceremony; someone spilled red wine on one of the beds and my mom was in a good enough mood to forgive them; I got my fucking period (will you never *leave me be*, fell ghoul!?); it poured down rain after a month of uninterrupted sunshine, then abruptly stopped just as we emerged from the tent to dance; Meagan killed everyone with a toast about how Great-Aunt Eleanor died believing Meagan and I were lesbian lovers; a friend of mine, post-late-night-hot-tubbing, got confused about the route to the bathroom and walked into my mom's bedroom naked. Oh, and Aham's one-hundred-year-old great-grandmother had a stroke on the way to the wedding, went to the hospital, got better, *and still came and partied*. It was a gorgeous, chaotic, loving, perfect day.

We scribbled our vows five minutes before the ceremony.

Aham's read:

You know that thing that I do that you hate? That thing where I talk about how years ago when we were friends and I always wanted to hang out with you and I would always text you, and I would see you and be like, "We should hang out!" and then you'd always cancel on me? I'm never going to stop bringing that thing up, because I like being right. And all those times that I tried so hard to get you to hang out with me, and I just wanted to be around you so much, I've never been more right about anything in my life. The only way I can think to say it is that you are better than I thought people could be.

I am happier than I thought people could be.

Slaying the Troll

One ordinary midsummer afternoon in 2013, I got a message from my dead dad. I don't remember what it said, exactly, and I didn't keep a copy for my scrapbook, but it was mean. My dad was never mean. It couldn't really be from him. Also, he was dead—just eighteen months earlier, I'd watched him turn gray and drown in his own magnificent lungs, so I was like 80 percent sure—and I don't believe in heaven, and even if I did I'd hope to nonexistent-god they don't have fucking Twitter there. It's heaven! Go play chocolate badminton on a cloud with Jerry Orbach and your childhood cat.

But there it was. This message.

It was well into the Rape Joke Summer and my armor was thick. I was eating thirty rape threats for breakfast at that point (or, more accurately, "you're fatter than the girls I usually rape" threats), and I felt fortified and righteous. No one could touch me anymore. There was nothing remarkable about this particular tweet—oh, some white dude thinks I'm ugly/fat/stupid/humorless/boring? Does the Pope fart in Latin?—and by all conceivable logic it shouldn't have even registered. It certainly shouldn't have hurt.

The account was called "Paw West Donezo" (Paw West because his name was Paul West, and donezo because he was done being alive, done making up funny songs, done doing crossword puzzles, done not being able to get the printer to work, done getting annoyingly obsessed with certain kinds of Popsicles, done being so strong, done being my dad).

"Embarrassed father of an idiot," the bio read. "Other two kids are fine though."

His location: "Dirt hole in Seattle."

The profile photo was a familiar picture of him. He's sitting at his piano, smiling, in the living room of the house where I grew up. Some of the keys on that piano still have gray smudges worked into the grain, the ghost of old graphite where he'd penciled in the names of the notes for me when I was small. I never practiced enough; he always pretended not to be disappointed. The day they sold that house, when I was twenty-five, I sat on the stairs and sobbed harder than I ever had, because a place is kind of like a person, you know? It felt like a death, I thought. My family was broken, I thought. I wouldn't cry that hard again until December 12, 2011, when I learned that a place is not like a person at all. Only a person is a person. Only a death is really a death.

Watching someone die in real life isn't like in the

movies, because you can't make a movie that's four days long where the entire "plot" is just three women crying and eating candy while a brusque nurse absentmindedly adjusts a catheter bag and tries to comfort them with cups of room-temperature water.

Saturday afternoon, when we could feel his lucidity slipping, we called my brother in Boston. My dad's first-born. "You were such a special little boy," he said. "I love you very much." He didn't say very many things after that.

I would give anything for one more sentence. I would give anything for 140 more characters.

The person who made the "Paw West Donezo" account clearly put some time into it. He researched my father and my family. He found out his name, and then he figured out which Paul West he was among all the thousands of Paul Wests on the Internet. He must have read the obituary, which I wrote two days after my dad's lungs finally gave out. He knew that Dad died of prostate cancer and that he was treated at Seattle Cancer Care Alliance. He knew that I have a brother and a sister. And if he knew all that, he must have known how recently we lost him.

My armor wasn't strong enough for that.

What was my recourse? What could I do? This was before Twitter had a "report" function (which, as far as I can tell, is just a pretty placebo anyway), and it's not illegal to reach elbow-deep into someone's safest, sweetest memories and touch them and twist them and weaponize them to impress the ghost of Lenny Bruce or what-the-fuck-ever.

Hell, not only is it not illegal, I'm told it's a victory for free speech and liberty. It's just how the Internet works. It's natural. It's inevitable. Grow a thicker skin, piggy.

"Location: Dirt hole in Seattle."

All I could do was ignore it. Hit "block" and move on, knowing that that account was still out there, hidden behind a few gossamer lines of code. "Paw West Donezo" was still putting words in my dead father's mouth, still touching his memory, still parading his corpse around like a puppet to punish me for…something. I didn't even know what.

I'm supposed to feel okay just because I can't see it?

Yes. You're supposed to feel okay just because you can't see it. There's no other way, we're told. We couldn't possibly change the culture, we're told.

There's no "winning" when it comes to dealing with Internet trolls. Conventional wisdom says, "Don't engage. It's what they want." Is it? Are you sure our silence isn't what they want? Are you sure they care what we do at all? From where I'm sitting, if I respond, I'm a sucker for taking the bait. If I don't respond, I'm a punching bag. I'm the idiot daughter of an embarrassed dead guy. On the record. Forever.

Faced with a lose-lose like that, what do you do? Ignoring "PawWestDonezo" wasn't going to chasten him, or make me feel better, or bring my dad back.

So I talked back. I talked back because my mental health—not some troll's personal satisfaction—is my priority. I talked back because it emboldens other women to talk back online and in real life, and I talked back because women have told me that my responses give them a script for dealing with monsters in their own lives. Most importantly, I talked back because Internet trolls are not, in fact, monsters. They are human beings who've lost their way, and they just want other people to flounder too—and I don't believe that their attempts to dehumanize me can be counteracted by dehumanizing them.

The week after it happened, I wrote about PawWest Donezo in a *Jezebel* article about trolling. I wrote sadly, candidly, angrily, with obvious pain.

A few hours after the post went up, I got an e-mail:

Hey Lindy,

I don't know why or even when I started trolling you. It wasn't because of your stance on rape jokes. I don't find them funny either.

I think my anger towards you stems from your happiness with your own being. It offended me because it served to highlight my unhappiness with my own self.

I have e-mailed you through 2 other gmail accounts just to send you idiotic insults.

I apologize for that.

I created the PaulWestDunzo@gmail.com account & Twitter account. (I have deleted both)

I can't say sorry enough.

It was the lowest thing I had ever done. When you included it in your latest Jezebel *article it finally hit me.*

There is a living, breathing human being who is reading this shit. I am attacking someone who never harmed me in any way. And for no reason whatsoever.

I'm done being a troll.

Again I apologize.

I made donation in memory to your dad.

I wish you the best.

He attached a receipt for a fifty-dollar donation to Seattle Cancer Care Alliance, designated "Memorial Paul West" for "Area of greatest need."

This e-mail still unhinges my jaw every time I read it. A troll apologizing—this had never happened to me before, it has never happened to me since, I do not know anyone to which it has happened, nor have I heard of such a thing in the wide world of Internet lore. I have read interviews with scholars who study trolling from an academic perspective, specifically stating that the one thing you never get from a troll is public remorse.

I didn't know what to say. I said:

Is this real? If so, thank you.

It was really hurtful, but I'm truly sorry for whatever you've been going through that made you feel compelled to do those things. I wish you the best. And thank you for the donation—it means a lot. I love my dad very much.

He wrote to me one more time, our final contact:

> *Yes it's true. Thank you for responding with more kindness than I deserve.*
> *I'm sorry for your loss and any pain I caused you.*
>
> *All the best,*
>
> *[REDACTED] (my real name)*

I returned to my regular routine of daily hate mail, scrolling through the same options over and over—Ignore? Block? Report? Engage!—but every time I faced that choice, I thought briefly of my remorseful troll. I wondered if I could learn anything from him, what he'd tell me to do, if he had really changed. And then it struck me—oh my god. I still had his e-mail address. I could just ask him. Even if he turned out to be a jerk, it would make a great story.

I sent the e-mail. After a few months of torturous waiting, he finally wrote back. "I'd be happy to help you out in any way possible," he said.

Within a few days, there I was in a recording studio with a phone—and the troll on the other end. We recorded it for *This American Life*, a popular public radio show.

I asked him why he chose me. In his e-mail he wrote that it wasn't because of the rape joke thing, so what exactly did I do?

His voice was soft, tentative. He was clearly as nervous as I was. "Well," he said, "it revolved around one issue

that you wrote about a lot which was your being heavy—
the struggles that you had regarding being a woman of
size, or whatever the term may be."

I cut in. I hate euphemisms. What the fuck is a "woman
of size," anyway? Who doesn't have a size? "You can say
fat. That's what I say."

"Fat. Okay, fat."

He told me that at the time he was about seventy-five
pounds heavier than he wanted to be. He hated his body.
He was miserable. And reading about fat people, particularly fat women, accepting and loving themselves as they
were, infuriated him for reasons he couldn't articulate at
the time.

"When you talked about being proud of who you are
and where you are and where you're going," he continued,
"that kind of stoked that anger that I had."

"Okay," I said, "so you found my writing. You found
my writing, and you did not like it."

"Certain aspects of it."

"Yeah."

"You used a lot of all caps," he said. I laughed, and
it got him to laugh a little too. "You're just a very—you
almost have no fear when you write. You know, it's like
you stand on the desk and you say, 'I'm Lindy West, and
this is what I believe in. Fuck you if you don't agree
with me.' And even though you don't say those words
exactly, I'm like, who is this bitch who thinks she knows
everything?"

I asked him if he felt that way because I'm a woman.

He didn't even hesitate. "Oh, definitely. Definitely. Women are being more forthright in their writing. There isn't a sense of timidity to when they speak or when they write. They're saying it loud. And I think that—and I think, for me, as well, it's threatening at first."

"Right." It was a relief to hear him admit it. So many men cling to the lie that misogyny is a feminist fiction, and rarely do I get such explicit validation that my work is accomplishing exactly what I'm aiming for. "You must know that I—that's why I do that, because people don't expect to hear from women like that. And I want other women to see me do that and I want women's voices to get louder."

"I understand," he said. "I understand." I really felt like he did. "Here's the thing," he went on. "I work with women all day, and I don't have an issue with anyone. I could've told you back then if someone had said to me, 'Oh, you're a misogynist. You hate women.' And I could say, 'Nuh-uh, I love my mom. I love my sisters. I've loved my—the girlfriends that I've had in my life.' But you can't claim to be okay with women and then go online and insult them—seek them out to harm them emotionally."

In my experience, if you call a troll a misogynist, he'll almost invariably say, "Oh, I don't hate women. I just hate what you're saying and what that other woman is saying and that woman and that one for totally unrelated reasons." So it was satisfying at least to hear him admit that, yeah, he hated women.

We talked for two and a half grueling hours. They flew by, but every second hurt. He was shockingly self-aware. He said he didn't troll anymore, that he'd really changed. He told me that period of time when he was trolling me for being loud and fat was a low point for him. He hated his body. His girlfriend dumped him. He spent every day in front of a computer at an unfulfilling job. A passionless life, he called it. For some reason, he found it "easy" to take that out on women online.

I asked why. What made women easy targets? In retrospect, I wish I'd been even more plain: Why was it so satisfying to hurt us? Why didn't he automatically see us as human beings? For all his self-reflection, that's the one thing he never managed to articulate—how anger at one woman translated into hatred of women in general. Why, when men hate themselves, it's women who take the beatings.

He did explain how he changed. He started taking care of his health, he found a new girlfriend, and he went back to school to become a teacher. He told me—in all seriousness—that, as a volunteer at a school, *he just gets so many hugs now.* "Seeing how their feelings get hurt by their peers," he said, "on purpose or not, it derails them for the rest of the day. They'll have their head on their desk and refuse to talk. As I'm watching this happen, I can't help but think about the feelings that I hurt." He was so sorry, he said.

Finally, I brought up my dad.

"How did you even find out that my dad died? How did you—" I trailed off as my voice broke. He saved me the trouble of finishing the question. "I went to my computer. I Googled you—found out you had a father who had passed. I found out that he had—you had siblings. I forget if it was three total."

"I have two siblings."

"So—"

"Did you read his obituary?"

"I believe I did," he said. "I knew he was a musician."

"Yeah, I wrote that." My voice started to crack, the rapport I'd felt started to harden. "I wrote his obituary."

He hesitated at the edge in my voice. "I created a fake Gmail account using your father's name, created a fake Twitter account using his name. The biography was something to the effect of, my name is—I'm sorry, I forget the name—the first name."

"His name was Paul West."

"I wrote, 'My name is Paul West. I've got three kids. Two of them are great, and one of them is—'" He hesitated again. "'An idiot.'"

"Yeah, you said 'embarrassed father of an idiot.'"

"Okay."

"'Other two kids are fine, though.'"

He exhaled. "Ohhh, that's much more worse."

"And you got a picture of him," I said.

"I did get a picture of him."

"Do you remember anything about him?" I was crying

at this point. "Did you get a sense of him as a human being?"

"I read the obit. And I knew he was a dad that loved his kids."

"How did that make you feel?" I wasn't going to be cruel, but I wasn't going to let him off easy either.

"Not good," he said. "I mean, I felt horrible almost immediately afterwards. You tweeted something along the lines of, 'Good job today, society,' or something along those lines. It just wouldn't—for the first time, it wouldn't leave my mind. Usually, I would put out all of this Internet hate, and oftentimes I would just forget about it. This one would not leave me. It would not leave me. I started thinking about you because I know you had read it. And I'm thinking how would she feel. And the next day I wrote you."

"Yeah," I whispered, "I mean, have you lost anyone? Can you imagine? *Can you imagine?*"

"I can. I can. I don't know what else to say except that I'm sorry."

He sounded defeated. I believed him. I didn't mean to forgive him, but I did.

"Well, you know," I said, "I get abuse all day every day. It's part of my job. And this was the meanest thing anyone's ever done to me. I mean, it was really fresh. He had just died. But you're also the only troll who's ever apologized. Not just to me, I've never heard of this happening before. I mean, I don't know anyone who's ever gotten an apology. And I just—I mean, thank you."

"I'm glad that you have some solace." He seemed surprised, and relieved, that I hadn't been more cruel. But I was just tired. I didn't have much anger left. We exchanged a few pleasantries, I thanked him, he thanked me, and we hung up.

It felt really easy, comfortable even, to talk to my troll. I liked him, and I didn't know what to do with that.

It's frightening to discover that he's so normal. He has female coworkers who enjoy his company. He has a real, human girlfriend who loves him. They have no idea that he used to go online and traumatize women for fun. How can both of those people share the same brain?

Trolls live among us. I've gotten anonymous comments from people saying they met me at a movie theater and I was a bitch. Or they served me at a restaurant and my boobs aren't as big as they look in pictures. Or they sat next to me at a bar five years ago and here is a list of every single bite of food I consumed. People say it doesn't matter what happens on the Internet, that it's not real life. But thanks to Internet trolls, I'm perpetually reminded that the boundary between the civilized world and our worst selves is just an illusion.

Trolls still waste my time and tax my mental health on a daily basis, but honestly, I don't wish them any pain. Their pain is what got us here in the first place.

If what he said is true, that he just needed to find some meaning in his life, then what a heartbreaking diagnosis for all of the people who are still at it. I can't give purpose and fulfillment to millions of anonymous strangers, but I can remember not to lose sight of their humanity the way that they lost sight of mine.

Humans can be reached. I have proof.

This story isn't prescriptive. It doesn't mean that anyone is obliged to forgive people who abuse them, or even that I plan on being cordial and compassionate to every teenage boy who pipes up to call me a blue whale.* But, for me, it's changed the timbre of my online interactions—with, for instance, the guy who responded to my radio story by calling my dad a "faggot." That guy does not have a good life. Since this conversation with my troll aired on *This American Life*, I've had to report six more Twitter accounts using my father's name and face, one that scolded me for writing about my abortion. "Why did you kill my grandchild?" it asked. It got easier every time.

It's hard to feel hurt or frightened when you're flooded with pity. It's hard to be cold or cruel when you remember it's hard to be a person.

---

* "Whale" is the weakest insult ever, by the way. Oh, I have a giant brain and rule the sea with my majesty? What have you accomplished lately, Steve?

Abortion Is Normal, It's Okay to Be Fat, and Women Don't Have to Be Nice to You

Just two weeks after my *This American Life* segment aired, copies of a leaked memo by Twitter's then-CEO Dick Costolo began flooding into my inbox from breathless friends. An employee had posted my piece on an internal forum, where it got the attention of Twitter higher-ups, Costolo himself ultimately responding with this blistering communiqué: "I'm frankly ashamed of how poorly we've dealt with this issue during my tenure as CEO," he wrote. "It's absurd. There's no excuse for it. I take full responsibility for not being more aggressive on this front."

Then: "We're going to start kicking these people off right and left and making sure that when they issue their ridiculous attacks, nobody hears them. Everybody on the leadership team knows this is vital."

"We've sucked at it for years," Costolo went on. "We're going to fix it."

I was floored. Like, literally on the floor, rolling around. Bloggers, activists, and academics had been throwing ourselves against Twitter's opaque interface for years—begging for help, compiling sheaves of data on online abuse, writing heartfelt personal essays and dry clinical analyses— and suddenly, in one stroke, we had their ear. There was a human being behind the bird, and he actually gave a shit.

The jury's still out on the long-term efficacy of Twitter's "fixes." It's notoriously difficult, if not impossible, to retroactively change a community once bad behavior has taken root—once users know how to exploit a system, it's hard to evict them without rebuilding the system itself from scratch. Still, to know that Twitter is aware and they're trying—to have the CEO publicly throw his hat in with the feminazis rather than the trolls—is a victory, and a sign that our culture is slowly heaving its bulk in the right direction.

Decisive victories are rare in the culture wars, and the fact that I can count three in my relatively short career— three tangible cultural shifts to which I was lucky enough to contribute—is what keeps me in this job. There's Costolo and the trolls, of course. Then, rape jokes. Comedians are more cautious now, whether they like it or not, while only the most credulous fool or contrarian liar would argue that comedy has no misogyny problem. "Hello, I

Am Fat" chipped away at the notion that you can "help" fat people by mocking and shaming us. We talk about fatness differently now than we did five years ago—fat people are no longer safe targets—and I hope I did my part.

All of those changes are small, but they tell us something big: Our world isn't fixed, the way those currently in charge would have you believe. It's malleable.

When I was a little girl, I was obsessed with a video-game developer named Roberta Williams. She made point-and-click adventure games—King's Quest, Space Quest, Quest for Glory—a largely extinct genre in which exploration, curiosity, and problem solving took precedence over combat and reflexes. As a corny king or a dopey spaceman, you wandered through brilliant, interactive landscapes, picking up random shit in the hope that it might help you rescue a pissed-off gnome from a swarm of bees, or break a talking collie out of dog prison so he'll reward you with the magic kerchief you need to blindfold the King of the Dead.

I wanted to be Roberta Williams; I wanted to build worlds.

In ninth grade, I enrolled in a beginners' programming class at a community college near my house. I was the youngest one there, the only girl, and the only one with no previous knowledge of coding (which wasn't a prerequisite); the teacher ignored me and chattered away with the boys in jargon I couldn't follow. I sat through two classes in a humiliated, frustrated fog and never went back. I drifted away from video games; they didn't want me. I forgot about Roberta and grew up.

I think the most important thing I do in my professional life today is delivering public, impermeable *"no"*s and sticking to them. I say no to people who prioritize being cool over being good. I say no to misogynists who want to weaponize my body against me. I say no to men who feel entitled to my attention and reverence, who treat everything the light touches as a resource for them to burn. I say no to religious zealots who insist that I am less important than an embryo. I say no to my own instinct to stay quiet.

Nah, no thanks, I'm good, bye. Ew, don't talk to me. Fuck off.

It's a way of kicking down the boundaries that society has set for women—be compliant, be a caregiver, be quiet—and erecting my own. I will do this; I will not do that. You believe in my subjugation; I don't have to be nice to you. I am busy; my time is not a public commodity. You are boring; go away.

That is world-building.

My little victories—trolls, rape jokes, fat people's humanity—are world-building. Fighting for diverse voices is world-building. Proclaiming the inherent value of fat people is world-building. Believing rape victims is world-building. Refusing to cave to abortion stigma is world-building. Voting is world-building. So is kindness, compassion, listening, making space, saying yes, saying no.

We're all building our world, right now, in real time. Let's build it better.

Acknowledgments

First, to the Wests and the Oluos, I am so lucky.

To my mom, Ingrid, for teaching me that there's a right way and a wrong way, for taking care of me, and for always following through. To my dad, Paul, for modeling kindness and ebullience, blazing creativity and unconditional love. I miss you. I wish you could have read my book.

To my agent and friend, Gary Morris, who is just the best, for being so patient and encouraging while I figured out WTF a book is. To the whole team at Hachette, especially Mauro DiPreta. It is so fucking cool that you hitched your wagon to this fat feminist abortion manifesto—your confidence in me means everything—and I'm sorry I said "fart" so many times even after you asked me to pump the brakes on that.

To Paul Constant, Rafil Kroll-Zaidi, Guy Branum, Corianton Hale, and Amelia Bonow for the guidance and reassurance. To every member of the Secret Book Writing

Accountability and Crying Group—you are my medicine. To Charlotte and John MacVane for the solitude and whoopie pies. To Hedgebrook for reaching out to me with such supernaturally perfect timing that I almost believe in god now (and/or wiretapping?). To Meagan Hatcher-Mays for being a better version of me. You ate the thirteenth biscuit. To Annie Wagner and Jessica Coen for my big breaks. To Ira Glass and Chana Joffe-Walt. To every fat person who's ever sent me an e-mail. To my *Stranger* family, my GHS family, and my Oxy family. To Tamora Pierce audiobooks and every flavor of Runts except banana.

Thank you.

And to my husband, Ahamefule J. Oluo: You are the best thinker and funniest joke writer and most brilliant artist in the whole world, but you're an even better partner. I love you, I love you, I love you.